We Come for Good

UNIVERSITY PRESS OF FLORIDA

Florida A&M University, Tallahassee
Florida Atlantic University, Boca Raton
Florida Gulf Coast University, Ft. Myers
Florida International University, Miami
Florida State University, Tallahassee
New College of Florida, Sarasota
University of Central Florida, Orlando
University of Florida, Gainesville
University of North Florida, Jacksonville
University of South Florida, Tampa
University of West Florida, Pensacola

We Come for Good

Archaeology and Tribal Historic Preservation at the Seminole Tribe of Florida

EDITED BY PAUL N. BACKHOUSE, BRENT R. WEISMAN,
AND MARY BETH ROSEBROUGH

University Press of Florida

Gainesville · Tallahassee · Tampa · Boca Raton
Pensacola · Orlando · Miami · Jacksonville · Ft. Myers · Sarasota

This book may be available in an electronic edition.

22 21 20 19 18 17   6 5 4 3 2 1

Library of Congress Cataloging-in-Publication Data
Names: Backhouse, Paul N. (Paul Nathan), editor. | Weisman, Brent Richards,
   1952– editor. | Rosebrough, Mary Beth, editor.
Title: We come for good : archaeology and tribal historic preservation at the
   Seminole Tribe of Florida / edited by Paul N. Backhouse, Brent R. Weisman,
   and Mary Beth Rosebrough.
Description: Gainesville : University Press of Florida, 2017. | Includes
   bibliographical references and index.
Identifiers: LCCN 2016043298 | ISBN 9780813062280 (cloth)
Subjects: LCSH: Seminole Indians—Florida—History. | Indians of North
   America—Florida—History. | Seminole Tribe of Florida—History. |
   Historic preservation—Florida.
Classification: LCC E99.S28 W4 2017 | DDC 975.9004/973859—dc23
LC record available at https://lccn.loc.gov/2016043298

The University Press of Florida is the scholarly publishing agency for the State University System
of Florida, comprising Florida A&M University, Florida Atlantic University, Florida Gulf Coast
University, Florida International University, Florida State University, New College of Florida,
University of Central Florida, University of Florida, University of North Florida, University of
South Florida, and University of West Florida.

University Press of Florida
15 Northwest 15th Street
Gainesville, FL 32611-2079
http://upress.ufl.edu

My father, King Phillip, told me I was made of the sands of Florida,
and that when I was placed in the ground,
the Seminoles would dance and sing around my grave.

Coacoochee (Wildcat)

CONTENTS

FIGURES

PREFACE

The heritage of the Muscogee peoples is central to our understanding of the southeastern region of North America. Indigenous communities are today active participants and players in the identification, management, research, interpretation, and preservation of this heritage. The development of the Seminole Tribe of Florida Tribal Historic Preservation Office (STOF THPO) is explored as a case study in the generation of Tribal capacity to struggle with the huge number of heritage management questions that face stakeholders in the Southeast. Federal and state officials, cultural resource managers, and the general public typically only have a limited understanding of Tribal government and the operation of a THPO. These chapters attempt to demystify these relationships and should be of considerable interest to anthropologists, archaeologists, historians, Native American studies scholars, and the aforementioned officials, as well as other THPOs seeking to build capacity to deal with the challenges associated with tribal sovereignty in the early twenty-first century.

The research presented herein represents expanded versions of papers originally given at the 2013 Southeastern Archaeological Conference held in Tampa, Florida. We are grateful to the Florida Archaeological Council for partially funding the THPO's participation at that conference. Permission to proceed with the publication of this volume was given by Tribal Council Resolution (C325-14), which passed unanimously at the August 2014 Special Council Meeting held on the Big Cypress Seminole Indian Reservation. All chapters were authored by practitioners actively involved with the operation of the THPO. We seek, in some small fashion, to redress the dearth of available literature written from within the Tribe. Completion of this manuscript has been a hard-won battle as there are no sabbaticals or study leave from our duties and service to the Seminole Tribe of Florida.

Tribal members affected by the activities of the THPO rarely have an opportunity to speak for themselves. Administrators, professional archaeologists, academics, and Tribal leaders often put a voice to their concerns but in a language that is not theirs, using the practiced words of accepted professional discourse. One of our main goals in this volume is to let Tribal members use their own words in telling how the THPO has impacted their lives. To do this, it is important to capture the rhythm of the speech and the points of emphasis and to respect that phrasing and word use are unique expressions of a person's voice. Consequently, we have used a light editorial hand in presenting these interviews in the hope that both teller and reader will feel honored by the experience.

Ultimately, the process has been both reflective and empowering. In August 2014, a *Seminole Tribune* reporter, Eileen Soler, asked Willie Johns, Tribal elder and author of a chapter herein, to describe what we were trying to accomplish. His answer was that he hoped the Tribe would take a leadership role in historic preservation, just as they have in other Tribal endeavors, such as housing and education. For Johns, it is about allowing the Tribe to be an active participant in telling their own story. "Right now, archaeology and Native history go hand in hand. When is enough, enough? When we say so," Johns said. "We wrote the book on it."

Note: For the Coacoochee quote on page v, see John T. Sprague, *The Florida War* (Tampa, Fla.: University of Tampa Press, 2000), 327.

ACKNOWLEDGMENTS

We would like to thank the Tribal communities and elected members of the Seminole Tribe of Florida Council for their guidance, involvement, and support of this project. In addition, individual members of the Seminole Tribe of Florida deserve special thanks for propelling our work forward: Bobby Henry, Herbie Jim, Lorene Gopher, Chief Justice Willie Johns, Jack Chalfant, Lewis Gopher, Jeanette Cypress, Geneva Shore, Danny Tommie, Mollie Jolly, and Quenton Cypress.

We are also grateful to all our colleagues and coworkers at the Tribal Historic Preservation Office (THPO). This book is a testament to your collective efforts. A sincere debt of thanks is also due the Florida Archaeological Council for generously sponsoring the initial symposium at the 2015 Southeastern Archaeological Conference. We also thank Meredith Babb of the University Press of Florida for her patience, encouragement, and wisdom during the writing and editing process. The perceptive insights and direction of James Quinn, Mohegan Tribe THPO; Ryan Wheeler, Peabody Museum Director; and one anonymous reviewer greatly improved the quality of the final manuscript. The writing team, however, is responsible for any and all errors that remain. This volume contributes to the mission of the Seminole Tribe of Florida THPO and the promotion of cultural preservation throughout Indian country. The views contained within this volume are solely the responsibility of the authors and are not intended to convey the official views of the Seminole Tribe of Florida.

Finally, we extend our love and sincere appreciation to our friends and family who patiently wait for us as we make the often three-hour round-trip to work, to do what we love.

Sho Na Bish / Mvto

ABBREVIATIONS

ACHP	Advisory Council on Historic Preservation
AIRFA	American Indian Religious Freedom Act
AOI	Area of Interest
AOR	Area of Responsibility
APE	Area of Potential Effect
ARPA	Archaeological Resources Protection Act of 1979
BIA	Bureau of Indian Affairs
C&SF	Central and Southern Florida Project for Flood Control and Other Purposes
CCD-ID	Civilian Conservation Corps–Indian Division
CERP	Comprehensive Everglades Restoration Plan
CFR	Code of Federal Regulations
CPD	Community Planning and Development Department (STOF)
CRM	Cultural Resource Management
CRO	Cultural Resource Ordinance
CRS	Compliance Review Section (THPO)
ERMD	Environmental Resource Management Department (STOF)
GIS	Geographic Information System
GPR	Ground-Penetrating Radar
ICTD	Incoming Correspondence and Tracking Database
NAGPRA	Native American Graves Protection and Repatriation Act
NHPA	National Historic Preservation Act
NPS	National Park Service

NRHP	National Register of Historic Places
SHPO	State Historic Preservation Office
SSF	Seminole Site File
STOF	Seminole Tribe of Florida
TAS	Tribal Archaeology Section (THPO)
TCP	Traditional Cultural Property
THPO	Tribal Historic Preservation Office
TRHP	Tribal Register of Historic Places
USACE	U.S. Army Corps of Engineers

1

"When Is Enough, Enough?"

Willie Johns on Seminole History and the Tribal Historic Preservation Office, the Creek Perspective

WILLIE JOHNS AND STEPHEN BRIDENSTINE

In order for a Tribal Historic Preservation Office (THPO) to successfully represent a tribe, it must be fully engaged with the community it serves. One way therefore to measure the impact of the program is to solicit feedback from the people themselves. Interviews were conducted with five citizens of the Seminole Tribe of Florida who are broadly representative of the diversity of perspectives within the Tribe. A cross section of age, gender, and personal biographies was deliberately selected with the common theme that all interviewees had interacted with the THPO in some capacity in the last five years.

Historically, the Seminole Tribe of Florida is made up of speakers of two related but culturally distinct languages—Miccosukee and Creek. Language affiliation and cultural identity are intertwined and distinct. Today this traditional dichotomy is made more complex by the cultural and biological influence of non-Seminole peoples. Willie Johns, who has a long history of working very closely with the THPO, offers a Creek historical perspective.

Author Bio

Willie Johns is a citizen of the Seminole Tribe of Florida and a member of the Wildcat Clan.[1] Born in 1951 and raised on the Brighton Seminole Indian Reservation, Johns grew up in a traditional camp. He is a fluent speaker of the Cow Creek language and a respected Tribal historian.[2] He earned an associate degree in agriculture from Abraham Baldwin Agricultural College and a bachelor's degree in history from Palm Beach Atlantic College.

Figure 1.1. Willie Johns, Tribal historian. By permission of the Ah-Tah-Thi-Ki Museum.

A longtime advocate of education, Willie Johns served twice as the Education Director for the Tribe. From 2005, he worked as the Outreach Coordinator for the Ah-Tah-Thi-Ki Museum, delivering lectures and workshops about Seminole Tribal culture and history to Tribal and non-Tribal audiences. In this position, Johns established an ongoing relationship with the THPO, becoming an informal cultural advisor. Since October 2013, he has served as Chief Justice of the Seminole Tribal Court.

On June 10, 2014, Willie Johns sat down with Ah-Tah-Thi-Ki Museum Oral Historian Stephen Bridenstine to discuss Seminole history and his work with the THPO. In this humorous and insightful interview, Johns relates how he came to know and understand Seminole history and shares his personal thoughts and feelings about the work of the THPO.

STEPHEN BRIDENSTINE: Can you start out by describing for us the camp setting and the family environment that you grew up in?

WILLIE JOHNS: I always said that I came up at the right time because a lot of the elder gentlemen that I was raised with are no longer here. So I used to probe them, ask a lot of questions. And they would give me good answers, but I came to realize that history in their minds wasn't really that important. They didn't remember anything about, for instance, Osceola. I asked several men about him. They knew very little other than the fact that he wasn't a full-blooded Seminole or Creek. They knew that fact and they knew that he died in captivity, and that's as far as it went with anything about him.[3]

So I knew that their main focus was survival, simply surviving the environment. They lived in Florida—camped the camp, hunting, fishing, you know, hunter-gatherer. They were forced back into that from the early people that came here. They were back into that hunter-gatherer mode, but they were finally calming down when I came around because by then, they were all on the reservation and working for the government or they had their cattle herd and that's how I got to know a lot of the guys. And I grew up with them. A lot of them were Medicine Men, especially in my family. They were medicine bundle carriers, so we have always passed down that tradition through our family. The strongest male would get it.

So history for the most part wasn't really there. The challenge was that I had a lot of non-Indian friends who would ask me questions and I wouldn't know the answers so I would have to come back home and ask my parents, ask my aunts. You see, I was brought up in a matrilineal environment. We had our great-aunt and she had seven sisters, so we had a large family, probably twenty chickees in our camp.[4] So we were very challenged at the beginning anyway because our families, our parents, were illiterate. So like I said, there wasn't a whole lot to talk about concerning history. Most of my knowledge I got through my self-study because the college that I went to, Palm Beach Atlantic College, their specialty was European history. So I learned a lot about the kings and queens in Europe, in Russia, France, Italy, and how they all intertwined, intermarried among each other. But that was good for me.

SB: Why?

WJ: Because it gave me a really broad perspective on different people. I wasn't clouding my history, my mind, with just total Native stuff. So I got a broad picture of why people would want to come to America too. You know, because they totally destroyed Europe so they needed a new place to go—(laughs)—a new place to destroy. So they came to the promised land. So it kept my door open with the Native people, the Native history, my own history. Then once I graduated from college, I began my own venture into Florida's history and then into Native history, into military history, and into Tribal history. I had to start somewhere so back in high school days, you always start at the *Mayflower*. (laughs)

SB: I did.

WJ: Yeah, I did too! Because nobody talked about Florida history or Seminoles in Florida, the rich history that the Seminoles have. Nobody even mentioned that because from the *Mayflower*, it seemed like you dove right into the Revolutionary War. And then right there is when they spoke of the Trail of Tears very little. And then Indian Removal, very little in American history books.[5] So I didn't get a whole lot out of that but I knew there was a rich history, and I knew by talking to guys like Sonny Billie,[6] I knew that I didn't originate from here.

SB: Where did you come from?

WJ: Our people come from the southeastern area like Alabama, Georgia, Tennessee, parts of North Carolina.

SB: Did you know that growing up?

WJ: I didn't. So when I learned that, it was a shocker because I always believed that I lived here. I was from here. And I've been challenged by other Tribal members for believing that we didn't come from here. They've told me, "Our grandparents say we've always been from here." And then my comeback would be, "Well you must be Calusa or Tequesta or Jeaga, one of those aboriginal tribes that were here.[7] That's who you are I guess." But I said, "I'm not. I'm a Creek guy and I come from North Florida for sure. And then I came into Florida. I don't know which way, Alabama or Georgia." I think my family came in after the Horseshoe Bend, when the Red Sticks and the White Sticks had their big fight and Andy Jackson came in there and helped the White Sticks, and the Red Sticks were repelled and sent all over the country and a lot of them fled into Florida.[8]

But that's not the beginning either because there were already Creek people in Florida before that fight. Because by 1760, there were already large Creek towns in North Florida. Like the Red House, [also called] Chocochatti, Bowlegs town, Micanopy up there in the Ocala area, and Alachua.[9] All those were settled by earlier Creek guys who were already in business selling cows in the cattle industry. So we're pretty progressive people, I realize that. But to touch base with the men that I knew growing up, they didn't know this stuff. You see, their moms and dads came out of the Everglades after the war just surviving, hunting and fishing. Nobody wrote anything down, just the military people and the government. So they didn't have a whole lot to give me.

SB: Do you differentiate between history and the legends and some of the other stories about the Tribe? Do you see these as different or the same?

WJ: I see them as different. I grew up listening to all the legends. Some of the best storytellers in the language, telling stories about the rabbit and how arrogant he was and then in our language it's very funny but when you translate it back into English, it doesn't make sense. I think that those gentlemen in those days that I grew up also understood the difference. Something did happen because theoretically we would never have gone down into the Everglades. Something forced us. You know the Creeks led the Miccosukees down into the Everglades.

SB: I didn't know that.

WJ: Yeah, the Creek leaders, they've always known the Everglades. They hunted it and fished it for decades before Europeans knew that the Everglades sat there.

SB: Is this something you learned growing up from the community?

WJ: Yeah. And so these men, their parents came out, came out of the Everglades after the Wars looking for a better way of life because there is no life in the Everglades other than hunting and fishing. And most of these Creek people that were down in the Everglades were cattlemen, horsemen, so they were looking for a new way, a new route back to the old life. So they came out into the prairies after the Americans pulled out after the Seminole Wars.

SB: So the Seminoles were pushed south and then after the War, they went north again?

WJ: Yeah.

SB: Okay.

WJ: And see, that's where my family starts because my great-grandfather was born in 1875 but I never knew him. And my grandmother's mother, we're not sure, but on the census they have her death in 1930 and she was ninety-six years old. So she would have been born around 1834.

SB: So she saw a lot?

WJ: Yeah. We like to push her back to the Second Seminole War and say, "Wow! She saw one Seminole War, a second Seminole War, the Civil War, World War I, and then she died just before World War II.[10] So hardship she had known."

SB: As you learned these new things about the history of the Seminoles, did that change your identity in any way, or how you saw yourself and your community?

WJ: It did in a way change me because I was all of a sudden speaking a different tune. I was telling people, "You know what, I'm learning." And then from what I've learned, they would add in or if I got called out and I was told that I was wrong, then I always gave them the opportunity to challenge me. "Show me where I'm wrong," I always used to tell them, "prove me wrong." And of course that meant they had to go back and do some studying or talk to grandma but usually grandma is already in the grave. (laughs)

So I was called, for a long time, and I still feel that every now and then, that I'm a "textbook Seminole historian." Everything I know is in the book but you know what, there's truth to that. Because when I was growing up, there was not much by way of the talking history, the interpretive, because nobody hardly knew much. I mean you could get medicine. There were medicines around, Medicine Men. And still today you can still do that. But culture is culture. You can ad-lib that real easy, you know, the way of life, but you shock a Seminole when you tell them that their ancestors, when they came to Florida, did not live in chickees.

SB: What did they live in?

WJ: They lived in log cabins. We're the ones who taught you guys how to build them. So it shocks a Seminole to hear that. "Oh no!" they say. We didn't start living in chickees till we got pushed into the Everglades and then they became survival huts. Because they were real easy to put up and you could get out of the environment real quick and they were harder to detect. So it boggles their mind because that's all they've seen. That's all they've seen. It was chickees all their lives. And then some smart Seminole guy with a history degree comes up and says, "Look, we lived in log cabins."

(laughter)

SB: So of the little history that you did hear from the community, how far back did it go? Did it begin at the Seminole Wars? Because that was still alive in the memory of the community, right?

WJ: Yeah. What kept it in perspective was cattle.

SB: How so?

WJ: There's a thesis written by a U.S. Marine titled ["American Military Strategy during the Second Seminole War"].[11] And he talked about cattle and horses. So as we fled we had to leave a lot of cattle and horses because you could follow us easy. They left a lot of tracks with grazing and the big herds so we had to slim down. So you can see that we knew how to change game plans.

SB: And were there specific stories about the Seminole Wars?

WJ: Yeah, but not a lot. Not a lot because you know these men that I knew probably didn't see a real white man up front for many years. They saw them from a distance because they thought that they were dangerous. They'd take your stuff from you. So they didn't really want to intermingle but then after the Third Seminole War, everything kind of loosened up and then we started doing a lot of trading with the traders: Stranahan, Storter's, the Browns.[12] So I think learning from the community, there was not a lot there. And there weren't that many educated people either. But as far as history goes, another thing that really got me into the swing of things was Chairman James Billie because he used to tell me a lot.[13] We used to hang out a lot together, and he would tell me things that I never heard of and it's about our people and I wanted to learn. I wanted to know.

SB: Would that be because he grew up in a different community, on a different reservation, surrounded by different people?

WJ: Yeah, I think so because he always ran with a different crowd. And then being in that Chairman's Office, you're always around people telling you things. Other historians, you're always around them. They're always near you.

SB: So within the Tribe, obviously you have different reservations. You have a Creek-speaking community. You have a Miccosukee-speaking community.[14] You have eight different clans.[15] Do those different designations change what people might know about the history or what they know about the community?

WJ: You know, I don't think so. We knew about our clans all along. We knew our designations, what we're to know, what we can say, what we want to put out there. But I learned a lot because I was inquisitive. There was one man in my life, Ollie Jones,[16] he used to teach me different songs all related back to war, war songs. He taught me a song that if somebody held a gun on you, you could sing that song and that bullet, while meant for you, would hit somebody else. And there was another song about when you're fleeing the enemy and you disappear in front of their eyes. Now this is all when I'm young and I'm interested but I'm not learning. I should have really learned them. If you wanted to learn you could, I guess, to an extent but you had to ask. Like if you wanted to learn a song to lead at the Corn Dance, there was nobody to teach you but maybe your uncle. But this day in time, it's changing because they're starting to have classes to learn how to lead a song. And that all involves the culture.

SB: Okay. So besides the Seminole Tribe of Florida, you also have the Miccosukee Tribe of Indians of Florida, you have a group of Independent Seminoles in Florida, and you have the Seminole Nation in Oklahoma.[17] I'm wondering if you feel any sense of shared heritage with these other Tribal communities?

WJ: You know, for a long time when I was growing up, I didn't like them.

SB: Why not?

WJ: They always had this warrior-type mentality. And they may have wanted to share, but I'm a renegade Creek who was still fighting a war, in my mind, in my thoughts. But as I got older and I started to get to know the people, I realized that they had things to offer, to teach me. And I had things to offer to them because they were coming to me. So with the Miccosukees, the Independents, the Oklahoma Seminoles—well not so much Oklahoma, but a little bit—we all have a shared investment because traditionally, culturally, religiously, we're basically the same people but one with a different language. And I haven't a clue what they say.

SB: So do you have any understanding of the Miccosukee language?

WJ: What I do is I sit and listen and I pick out Creek words to keep me on track, what's going on. If I don't hear a Creek word, I don't have a clue. And I can talk to them and it's the same way. They don't understand me. Even like some of our Corn Dance songs, it's all pure Creek. And a lot of the Miccosukee guys, they know the title of the song but they memorized it and they can lead it, but they don't know what they're singing. You have to know the Creek.

SB: What about with other Creek-speaking communities: the Creek communities that are left in Alabama and Georgia and the Creek Nation in Oklahoma.[18] Do you feel any sense of shared heritage with them?

WJ: I do, you know, linguistically I do. But the Alabama and the Georgia bunch, they're trying to speak Creek but I don't understand them. I can pick out a word here and there. It's because they've been Americanized too long, and then all of a sudden somebody told them they might have Native blood in them and they get this intent to learn. I have a cousin. When she talks to you, she's talking Creek, but you can tell by the way she says the words that it's coming out of a book. It's too proper. (laughs)

SB: What would you say was the biggest legacy or impact of the Seminole Wars on the Seminole Tribe?

WJ: Well, you know like all wars, there was a lack of men. You can pick up history papers and they'll say we committed polygamy, that you would see men with more than one wife or stuff like that. Also, food and sense of direction because by then, after the Third Seminole War, central Florida was already populated by probably 100,000 Americans. Some of the wealthiest ranchers today are descendants of those people that came to central Florida. Landgrabbers, you know, and they made a life with the cattle industry. So all the trails, all the hunting grounds, were almost all dried up. Seminoles were left to be almost like a vagabond, like gypsies staying wherever they could. A lot of them were not welcome. They were run off the property. And then when Florida passed the fencing law, that really shot them in the foot because all these large ranchers and landholders had to fence their property off. So they couldn't go back and forth through the old trails. So we're talking like prereservation.

SB: That would be like 1880s, 1890s, 1900s?

WJ: Yeah.

SB: So I wanted to ask you then, in this time period, late nineteenth to the early twentieth century, how much did people travel?

WJ: A lot.

SB: Why?

WJ: They were following the game or they were following farmers going to different areas or some of them were following the herds. Some of them had cattle, large herds.

SB: As we get into the twentieth century, there were some big changes in the environment with the canals and the draining of the Everglades.[19] What was the impact of that on the Seminole way of life?

WJ: It made it easier for non-Natives to get to you. (laughs) It made boating easy and it split your hunting grounds, and a lot of them in those days were alligator hunters. You know where the Seminoles go into camp in Miami and they service the tourist world like at Tiger Tiger camp? It's because it's pushing them. It's moving them out of the swamps because they need a regular paycheck so they become actors and they start to alligator wrestle. They start to sell trinkets to the northern people.[20]

SB: So the changes in the environment directly related to the change in where they lived and how they lived?

WJ: Yeah, you're drying it up when you start digging.

SB: Were you around in 1957 when they signed the Seminole Constitution?[21]

WJ: I was seven years old. I was there when they signed it. I was there when Chairman James Billie was a young teenage boy and he did the Pledge of Allegiance.

SB: Did you know at the time how significant it was?

WJ: You know, not really. It was just a big party because I was a kid, right, seven years old so what do you expect? (laughter) I do remember getting up early in the morning and getting into the cattle truck with maybe twenty other families and making that trek across the Everglades to Hollywood.[22] Because I knew we got there around ten o'clock.

SB: What did receiving federal recognition change for the Tribe?

WJ: Well, I know the power struggle changed because—remember the Corn Dance? That was our power base. Each clan was represented. Now we have elected officials. So that didn't sit well with the old boys.

SB: You brought up your new job as Chief Justice. Could you share with us what are some of the different positions you've held both within and outside the Tribal government?

WJ: Well, I worked for the state for many years as an animal livestock inspector but I always had a degree so doors starting opening up for me. And then I came to the Tribe as an Education Director. I'm probably the only one that's held that job twice.

SB: What was your degree in?

WJ: History. I left my degree open so I eventually went back to finish up. There was a time span that I actually just worked for myself.

SB: Okay. So eventually you worked at the Seminole Tribe's Ah-Tah-Thi-Ki Museum, correct?

WJ: Yeah, I was the Outreach Coordinator but since October 2013 I have been the Chief Justice of the Seminole Court.

SB: So I want to ask you about the Tribal Historic Preservation Office. In your own words and in your own experiences, what does the THPO do? What service does it provide to the Seminole community?

WJ: You know, for a long time, when I worked for museum outreach and Bill Steele was the THPO Director, I always thought that all they were doing was digging, you know, finding remains and marking camps.[23]

But as time went along, I started getting involved with THPO. They started involving me from museum outreach. I was doing more work for THPO than I was for outreach. Going to sites, going to different states to look at remains, and so I come to realize, they're really important for the museum even though outreach is really important too because we're out there with the enemy, us outreach guys. You're out there with them and teaching them about yourself whereas THPO, they're around the Rez. Some of them do go off for training and higher learning, but you know what I went through with Bill Steele?

We went to Boston to check some bones out, which was the first time I ever went all the way through the NAGPRA [Native American Graves Protection and Repatriation Act] process from the spotting of the bones, to doing all the paperwork, walking it all the way through till where the girls pick the bones up and we meet them at their final destination, then finally seeing the remains going into the grave and being covered. It was the first time.

And you know, there are a lot of Tribal members that say, "Yeah we don't need to be involved in that kind of stuff." But we do. We should be the caretakers of the people that can't take care of themselves anymore. So it did my heart good not too long ago to see those bones go back into the ground. I know the girls [THPO Bioarchaeologist Domonique deBeaubien and THPO Collections Manager Kate Macuen] got emotional. And it was an emotional moment because there was an infant and one of the tribal members from the other tribe in Boston sent a baby blanket. And so the box that the remains were in, they wrapped the baby blanket around it and buried it. That really got them crying.

So THPO, do they dig bones? Yes, they find bones, but not always. There's always archaic stuff that they find, arrowheads and military stuff. And then forts, several forts around. And here recently, in this last twenty years, they've gotten involved in housing. When a Tribal member wants a house, they check it to make sure you haven't picked a burial mound which could be real easy around here.

So I think it's all cool. They bring in all these educated people and then you get to mingle with them and they're a good bunch of people that share what they know. You know, like Domonique deBeaubien. She's always telling me about what she's looking at. Like when we went to Philadelphia to look at twenty-one skulls, I was really surprised at her professionalism with it, doing the work and what she knew. It's always good to watch another professional at work like when she was handling the skulls. So that's a project that we're working on.

And sometimes THPO, I don't know if you'd call it rewriting history, but take Egmont Key for example. THPO has gotten very involved in that one. And when you start talking about Egmont Key, you have to talk about Fort Myers, Punta Rassa, all those because those are ports where the Seminoles were shipped to Oklahoma. And then it all breaks down to Polly Parker. Polly Parker is that trip we took commemorating her voyage until she escaped. So all that's driven by THPO.[24]

And these events are fine but my thing is—I'm in for the history part of it. That's why when we went to Philadelphia, each skull had a history paper written on it, but it wasn't by any twentieth-century person. It was by the surgeon himself, Dr. Abadie. He wrote different things about where he picked the skull up, where he dug this skull out of a grave, or took it off a battlefield. I hear this practice went on clear into the Civil War, taking skulls off of dead soldiers and warriors. They were trying to decide what made each other angry. (laughs)

SB: Do you think there's a bad side to archaeology? Can archaeology be done wrong?

WJ: I think so, maybe. I did a talk at archaeology day at the [New College of Florida in Sarasota], and they wanted me to be their guest speaker so I talked about archaeology. I left them with these final words, "When is enough, enough? How much more can you learn digging around? When's this going to end?" Because I know THPO every day gets calls about remains of something. So you could spin your wheels, get bogged down. And they have to be selective or else you'd always have a funeral crew around. But yes, I think that it can be misinterpreted, but it just depends on who is in control. I think they have a good team now with Dr. Backhouse and his team. I think they mean well, and they're always checking to make sure what Native people think. They involve them.

SB: Have you ever worked directly as a cultural advisor for THPO or you just happened to do it while you were working in museum outreach?

WJ: Yeah, they just shanghaied me! (laughter) Like they're doing now. They call me all the time. But the way my position is, I have some down time that I don't mind giving it to them. Like today, you know.

SB: Well, we're glad to have you participating.

WJ: Well you know, when they started this project, I was supposed to go up to Tampa for the conference.[25] I was supposed to be there, but I was already booked for something else. And I was supposed to write my story and turn it in like everybody on this list here. I was looking at this one here [points to book chapter list], "Bringing the Ancestors Home." I was very involved in that one there with Domonique and Kate.

SB: I want to ask you about your experience with historic preservation, preserving historic sites and historic structures. What do you think that does for the Tribe? Do you think it's important that these sites are preserved?

WJ: Yeah, I think they do a great job with researching and documenting what we have, even going out to other places like I believe we're involved with researching Pensacola, the site there.[26] So I think as far as the dollar can stretch, they're doing pretty good. Of course, I'm a history guy so I understand archaeology, why it's important. But a layman Seminole person may not understand it.

SB: That ties into my next question. Things like the Red Barn in Brighton and the Council Oak in Hollywood went through a process with the THPO of formally being preserved and being listed as historic sites.[27] Do you think that would have been done without the THPO? Did the community feel these places were important and worth preserving?

WJ: You know, Red Barn maybe so because it was a small community effort but THPO brought it to the point. I think that once it was registered, it just sat on somebody's desk. I think it was Carrie Dilley who discovered it and brought it to my attention and Paul's attention. So we went to the community there and they liked the idea of preserving it, and so the rest is history. When Carrie was with the THPO, she pushed it right on through until it is what it is today. But the Council Oak, you know, that would have made some good firewood right there. In a way, it's all show I guess. It probably isn't even the tree that they sat under. (laughs)

SB: Where would you like to see the THPO office go in the future? Any different directions than it's going now? Or do you see it heading in a good direction?

WJ: I see them heading in a good direction right now. And I don't see any reason why they should change. But there's going to be change because subjects change or the miles change. You asked me a question about preservation of grounds, the Battle of Okeechobee is one of them.[28]

The state of Florida bought that and the Seminole Tribe has been very involved in that. Well, not so much the THPO but the THPO is now starting to get involved with that particular location. The fact is that site in Okeechobee, it's only 1 percent of the battleground. So it's only good for reenactment once a year because the whole island around the lake, that's the battleground. From Taylor Creek to Nubbins Slough, probably a mile and a half across there on the white sand dunes on the beach. That's the real battleground, but now it has people living there, homes and roads. We're lucky to get that 1 percent.

And Egmont Key, the Tribe is involved with that.[29] There's real genuine heartfelt effort of non-Natives who are really trying to step it up because I've been to Egmont Key three times and I've seen three pictures of how the waves and the erosion are working. The island is going away, and if man doesn't do anything about it, it could be no more. And you know, for most Seminoles, it's "Que sera, sera." But for some of us, it's our Auschwitz because Seminoles were held there. It's our concentration camp. It's our history.

Put the shoe on the other foot now with these new kids coming up. You have history-minded kids, but who are they going to go to? All these elders are gone. I think here on the Brighton Reservation, the oldest guy is like seventy-five years old. And by our standards, that's not very old. That's nothing when you put him against my great-grandmother. She was ninety-six. (laughs) So where do these kids go? They go to the textbook, they go to the museum, to find out who they are.

SB: But isn't that what you did?

WJ: That's what I did. I didn't learn much at the museum but—(laughter)— I was good enough to understand people like Brent Weisman and Bill Steele, their work. Also, there's a Seminole War Society. I got myself connected with them. I even became an officer. But those historians would always like to tick me off, tell me stuff, military stuff.

So in my later years, all of a sudden, I might be the go-to person. Not to learn it all because I don't want to tell them everything, I want them to research it, because it's there. You can't be afraid of the written stuff. And that's the era that I came through, so they would mark me as a textbook historian. (laughs) I say, "Well I don't feel too bad. That's what all the white guys do. They're all textbook." One thing I do regret, I wish I had thought of it when I was younger, the guy that wrote *Bury*

My Heart at Wounded Knee, I would have loved to have studied under him.[30]

SB: Did you ever consider making history your career more formally?

WJ: Nope. I have a good time doing what I'm doing now.

SB: Anything else about the THPO office?

WJ: I can't say enough about them. They really are like the museum outreach, the arm and the leg, because if they weren't out in those woods checking things out and doing their little test digs, we wouldn't know a whole lot.

SB: Is there anything in particular you want readers of this book to know about the Seminole Tribe or how our THPO operates when they go about their own work?

WJ: Well yeah, it takes a lot of work, a lot of planning. And for tribes, you have to sell it to your Councilmen too, your Chairman. If they're not on board, you're not going to get it. We're lucky that our Chairman is on board with it. He's the one that built the Ah-Tah-Thi-Ki Museum back when it almost couldn't be done.[31] But he understood. And it's flourished from there. It hit a couple snags, but that's expected when you have growing pains. So my advice to anybody that wants to get involved with this, it's not for the lighthearted. You have to be willing to put in the work and get out there. I'm amazed at what the THPO group here does.

I have a little joke. A friend of mine saw THPO people out there on the side of the road. They had their shovels or they're doing something. And my friend asked me, "What are they doing?" I go, "You didn't hear?" He goes, "No, what?" I said, "They discovered gold around here." (laughter) He got all excited. He wanted to go get a shovel and go to work. (laughter) But it's been fun. It's been a good life. I wouldn't change anything.

Notes

1. When the Seminole Tribe gained federal recognition in 1957, the Bureau of Indian Affairs (BIA) only recognized eight traditional matrilineal clans. Some Tribal members, including Willie Johns, identify with older clans such as Wildcat, which is subsumed into the larger Panther Clan.

2. Cow Creek is an alternate name for the Mvskoke, or Creek, language spoken by members of the Seminole Tribe. According to Johns, its name derives from Seminole leader Cowkeeper (ca. 1710–1783) and his followers tending to herds of cattle while

living along the St. Johns River south into St. Lucie County (east-central peninsular Florida). Johns affirms that descendants of this community eventually moved onto the modern Brighton Reservation (Covington 1993).

3. Osceola, also called Billy Powell, was born in the Upper Creek town of Tallassee ca. 1804. He was a prominent warrior in the Second Seminole War famously captured under a white flag of truce and shipped to Fort Moultrie in Charleston, South Carolina, before his death in 1838 (Wickman 1991).

4. A chickee is an open-sided, palmetto-thatched-roof shelter supported on posts that served as the primary dwelling of Seminole people from the mid-nineteenth century through the mid/late twentieth century (Dilley 2015).

5. The Trail of Tears refers to the forced relocation of Native Americans from their homelands in the American Southeast to Indian Territory (Oklahoma) west of the Mississippi River prompted by the Indian Removal Act of 1830 (Foreman 1974; Howard 1984).

6. Sonny Billie (1935–2003) was a Seminole Medicine Man and member of the Panther Clan from the Big Cypress Reservation.

7. The Calusa (southwestern Florida), Tequesta (southeastern Florida), and Jeaga (southeastern Florida) were the European names identifying three prominent Native American cultural groups encountered along the Florida coast (Milanich 1998).

8. The Battle of Horseshoe Bend (1814), the last major conflict in the Creek War (1813–1814), pitted a coalition of state militias (commanded by Andrew Jackson), White Stick Creeks, and Cherokee allies against the more traditional Red Stick Creeks who opposed European encroachment. Some surviving Red Sticks fled south and joined Seminoles already living in Florida (Weiss 2014).

9. Larger settlements (towns) were being established throughout Florida by the second half of the eighteenth century, including Chocochatti (Red Town), located as far south as Hernando County, just north of the modern city of Tampa (Weisman 1989).

10. The Seminole Wars were a series of armed conflicts between the U.S federal government and the Seminoles. Historians have split them into three main conflicts: First Seminole War (1817–1819), Second Seminole War (1835–1842), and Third Seminole War (1855–1858). In reality, the period from the Creek War (1813–1814) until 1858 marked a time of intense conflict and hardship. Citizens of the Seminole Tribe of Florida are descended from those who remained in Florida at the end of the Third Seminole War (Covington 1993).

11. White (1995).

12. Seminoles traded at several trading posts in South Florida in the late nineteenth and early twentieth centuries, including the Stranahan Trading Post on the New River in Fort Lauderdale, G. W. Storter's Trading Post in Everglades City, and Browns Trading Post located in Big Cypress (Kersey 1974).

13. James E. Billie, Bird Clan (1944–) served as Chairman of the Seminole Tribe of Florida from 1977 to 2001 and from 2011 to the present.

14. Seminoles in Florida historically speak two related but distinct languages. Creek, or Mvskoke, is spoken primarily on the Brighton Reservation and areas north of Lake Okeechobee. Miccosukee is spoken on the Big Cypress Reservation and areas south of Lake Okeechobee. Seminoles from older generations were often fluent in both languages (Covington 1993).

15. The eight Seminole clans currently recognized are Wind, Otter, Bear, Snake, Panther, Toad/Big Town, Bird, and Deer. Historically, there were many more clans prior to the intense conflicts and forced demographic dislocations that took place throughout the nineteenth century.

16. Recognized as a pioneer of the Seminole cattle industry, Ollie Jones (1928–1987) was a member of the Bird Clan and lived primarily on the Brighton Reservation.

17. In Florida, there are two federally recognized groups of Native Americans: the Seminole Tribe of Florida and the Miccosukee Tribe of Indians of Florida. Additionally, there is a group of Independent Seminoles who do not wish to be federally recognized. In Oklahoma, there is the Seminole Nation, comprised mostly of Seminole people forcibly relocated during the Seminole Wars (Covington 1993; Howard 1984).

18. The Mvskoke, or Creek, Nation is a federally recognized tribe of Mvskoke people in Oklahoma. There are other federally recognized and state-recognized Mvskoke communities, including ones still residing in their ancestral homelands in Alabama and Georgia and then others in parts of Oklahoma, Louisiana, and Texas (Wickman 1991).

19. From the late nineteenth through the mid-twentieth century, a systematic effort to drain the Everglades for flood control and agricultural development resulted in thousands of miles of canals and levees that compartmentalized the land and altered water levels and flows throughout the Everglades ecosystem (McVoy et al. 2011).

20. Beginning in the early twentieth century, Seminoles lived and worked in "tourist camps," purpose-built Seminole villages along the Tamiami Trail or near resort locations, where they produced and sold Seminole crafts, wrestled alligators, and engaged in otherwise everyday cultural activities for a paying tourist audience (West 1998).

21. On August 21, 1957, the Seminole Tribe of Florida was formally established with the signing of the Seminole Tribe of Florida Constitution and Bylaws.

22. Hollywood is a city located on Florida's southeast coast, a subdivision of the modern city of Fort Lauderdale. The adjacent Hollywood Seminole Indian Reservation is the seat of the modern Tribal government and is located roughly 108 miles from the Brighton Reservation.

23. Willard (Bill) Steele was Director of the Seminole THPO from July 2002 to February 2012.

24. On December 1, 2013, a group of Seminoles, Tribal employees, invited media, and guests embarked on a chartered fishing boat to retrace the historic 1858 water route traveled by a group of Seminole captives being forcibly relocated to Indian Territory (Oklahoma). The Seminole captives traveled by steamship from a stockade on Egmont Key at the mouth of Tampa Bay up to old Fort San Marcos south of Tallahassee. It was there that Seminole Polly Parker escaped her captors and walked 200 miles through the Florida brush to her home near Lake Okeechobee. Many of Polly Parker's descendants are Florida Seminoles who joined this commemorative trip (Gallagher 2013b).

25. The 2013 Southeast Archaeological Conference was held in Tampa November 6–9.

26. The THPO has an active and ongoing program of research in the Florida panhandle and particularly the Pensacola area. The goal of this research is to develop a stronger understanding of Native American history in this critical region.

27. The Council Oak was the site of the meetings that led to the creation of the Seminole Tribe of Florida Constitution and Bylaws, which gave official recognition to the Tribe in 1957. The Brighton Red Barn, built by the U.S. Civilian Conservation Corps–Indian Division in 1941, marked the beginning of the Seminole cattle industry and quickly became a social center for the Brighton community. Both sites are listed on the National Register of Historic Places (Dilley, this volume).

28. The Battle of Okeechobee was a major battle of the Second Seminole War fought on December 25, 1837 (Covington 1993; Mahon 1967).

29. Egmont Key is a small barrier island located at the mouth of Tampa Bay on the West Coast of Florida. U.S. federal troops imprisoned Seminoles on the island during the Third Seminole War, many of whom died and were buried there. Severe erosion now threatens the integrity of the island and the sanctity of these unmarked graves (Covington 1982; Gallagher 2013a).

30. The historian and author Dee Brown worked at the University of Illinois at Urbana-Champaign.

31. Thanks to the leadership of Chairman James E. Billie and Seminole Tribe of Florida Resolution C-96-89, the Ah-Tah-Thi-Ki Museum was established as a not-for-profit corporation on February 3, 1989. Located on the Big Cypress Reservation, the museum opened to the public on August 21, 1997.

References Cited

Covington, James W. 1982. *The Billy Bowlegs War*. Chuluota, Fla.: Mickler House Publishers.

———. 1993. *The Seminoles of Florida*. Gainesville: University Press of Florida.

Dilley, Carrie. 2015. *Thatched Roofs and Open Sides: The Architecture of Chickees and Their Changing Role in Seminole Society*. Gainesville: University Press of Florida.

Foreman, Grant. 1974. *Indian Removal: The Emigration of the Five Civilized Tribes of Indians*. The Civilization of the American Indian Series. Norman: University of Oklahoma Press.

Gallagher, Peter B. 2013a. "A Visit to Egmont Key as It Slides into the Sea." *The Seminole Tribune*, August 30.

———. 2013b. "Emateloye Estenletkvte: Polly Parker Got Away." *The Seminole Tribune*, December 20.

Howard, James H. 1984. *Oklahoma Seminoles: Medicine, Magic, and Religion*. The Civilization of the American Indian Series. Norman: University of Oklahoma Press.

Kersey, Harry A., Jr. 1974. *Pelts, Plumes, and Hides*. Gainesville: University Press of Florida.

Mahon, John K. 1967. *History of the Second Seminole War*. Gainesville: University Press of Florida.

McVoy, Christopher W., Winifred Said Park, Jayantha Obeysekera, Joel Van Arman, and Thomas Dreschel. 2011. *Landscapes and Hydrology of the Predrainage Everglades*. Gainesville: University Press of Florida.

Milanich, Jerald T. 1998. *Florida's Indians from Ancient Times to the Present*. Gainesville: University Press of Florida.

Weisman, Brent Richards. 1989. *Like Beads on a String*. Tuscaloosa: University of Alabama Press.

Weiss, Justin Scott. 2014. "The Ghosts of Horseshoe Bend: Myth, Memory, and the Making of a National Battlefield." http://repository.asu.edu/attachments/135087/content/Weiss_asu_0010N_13935.pdf.

West, Patsy. 1998. *The Enduring Seminoles: From Alligator Wrestling to Ecoturism*. Gainesville: University Press of Florida.

White, John C., Jr. 1995. "American Military Strategy during the Second Seminole War." Master's thesis, Faculty of the Marine Corps Command and Staff College, Marine Corps University.

Wickman, Patricia R. 1991. *Osceola's Legacy*. Tuscaloosa: University of Alabama Press.

2

"Bending and Not Breaking"

Seminole History and the Tribal Historic Preservation Office, the Miccosukee Perspective

MARTY BOWERS AND STEPHEN BRIDENSTINE

Working in the Tribal Historic Preservation Office (THPO) as the primary liaison to the community and later as an observer of the program, Marty Bowers offers a perspective that transcends both institutional and reservation boundaries. His involvement in the establishment and formation of the THPO was foundational to a new staff who were largely initially unfamiliar with working on a reservation or how to appropriately engage with the community. By reviewing incoming on-reservation projects for oftentimes intangible cultural areas of concern, Bowers introduced the staff to a new paradigm that prioritized community input as the primary driver of heritage management.

Author Bio

Marty Bowers is a citizen of the Seminole Tribe of Florida and a member of the Wind Clan. Born in 1971 and raised on the Big Cypress Seminole Indian Reservation, Bowers rode the bus 80 miles round-trip every day to attend public school in Clewiston, Florida. On the weekends, he joined his father's Creek-speaking family for services at a Baptist church on the Brighton Reservation. Raised in a bilingual household, Bowers is today more fluent in the Miccosukee language, the dominant language on the Big Cypress Reservation.

Throughout his career, Bowers worked for the Seminole Tribe as a ranch hand, librarian, and museum exhibits specialist. In 2004, he left Big Cypress to pursue other opportunities in Tampa. From 2007 to 2010, Bowers returned

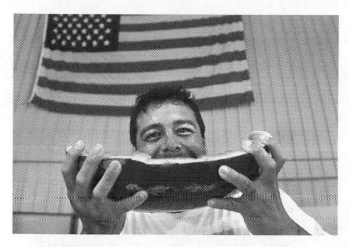

Figure 2.1.
Marty Bowers.
By permission
of *The Seminole
Tribune.*

to Big Cypress to serve as a cultural advisor to the THPO. He has since returned to Tampa where he currently resides.

On June 23, 2014, Marty Bowers sat down with Ah-Tah-Thi-Ki Museum
Oral Historian Stephen Bridenstine to discuss Seminole history and his work
with the THPO. In this wide-ranging and insightful interview, Bowers relates
his personal journey of cultural discovery and shares his thoughts and feelings
about Seminole history and the work of the THPO.

STEPHEN BRIDENSTINE: Could you start off by telling us about the
   setting that you grew up in, both the physical surroundings and the
   family environment?
MARTY BOWERS: I was raised with four sisters. I'm the youngest.
   Both of my parents worked. My father worked with the Land Use
   Office, I think it was funded by BIA [Bureau of Indian Affairs], and
   my mother worked with the Indian Health Service. She helped out at
   the clinic. I grew up in Big Cypress around the horseshoe.[1] I didn't go
   to the school on the Rez so I caught the bus every morning, probably
   six o'clock or so. The bus stopped at the public school in Clewiston
   and then bussed back every afternoon.[2] A lot of my peers went to the
   Ahfachkee Tribal School, but I didn't go there at all.
SB: Did you speak either Creek or Miccosukee in your family?
MB: Miccosukee. My father was a Creek speaker, but he spoke both. And
   back then, in his time, everybody spoke both from what I understand.
   He spoke Creek and Miccosukee in the house so there was a little bit
   of both, but I was more fluent in Miccosukee because we were on Big
   Cypress and that was the language there.[3]

SB: What roles did your family members have in your upbringing?

MB: My immediate family was just like any other nuclear family. I suppose we hung out, had good family vacations. My oldest sister was kind of a surrogate mother because both my parents worked so she was around more than they were a lot. And we were also raised by aunts and uncles, and with my dad's family in Brighton.[4] We didn't do a lot of the traditional Seminole cultural ways where we go off with our aunts and uncles. We didn't do that. We were raised in the Baptist Church.

As traditionalists, we go on our mother's family, our mother's side, our mother's clan, and it's the mother's family's responsibility to raise us and teach us the family ways. In biblical teachings, you take the name of the father and the father is the head of the household. So we were raised in church with my dad's family spending weekends in Brighton. We hung out with my dad's brothers and my dad's sisters and my dad's family, not my mom's. That's how it was with us.

SB: Growing up, would you say that you had a traditional Seminole education in addition to your school in Clewiston?

MB: No, we didn't. That wasn't the direction our father took us. It was school, and he wanted us to be hard workers like he was. But he would make jokes, like we'd be sitting at the table and I'm blowing on my food to cool it off and he'd say, "Face the direction of the sun," and I didn't get it. My mom would giggle and nudge him but I didn't get it. Throughout my early childhood, I remember little comments like that, and as I got older and my curiosity grew about the other part of who I am culturally, I started going to Corn Dance on my own and started branching out into cultural stuff on my own. That's when I started getting the jokes. When we're out touching medicine or practicing a ritual, there are certain directions we have to face and when I was older, I finally got them, I got the joke. "Oh, that's what Dad was talking about!" (laughs)

So my dad was raised in those ways but for some reason it didn't translate to us, he didn't instill that knowledge in us, nor did my mom. I don't think she was raised in that real traditional manner either. My mom was raised in places like Coppingers and Silver Springs, so she spent a lot of time in the tourist camps.[5] So as far as living in a camp setting, that part we got, but as far as traditional practices and a religious belief system that comes from our culture, that part wasn't imparted upon us.

And my dad had the scars that showed he did practice in his former life. He just didn't impart it upon us. His family in Brighton were some of the first Christian converts, and I think that is kind of what happened with his family. They broke away from the cultural stuff and started going to the Christianity. It just severed it.

SB: When you were young and saw the scars on your father's arms, did you know what they were or why they were there?

MB: No, I never thought to ask and I didn't find out until later. In my house, Dad wasn't around. He worked from sunup to sundown, so when he was around he was tired. Sometimes he'd take me out with him to work but that stuff just never came up. It was like a secret. (laughs)

SB: Growing up, did you ever hear stories about the origins of the Seminole Tribe?

MB: Yeah. My mom was raised by her aunt instead of her mother. They settled out in Big Cypress with Frank Billie, who was one of the founding members of the Tribe and is my grandfather. So when we weren't going to church in Brighton, we were with Frank Billie and my mom's aunts. He was a pastor in Big Cypress so we had the church family in Brighton and we had the church family in Big Cypress, so we were definitely doing the Christianity thing.

As I said, we would go over to Frank Billie's house from time to time and he would sit with us and tell us the history of the Tribe as he lived it, how the Tribe was formed. So from really early on, I got a lot of that information before I really understood it. I was really young. I can't remember how young I was. I have memories, many memories, of sitting with my grandpa Frank. I was a kid though. I thought we listened to him because we were supposed to. I really didn't get what he was saying until later.

SB: Did you have any expectation or feeling that you had to learn it or was it just stories that you listened to?

MB: We had an expectation that we had to learn it. It seemed that way. And the way he told it, it just seemed like it was something we were supposed to know.

SB: Would you be willing to share your story about where the Tribe came from? An origin story?

MB: So the creation story to me—I'll tell you what I think about it. It's a story. It's a story. And it's a story that I kind of grew in to because I guess I was raised in church with Adam and Eve and all that stuff. That's a story also. But what I like about the Seminole creation story, how I learned it, it just seems more cool. (laughs) I was taught—they call it the backbone of the earth. It's a mountainous region and we were in a pit that was void of everything and dark. There was a hole up on top and there were different life forms within this pit. Some of them were animals and some of them were us. The Breathmaker made the animals and their songs and their wails and their cries.

This coincides with our celebration songs we have at Corn Dance. There are songs that celebrate elements and animals, but there is no song that celebrates man. And so I guess, from what I was taught, it's a humility thing. And then here in the story of our creation, that's where we get it from. He kind of left us alone, to our own devices. So different clans would try to escape, and they couldn't come out of this void. One of the strongest animals, the Bear Clan, they thought that they could muscle their way out and they couldn't. The Panther, he thought that he could climb out and he couldn't. Then the Bird thought he could fly out and he couldn't. Finally, there was a form off in the corner, kind of humble, and he's just watching everything. And that's how they say Wind Clans are, we take everything in. We're like wind. We're everywhere. We see things. We hear things.

So he's doing what he's supposed to do. He's watching and he's learning and they ask him to help so he says he thinks he can help. He starts singing songs and chanting and takes the form of wind and goes through the opening and breaks it open wide enough for the cat to come through and then the bird to fly through and then the other animals follow. That's what I learned. I've been told by my aunts, my uncles, the Chairman, that that is how Wind Clan people are. Back before we were tribes and we were just different groups of people, they say that decisions weren't made unless there was a Wind on the council or a Wind present as a counselor to listen, to make sure all sides were being heard. So that story of our creation kind of put us in that responsibility since we helped then, we help now. That's what I was taught about our creation.

SB: Now this is the Wind Clan version of the story?

MB: (laughs) Yes.

SB: So between clans, between families, between reservations, the stories do differ?

MB: Yeah.

SB: Did you ever hear stories about the other tribal peoples who lived in Florida like the Calusa, the Tequesta, or the Jeaga?[6]

MB: Yeah. What I was taught is that we're a part of them. We're their descendants. Not all of us, some of us. That's what I was taught. And I remember being a kid and my mom, she would always talk to us about not getting tattoos. "Don't get tattooed. Don't get tattooed." And we would ask her, "How come?" and she would tell us, "That's how the soldiers knew who to capture. That's how the soldiers knew who to chase and knew who you were, by your tattoos." To me that sounds old, like really ancient people. I don't hear about the Miccosukees or Seminoles being tattooed up in a way that's significant. So that's the story that my mom told me, but she's Otter Clan and I'm Wind Clan so some of the stuff that I learned from her was coming from an Otter family perspective. I was adopted from the hospital.[7]

SB: Do you find that in different situations or at different times in your life, you might identify yourself differently?

MB: Right now, I feel like I'm Seminole and I'm Wind. I feel like all I'm doing what I'm supposed to be doing. I come out here and I don't live on the Rez. Like my friends on the Rez, they always say I live behind enemy lines. (laughter) I've never had that really strong bias or almost racist outlook. I've been around other people all my life. From kindergarten, I was going off the Rez and mixing with non-Tribal people so it was always easier for me to mix with non-Tribal people. Sometimes it's even easier to mix with non-Tribal people than it is people on the Rez.

So right now, I'm doing what I'm supposed to be doing like we were taught. I talked with my uncles and my aunts of my Wind family and started to learn who I am as a Wind. What does it mean to be Wind Clan? What are my responsibilities as a Wind Clan? Part of that is to be places. It's to go and learn and bring back knowledge to your people from what my family taught me. So now I just feel like I'm doing what I'm supposed to be doing. I live out here and I go home and say, "This is this and that is that." It's not anything formal, it's just how I carry myself within my clan duties.

SB: In your formal education, did you ever learn anything about the Seminoles?

MB: (laughs) No. When I was in eighth grade, they had Florida history and there was one thing, just two or three paragraphs, a page maybe, about Osceola. That was it. That was it! There were the [Seminole] Wars and they would glance over that stuff, but as far as what we know now, nah. Nah.

SB: Besides the Seminole Tribe of Florida, you also have the Miccosukee Tribe of Indians of Florida, you've got Independent Seminoles in Florida, and then you have the Seminole Nation over in Oklahoma.[8] Do you feel any sense of shared heritage with these other communities?

MB: Oh yeah. We're all basically the same. The Seminole Nation, they were once here with us. So yeah, I think that we're all the same.

SB: Were there many stories about the Seminole Wars that you heard from family growing up?[9]

MB: Not stories. When I think about my experience growing up on the Rez, in my family it seemed very fearful. You'd have to be careful like it could happen again. For example, when my mom would call my name from across the house, I made the mistake several times of going, "What?" Then she'd come and get me and pull me into wherever she wanted me to be at and she'd say, "When I call you, you don't say 'what?' you come to me because you don't know what's happening. You have to listen. You don't know if a soldier is taking me away. I may not be able to say your name again. So when I call you, you come." So it was more stuff like that, teachings about being careful and warnings. She would always say soldiers or *sholetaawe*, that's soldiers in our language, and I didn't understand it. I didn't. It was not be afraid, but be cautious. That was the main vein that went through my childhood. You had to be careful, something could happen.

SB: Did you hear any specific stories about how the Seminoles ended up in the Everglades and on the reservations? Any stories about movement?

MB: Now this stuff started when I got older. I guess I was about sixteen, seventeen, or eighteen when I became more interested and started living the more traditional lifestyle. I learned from people like Sonny Billie who has since passed on.[10] I just became really curious and started asking questions, having heard his version of it and other people's version of it.

Take Abiaka.[11] Some people say he didn't exist. There are some stories that say he was a made-up character by the Natives who were here at the time. He was like a boogeyman to scare the soldiers during the Seminole Wars. But then you hear other stories that say he's the reason we're here in Florida. That from when the time he was born, his life wasn't his. He was trained in the medicinal ways, and he knew stuff that he was taught. He was born in the late 1700s, so he was taught old, old stuff, and he lived till past [the] 1850s, if it's real.

And they say that he's the one that was living in, not Georgia or

Alabama, but in Florida beneath the panhandle and that he knew war was coming. He was the one that came and mapped out the bottom of the state. Abiaka and others with him were coming down and preparing and mapping and getting ready, saying war was coming, "This is it. This is our dying ground." So that's what I was taught oral history wise, that he came down with several other Natives that were around at that time and they learned the lay of the land.

SB: What about some of the other historical figures who are prominent in the Seminole Wars, like Osceola?[12] Were there stories about him that you heard from the elders?

MB: Yeah, he was the one I heard of most because he's just a popular guy, right? And hearing stories from different families, I asked about him. Some say that he was just a white man. Some say he didn't have a clan so he really had no place. The stories are so twisted up that in some people's minds he didn't have a place because he had no clan, but then you hear the other version of it saying he rose to prominence as a warrior or a chief. You hear all those things.

My mom is one of the ones who taught me that he weakened his group. That he killed one of his own leaders and took over, like a coup, for lack of a better term. He wouldn't let them eat. He ruled them with an iron first. It was his way or the soldier way. My mom said that he did that because he didn't want his group shipped out West or shipped from their new homes, but he also didn't want them listening to anyone else. He was power hungry.

Some other families, some friends I grew up with, they say that he was just a white man. Then you see other families in the Tribe where he's revered. How I see it is that he was someone the military built up so when they captured him, they could say they caught the great Osceola.

SB: What about the role of Black Seminoles, both the role in the community and during the Wars?[13] Had you heard much about that?

MB: Not growing up. James Billie talked to me about them.[14] They were just groups. It wasn't anything ever like a mass exodus from slavery. They had just escaped and learned our ways and we traded with them. We learned the names of certain animals like the lion. We had never seen a lion, but there's the story of the landmass, right? The story of how the lion got the rabbit.[15] There are stories and then there is what I guess your faith will allow you.

SB: I suppose that makes sense because there are no lions around here.

(laughter)

SB: I never thought about that.

MB: It's the same with zebras. We have names for animals we never saw. And then I think that some of that stuff came from interactions with escaped slaves. Then there is some stuff that we cook which is like stuff that they cook. And I kind of see things that way, like how we view owls, how they're a bad omen. I was talking to James Billie one time, and he talked about his legend when he was a baby that a bunch of owls came and perched up by his chickee, that it was supposed to be an omen or something. Talking to him he goes, "Just a bunch of bugs. Rodents eat bugs, lizards or whatever. It's just the food chain. It has nothing to do with me. I'm not special. They just all saw a bunch of bugs and it may be time to eat. That's why they came down. They weren't interested in me."

Then I was talking to him about Corn Dance and how it seems kind of similar to a Catholic Mass. It makes sense really. Florida was Spanish at one time, and there's no way that we could have been here and interacted with them and parts of their ceremonies didn't get mixed in with ours. Like when you're at Corn Dance, you see altar boys. They're following the Father around, or the main head guy, preparing the medicines. They walk around with the water, like holy water blessing things. We drink it, like the Blood of Christ. We eat the corn, which to me is like eating the Body of Christ. So there's a whole bunch of similarities that I didn't start seeing until I started talking to James Billie more often.

With the history and our religious beliefs and faith, if I sat and thought about it too long, I'd just be challenged, I wouldn't move. So it's like a choice. What am I going to follow? And what I follow is our traditional ways. It just seems kind of funny. There's a lot of stuff that contradicts how I was raised and what I was taught. But, hey man, I'm Seminole. I've chosen what I believe. (laughs) But I'm not blind to the facts.

SB: I'd like to ask you about Indian Removal and the story of Seminoles moving west.[16] Was that a prominent part of what you heard from the elders? What were some of the feelings toward the people who left?

MB: There are several. People say, "We're unconquered," but during my own interviews, when I talked to the elders, they said, "No, we were beat up." They say, "They beat us up and we were just running around." When you hear about the people who were moved out West, it's a very sad story because families were broken up. I'm sure you've heard in interviews about babies who were held underwater to keep them quiet or about running through the swamp, raiding settlers or soldiers' forts for corn, like feed corn, and eating it. Even eating parts of animals that the soldiers threw out, rummaging after them because things were so unorganized and it was unsafe to go out venturing. You hear about them trying to hunt but the gunshots would bring the soldiers, so a lot of times they would steal food from the soldiers or steal food from other camps. It was a time of great sorrow. That's what you hear when you talk to the older folks. But then the younger crowd, you hear a lot of, "Oh, they got beat. They're not Florida Seminoles. They got beat. They're not unconquered, we are." So there's that. And personally I think it was very sad. Like I said, we're a part of them. We were all one at one time.

SB: Moving into the late nineteenth, early twentieth centuries now, what changed but what remained the same?

MB: I think that a lot of what changed was how young the women or girls were who were married out to start their own families. I think that's huge. No one really knows how many of us were left after the last Seminole War, when we were finally left alone and the dust settled, but it seemed like hearing the stories, young girls, young teenagers were married off to older men and that it was all to bring our numbers back up. That's what I surmise from hearing the different stories. So I think that was the biggest thing, is that our numbers were gone and we needed a way to bend and not break. I think that was one of the bending points.[17] Historically, Seminole men had more than one wife but they were grown women, not three fourteen-year-old wives. So I think that was the biggest thing.

SB: So after the Seminole Wars, how did people make a living? How did they get by?

MB: Picking peppers, tomatoes, stuff like that. Moving from farmstead to farmstead, kind of like how the immigrants from Mexico do it now. They went to different parts of the country, picking crops in different farm regions. But that was after the draining. Then there were the different tourist camps. Like I said, my mom lived at Silver Springs for a lot of her life. My dad, he was a mechanic. He was a self-taught diesel mechanic and he lived in Brighton. I think the Brighton group living outside Okeechobee were a little different than our groups down south of Lake Okeechobee. The Brighton group, the cowboys, the Creeks, I think they had a more friendly thing going on with their neighbors. So I think my dad was able to get work. He was born around 1920 so he was a teenager in the '30s. I think the Brighton group was able to do a lot of things different than the groups down south.

SB: I was going to ask you about that. Feelings toward people outside the Tribe have changed, right?

MB: Yeah.

SB: Certainly since your parents and grandparents generation, right?

MB: Yeah, it's changed, but I go down to the Rez and I still hear it. I do. And it's not like how it used to be, but it's still there. I remember one time, James Billie and I were talking, and he says, "You hear these people talking about white people this and white people that. They're the ones coming to our casino." He says, "Man, treat them better." (laughs) "You all run around talking about 'unconquered.' You all have no idea what that means. You have no idea what our people went through for this." And on some level he's right. And it's not because they're just white people, it's because they're outsiders. And so I think that has toned down a bit, but it's still there.

SB: How do you understand Tribal sovereignty? What is that to you?

MB: What I understand it to be is we are our own governing body. On certain levels, they look at us like we're another nation, but that's not what we are. We're still tied in. We're able to set our own laws, how we govern our own people. We're supposed to be treated as another country.

SB: So then in your lifetime, you've seen the rise of smoke shops, bingo, and casino gaming. How have those changed the Tribe?

MB: Housing is huge and our health care, too. For example, my dad, when he got older and we didn't have the resources to have him live at home with us and be around family, the Indian Health Service provided money to send him to a home, so that's what we did. And I think now, with how it's structured with our businesses bringing in income, we have an option to have our elders live at home with us and be taken care of at home, just like it always was. Just like it always was. And I think that to me is the biggest thing right there. Along the way, we lost that.

Like I said before, my dad wanted us to work hard. He came from a hard-working family. The family was all work, work, work, but the money they were making had to go to feeding the family. Being a kid, I remember going to visit his sister in a nursing home because the funds were not there to give her the care she needed at home. There wasn't any money for that. So we'd go and visit her at a nursing home almost every other weekend.

My dad always seemed distant and kind of standoffish, but there were also some gentle things about him. I would see him cry almost every other weekend visiting his sister because she didn't remember his name. It was like a reintroduction every time. So for me, that's the biggest thing. I had to watch my dad go through it with his sister and with us because we went along with them. Then we had to do that same thing with my dad. Now my mom, she's in care, but she's doing it at home. My dad was probably thirty years older than my mom so we had to do it how we did it, but now Mom is at home. So that's the biggest thing to me. Seeing it with my dad's sister and then my dad but now my mom gets to be at home.

SB: So I'd like to move on to the Seminole THPO. In your own words, and from your own experience, what does the THPO do?

MB: To me, they are the Tribe's archaeological firm, and they help us stay away from places we're not supposed to be at and help us build our houses. I think THPO does an awesome job with doing that.

SB: Before you started to work for THPO in 2007, did you have any experience with archaeology?

MB: No, but it's fun. I love it.

SB: During your time there, did you go out into the field and do some fieldwork?

MB: Uh-huh. Yep.

SB: So what specifically would you say that archaeology can offer to the Tribe and to the community?

MB: A different perspective on our history. Like I said, there is what I was taught and I know a lot of it is oral history and a lot of it is different than the facts. Sometimes, you don't want to hear what THPO found out or what they dug up. Sometimes you don't want to hear that because it kind of challenges that belief.

SB: Especially if it's on your home site.

MB: Yeah!

(laughter)

MB: Sometimes you don't want to hear it but I think in the end, it just adds to the knowledge base of what I can either take with me or leave it. It's just giving me more options.

SB: Okay. So you obviously like THPO?

MB: Uh-huh.

SB: And other people in the Tribe, what are some of their opinions? Have people's opinions changed over time?

MB: I don't know if they've necessarily changed. I haven't talked to too many people about it since I stopped working there. But my Wind family, my aunts and my clan sisters, they didn't want me working there. They were telling me, "You're going places and doing things that we taught you not to do and we taught you not to go there." So they didn't want me working there. And I'm saying my aunts and my sisters because one of my uncles worked at the THPO after I left. And maybe he wasn't doing the same things I was doing but that it's that same "bend not break." I was talking to Brian Zepeda one time. He's the one that put that little thing in my ear. That we have a lot of rules to live by, but not everyone follows every rule to the letter.

One time I was working with THPO and we found what we thought were human remains or burial objects or something like that and somehow it had gotten out. My aunts came and found me and performed medicine rituals on me, and it wasn't because, "Oh we don't like THPO," it was because we're doing things that we were taught not to. Going into a site and digging up midden material, right? You're essentially invading someone's home. Then you have a place like Waxy Hadjo's Landing where for hundreds of years people have been living there.[18] So at some point, somebody went in and invaded someone's house. (laughs) So it's stuff like that. You have that flash of traditional teaching and opinions and rules but then this was happening also. Bending and not breaking.

And there's some people that will call the Ah-Tah-Thi-Ki Museum the "science fiction museum" because some of the stuff in there isn't real, isn't true. Like some of it will tell just a part of the story. Like the Corn Dance exhibit where you had a scarifier in a glass case. The label said scarifier but it's never about scars, it's about bleeding. So those same people that call it the "science fiction museum," if we were telling everything accurately, they'd be pissed that we were telling everything, so it's a two-edged sword. The museum isn't telling enough so it's a "science fiction museum," and if they were telling everything then it'd be an abomination to the Tribe. (laughs)

SB: Did you have any experience with historic preservation before you started working for THPO?

MB: No, it never crossed my radar. I didn't even think about it. I look at old buildings in town and think, "Oh, who knew what that history is or where that came from."

SB: Two examples in recent years are the Red Barn in Brighton and the Council Oak in Hollywood, both now listed as historic sites.[19] Do you think they would have been preserved without the THPO?

MB: Well I was still there at THPO when we first started looking at the Red Barn in Brighton, and I know that the Brighton community is really excited about preserving that. Would they have done it without THPO? That's hard to say because on some level it was being done already, just not to the level that THPO has done it. They've completed the laser imaging, and they're doing stuff to preserve it on a level that adds to how the Brighton community would preserve it. You know the Brighton community would go there and have family cookouts and outings, so it was still part of the community lore. And the same with the Council Oak, I think that THPO just added another dimension of preservation to it.

SB: So this book is aimed at a few specific groups: federal agencies, other THPOs, cultural resource management professionals, museums dealing with NAGPRA [Native American Graves Protection and Repatriation Act] issues, and academics. Did you have any experience working with any of these groups during your time at the THPO? What do you feel people should know about the Seminole THPO and what they do and how things work differently with the Tribe?

MB: I never worked directly with any of them, just on the periphery. Things were run a lot differently than they are now. When Bill Steele was the THPO Director, he wanted to be the one taking on NAGPRA and talking to the officials from those agencies so I didn't deal with them directly, but I think NAGPRA is good.[20] I don't think how we set our guidelines as a Tribe and what we think needs to be returned or needs to be left alone is what outsiders expect.

Here's a perfect example, Egmont Key on the Gulf Coast.[21] It's eroding away and some bodies or remains are coming up. I don't know if it's changed now, but I remember when that first started happening, when it first started being discussed, Bobby Henry said, "Well let them. Let them wash away," because that's nature.[22] That's God. That's the Breathmaker's way. He's doing it. And when we come in and say, "Hey no don't," then try and preserve it, we're going against what the Breathmaker wants. So I think that sometimes a lot of that preservation stuff is deemed more important and put on a different plane of importance than how sometimes more traditional members of the Tribe might think.

Because when someone dies, when someone passes on, once that last ceremony is done, you walk away. You don't go and visit the grave. It's done. And that's just something that worked out. We're taught that at a funeral when someone passes, there's the regular emotions, but the crying and the grief we're taught not to do because it confuses the soul. If the soul hears family grieving in such a way, it makes the soul not want to leave.

So looking at that teaching and then looking at stuff like NAGPRA and what other groups think should be preserved versus what we as a Tribe think should be preserved, THPO sought the input of different Tribal members to decide what is important. I think it's important to show that just because some group out West might want clothing back that was unearthed from a burial from 200 or 300 years ago, that necessarily isn't what we want. Because we've had finishing ceremonies and now whoever touches that material is cursed for lack of a better term.

SB: In your role as a cultural advisor at THPO, what did you do?

MB: I just helped the office run in a manner that was more in tune with Tribal beliefs, as much as I could. One of the things that Bill Steele had said about me was again, the bending not breaking. I didn't mind going to places. I didn't mind helping to dig at the sites. But there are a lot of Tribal members that aren't going to do that. So I was walking a fine line between what's okay and what's not. And then it got to where I just had to make sure that it wasn't my own opinion. I had to go talk to somebody. (laughs) That was the whole plan. It was to not rely on my own opinion but to go ask and then get a consensus.

SB: Anything else you want to share about THPO or the Tribe or the history? Anything important that you feel people should know?

MB: Nope. I think we covered it.

SB: Alright, thank you very much for chatting with me today.

Notes

1. The "Horseshoe" is a semicircular street configuration on Big Cypress that still contains some of the original BIA Housing and Urban Development (HUD) concrete block and stucco (CBS) housing dating to the 1960s.

2. Roughly 40 miles from the Big Cypress Reservation.

3. Seminoles in Florida historically speak two related but distinct languages. Creek, or Mvskoke, is typically spoken on the Brighton Reservation and areas north of Lake Okeechobee. Miccosukee is typically spoken on the Big Cypress Reservation and areas south of Lake Okeechobee. Seminoles from older generations were often fluent in both languages (Sturtevant and Cattelino 2004).

4. The Brighton Seminole Indian Reservation is located on the northwest side of Lake Okeechobee and is roughly 60 miles by road from the Big Cypress Reservation.

5. Beginning in the early twentieth century, Seminoles often lived and worked in "tourist camps," purpose-built Seminole villages along the Tamiami Trail or near resort locations, where they produced and sold Seminole crafts, wrestled alligators, and engaged in otherwise everyday cultural activities for a paying tourist audience (West 1998).

6. The Calusa (southwestern Florida), Tequesta (southeastern Florida), and Jeaga (southeastern Florida) were the European names identifying three prominent Native American cultural groups encountered along the Florida coast (Milanich 1998).

7. While Bowers's biological mother was an Otter Clan member, he associates his clan identity to the woman who raised him in the Wind Clan camp.

8. In Florida, there are two federally recognized groups of Native Americans: the Seminole Tribe of Florida and the Miccosukee Tribe of Indians of Florida. Additionally, there is a group of Independent Seminoles who do not wish to be federally recognized. In Oklahoma, there is the Seminole Nation comprised mostly of Seminoles forcibly relocated during the Seminole Wars (1817–1858).

9. The Seminole Wars were a series of armed conflicts between the U.S. federal government and the Seminoles. Historians have split them into three main conflicts: First Seminole War (1817–1819), Second Seminole War (1835–1842), and Third Seminole War (1855–1858). In reality, the period from the Creek War (1813–1814) until 1858 marked a period of intense conflict and hardship. Citizens of the Seminole Tribe of Florida are descended from those who remained in Florida at the end of the Third Seminole War (Covington 1993).

10. Sonny Billie (1935–2003) was a Seminole Medicine Man and member of the Panther Clan from the Big Cypress Reservation.

11. Abiaka (ca. 1768–ca. 1868), also called Arapeika or Sam Jones, was a prominent Seminole leader during the Seminole Wars who resisted all attempts at removal and remained, with his people, in the Big Cypress area after the end of hostilities (Covington 1993).

12. Osceola, also called Billy Powell, was born in the Upper Creek town of Tallassee ca. 1804. He was a prominent warrior in the Second Seminole War famously captured under a white flag of truce and shipped to Fort Moultrie in Charleston, South Carolina, before his death in 1838 (Wickman 1991).

13. "Black Seminoles" refers to free blacks and escaped slaves who fled south into Florida and allied themselves with Seminoles (Porter et al. 1996).

14. James E. Billie, Bird Clan (1944–), served as Chairman of the Seminole Tribe of Florida from 1977 to 2001 and from 2011 to the present.

15. See "The Rabbit and the Lion" in Jumper 1994, 76–77.

16. Indian Removal refers to the forced relocation of Native Americans from their homelands east of the Mississippi River to territory west of the Mississippi River, prompted by the Indian Removal Act of 1830 (Covington 1993).

17. For a more thorough discussion of this analogy, see Wickman 1999.

18. Waxy Hadjo's Landing is an archaeological midden site located on a large tree island on the Big Cypress Seminole Indian Reservation. The site was investigated by the THPO in 2011. Marty Bowers worked in the field during those investigations.

19. The Council Oak was the site of the meetings that led to the creation of the Seminole Tribe of Florida Constitution and Bylaws, which gave official recognition to the Tribe in 1957. The Brighton Red Barn, built by the U.S. Civilian Conservation Corps–Indian Division in 1941, marked the beginning of the Seminole cattle industry and quickly became a social center for the Brighton community. Both sites are listed on the National Register of Historic Places (Dilley and Gopher, this volume).

20. William (Bill) Steele was Director of the Seminole THPO from July 2002 to February 2012.

21. Egmont Key is a small barrier island located at the mouth of Tampa Bay on the west coast of Florida. U.S. federal troops imprisoned Seminoles on the island during the Third Seminole War (1855–1858); it is unknown how many died and were buried there. Severe erosion now threatens the integrity of the island and the sanctity of these unmarked graves (Covington 1982; Gallagher 2013).

22. Bobby Henry (1937–) is a Seminole Medicine Man and member of the Otter Clan who currently resides in Tampa.

References Cited

Covington, James W. 1982. *The Billy Bowlegs War*. Chuluota, Fla.: Mickler House Publishers.

———. 1993. *The Seminoles of Florida*. Gainesville: University Press of Florida.

Gallagher, Peter B. 2013. "A Visit to Egmont Key as It Slides into the Sea." *The Seminole Tribune*, August 30.

Jumper, Betty Mae. 1994. *Legends of the Seminoles*. Sarasota, Fla.: Pineapple Press.

Milanich, Jerald T. 1998. *Florida's Indians from Ancient Times to the Present*. Gainesville: University Press of Florida.

Porter, Kenneth, Alcione M. Amos, and Thomas P. Senter. 1996. *The Black Seminoles: History of a Freedom-Seeking People*. Gainesville: University Press of Florida.

Sturtevant, William C., and Jessica R. Cattelino. 2004. "Florida Seminole and Miccosukee." In *Handbook of North American Indians Southeast*, Vol. 14, edited by Raymond D. Fogelson, volume editor, and William C. Sturtevant, general editor, 429–449. Washington, D.C.: Smithsonian Institution.

West, Patsy. 1998. *The Enduring Seminoles: From Alligator Wrestling to Ecotourism.* Gainesville: University Press of Florida.

Wickman, Patricia R. 1991. *Osceola's Legacy.* Tuscaloosa: University of Alabama Press.

———. 1999. *The Tree That Bends: Discourse, Power, and the Survival of the Maskoki People.* Tuscaloosa: University of Alabama Press.

3

Building Capacity in a Tin Can

A Short History of the Seminole Tribe of Florida Tribal Historic Preservation Office

PAUL N. BACKHOUSE

I'm glad to talk about my ways of life to others who want to learn. I don't know
everything but I will speak on what I know.

Willie Frank, Wind Clan

Institutional histories are often rarely considered when measuring the performance of an organization. This is largely because the metrics that are used to
measure performance are derived from the world of business and are therefore
geared toward optimization. This chapter goes against the grain in presenting a
biographical institutional history that examines the temporal evolvement of the
Tribal Historic Preservation Office (THPO). As the Seminole Tribe of Florida under-
takes to launch a Tribal-wide computerized permitting system for on-reservation
development, the reality is that less than a decade ago requests for cultural review
were more typically obtained by happenstance during trips to the on-reservation
trading post for gas. Examined through a historical lens, the fluidity of organizational dynamics underscores the administrative and technological leaps felt necessary by the Tribe to productively conduct heritage management in the early
twenty-first century.

Author Bio

On an incredibly hot afternoon huddled over an excavation unit in Yellow-
house Canyon, West Texas, a seasoned cultural resource management (CRM)
practitioner told me that archaeologists do not get promoted, they just survive
and garner more responsibilities through an ongoing and invisible process of

attrition. I would agree. I am not a member of the Seminole Tribe of Florida. In fact, I grew up in the small fishing community of Steephill Cove on the Isle of Wight, England. Interestingly, I now find myself faced with the challenge, as a government employee, of representing a culture not my own. Archaeology had found me among the dust and tumbleweeds of the beautifully desolate landscape of the North American southern high plains. A decade later, an opportunity to help build the incipient THPO for the Seminole Tribe of Florida presented itself, and I swapped the hot, dry plains for the equally hot but low and wet South Florida swamp. The better part of a decade later, I now find myself directing the THPO and Ah-Tah-Thi-Ki Museum. The workload and responsibilities are enormous, and we seem to ply new cultural waters daily. The sage CRM veteran in Texas would have smiled. Fortunately, my staff does a fine job of carrying me, and it is an honor to aspire to be a true servant of the Seminole Tribe of Florida. My goal in this chapter is to set out what a THPO can be and how it is operationalized by the Seminole Tribe of Florida.

Introduction

There is no blue print for the successful development of a THPO. In fact, more than 150 THPOs now exist across North America, with many different individual missions and personnel configurations. In this chapter, the history of the Seminole Tribe of Florida THPO is explored as a vehicle for tribal capacity-building and an expression of sovereignty.

The Big Cypress Seminole Indian Reservation is the most isolated of the Seminole Tribe of Florida Trust lands. This contested landscape was the backdrop during the nineteenth century in which Abiaki (Sam Jones) led an indigenous community to resist colonialism through exceptional leadership, isolationism, and a superior understanding of the environment. Today, the Big Cypress Reservation is home to the Ah-Tah-Thi-Ki Museum. Its position, as James Billie, the Tribal Chairman, points out during the orientation film for the facility, is deliberate. Sited at a point 3 miles from the final resting place of Abiaki, the museum stands in front of a beautiful cypress dome where the present Chairman, in more recent times, built his camp and challenged the authorities for hunting a panther (*New York Times* 1984). Tribal elders sometimes call Big Cypress the Old Grounds. Behind the museum building, at the edge of a parking lot, sits a modular building that in many ways resembles a large indistinct tin can (Figure 3.1). Inside this unremarkable and ailing structure, a team of eighteen historic preservation professionals wrestle

Figure 3.1. Aerial image of the Tribal Historic Preservation Office located on the Ah-Tah-Thi-Ki Museum campus on the Big Cypress Reservation.

with the question of what a THPO is, what it should do, and how on earth they are going to keep up with the requests for government-to-government consultations that pack the small mailbox on Josie Billie Highway to capacity each day. Operating within the system of Tribal government and with regulatory responsibilities to outside federal agencies, the THPO straddles two very different worlds.

For the Seminole Tribe of Florida—and most, if not all, other North American Indian organizations—the concept of a THPO is culturally at odds with traditional learning and belief systems. Seminole Tribal members do not require an organized governmental institution to protect the important sites of their loved ones who have passed. After all, they have strong proscriptive cultural rules to avoid such places and things. External officials contact the THPO with some frequency, earnestly concerned that they learn the correct words, acts, or Tribal member authority to ensure that excavated human remains be laid back to rest in the proper manner. The reality is that Seminole Tribal members would not be so foolish as to disturb them in the first place. As archaeologists, we wring our hands and attempt to classify remains to fit our arbitrarily constructed ideas of cultural group, site type, period, and/or phase. Tribal members do not typically view the archaeological record with the same gaze, and it is with this difference that external researchers greatly struggle. Consultation too often breaks down when the conversation fails to acknowledge that it takes place between equals and is not dictated by the theoretical archaeological structures that non-indigenous scholars impose on the material we encounter. Assertions of archaeological affiliation to categories such as "prehistoric" and "culturally unidentified" are not only derogatory but serve to erect an artificial wall. Officials too often erroneously presume that wall requires contradictory evidence to be presented and the wall effectively assailed before the indigenous claimant can even be heard.

Many of the THPO staff, including myself, are not Tribal members. This apparently dichotomous situation is rationalized when the cultural relationship between Seminole people and archaeology is explored. Most Tribal members deliberately do not engage with the material past. Indeed, cultural tradition explicitly holds against such engagements. Important Seminole leaders who have passed are not commonly discussed in the way that Western academic traditions memorialize standard history. The historical narratives of their lives, therefore, have often only come to the attention of Tribal members today largely because of the work of Western academics. Does this mean that Tribal archaeology is in itself an unnecessary cultural contradiction, the imposition of well-meaning Western academics and federal officials? Colonialism wrapped in a more liberal and well-meaning package? A definitive answer is, of course, complex, dynamic, and illusory. Billy Cypress answered the question most succinctly when he noted that the Seminole Tribe today *needs* archaeologists (Cypress 1997, 156–160). Tribal archaeology then awkwardly straddles the fusion of two opposing worldviews.

When external agencies approach the THPO for government-to-government consultation, they are often somewhat surprised that many of the THPO staff are also non-Tribal. They may be forgiven for thinking that not only is conventional Tribal historicism lacking but also that Tribal members do not want to engage and therefore have no interest in a cultural perspective. These statements could not be further from the truth. Rather than a demonstration of the erosion of Seminole culture, this situation reaffirms the strength of the opposing worldview. Non-Seminole practitioners are not only preferable, they are absolutely necessary. A dramaturgical perspective tells us that much occurs backstage (e.g., Brissett and Edgley 2005). It is in this arena, unseen by the consulting official, that the close coordination between the THPO and the Tribal government and communities it serves occurs. This relationship above all others is the most important and least understood aspect of THPO programs. The THPO must attempt to navigate the tension and revision of these relationships if we are to be successful. Unlike academics, cultural resource professionals, and researchers, the THPO must remain in situ, working with and being part of a community and a system of government. Non-Tribal staff are proud to serve. They must wake at dawn to make the 80-mile commute into Florida's interior, dodging alligators and half-awake agricultural truck drivers as they go. They stay on-reservation to attend community meetings that oftentimes go deep into the night, as anyone who has attended a Big Cypress cattle owners meeting can well attest. Above all else they care about what they do and the community they serve.

Today, the THPO celebrates more than a decade of serving the Seminole Tribe of Florida. During the October 2013 Tribal Council meeting, the Seminole Tribe of Florida THPO presented, for the consideration of Tribal Council, a Cultural Resource Ordinance. This ordinance, the drafting of which has been a monumental undertaking, takes advantage of a provision of the National Historic Preservation Act (NHPA) that allows tribes to develop their own rules for the consideration of cultural resources. The adoption of the ordinance is a huge step forward in terms of Tribal sovereignty over cultural resources. In order to place this development in context, it is necessary to set out a thumbnail sketch of the history of the THPO and the path that has led us to this point.

Asserting Sovereignty

The development of THPOs in Indian Country should be viewed within the wider economic and political perspectives of tribal capacity-building and assertions of sovereignty. Since the early 1990s, the number of such offices has increased exponentially, and today 142 of the 332 tribes eligible to request THPO status have done so (National Park Service 2013). Every year, more offices are created, and all are eligible for the tiny National Park Service (NPS) Historic Preservation Grant. Unfortunately, this grant decreases every year as the pool of applicants enlarges. Today the grant yields funding roughly equivalent to one full-time midlevel manager's salary. Can one midlevel manager cope with the workload necessary to operate a THPO? A review of the last five years of Seminole Tribe of Florida Annual Reports suggests not (Seminole Tribe of Florida 2009, 2010, 2011, 2012, 2013). Annual reports are produced yearly in order to communicate to the community major activities undertaken by the department, as well as to satisfy the NPS THPO reporting requirements. These reports reveal that the office receives several thousand requests for consultation from outside agencies every year; conducts and reports on between 200 and 400 cultural, architectural, and archaeological investigations on-reservation; juggles multiple Native American Graves Protection and Repatriation Act (NAGPRA) caseloads; processes and curates items collected during on-reservation archaeological survey; advocates for historic preservation and participates in numerous Tribal and general public education efforts; maintains comprehensive lists of sites on the reservation (that is, a comprehensive site file); develops cooperative agreements with relevant federal agencies; and perhaps most important plays an active role in Tribal government and in the six Tribal communities spread out across southern Florida.

Some projects are, of course, much more complex than others. By way of example, during the 2010 Deepwater Horizon Oil spill the THPO was engaged with conference calls that ran on military time and had a roll call of officials that took up the first thirty minutes of every call. Calls began at 5 p.m. and rarely finished before 7 p.m. Every Wednesday the Backhouse dinner table became a quiet listening station as federal officials chased the ever elusive carrot of agreeing with one another about creating a cultural resource protection plan to deal with the situation.

Section 101(d)(2) of the NHPA is deceptively simple and straightforward. It states that the THPO can assume some or all of the functions otherwise assumed by the State Historic Preservation Officer (SHPO). The workload for a THPO is, theoretically at least, a function of the level at which the tribe wants to assume such responsibilities. Indeed, I suspect Robert Bendus (the present Florida SHPO) would be delighted if such an option existed for his office. Nevertheless, in order to assume such responsibilities, a detailed THPO Plan must be submitted and approved by the NPS. Assumption of tribal capacity, sovereignty, and optimistic enthusiasm are all tied up in the generation of the THPO Plan. After all, individual tribes are unlikely to know what the development of a THPO actually entails until they jump in and do it. Federal agencies are not directed to treat THPOs unequally; they typically assume that each THPO has taken the full responsibilities as set out in Section 101(d)(2) of the NHPA. Attempts to fend off the deluge of consultation requests would likely require greater tribal capacity than the effort to sift through them—to find the few that have important ramifications for tribal interests.

Where Is the Manual? Building the Seminole Tribe of Florida THPO

The Seminole Tribe of Florida is a sovereign government. The governmental organization structure comprises more than seventy individual departments, each of which reports to a Tribal Council of elected officials and ultimately, a Chairman, at the time of this writing James E. Billie of the Bird Clan. Prior to 1998, the Chairman and Tribal Council of the Seminole Tribe of Florida were only peripherally aware of that possibility for creating a dedicated THPO to serve the Tribe. Two legislative developments in the early 1990s are directly responsible for the creation of THPO programs that now account for more than 154 organizations throughout Indian Country. The first was the passing of NAGPRA in 1990. The second was the addition of a provision for the development of a THPO during the 1992 amendments to the NHPA (Pub. L. No. 89–665; 16 U.S.C. §470 et seq.). Specifically, Section 101(d)(2) of the NHPA allows for federally recognized tribes to appoint an official to take over some of the responsibilities of the SHPO on tribal lands. The cumulative effect of these two laws was to place a greater burden on tribes to develop mechanisms to deal with external agencies, institutions, and officials. The Seminole Tribe of Florida reacted to these developments in less than a decade. The ripples, however, are being felt across Indian Country today as tribes continue to struggle to develop the capacity required to match the expectations of the federal government.

The National Parks Service, as administrator of the THPO program, has established procedures that federally recognized tribes must follow to be recognized as an official THPO and be eligible for the annual National Park Service Historic Preservation Grant. Application is a two-step process. The first step is the submission of a request to develop a THPO accompanied by a Tribal Council resolution. The second step requires the submission of a detailed work plan (often referred to as a THPO Plan) and THPO application form. Following review and possible revision to the plan, THPO status is conferred by the designated NPS official. As a federally recognized position, changes in the Tribal Historic Preservation Officer must also be communicated to the NPS. By 1992, then, the potential to develop a THPO existed but likely went unnoticed by the Tribe.

Although a legislative mechanism existed for the development of the THPO in 1992, by 1998 the Seminole Tribe of Florida THPO was born out of necessity as the trickle of incoming consultation requests and NAGPRA inventories had become a torrent. On-reservation capacity was also being built in other ways that would put Tribal members and archaeologists within the same spheres for extended periods of time. The Seminole Tribe had pioneered Indian gaming, and the proceeds were benefiting the Seminole communities directly. Large-scale housing and infrastructure projects on-reservation required compliance review by the Bureau of Indian Affairs (BIA) with a slew of cultural resource laws. Despite the land being held in trust for the Seminole Tribe of Florida, very few areas of the Tribe's reservations had been archaeologically surveyed by 1990. Individual surveys were contracted out by the Tribe's Water Resources Department on an as-needed basis. Surveys were infrequent, and the resultant artifacts and documentation were removed from the reservation and retained by the CRM firm hired to perform the work. Very few CRM firms served South Florida in the early 1990s. Indeed, one firm was typically selected, and invariably the process of contracting archaeological surveys brought archaeologists and Tribal members into the same sphere for the first time on a consistent basis. The development of interpersonal relationships through this process would eventually result in the creation of the THPO.

A survey on the Brighton Reservation was in many ways the touchstone of these early interactions. Willard "Bill" Steele was working for the CRM firm that had been contracted to complete a survey of a parcel of land on the 36,565-acre Brighton Reservation. The remote Brighton Reservation was a long way from his home on the East Coast, and details of the project's area of potential effect were severely limited (Bill Steele, personal communication). The unique ecological setting of the Brighton Reservation, with its open pastures punctuated by cabbage palm hammocks (or tree islands), proved to be fascinating. With no clear project boundary, Bill began systematically testing the hammocks for archaeological sites. This process not only gave the earliest indications of the archaeological potential of the vast Brighton Reservation, it also put him in contact with Brighton residents. An incident occurred during that survey that typified the relationship between archaeologists and Tribal members. Arriving late in the day on-reservation and parking his small truck by the side of the dirt road, Bill set off on foot across the open pastures to reconnoiter a far-off tree island target. Bill always had a plethora of archaeological equipment in his vehicle and that day was no different. After a long hike through the pasture he returned to his vehicle to discover that someone had taken some of his equipment while he had been away. Closer inspection revealed that a specific piece of equipment had been targeted—his shovels (Bill Steele, personal communication). The message was clear and one that Bill never forgot; archaeology as practiced off-reservation at the time, with little community involvement, was never going to work on-reservation. This incident and the protracted Brighton survey were perhaps the catalyst that allowed for the time necessary to form the relationships and dialogue that would pave the way for the development of the THPO.

While Tribal capacity on-reservation continued to gather pace, the aforementioned passing of NAGPRA and amendments to the NHPA resulted in increasing numbers of external agencies contacting the Tribe to seek consultation on matters of potential cultural importance. At that time, such requests were invariably directed by the Tribal government to the Anthropology and Genealogy Department. THPO records demonstrate that as early as 1998, the Tribe was actively involved in consultation at Fort Benning and the Ocmulgee National Monument in Georgia (Wickman 2000). The flow of consultation continued to increase as a function of time, and by 2000 the role of Tribal Historic Preservation Officer was conferred on the director of the Anthropology and Genealogy Department. An internal memo dated June 20, 2000, provides some insight as to the discussion occurring as Tribal government sought to meet the demand for consultation (Wickman 2000). Review of the extensive inventories submitted to the Tribe as a result of the passing of NAGPRA in 1990 was clearly of some concern. Additionally, the ability for the Tribe to assert sovereign interest in areas outside the geographic extent of its reservations but within lands considered to be ancestral, aboriginal, or ceded was being explored. By 2002, recognizing the need to establish the necessary authority for such consultation, the Anthropology and Genealogy Department put forward Tribal Resolution C-185-02 for the consideration of the Tribal Council. The passing of this resolution laid the groundwork for a federally recognized historic preservation department by establishing the responsibilities of THPO to be carried out by the Director of the Anthropology and Genealogy Department. In 2004, this responsibility was shifted to Billy L. Cypress, the Executive Director of the Ah-Tah-Thi-Ki Museum. Day-to-day responsibilities for the THPO were carried out by Bill Steele, who began to develop the structure and organization of a fully realized historic preservation office. On October 4, 2006, with the passing of Tribal Resolution C-281-06 and the approval of the Seminole Tribe of Florida NPS Work Plan, the Seminole Tribe of Florida THPO began to officially shoulder the responsibilities of Section 101d(2).

We Have a THPO—Now What?

The approved NPS Work Plan became the immediate road map; however, the implementation was equivalent to attempting to walk blindfolded through the Everglades without getting your feet wet! Key issues revolved around finding a home for the office and building capacity. After a brief flirtation with Hollywood, Florida (the geographic seat of Tribal government), a core staff of seven employees set out to develop a functioning THPO on the Big

Cypress Seminole Indian Reservation situated in the heart of the Everglades. The decision to place the THPO in Big Cypress was one of practicality. Big Cypress is centrally located to the other Tribal reservations, and the existing museum campus allowed for the use of resources (research library, laboratory) the THPO would require. A Compliance Review program was initially established in Hollywood for a short while; however, former Tribal Historic Preservation Officer Bill Steele was a strong believer in centralization and early on made the choice to keep all aspects of the program together on the Big Cypress Reservation.

The organizational structure of a THPO is not prescribed, nor should it be. Each office must serve the cultural group it represents by fulfilling the obligations set out by the NPS Work Plan. An examination of the myriad of structural organizational changes that characterize the period from 2007 to 2012 underscores the massive workload that was assumed by the THPO (Figure 3.2). Two pivotal events shaped the staffing and internal organizational structure of the office. The first was recognition by the NPS and conferment of official THPO status. As Steele acknowledges in the 2007 Annual THPO Report, the additional responsibilities required a professional staff willing to build a program from scratch (Steele 2007, 3–4). For the most part, staff with the necessary specialist skill sets were not available locally. During this initial capacity-building phase, the staff of the office increased from seven in 2006 to twenty-eight by the second decade of the millennium. During this time, the basic structure of the office emerged. Distinct practice areas, or "Sections," were formulated and consisted initially of Tribal Archaeology, Compliance Review, and an Archaeological Laboratory. Archaeometry (which was not well understood and amusingly referred to as Goniometry for several months by management) and Architectural History were added shortly thereafter. Cultural and Research Sections were both experimented with between 2007 and 2009, with the eventual realization that both areas should permeate all aspects of the operation of the office. Lastly, the Archaeological Laboratory was retitled the Collections Section to more accurately capture the scope of its responsibilities. A hands-off approach to management during this time by Tribal leadership, coupled with an ever-increasing need to add capacity by ramping up staffing in response to the workload generated by external agencies, led directly to a disconnect at the community level between the THPO and the people it served.

Outside of Indian Country, federal agencies were themselves building capacity. In the early 2000s, the BIA hired a single archaeologist for the Eastern Regional Office based out of Nashville, Tennessee. The trust status of tribal

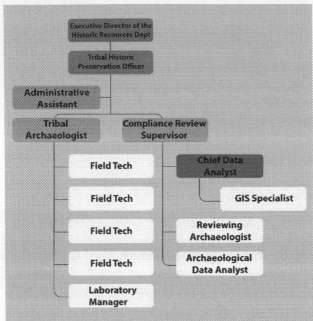

a

Figure 3.2. Tribal Historic Preservation Office organizational structure from 2007 to 2014: *a*, February 2007 (THPO *minor*); *b*, February 2010 (THPO *major*); *c*, June 2014 (THPO *optimus*).

land requires that federal agencies review undertakings that take place on tribal reservations. Although the BIA was conspicuously absent from completing systematic cultural resource surveys of reservation land prior to the 2000s, the arrival of the nominal capacity to complete cultural resource reviews for all undertakings was mirrored across a raft of different agencies. Unfortunately, the BIA Eastern Regional Archaeologist and many other federal reviewing offices are in the unenviable position of having the authority without having the time or resources to carry out the task. For instance, the BIA Eastern Regional Archaeologist is responsible for activities on all federally recognized tribal reservations east of the Mississippi River. A rough calculation puts the enormity of the task into context. She or he has about a week of work time to devote to each tribe every year. Technically, the BIA is the lead agency in a great many on-reservation Section 106 actions and would therefore be required to complete cultural resource surveys of all unsurveyed properties (indeed, all of them) prior to construction. In order to get Tribal members into home sites within their lifetimes, the THPO has assumed the role of field investigator, thus greatly expediting the review process.

The second pivotal event in the history of the THPO occurred as a consequence of the 2011 Tribal elections. The new leadership immediately began to review all Tribal programs against a backdrop of prior uncontrolled expansion

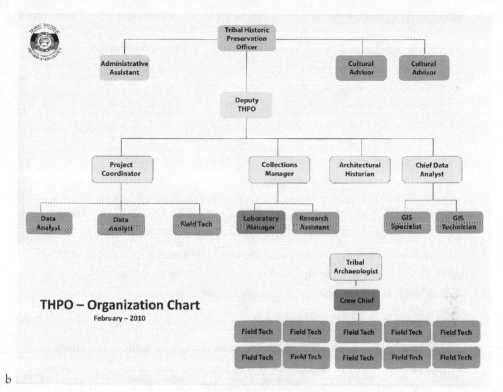

b

THPO – Organization Chart
February – 2010

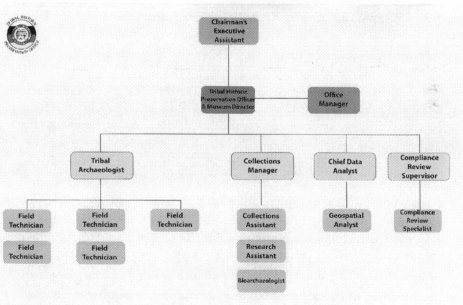

c

THPO – Organization Chart
January 2016

and the broader economic downturn. The THPO was no exception to this process. By struggling to fulfill the high-level mission to defend and promote Tribal sovereignty beyond the boundaries of the reservations, the THPO had lost relevancy to the Seminole people themselves. Ironically, the staff size had likely exacerbated this situation. Indeed, a Tribal member on Big Cypress remarked to me that he had "no idea what went on at the THPO," and even more sadly that he felt excluded to the point that he didn't want to know. The new government direction post-2011 presented an opportunity to fully engage with Tribal communities, an endeavor that took a huge effort by the entire THPO staff, fundamentally changing their work practices in order to find community relevancy. The hiring of a Tribal member from the Brighton Reservation greatly facilitated this transformation and allowed the THPO staff to work much more closely with the Seminole people as well as with Tribal leadership. The importance of participation at any and all community events was key to this growth in the office. Prioritizing handing out Halloween candy at the Brighton preschool rather than completing the review of a large building development (that threatens the site of a historic Seminole village within the thirty-day federal review window) may seem like a poor use of time to most historic preservation professionals, but we have learned that way of thinking to be entirely incorrect when working with a community.

THPO Operations

The on-reservation permit review process is but one of a huge range of activities that the THPO performs. An active NAGPRA program, off-reservation review of projects for compliance with the NHPA, and development of a Tribal Register and Seminole Site File are some of the myriad activities expected and prescribed by the NPS Work Plan. These occur simultaneously as different cross sectional teams work toward individual goals. There are other regular activities that are not prescribed, and in the performance of these we aspire to provide the greatest service to the Tribal communities. The nonprescribed activities are often organic, in the sense they are socially vital and owned by multiple stakeholders. They typically require greater interpersonal communication, coordination, and an ability to approach heritage management from perspectives that run contrary to the preparation provided by our higher education and professional experience in nontribal contexts. An example of this type of activity is the development of a participatory mapping program that sets up and holds regular community meetings to discuss the locations and meaning of places on the reservation (see Cancel, this volume). The federal government would recognize these as Traditional Cultural Properties (TCPs); however, at a community and individual level, these can be biographical. The process of bringing Tribal members together to discuss them promotes a dialogue and potentially facilitates cross-generational transmission of knowledge. Meetings are often unplanned and organic. They can take place over lunch, at a family or clan camp, or even at the gas station. Flexibility allows for greater respect of Tribal members' personal schedules and requirements as to the right time and place to share knowledge. It allows such programs to be less rigid and affords greater opportunity to facilitate traditional transmission of knowledge. Traditional Seminole learning occurs outdoors. Bobby Henry, Tribal elder and spiritual leader, told me during a particularly difficult NAGPRA consultation that buildings capture words and don't allow them to go where they need to in the world. Cultural respect and understanding therefore are the cornerstones of the success of the THPO.

Programs such as the participatory mapping example seek input not just in providing information for use in the on-reservation planning process and Tribal archives but also in how the information should be captured and communicated. Community input dictates that these records are typically kept secure and are oftentimes restricted even from members of the THPO staff.

There are many other examples, and for the most part these will not be written or presented as academic discourse, for they represent the core cultural component of the project of the THPO. Our most notable achievements in historic preservation are those that go unsaid here or in any public forum. The THPO is of course only as successful as its ability to communicate with Tribal leadership, the communities we serve, and the external agencies and partners with whom we must consult. There is no doubt that the process of consultation is difficult, oftentimes frustrating, and time consuming for all parties, but the rewards are occasionally culturally staggering.

This process is perhaps most difficult for the agencies that engage but do not see the other side of the story and the difference it makes to Tribal communities. Again, the THPO remains in situ, not as a flash-in-the-pan fleeting project that takes as much from the community it serves as it gives, but as an institution that listens and works through the many difficult questions that come at the intersection of greatly differing worldviews. Cultural positions can change and sometimes seem contradictory, and this must be difficult for the agencies with which we work. Efforts by forward-thinking agencies such as the U.S. Army Corp of Engineers, Jacksonville District, to undertake cultural immersion training on-reservation allows anthropologically and non-anthropologically trained employees to gain a critical glimpse of a culturally inscribed perspective.

The THPO of the Seminole Tribe of Florida acts as a bridge and, most important, as a cultural filter to communicate the strange and oftentimes culturally alien ways of archaeologists and other heritage workers, working on- and off-reservation, to various Tribal communities. We practice Tribal archaeology in the sense that we try to incorporate traditional values and beliefs into everything we do. This process is ongoing and reflexive, formed in situ. We cannot go anywhere or hide from our actions; we must work through them with the community members and government we serve. For the Seminole Tribe of Florida, this is Tribal archaeology.

Viewed through a historical lens, it is clear that the passing of NAGPRA and amendments to the NHPA made the creation of THPOs inevitable. The Seminole Tribe of Florida was required to respond to this "opportunity," as not doing so impacted its ability to retain ownership of its history and culture. By developing a THPO, traditional systems of heritage conservation and transmission were undoubtedly disrupted. The placement of the THPO within Tribal society is therefore an extremely complex issue. The solution for the Seminole Tribe of Florida is communication and engagement. We are always cognizant that we are a part of Tribal government and work within that framework. Continued and persistent meaningful engagement with citizens, reservation communities, and leadership continues to be our strategy. By doing anything else we risk the potential of responding to the volume of the requests without the cultural input that makes the THPO such a unique institution.

Building Capacity: A Cultural Resources Ordinance

Following recognition by the NPS in 2006, the day-to-day operations and long-term goals of the THPO were set out in the approved NPS THPO Work Plan. Expectations of tribal and federal governments are different, however, and not necessarily complementary. This dichotomous relationship is tempered by the realization that the work plan is written but once. In contrast, the cultural position of the Tribe is of course dynamic. The solution for the Seminole Tribe of Florida was to develop a Cultural Resource Ordinance that allows the Tribe much greater internal control of its cultural resources both on-reservation and throughout the vast area of cultural interest comprising much of southeastern North America. When we consider that on October 1, 2013, the federal government closed down its normal services due to a row about health care, the importance of the development of the ordinance is bought into sharp perspective (Indian Country Today Media Network 2013). The closure of the BIA Eastern Regional Office for what was then an unknown amount of time could have had serious consequences for Tribal member X who required an NHPA Section 106 determination prior to being approved a loan.

In order to cut through the red tape, the Seminole Tribe of Florida sought actively to meet the criteria to be approved under the 2012 Helping Expedite and Advance Responsible Tribal Homeownership Act (HEARTH) (H.R. 205). In parallel with this effort, the THPO worked to generate an ordinance (a copy of the complete ordinance can be found in the Appendix) as a mechanism by which the legal foundation for cultural resource decision making is placed firmly back within the control of the Seminole Tribe of Florida. Our initial analysis suggests that in addition to providing protection for the places and things the Tribe considers significant, the adoption of such an ordinance will greatly streamline the on-reservation permitting review process and reduce the time necessary to get Tribal housing and Tribal businesses clearances.

One of the important benefits of the ordinance is that it seeks to set in place the legal framework by which the THPO can enter into agreements with federal agencies to assume the responsibilities for such reviews directly. Another benefit is that the ordinance allows the THPO greater responsibility in the level and type of survey that is necessary for the clearance of a particular project. This provision should result in substantial savings in terms of time and staffing requirements. For example, no longer will it be necessary for the THPO to conduct intensive surveys in areas that are known to have very limited potential for encountering cultural resources.

The ordinance has several other significant advantages, including the following provisions:

+ Provides a legal framework through which the Tribe can take control of various federal responsibilities currently burdening the on-reservation permitting system;
+ Affords the Tribe greater discretion on what is and what is not culturally important and therefore worth preserving;
+ Codifies the importance of a network of cultural advisors in the decision-making processes of the THPO;

+ Allows for the issuance of general permits for activities that are un-likely to affect cultural resources, such as is the case with a consider-able number of agricultural practices that currently require surveys;
+ Plugs a gap by which the planned implementation of provisions of the HEARTH Act potentially leave Tribal resources vulnerable;
+ Squarely situates the on-reservation permit review process within the Tribal government system; and
+ Provides a clear statement to outside agencies as to how Seminole Tribe of Florida views cultural resources, greatly saving time and money on future consultation efforts.

The ordinance (C02-14) was passed unanimously by the Tribal Council in October 2013. As with everything else that the THPO does, the communi-cation of the provisions and implementation of the ordinance is of critical importance. The THPO takes advantage of ongoing opportunities to engage leadership and Tribal communities at various community meetings and func-tions by providing information on the THPO program and the ordinance, us-ing simple leaflets that detail its main provisions (Figure 3.3). We have found that these are a good starting point to generate dialogue but cannot replace the one-on-one personal engagement that is perhaps the most vital part of the ordinance's implementation.

Conclusion

George Orwell famously wrote that "He who controls the past controls the fu-ture. He who controls the present controls the past" (Orwell 1950, 35). Tribes and their various THPO programs are attempting to do just that by redress-ing centuries of the presentation of their heritage being controlled by external citizens, academics, and governmental agencies. By pulling up a seat to the table, the THPO has at least a voice in the production of the story. The meta-phorical seat that is selected to be pulled to the table, and indeed the table it-self for that matter, need not be regulated. It should be expected that the voice of the Tribal participant will be different from those of the other people sitting there. The value of this contribution is powerful. It is our experience that a far richer story emerges when all participants are involved in its creation.

The THPO is a part of Tribal government, and its relevance is dependent on the ability of its staff to communicate the important work they do every day to serve the Seminole Tribe of Florida. We have come a long way since 1998.

Clearance & Permit Types

- **General Clearance Letters** are issued for most undertakings submitted to the THPO.

- **Class A permits** are issued for undertakings, including activities constituting "development" by the Seminole Tribe.

- **Class B permits** are issued for undertakings by local, state, and federal agencies on reservation lands, including undertakings conducted in partnership with the Seminole Tribe.

- **Class C permits** are issued for undertakings by Seminole Tribe tribal members.

- **Class D permits** are issued for undertakings that utilize, affect, or may affect historic structures or historic buildings.

- **General permits** are issued for similar activities that cause no or acceptable impacts to cultural resources and/or historic properties.

Questions?
CONTACT US

30290 Josie Billie Highway
Clewiston, FL 33440

Phone: (863) 983-6549
Fax: (863) 902-1117
www.stofthpo.com

The Cultural Resource Ordinance
A Departmental Guide

Tribal Historic
Preservation Office

Introduction

Since October 3, 2006, the Tribal Historic Preservation Office (THPO) has assumed the role of the State Historic Preservation Office on tribal lands for compliance with Section 106 of the National Historic Preservation Act. The review of cultural resources is mandated by Federal law. By setting up a THPO, the Tribe assumes the responsibility for decision making with regard to its own resources.

In October 2013, the Tribal Council passed the Cultural Resource Ordinance (CRO) (Ordinance C-02-14), which pertains to any areas within the reservation lands as well as those where the Seminole Tribe of Florida (STOF) has defined customary usage rights. The main goals of this ordinance are to allow the THPO to better preserve the cultural heritage throughout the reservations and to set out a transparent process for on-reservation project review.

The On-Reservation Review Process

The Cultural Resource Ordinance helps make the on-reservation review process easier for everyone. While much of the process will remain the same, the documentation changes slightly. Each project request will follow the below steps:

1. Project is entered into Energov. Each project should include a locational description, federal agency involvement, a clear project description (i.e. construction of a road or a home site), and the project's funding source.

2. The THPO reviews the project to determine if cultural sites, archaeological sites, or historic structures are within the project area

3. If the project is receiving federal funding, the work completed by the THPO is reviewed by the applicable federal agency.

4. If the project contains no significant sites, the THPO will issue a General Clearance Letter in Energov. If the project contains a site that is considered significant, the THPO will work with the STOF departments and tribal members to both preserve the cultural resources and to continue the Tribe's developmental processes.

Did You Know?

The average time for the THPO to complete an On-Reservation Project Request is:

— 37 days —

Proper planning of projects can significantly decrease this time and allow the THPO to better look after the Tribe's non-renewable cultural resources.

Administrative Remedies and Enforcement

The THPO will work with the STOF Tribal Council to determine the appropriate measure to take when any person does not agree with a CRO permit. However, any person who is affected by a decision, determination, action, or enforcement action under the CRO may request an administrative hearing within thirty days after receipt of the Notice of Violation, Cease and Desist Order, or Citation.

Additional Information

Any changes or additional work that might occur within the project area should be sent to ERMD, who will notify and work with the THPO to address these changes.

The THPO may reevaluate the circumstances and conditions of any permit at any time which may result in the modification, revocation, or suspension of the permit in order to preserve cultural resources or to protect the best interest of the Tribe.

Contact the THPO at any time if there is a question about the review process or about a permit.

Figure 3.3. Cultural Resource Ordinance pamphlet distributed to Tribal departments by the Seminole Tribe of Florida Tribal Historic Preservation Office.

Figure 3.4. Artist's drawing of the proposed Abiaki Learning Center (*left*) and Tribal Historic Preservation Office offices (*right*) on the Big Cypress Seminole Indian Reservation. By permission of Wolfberg Alvarez & Partners.

The tin can referenced in the subject of the title of this essay, within the walls of which we have built our program, is about to be demolished as we move to a new chapter in the organization. A new THPO facility is to be constructed on the museum campus as part of the work to create the Abiaki Learning Center (Figure 3.4). The new structure respects cultural design aesthetics and includes a dedicated laboratory, collections vault, and archives spaces as well brick-and-mortar offices for team members. The design includes both outdoor and indoor spaces that we hope will be suitable for dialogue, discussion, and engagement. As THPO programs mature and become more organizationally and procedurally stable, it will be imperative that we redouble our efforts to maintain connections with the communities we serve. By providing programs that appeal to intergenerational families, the THPO facilitates Tribal members being active participants in the preservation of their own heritage and ultimately their own identity.

Extending underground from our tin can on Big Cypress, a cable snakes its way eastward, connecting the THPO office with Tribal headquarters in

Hollywood and in turn the external world. The cable and the office are more than physically linked, as both are constrained by location and capacity. There is no difference between the nineteenth century and twenty-first century; indigenous groups still oftentimes face seemingly insurmountable odds to retain their culture. Today, aggression has turned to corrosion. The story of THPOs is that the promise of capacity is always illusory as the bar is lifted ever higher and indigenous cultural traditions are eroded or homogenized to conform to external value systems. The development of a Tribal legal framework, by which the exponential and oftentimes unnecessary ramping up of capacity on both the federal and Tribal levels can be avoided, is one solution that respects Tribal sovereignty and puts more of the decision-making process back on the Tribe. After all, we have just completed our 10,000th shovel-test on-reservation. Aren't we now well positioned to model where archaeological sites are located and where they are not?

Figure 3.5. Paul Backhouse. By permission of Annette Snapp, Operations Manager, Ah-Tah-Thi-Ki Museum.

References Cited

Brissett, Dennis, and Charles Edgley. 2005. *Life As Theater: A Dramaturgical Sourcebook*. Piscataway, N.J.: Transaction Publishers.

Cypress, Billy L. 1997. "The Role of Archaeology in the Seminole Tribe of Florida." In *Native Americans and Archaeologists: Stepping Stones to Common Ground*, edited by Nina Swidler, Kurt Dongoske, Roger Anyon, and Allan Downer, 156–160. Walnut Creek, Calif.: Altamira Press.

Indian Country Today Media Network. 2013. "Limited Services Provided by Indian Affairs during Government Shutdown." http://indiancountrytodaymedianetwork.com/2013/10/02/limited-services-provided-indian-affairs-during-government-shutdown-151558.

National Park Service. 2013. *2013 Annual Report*. Washington, D.C.: National Park Service Tribal Preservation Program.

New York Times. 1984. "Indian Leader Faces Trial in Panther Slaying." February 12.

Orwell, George. 1950. *1984*. New York: Signet Classic.

Seminole Tribe of Florida. 2009. *Tribal Historic Preservation Office 2009 Annual Report*. Big Cypress Seminole Indian Reservation: Seminole Tribe of Florida.

———. 2010. *Tribal Historic Preservation Office 2010 Annual Report*. Big Cypress Seminole Indian Reservation: Seminole Tribe of Florida.

———. 2011. *Tribal Historic Preservation Office 2011 Annual Report: 5 Year THPO Anniversary*. Big Cypress Seminole Indian Reservation: Seminole Tribe of Florida.

———. 2012. *Tribal Historic Preservation Office 2012 Annual Report: Branching Out*. Big Cypress Seminole Indian Reservation: Seminole Tribe of Florida.

———. 2013. *Tribal Historic Preservation Office Annual Report: Sustaining Sovereignty*. Big Cypress Seminole Indian Reservation: Seminole Tribe of Florida.

Silliman, Stephen W., and T. J. Ferguson. 2010. "Consultation and Collaboration with Descendant Communities." In *Voices in American Archaeology: 75th Anniversary Volume of the Society for American Archaeology*, edited by Wendy Ashmore, Dorothy Lippert, and Barbara J. Mills, 48–72. Washington, D.C.: Society for American Archaeology.

Steele, Willard. 2007. *THPO Annual Report*. Big Cypress Seminole Indian Reservation: Seminole Tribe of Florida.

Wickman, Patricia. 2000. Memorandum to James E. Billie, dated June 20 with the subject: THPO. Document on file at the Tribal Historic Preservation Office, Big Cypress Seminole Indian Reservation.

4

"We're Just Small Little Circles Inside One Big Huge Circle"

Tribal Governance, Sovereignty, and the Tribal Historic Preservation Office

DANNY TOMMIE AND STEPHEN BRIDENSTINE

The emic perspective as derived from experience within the upper tier of tribal government is rarely presented as academic discourse. This is likely a direct result of the burden of commitments and workload inherent in such positions, as well as the specific objectives of the government itself. The following interview, from the perspective of someone with responsibility for oversight of the day-to-day operations of the Tribal Historic Preservation Office (THPO), therefore provides vital context for the role the THPO plays within the broader governmental structure of the Tribe.

Author Bio

Danny Tommie is a citizen of the Seminole Tribe of Florida and a member of the Bird Clan. He was born in a traditional Seminole camp in Bluefield, Florida, delivered by his grandmother Sally Tommie. Raised in a bilingual household and surrounded by his extended clan family, Tommie worked as a farm laborer from a young age through his teenage years. After he moved into town with his mother, Tommie still made regular visits to his family camp until the passing of his grandmother many years later.

Danny Tommie attended public schools and graduated from Fort Pierce Westwood High School. He then graduated from Florida Atlantic University and is currently pursuing an MBA at Nova Southeastern University. He is the

Figure 4.1. Danny Tommie. By permission of the Tribal Historic Preservation Office of the Seminole Tribe of Florida.

Executive Administrator under the Seminole Tribal Chairman and directly oversees the THPO.

On July 8, 2014, Danny Tommie sat down with Ah-Tah-Thi-Ki Museum Oral Historian Stephen Bridenstine to discuss the Seminole Tribal government and his role as Executive Administrator. In this interview, Tommie shares some of his childhood experiences living in a traditional camp and obtaining an education before discussing the structure of the Seminole Tribal government, the role of the THPO, and the many issues that arise from working with state and federal agencies.

STEPHEN BRIDENSTINE: If you can start by telling us a little bit about the type of setting you grew up in. What was that like?

DANNY TOMMIE: As a kid, I recall mainly being together with my mom's sisters and brothers, hanging around the camp which was sort of like the center of our little world. Then as we got a little older, our parents moved into town settings, but we still always frequently got together and visited the camp for years until the passing of my grandmother Sally Tommie, who was the matriarch of the camp. But the main focus during that earlier time was family togetherness because my mother and my grandmother were all big on that as far as keeping that togetherness as a family. That's always been a big thing with different clans. That's why you see in a clan camp uncles and aunts and so forth all still living there amongst each other. Initially, that's the way things began for me. Then we sort of moved out into what I guess you would call mainstream society—living amongst the normal communities.

SB: Do you remember how old you were when you moved out of the camp into town?

DT: Well, first of all, I was born in Bluefield where my grandmother delivered me right there in the camp. And Bluefield sits right at the edge of the St. Lucie County–Okeechobee County line.[1] During that time, you had families from Big Cypress and Brighton that always used to converge on this area. It was explained to me that that setting was more like a migrant setting for Indians. A lot of the Indians came together for work during the different growing or harvest seasons. So I was born there and then a little later on, we had a camp out near this place called Ideal Holding Road.[2] And that was just a little west of the final camp which would be on Midway Road. So I sort of slid from Bluefield on up to Ideal Holding on over to Midway Road camp.

Most of the families were together for a period there, but the sisters moved into town settings as they got married. Ironically, the brothers all sort of resided most of the time on the Brighton Reservation, which is where a lot of our family is from. But growing up we had several families. We had Willie Jones, he lived on a road down from our camp called Eleven Mile Road. There were several families that grew up over in that area and there were some that were even over at Indiantown and so forth.

SB: When you say camp, do you mean a traditional Seminole camp with chickees?[3]

DT: Yes, chickees, gardens, pigpens, a few head of cattle, raising animals for harvest each year. It was all chickees and the only thing that had a little metal roof on it was a little small kitchen that my uncle built over time for my grandmother. It had doors and a few things in there like a refrigerator, though that was later on in years. That was the only structure there that wasn't a chickee. It was made to house the food that they prepared because the cookhouse was right directly out from there. A lot of times, instead of leaving the food out they would put it in that little kitchen on the table and sometimes when it was raining or at nighttime or if you had guests, you would go in there and sit underneath the roof.

SB: What language was spoken in the household?

DT: Coming up as a kid, mainly the Creek language, also called the Mvs-koke language. But all my uncles and even the sisters grew up speaking and understanding both Miccosukee and Creek. My grandma was Sally Tommie and my grandpa was Jack Tommie who spoke the Miccosukee language and the Creek language, so as a result, the kids all ended up understanding it and the brothers mainly all spoke both languages.[4]

SB: What type of schools did you attend growing up?

DT: From elementary on up, I went to public schools. I went to the old Fort Pierce Central High School for three years, and then my senior year I graduated out of the new Fort Pierce Westwood High School.

SB: In addition to attending public school, would you say that you had a traditional Seminole education, whatever that may be?

DT: Yes, I would say I did. It was something that you weren't going to get around not learning during that time. I always say that I was right at the cusp of the group that probably was the last to learn a lot of things as far as being Seminole and some of the teachings and the ways of how they lived and so forth. I was right at the break then, and I got the advantage of having that education as far as growing up as a Seminole and understanding some of the things that was a part of survival and making a living. I had uncles who disciplined me and I had a mother who spent a lot of time with her mother, and then we went out and did certain things. I guess you could call it Seminole, but at the same time I think what it really refers to is surviving—doing whatever it took based on the resources that were available in order to survive.

SB: How did your parents make a living? How did they bring up the family?

DT: They grew up in a camp, so the migrant labor type of work was the biggest form of making a living. That's picking tomatoes, squash, bell peppers, and planting farm fields. Then as I got a little older, we went into citrus, where we were harvesting the fruit. That was a big job because during that time you had citrus groves that ranged from upper Martin County, the Stuart area, all the way up to Wabasso, Florida.[5] The majority was owned by a big company named Becker Groves. Then you had Coca-Cola Groves. You had a couple of other groves that were privately owned, but they still had to use harvesters that would come in and harvest. I always say I probably picked 80 or 90 percent of those groves at one point or another growing up.

SB: How old were you when you got started doing that?

DT: Well, when you were old enough to carry a bucket, you got out there and picked tomatoes or squash. You helped. I used to go to the fields with my mother as a little kid. We started citrus when I was somewhere around nine or ten years old, probably till I was about fifteen or sixteen. We stopped working the fields, or didn't go as often, when my mother took a job in a bowling alley. She ended up doing the maintenance for the bowling alley. When she took on that job, it got her out of the fields, out of the heat, so I was glad. I was happy. We'd still go occasionally on a weekend just to sort of subsidize that little income that she had coming in. She probably worked at that bowling alley for a good twenty-five years. She stayed there a long time. And my mother, she became a pretty good bowler. She was probably one of the top bowlers in the county, as a matter of fact, in the South. She was a very good bowler.

But she had no education, never went to school. Same with a lot of my uncles and aunts, they never went to school growing up. So I was lucky that I had a mom that sort of pushed me, and she pushed me because of that reason. When I was eight or nine years old, I was filling out her bills in her checkbook to pay her bills for her. I could actually fill out a check legibly and the amounts based on her bill. And one of the things I always admired about my mom was that at a later age she took on an adult education class where she learned how to write a little better and write her name. She had a generic way. I can remember years ago she used to put an X for her name for her signature. After she took that class, she actually learned to write her name, Hope Tommie.

She used to get home at nighttime being tired but she'd still get her book. And it was funny because I remember they were adult education books for someone who had never gone to school, and it was just like the same things that I did in first grade or in kindergarten where you'd have to follow the dotted line to do the "a" to do the "b." She did the same things. She religiously went home and did that for several years, and her handwriting got pretty decent.

She was always one to tell her kids to go to school and get an education because that's not what she had. I think that was a lot of the emphasis because as kids we all heard our language, but then at some point, probably in those important learning years at a younger age, I noticed she was one that sort of got away from it. I was one of those victims where your parents wanted you to learn the other side, so as a result it hurt my retention, as far as remembering or retaining a lot of the language. You lose so much doing that but I guess she had a purpose and a reason, and her main thing was she wanted to give her kids an opportunity to try and be successful or succeed in the big world that was surrounding our little small world. She knew that you had to get out there. That was one of her, I'm not going to call it a downside, but it was just one of those things that affected us in a way that you wish you could go back and figure out a way to have equally divided it so that you got enough of both.

As a result, it hurts you on one side because the big push was to learn those other things for the purpose of succeeding in the world. So I never held that against her, but I just think that she didn't know that fine line there. She did what she thought was best, and as a result, all of her kids graduated from high school. I thought that was a success story in itself.

SB: Did you go on to college?

DT: Yes, I graduated from Florida Atlantic University, and here recently, I decided to go back to school. I'm in an MBA program at Nova Southeastern University.[6] I haven't decided what concentration yet, but I was thinking about international finance.

SB: Let's move on to the modern Seminole Tribal government. One of the biggest things that is important to the Seminole Tribe is sovereignty. Could you share how you understand sovereignty and how it applies to the Seminole Tribe?

DT: You know, sovereignty is one of those things that I've tried to figure out for a long time. I've heard that over time Indian sovereignty is getting weakened because everybody likes to put that out there and use that as a way of getting around certain circumstances that come about with getting a decision handed down. They try to invoke this sovereign immunity thing, and it's slowly etched away at what everybody considers to be a sovereign right to Native American tribes because once that decision is rendered, it applies to all tribes across the country. If you have a certain situation where there's a court action being pushed and that particular court action ends in an opinion that is negative to one tribe, now it becomes case law so it affects every tribe across the country. You might have a decision out in California, but it's going to affect every tribe east of California because of that decision.

I think that it used to be that having sovereignty meant that we were a nation within a nation and we had an ability to govern ourselves when we got to that point. But I think that the problem with self-governing is that it has a learning curve. It's a road you have to take to get to a certain point, and everybody can't start out being able to do those things as a tribe, as a nation of people. It's almost like any developing country; it takes time before you can say they've developed to a point that they now have a sustainable government.

Just seeing this over years, I don't think there's really any clear definitive way of describing sovereignty. I've looked up the meaning in the dictionary several times and tried to apply it and it's just one of those things where I don't want to call it a roll of the dice at times, but I think when you keep throwing it out there, no matter what tribe you are, that impending decision is going to affect all your Native people across the country. So as tribes they need to be very careful about those things.

You hear every day about waiving sovereign immunity or limited waiver of sovereign immunity for particular types of actions that might come about at that specific moment, mainly to get someone paid. That's where it mainly comes in, when there's an agreement in place for an exchange of moneys or services. So I know a lot of people have a dislike for hearing that but at the same time in the normal course of business you have to have recourse in the event that something happens. If you're going to have outside companies do business with tribes, you have to sign a limited waiver of sovereign immunity or grant that limited waiver to a particular entity so that in the event something happens, they have a process to recover their losses.

And that's understandable because that's a normal action you take in business. If you're going to do business and you're going to propel your tribe forward, there are times where that has to take place. If not, you don't have very many companies out there, or any hardly, that are willing to assume that liability of not being able to recover their losses in an event that something happens, or don't have any recourse to resolve a dispute or an issue. You almost have no choice. So even though you have sovereign immunity, there's still a limited waiver to a degree so that you can do business in the real world. Without companies willing to give that limited waiver in exchange for either lending dollars or providing services or whatever it may be, tribes couldn't move forward. So that's why I say that about sovereignty. It's one of those things where even though it's there, I think the old sense of what it might have represented, doesn't really—well, it applies today, but it has to be applied in more of a customized way.

SB: I understand that the Seminole Tribe today has a Tribal Council and then there's also a Board of Directors. Could you speak to the difference between the two and how they're structured and what each does?

DT: Yes. Let's start with the Tribal Council. The Tribal Council is structured as such that you have a Chairman who is elected at large by the general population. His responsibility is the oversight of the Tribe on a day-to-day basis. He's that immediate point to go to in the event that there needs to be an answer or a decision on something that deals with our day-to-day operations. In the event that something comes up that he feels needs input from all the Councilmen as a whole, that they need to come up with a good answer or right answer to address a certain situation, the Chairman will call a meeting. It can be an emergency meeting or just a general meeting for them to get together.

Then you have Representatives from each reservation: Big Cypress, Brighton, and Hollywood.[7] Their job, or the entire Council's job really, is governance. That means they determine what policy or body of law is going to be used on a day-to-day basis to run the Tribe. They determine what that policy is or what that law is and then they send it down the chain to the Executives. It's the Executives' role to execute those policies or those laws as adopted.

Then you have a President and he's utilized on the Council side as the Vice-Chairman. He's not elected as a Vice-Chairman, he's elected as a President, but he's that fifth vote on the Council so he slides over and he becomes the Vice-Chairman. He's elected at large just like the Chairman, but he's elected at large as a Board President. He serves on the Council to be that fifth deciding vote in the event you need a tiebreak.

Going onto the Board of Directors, that has also five members. Those members start with the President, who again is elected at large by the people. Then you have three Board Representatives and they are from Brighton, Big Cypress, and Hollywood as well. Just as you have the President serving as a Vice-Chairman, now you take the Chairman, who is elected as a Chairman, and have him put on a

Vice-President hat and serve on the Board to be that fifth person, that deciding vote.

The Board is the Seminole Tribe of Florida, Inc. They're the corporation, established as the economic arm of the Council. They are the business entity, and they were set up as such so that all things that were considered business would fall under the Board. The Board consists of shareholders, and those shareholders are every Seminole who is a member of the Tribe. The Board initially started out with the cattle program and citrus, those kinds of things.

The Council is set up as your government or your governing body, and they oversee things that pertain to the general welfare of its people. So all your direct or indirect services in the Tribe fall under the Council, whereas all your business ventures and so forth will go under your Board. That's the way it was intended to be set up. Today, the one large thing that the Council has, and has always had, is the one business that probably makes us what we are today. It gives us the ability to run a government and to fund that government to a degree that it represents a good example for the Native American world, or for any other government or country really. And that's gaming. Gaming has been that lifesaver.[8]

SB: How do elections work in the Tribe?

DT: We don't have primaries but instead a win or loss kind of vote. If you get the most numbers, you win. If you don't, then you don't win. That's been a topic of discussion for years. Some propose changing it to where you need a majority, 50 percent or better, to take an office. They would thus have a runoff or a primary. It hasn't happened yet, so today our vote is if you get five individuals who are running for Chairman or President, whoever gets the most votes on the Chairman's side or the President's side is declared the winner. And it's the same way with your local Representatives. Whoever gets the highest number of votes wins.

As far as the elections go, we have a President and a Chairman election every four years which fall in the odd years. So this coming May 2015, we have an election. That's for everyone: your President, your Chairman, all your Representatives. Then every two years subsequent to those, you have a Representative election. So the Representatives are only elected for two years, the President and Chairman for four years.

SB: Could you speak briefly about some of the different direct and indirect services that the Tribal government provides to Seminole Tribal members?

DT: Yes. The government provides health care for every Tribal member so we're 100 percent covered with health care, which is great. Health care is that main, primary concern. I think second on that list, they like to make sure to give every Tribal member an opportunity for an education. Whether it's preschool on the reservation or even if you're off, they help cover some of the expenses all the way up to college, as long as you're maintaining at a certain level. They have a criteria for that. Then you have recreation. You have the seniors program or the elderly programs. All of these programs will fall under the Executive Administrator's Office. He's in charge of the majority of the direct services to Tribal members.

Then you have community planning and development. Their main emphasis is to continue to try and provide housing for the growing population of Tribal members.[9] I know you see a lot of other development happening on the reservations. They are responsible for that, but our reservations can only hold so much development anyway. We're limited in the landbase and available land to do those things, but you'll always have a continuous need for housing. So that's their main emphasis, to provide housing, but they're also in charge of planning and doing all the design concepts, all the studies to make sure that it's even something that makes sense to do.

Outside of that, we also have under the government, museum, and THPO. Even though it's an indirect service, it still provides a service for the Tribe. The Ah-Tah-Thi-Ki Museum educates the outside public and gives people a feeling of what Seminole life and being Seminole is like, not just today but in the past.[10] So we have these different programs that again fall under the government, that provide all these services to our Tribal members.

SB: What is your current title?

DT: I'm the Executive Administrator under the Chairman. We have other executives like Human Resources and we have an Executive Administrator's Office that deals with the direct services for the Tribal members. We also have Community Planning, which takes in several areas. But on a day-to-day basis, when you need approvals for funding for many of these things, that's something that I do in my position. I'm that last person in that process before it goes up for final signature.

Also, when it comes to certain government matters, I work directly with the Chairman in presenting those to the communities. For instance, if we have a ballot coming up to amend the Constitution or such, I try to assist with those things. Just a multitude of different responsibilities, like getting out to the communities because under the Chairman, even though we have three main reservations, and three smaller reservations [Immokalee, Tampa, and Fort Pierce], you still have nearly 2,000 Tribal members who live off-reservation and they're all across the country. So we have been traveling and meeting with Tribal members in Texas, Oklahoma, Arizona, Tennessee, Georgia, Colorado, and giving them updates on things that are available to them. They fall under the Chairman so it's his responsibility to maintain that connection with them, to let them know what's available and if there are any major changes in the Tribe. The Chairman also wants to know his Tribal members, know who he's representing, and they need to know who he is.

SB: In your position, how much do you interact with state and federal agencies, and what has that experience been like for you?

DT: I have quite a bit of involvement because of the Chairman. He's always involved in those things because he's that point to go to in the Tribe whenever correspondence comes in. He's that point of contact for every agency or every official. He's that person that they want to have that conversation with. So in most instances, I'm there with the Chairman on those things, on those matters. Whether it's meeting the governor or state representatives or just meeting individuals from federal agencies like Army Corps of Engineers or EPA [Environmental Protection Agency], whoever it might be, I'm always involved. I'm always in the loop, and I'm usually that point of contact or correspondence when there's follow-up or different things like that.

It's always changing, and in my position, I'm involved with a range of issues from small to large. I never know what I'm going to be involved with. And that's what makes it sort of intriguing and fun because I've always been the type who likes it different. I don't like the same redundant thing over and over every day. So it benefits me, and it's probably the reason why I like being there. I don't like to know what I'm going to do on a day-to-day basis. I like to know I'm going to be busy and I'm going to work. That's what I want. No matter what pops up, just work with it, just deal with it.

SB: We'll end with some questions about the Tribal Historic Preservation

Office. In your own words and based on your own experience and understanding, what service does the THPO provide to the Seminole community?

DT: I guess most importantly, they're in that approval process for certain things to help them move along for clearance purposes. I think that's the way the community has always viewed them, as the department that has to come in and give you the okay to proceed forward with things. The THPO gives you clearances on whether there's something there that's historically important or something that should be of value to the Tribe as a whole from a cultural or historical standpoint. They make sure that none of that is being interfered with, that those things aren't being decimated before we have knowledge of it. We don't want to go out there and stick a backhoe in the ground if no one has ever checked to see if that site has some big importance to the Tribe.

They give that approval, and I think what it does is it assures people that you have a department out there helping preserve something for the Tribe. And that something is important because even though it might not have had great significance back in the day, it's what makes us what we are as far as Tribal members today. They left something behind for us as Tribal members to learn from. But if we go and destroy all those things or if we don't have something in place to assure that we're not destroying those things, then we could lose what little we still have today. We could lose a lot of that, and THPO plays an important role there and I think they do an excellent job.

SB: Did you have any experience in archaeology before you started in this position overseeing the THPO?

DT: No experience in archaeology.

SB: Did you have any impression of what it was?

DT: Yeah, I understand what archaeology is to a degree and what they do. Reading and keeping up with public interest issues across the country that involve archaeology, you sort of get a pretty decent perspective on what they are. Specifically, I know their job really drills down and gets really detailed. With the stuff that they can do based on just going in and taking an area and determining so many different things from it, I think it's very exciting. It's not an easy area and for them to come up and make some of these assessments and make sense of it in the end is a really cool thing. So it's an interesting field, it's an interesting area. I mean, I couldn't do it on a day-to-day basis.

SB: Can you describe briefly how the on-reservation permitting process works for home sites and other Tribal construction projects?

DT: For home sites, it basically starts when a Tribal member goes in and gets an application to draw for approval for a home site. They get that application and they go through land use committee and ERMD [Environmental Resource Management Department]. They will determine sometimes for Tribal members if certain large areas are available for home sites or can be permitted. In addition to land use, you have your water commission and then you have your THPO. When THPO gets involved, they go out and inspect the site to make sure that again we're not approving something that might have some historical importance to the Tribe. Then at that point, they send it up for resolution to go before Tribal Council, and they will approve the home site based on the fact that all the clearances have been done from water, land use, natural resources department, ERMD, and THPO.

But THPO is that important piece that a lot of Tribal members have griped about because there was a point when THPO was the biggest holdup in that whole entire process—not THPO itself, but rather the agency they had to send the documentation up to for approval. It was so drawn out because of again those federal mandates put in place that create more of a hindrance. It was like this for a long time until these federal agencies started realizing that it threw a lot of work on them. Then at some point, they started passing it back over, but it takes a while for them to get to that point, to sort of streamline the process.

SB: What does the term "held in trust" mean to you as related to Tribal lands?

DT: In my opinion, the federal government has a fiduciary or responsibility to the tribes to make sure that the lands that were designated to tribes stay in place. They oversee it to make sure nothing affects that usage or that right to that land. In my opinion, I take it as forever because when tribes have this property that's held in trust, it's something that they were actually entitled to anyway. It's just protecting those lands. That's sort of my take on it.

SB: The THPO is charged with reviewing all the projects that are on the Tribe's ancestral, aboriginal, and ceded lands that extend all the way up to Georgia and Alabama. What are your thoughts on the importance of this to the Tribe, because there are no trust lands or reservations in

Alabama or Georgia and yet the THPO deals with things that come up there. How do you feel about that?

DT: There are no trust lands up there—yet.

(laughter)

DT: I think it's very important because everyone knows that even though we're down on Big Cypress or Brighton or Hollywood, this wasn't our original region or this isn't where we originally come from. Now we have your State Historic Preservation Offices and they're involved, and they're recognizing the importance of making sure that certain Tribal rights or culturally sensitive things that belong to the Tribe aren't destroyed or aren't interfered with. And not only does this process identify the items but also that there was a group of people in those areas and that still should have rights or ownership to certain things. In addition to that, I think there are certain inherent rights that should be granted somewhere, hopefully in the near future, as far as having more land put in trust for that group.

So I think it's important to have THPO in place to do these things because at some point or another, it's going to benefit the Tribe. It identifies a lot of things that maybe aren't acknowledged today that should be acknowledged. And again like I said, it could potentially open up doors to allow us to regain some of those areas that were inhabited by our people. And we should have a place, since we inhabited a lot of Georgia and Alabama. We should be entitled to some of that recognition. You know, "Hey, there was the Seminole Tribe here. They originated here and they're back home to be part of Alabama or Georgia or wherever."

SB: Speaking to the audience of this book, is there any advice or counsel you want to give them to help them work better with tribes in this country?

DT: After different conversations with different individuals involved in these organizations, I think the one thing we've agreed upon is that we need to consider the effect of the decisions prior to making those decisions. In order to do that, we have to thoroughly examine what those effects are going to be before we move forward. Sometimes the only way to get the full impact of what might be taking place or could take place is to have the Tribe involved in those discussions because we have had to deal with the overall effects of things in the past. We have had to live with these decisions.

We're just small little circles inside of one big huge circle so it's more impactful to us than what a lot of agencies realize until the damage is done. And then to go in and try to undo something, it just creates a chain effect from one move, from one action, from one approval, or from one proceed ahead with something. It just shows that they didn't consider how it's going to affect the overall Tribe and overall lands and our people.

I guess what I'm trying to say is that it's not smart decision making sometimes. It's not done in a way like they always taught us. Let's brainstorm. Let's get together. Well, in order to brainstorm, you can't leave some of the most important people out. You have to let them have that input. And I think for the most part, there tends to be a little more effort towards that trend now than there has been in the past. But it still has a long way to go. Like I said, we're just a small group inside of a big circle but it's important to us. What belongs to us or the things that we belong to, our surroundings, our land, our people, our cultures, our traditions, all the things I just mentioned, they're important to us just like the issues on the outside are important to these agencies.

I think a lot of times, they're doing a job, and I understand that, but they have to also understand that while they go home at the end of the day, we have to live with their decisions for a long time. We're the ones stuck with now having to reverse that battle and having to take those conversations the other way, go backwards with it to try and undo some of these things, whereas if we had been brought into the initial start of that process, of deciding what's the best route to take, we could have avoided a lot of that. You know, we're dealing with that now, all the things that are above us that affect us so much. It's the water and the drying up of the land and all the nonnative species of plants that are taking over certain native plants in Florida. The species that have inhabited these areas for a long time are just being choked out, so it's changing the whole terrain of the land. And then access to water. There are so many things that affect us here from that standpoint.

One of the issues that I think I talked about earlier was that sometimes these legal opinions affect tribes across the country. Well it's the same difference with a lot of these federal mandates that take place. They affect a tribe down here maybe a little more awkwardly than a tribe further north or out west. One of my biggest concerns is that they make these changes and they make these decisions about federal policy but they don't attach a budget to it. They leave that on the expense of the tribes. If you're going to make decisions that affect us, you should also help alleviate that financial burden by saying, "We're going to help you all pick up the expense on it." For example, having to do all the surveying and the plotting of the reservation lands. They wanted us to do all these things when we first started, but when they put us down on the federal itinerary, they didn't put us over in the other column, the federal budget. Their push is really to slowly get away from funding tribes. The whole idea behind BIA [Bureau of Indian Affairs] or Department of Interior was to minimize its involvement with tribes. As we developed and became more self-sustaining and our ability to govern ourselves got a little firmer and firmer, they were going to back off. Twenty-five years they said they were going to give tribes to become more self-sufficient. Well, they stayed with us longer than twenty-five years, but you'll notice over the last ten years, funding for so many tribes has decreased tremendously.

I think one of the determinants of that is really the one thing that people see today. They see tribes being so successful in gaming and having money, but they don't realize that's probably around 20 percent of the tribes—20 percent that are really able to do that—but you have the other 80 percent that are really suffering. Everybody lumps us into one big basket and says, "Oh Indian tribes are doing so great these days," but no. There are some tribes out there, Seminole Tribe being one of them, that does well for itself. People see the big glitz and glamour and success of some of these tribes, or what appears to be success, and they apply it to every tribe out there. That's unfair for a lot of tribes because most of them are still poverty stricken and doing very tough for themselves. That's the sad part about the whole thing.

And at the same time, the other thing I want to say is I don't want, whether it's federal agencies, U.S. government, or whoever, to view us as Hard Rock Seminoles. We're Seminoles and that's what we are. We're Seminoles and we have a history. We have a tradition and a culture that we are going to continue to keep handing down to our young people and continue to pass it on for generations to come. But we still have to get past that dilemma, that they equate us to just Hard Rock and gaming. No, we're not just Hard Rock and gaming, that came after. We're Seminole first. We're Seminole and then underneath that we own Hard Rock as a business. That helps us to be what we are today. But that's the thing, everybody comes to Hollywood or they go to Tampa and that's what they see. Well, I'd like for them to come out to Big Cypress or go to Brighton and see that it's not Hard Rock out there. It's still reservation. You still see cattle. You still see people that are living and trying to hang on to what they were born to be, and to me, they were born to be Seminoles.

SB: Anything else you'd like to add about yourself, the Seminole Tribe, or THPO?

DT: As I said earlier, I think THPO has been doing a great job. One of the big issues that was out amongst the community and the members was the time period for approvals. They've really worked towards reducing that, and they keep statistical data from the last couple years which shows how it has reduced in time. I think the members are starting to see that. And even on the process side, when it deals with the government projects, not just individual homes, they've reduced that approval time. I think those departments are starting to realize that THPO is a big part of that process and now they're more considerate when these things start taking place. Their name comes up in the conversation a little more often now, so I think that's great because now they're getting a little more awareness in the Tribal-wide communities. People realize they exist, that THPO is there.

As far as the Tribe and the government, I think the Seminole Tribe today is doing very well to the degree that it's able to fund the museum and different things that may not be considered direct services. It is an indirect service as far as the benefits it gives to the Tribe, yet it's still something that is much needed. I know on the outside, during the economic downturn, there were a lot of things that were considered luxuries that were wiped out and done away with or they were reduced to a point that they had to operate on a skeletal crew and a skeletal budget. But we've managed to move along even during the downturn. Between the museum and several other entities in the Tribe, we've managed to hang on and keep those things moving forward. I think that's good and in addition to that, the amount of things that have gotten better. I think people can see there's a lot of forward movement on the reservations with the new construction projects. So I think it is good times for the Seminole Tribe and its people.

Notes

1. Immediately north and northeast of Lake Okeechobee in southern peninsular Florida.

2. Broadly, the location of the modern Fort Pierce Seminole Indian Reservation.

3. A chickee is an open-sided, palmetto-thatched-roof shelter supported on posts that served as the primary dwelling of Seminole people from the mid-nineteenth century through the mid/late twentieth century (Dilley 2015).

4. Seminoles in Florida historically speak two related but distinct languages. Creek, or Mvskoke, is spoken primarily on the Brighton Reservation and areas north of Lake Okeechobee. Miccosukee is spoken on the Big Cypress Reservation and areas south of Lake Okeechobee. Seminoles from older generations were often fluent in both languages (Covington 1993).

5. East coast of southern peninsular Florida, northeast of Lake Okeechobee.

6. Florida Atlantic University is located in Boca Raton, and Nova Southeastern University is located in Fort Lauderdale. Both schools are geographically the closest higher education facilities to the Hollywood and Big Cypress Seminole communities.

7. The Big Cypress Seminole Indian Reservation, the main center for the Miccosukee-speaking population, is located on the western boundary of the Everglades. The Brighton Seminole Indian Reservation, the main center for the Creek-speaking population, abuts the northwestern shore of Lake Okeechobee. The Hollywood Reservation, the seat of Tribal government, is located in the Fort Lauderdale area. The Big Cypress and Brighton Reservations comprise the largest reservation land bases.

8. The Seminole Tribe of Florida was the first to develop bingo and later casino-style slot machines and table games. Today, the Tribe owns Hard Rock International with facilities and interests around the world (Cattelino 2008). Profits from gaming are distributed back to the Tribe, funding both infrastructure and essential services.

9. Historians estimate that the total Tribal population at the cessation of the Seminole Wars in 1858 was only several hundred people. Since then, the population has increased significantly and today consists of approximately 4,000 enrolled members.

10. Thanks to the leadership of Chairman James E. Billie and Seminole Tribe of Florida Resolution C-96-89, the Ah-Tah-Thi-Ki Museum was established as a not-for-profit corporation on February 3, 1989. Located on the Big Cypress Reservation, the museum opened to the public on August 21, 1997. It features exhibits on Seminole history and culture, an extensive collection of Seminole cultural items, and a 1-mile raised boardwalk through a 60-acre cypress dome.

References Cited

Cattelino, Jessica. 2008. *High Stakes: Florida Seminole Gaming and Sovereignty*. Durham, N.C.: Duke University Press.

Covington, James W. 1993. *The Seminoles of Florida*. Gainesville: University Press of Florida.

Dilley, Carrie. 2015. *Thatched Roofs and Open Sides: The Architecture of Chickees and Their Changing Role in Seminole Society*. Gainesville: University Press of Florida.

5

On-Reservation Projects and the Tribal Historic Preservation Office's Role within Tribal Government

ANNE MULLINS

The Seminole Tribe of Florida (STOF) reservation system consists of five geographically dispersed parcels of land that are spread out across the length and breadth of South Florida. These lands, held in trust by the U.S. government, give the STOF the unenviable distinction of being the most geographically dispersed of any federally recognized Tribal entity residing in North America. The distance from the Hollywood Reservation on Florida's southeast coast to the Tampa Reservation is 258 miles by road (longer than the distance from Washington, D.C., to New York City or from London to Paris). The seat of Seminole government resides in Hollywood, Florida, with reservation land set aside for the utilization and development of the Tribe. The on-reservation project cultural review process undertaken by the Tribal Historic Preservation Office (THPO) is central to all but one of its component sections—that is, the Tribal Archaeology, Collections, and Archaeometry Sections. Geographic distance, technological constraints, and interdepartmental goals are all significant challenges that must be overcome in order to achieve the goal of facilitating better housing. Waiting lists often approach a decade, and the job of the THPO is to complete quality cultural reviews in a timely fashion. During 2014, the average turnaround time for a typical project on-reservation was 37.2 days.

While the THPO staff work closely with a group of local reservation-based cultural advisors (Preservation Review Board), the on-reservation cultural review process holistically encompasses both the tangible and intangible when considering a determination of effect under the Tribal Cultural Resources Ordinance. It is important to note that some tangible resources, like medicinal plants, move across the landscape. It is therefore vital that determinations represent the result of an ongoing dialogue with the community. Working at the reservation scale, this is a possibility that might not be practically achievable at the state or national level.

Author Bio

Currently the Deputy Tribal Historic Preservation Officer since 2012, Anne Mullins was initially hired in 2009 as the Project Coordinator responsible for facilitating the THPO on-reservation project review process. She was the Compliance Review Supervisor from 2011 to 2012, with oversight of federal Section 106 consultations under the National Historic Preservation Act (NHPA). Mullins holds a B.A. in historic preservation (1989) from the University of Mary Washington in Fredericksburg, Virginia, and a master's in city and regional planning (1993) from Clemson University in Clemson, South Carolina.

Her early career was spent working in archaeology, anthropology, and museum studies to find her professional niche. Only after she obtained a degree in city planning did her path become clear. This was followed by sixteen years of experience in the city planning arena. Mullins has worked for municipal governments in South Carolina, Florida, and Arizona. While working in Arizona she was exposed to the consultation process under Section 106 of the NHPA. As the Historic Preservation Planner, she reviewed federally funded projects for impacts to ancestral, aboriginal, and ceded lands for Native American tribes. This experience led to her current position within the THPO. Her historic preservation and regulatory background provides a unique "big picture" understanding for the administration of the STOF Cultural Resource Ordinance (C-01-16) (CRO) (Appendix) as applied to on-reservation projects as well as working with Compliance Review to address federal agency consultation responsibilities to Native American tribes. This insight provides her the ability to apply Tribal, state, and federal laws in order to address cultural concerns of Tribal members and uphold the sovereignty of the STOF.

Introduction

The THPO is an integral part of the planning process for all land use determinations made by STOF for their trust lands (Tribal Historic Preservation Office of the Seminole Tribe of Florida 2006). The THPO coordinates with other Tribal departments, Tribal members, and outside entities to facilitate Tribal development across the six reservations that include Big Cypress,

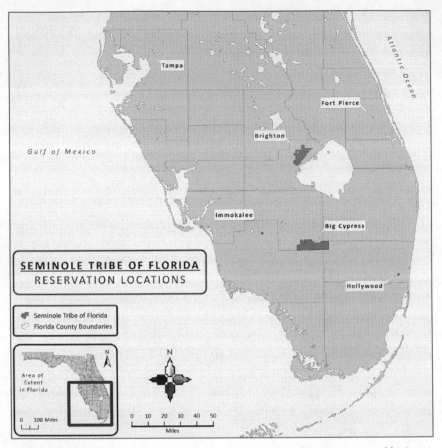

Figure 5.1. Map of Seminole Tribe of Florida Reservation locations, created by Juan Cancel, Chief Data Analyst, Seminole Tribe of Florida Tribal Historic Preservation Office.

Brighton, Tampa, Hollywood, Immokalee, and Fort Pierce (Figure 5.1). This assures that historic properties present on Seminole reservations are considered at an early stage of the planning process (Tribal Historic Preservation Office of the Seminole Tribe of Florida 2006). The reservations are not contiguous within the state and in fact are located across the southern peninsula of Florida from coast to coast. The THPO is centrally located on the Big Cypress Reservation in the Big Cypress Swamp between the two coasts (Figure 5.2). Project reviews take into account the logistics of distance and time involved to travel to the respective reservations for each project. When evaluating each project, THPO staff work within multiple cultural frameworks that often have different expectations and culturally mandated requirements. The Tribe is made up of both Creek and Miccosukee speakers; the Creek are largely located in the area northwest of Lake Okeechobee (Brighton Reservation) and the Miccosukee farther south across the interior of the peninsula, largely to the west of the Everglades in the Big Cypress Swamp (Sturtevant and Cattelino 2004).

Between 100 and 300 projects are submitted annually by outside entities and Tribal departments. These include housing for Tribal members, commercial ventures, public works and infrastructure improvements (that is, water and sewer, service lines, and road improvements), pasture improvements, and traditional development (chickee construction). Historically, Tribal members have had to wait for many years to obtain a home site lease to build on one of the Tribe's reservations due to the lengthy process of lease approvals. The Bureau of Indian Affairs (BIA) is the lead agency for on-reservation project reviews, but due to the limited capacity and staffing of the BIA, the THPO has assumed the role of principal investigator in order to expedite the project reviews (see Backhouse, this volume). The potential for ground disturbance and encountering cultural resources is increased by the existence of several construction-related Tribal departments. In order to manage this monumental task, it requires engagement and coordination with a variety of stakeholders across the Tribe that includes: Tribal leadership; the Community Planning, Real Estate, Construction Management, Environmental Resources

Figure 5.2. Tribal Historic Preservation Office signage, looking west from W. Boundary Rd. By permission of Kate Macuen, Collections Manager, Seminole Tribe of Florida Tribal Historic Preservation Office.

Management, Housing, Public Works, and Information Technology Departments; the Land Use Commission; cultural advisors; and Tribal members, families, clans, and communities on each of the reservations.

Three regulatory guidance documents are utilized by the THPO to evaluate these projects: the STOF Historic Preservation Program Plan (THPO Plan), the BIA/ACHP Programmatic Agreement (Programmatic Agreement), and the STOF CRO. In addition, the THPO initiates review of each project to include oversight by Tribal cultural advisors that determines a project's cultural appropriateness. This coordination is at the core of the THPO review process and may involve site visits by staff and cultural advisors and oral interviews of Tribal members familiar with a project area, as well as review of the Seminole Site File (SSF) to determine existing cultural resource information. Those sites that have been elevated to the Tribal Register of Historic Places (Tribal Register) are particularly important to the STOF and will be considered and protected when there is an adjacent proposed project. Four case studies will be utilized to explore the on-reservation project development process on the Big Cypress, Brighton, Hollywood, and Immokalee Reservations. Focus will be placed on the importance of communication, collaboration, and coordination between departments, tracking mechanisms, and internal controls to review and evaluate the potential impacts of a project early in development.

Regulatory Guidance Documents

Currently, three guidance documents regulate the on-reservation review process: the THPO Plan, the Programmatic Agreement, and the STOF CRO. Each of these guidance documents will be examined in turn for its relevance to the permitting process.

Historic Preservation Program Plan

Approval by the National Park Service in 2006 made the STOF the sixty-fourth federally recognized tribe to have a Historic Preservation Program Plan (National Park Service 2006). The THPO Plan outlines the responsibilities of the THPO and processes that will be implemented to carry out the NHPA Section 106 duties (Tribal Historic Preservation Office of the Seminole Tribe of Florida 2006). As a division of a federally recognized tribe, the THPO may assume all or any part of the functions of the State Historic Preservation Office (SHPO) on Tribal lands (Advisory Council on Historic Preservation 2004). The Code of Federal Regulations (36 CFR Part 800) notes that tribes that have assumed the duties of the SHPO on tribal land appoint a Tribal Historic Preservation Officer as the designated point of contact and official representative for purposes of Section 106 on the reservation. Additionally, federal agencies shall consult with the THPO instead of the SHPO regarding undertakings occurring on or affecting historic properties on tribal lands (Advisory Council on Historic Preservation 2004).

The duties assumed on reservation lands by the THPO as related to on-reservation permitting include: conducting a comprehensive survey of historic properties and maintenance of inventories of such properties; identification and nomination of eligible properties to the National Register of Historic Places; and the responsibility of implementing a comprehensive Tribal historic preservation plan. A primary duty of the THPO is to perform cultural resources surveys for all on-reservation projects, as it is responsible for cultural resources, which includes oversight of archaeological, historic, and cultural sites of significance to the STOF. This allows the THPO to maintain lists of sites on-reservation, effectively excluding the SHPO.

A second major function of the THPO is the identification and nomination of eligible properties to the National Register. For those projects surveyed that are determined to be an undertaking as defined under Section 106 of the NHPA, a determination of eligibility for the National Register is required for any site identified within a proposed project boundary. This determination is captured in the survey report completed for all projects in order to meet the requirements Section 106 of the NHPA.

Finally, the Historic Preservation Program Plan directs the THPO to develop a Tribal historic preservation plan (National Park Service 2006). The plan must incorporate existing regulations that govern historic preservation on Tribal trust lands as noted in 36 CFR 800 and the protection of archaeological resources. Furthermore, the THPO is directed to develop a Tribal Register to record significant Seminole sites that reflect the interest and values of the Seminole people (National Park Service 2006).

BIA/ACHP Programmatic Agreement

A Programmatic Agreement between the BIA and the Advisory Council for Historic Preservation (ACHP) for the Indian Land Lease Program on the Reservations and Trust Lands of the STOF (Programmatic Agreement) was approved by Tribal Council in 2012. The focus of this document was to create a streamlined process to coordinate on-reservation residential, commercial, and agricultural leases for Tribal members under Section 106 of the NHPA. Through consultation with the THPO, the BIA has determined that project undertakings addressed within the Programmatic Agreement may have an adverse effect on historic properties (Bureau of Indian Affairs, Seminole Tribe of Florida, and Advisory Council on Historic Preservation 2012). The intent of the Programmatic Agreement was to facilitate timely review and approvals of development projects by grouping activities in one of three categories: No Potential to Affect Historic Properties, Exempt undertakings, and Non-exempt undertakings for which a determination is required (Bureau of Indian Affairs, Seminole Tribe of Florida, and Advisory Council on Historic Preservation 2012). Projects within the No Potential to Effect category include renewal or transfer of a lease with no construction, changing the name of a lessee, mortgage payouts, renovation of existing buildings less than fifty years old, demolition of structures less than fifty years old with reconstruction, and landscaping without use of heavy equipment (Bureau of Indian Affairs, Seminole Tribe of Florida, and Advisory Council on Historic Preservation 2012). Exempt undertakings consist of lease renewals and transfers with proposed construction, new leases for areas with no historic properties identified, and new leases with historic properties identified but no adverse effects (Bureau of Indian Affairs, Seminole Tribe of Florida, and Advisory Council on Historic Preservation 2012). Finally, the Non-exempt category includes all undertakings in which a finding must be made and require concurrence by the federal agency (Bureau of Indian Affairs, Seminole Tribe of Florida, and Advisory Council on Historic Preservation 2012). This streamlined approach was designed in an effort to identify projects that did not qualify as Section 106 actions and/or were solely funded by the Tribe and thus would not require review by the federal agency. However, the effectiveness of the Programmatic Agreement has been limited with respect to project revisions. The Programmatic Agreement did not take into account a provision for changes to on-reservation project boundaries after initial approval. Each change, however small, must be reviewed by the BIA. Fixing the process requires an amendment to the adopted Programmatic Agreement that will take extensive time, legal involvement of all parties, and adoption by the Tribal Council through a resolution. Thus, the effort to streamline the process and reduce review time has had the opposite effect.

Cultural Resource Ordinance (C-01-16)

In October 2013, the Tribal Council passed the STOF CRO to preserve cultural resources and property on and off reservation lands to include historic resources and archaeological, ceremonial, and sacred sites that hold cultural and religious significance to the STOF (Seminole Tribe of Florida 2013).

Thus, all proposed projects on-reservation that may cause ground disturbance and have the potential to affect cultural resource on-reservation require approval from the THPO prior to commencement (Seminole Tribe of Florida 2013). The ordinance requires that the THPO be provided adequate time to evaluate the proposed project, survey the area of effect, and complete internal reviews to assess potential impacts to cultural and/or historic resources (Seminole Tribe of Florida 2013). The adoption of the CRO has many implications both on and off the reservations. The creation of the ordinance established the legal mechanism for on-reservation project review that had been developing organically since the inception of the THPO in 2006. Additionally, the CRO expanded upon the basic lists first authorized in the 2006 THPO Plan to include a three-tiered site file system that could encompass resources both on and off the reservation, known today as the SSF (Seminole Tribe of Florida 2013). The Tribal Register was established as the top tier for cultural resources considered of special importance to the STOF (Seminole Tribe of Florida 2013). The CRO further acknowledged that the THPO, in consultation with the Tribal Historic Preservation Review Board (Cultural Review Board), may identify and nominate properties that are eligible for both the Tribal Register and the National Register (Seminole Tribe of Florida 2013).

When considering listing a property on the Tribal Register, it is both a land use and legal issue, as use of trust lands of the STOF are reviewed by the STOF legal counsel and approved by the Tribal Council through a resolution (Tribal Historic Preservation Office of the Seminole Tribe of Florida 2006). In addition to this legal process, consideration is also given to both Tribal members and traditional cultural authorities within the Tribal community (Tribal Historic Preservation Office of the Seminole Tribe of Florida 2006). Thus the incorporation of the Cultural Review Board addresses both the cultural decision-making process and the legal requirements as laid out in the NHPA (Tribal Historic Preservation Office of the Seminole Tribe of Florida 2006).

With the passage of the CRO, "the THPO is authorized to coordinate with appropriate federal agencies the development of agreement(s) that will authorize the Seminole Tribe to substitute its own review procedures for those established by the Advisory Council on Historic Preservation" (Seminole Tribe of Florida 2013). Thus, concurrency reviews of THPO reports by the lead federal agency as required under the Section 106 process could be eliminated if the THPO is allowed to substitute its own review procedures. Through the passage of the CRO, the Tribe has now officially established its own review procedures, another step toward sovereignty from federal oversight. By late

2013, the THPO had initiated discussions with the ACHP and other federal agencies to establish agreements that facilitate the substitution of its review procedures based on the adoption of the CRO.

On-Reservation Project Review Process

Since establishing the THPO Program, the role of the Tribal Archaeology Section (TAS) focuses on completion of all cultural resource surveys based on cultural sensitivity and understanding of the resources. THPO reviews commonly involve engagement with a variety of departments and entities within the Tribal community. Reviews involve coordination with not only the Environmental Resource Management Department (ERMD) but also, depending on the location of the project, with Tribal Community Development for housing and commercial projects, the Cattlemen's Association for all projects relating to pastures and their improvements, and the Forestry Section within the STOF Fire Department to address review of controlled burns and invasive species eradication. Coordinating with the federal agencies for the completion of report reviews can be time consuming. The federal agency concurrency review may take anywhere from a week to a month to complete, extending the permitting process. The reservations are administered as federal trust lands, and development must be compliant with a host of federal regulations, including Section 106 of the NHPA. The THPO is an integral piece of the planning process, as it is entrusted with the responsibility of making sure that cultural and historic resources are taken into account at every level of the planning process (Tribal Historic Preservation Office of the Seminole Tribe of Florida 2006). Although on-reservation projects may be initiated, funded, and/or permitted by other federal agencies, approval of a land lease assignment by the BIA is required and categorized as an undertaking subject to review under Section 106 of the NHPA (Bureau of Indian Affairs, Seminole Tribe of Florida, and Advisory Council on Historic Preservation 2012). Cultural resources identified within a project area are evaluated for their eligibility to both the Tribal Register and National Register.

The on-reservation project review process is initiated when an outside entity or internal STOF department submits its project (via a project request form and map) to the ERMD for review (Figure 5.3). The THPO may also initiate a project internally to investigate disturbance from a project initiated without review or as a research project to fully document a site if identified during fieldwork. Under the current protocols, the ERMD is responsible to forward projects to the THPO for concurrent review in order to evaluate

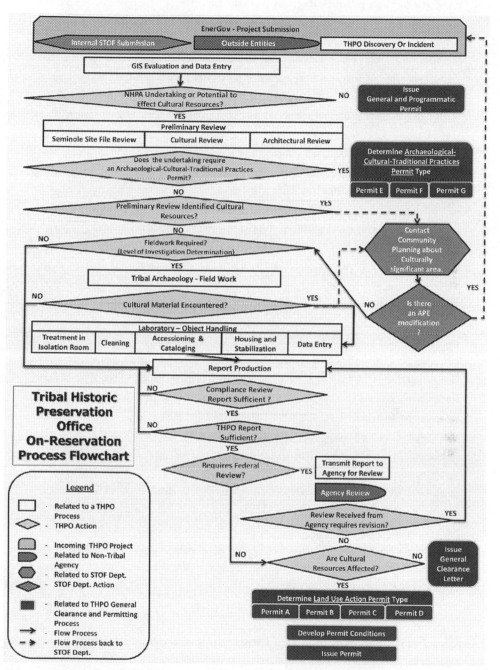

Figure 5.3. On-reservation Tribal Historic Preservation Office review process. Chart created by Juan Cancel, Chief Data Analyst, Seminole Tribe of Florida Tribal Historic Preservation Office.

potential impacts to cultural resources. The THPO logs each project and distributes for internal review to evaluate against the SSF for known cultural sites; architectural review for known structures; and cultural review for tangible and intangible cultural resources. These can include medicinal plant gathering locations or places where ceremonial dances are held. Cultural reviews are completed by community-based traditional practitioners who are familiar with a project area (formally known as the Tribal Historic Preservation Review Board). Cultural review may require site visits by the cultural advisors, oral interviews with Tribal members familiar with an area, and comparison to the SSF to determine any potential impacts to known cultural resources from a project. Coordination with cultural advisors ensures that every effort is made to address potential cultural concerns prior to development.

Upon successful completion of the three-part background review, the project is then routed to the Tribal Historic Preservation Officer to determine the amount of effort, if any, required by the TAS. Some projects may only require a desktop analysis by the TAS, while others will require more extensive fieldwork to determine a site's significance.

If fieldwork is required, then any artifacts recovered will be transferred to the THPO Collections Laboratory. It is important to note that a bioarchaeologist examines collected archaeological materials and ensures that no human remains or funerary items enter the collections. Once recovered, all items are held in isolation until proper cultural treatment is completed. Each project requires that a final report be produced with the inclusion of lab results and a recommended determination of effect under Section 106 of the NHPA and determination of eligibility to the National Register. With respect to the CRO, the THPO shall issue a determination as to whether the proposed project will have an effect on cultural resources. Either a "no cultural resources affected" or "cultural resources affected" determination will be rendered (Seminole Tribe of Florida 2013). If there is no Section 106 action and no federal funding, permit, or action, a clearance may be issued for the project. Otherwise, the report is forwarded to the lead federal agency for review and concurrence.

Seminole Site File

Under the duties outlined in the Historic Preservation Plan, per 101 (d) 2 of the NHPA, the THPO, in cooperation with federal and state agencies, local governments, and private organizations and individuals, will direct and conduct a comprehensive statewide survey of historic properties and maintain inventories of such properties (Seminole Tribe of Florida 2006). The SSF is a repository for the STOF's cultural resource information (for example, archaeological sites, traditional cultural properties, historic buildings and structures). It provides the Tribe the ability to manage its extant cultural resources in an appropriate manner and creates an organizational structure to curate the cultural resource records. These records include archaeological and historical survey reports, maps, and also hyperlinks to associated artifact information captured in the collections electronic database (PastPerfect). The cultural resources that are documented within the SSF are potentially significant to the Seminole Tribe's heritage and culture regardless of eligibility for inclusion in the Tribal Register or National Register. Information regarding these culturally sensitive sites is further protected by records access restrictions and database permissions and is not distributed, published, or shared with persons not enrolled as Seminole Tribal members unless specifically authorized by the THPO in consultation with the Cultural Review Board (Seminole Tribe of Florida 2013).

Tribal Register of Historic Places

The top tier of the SSF is the Tribal Register. Created in 2011, the Tribal Register closely mirrors the National Register in many ways. However, it was developed to preserve exceptionally significant Seminole sites that may not meet the National Register criteria or that contain culturally sensitive information that is not suitable for inclusion on the National Register, creating criteria specific to the culture, history, and beliefs of the STOF. The Tribal Register, therefore, holds the sites that have been evaluated by the staff and the Cultural Review Board, and determined by the Tribal Council, through a land set-aside process, to represent the most culturally significant sites on the reservation worthy of protection. These sites consist of places within reservation lands, land holdings not in trust, areas where there are customary usage rights, and areas within ancestral lands (Seminole Tribe of Florida 2013). Close collaboration between the THPO and Cultural Review Board is necessary to make determinations of eligibility, and often collective decisions require additional forums for presentation and discussion, such as community meetings and events. Preservation and interpretation decisions are also collectively made through an ongoing dialogue with the stakeholders—that is, individuals, families, clans, and communities. In some cases a site might be preserved by record only and the physical space continued to be occupied by a descendant in a new house. In some instances the stakeholders will want interpretative signage and protection of the site, which will require approval by the Land Use Commission and ultimately the Tribal Council. Good examples of this are the Billy Bowlegs III Camp and Red Barn. These types of Tribal Register properties are often used by the community for traditional cultural teachings and are excellent outdoor classrooms.

National Register of Historic Places

The National Park Service's National Register is a list of the nation's most significant historic places authorized by the NHPA of 1966. Consistent with the THPO Plan and the CRO, the THPO will consider nominating places that are eligible for both the Tribal Register and National Register and those that are eligible for the National Register but are not eligible for the Tribal Register. These places are of high cultural and historical value that are well known and for which there is no restriction in sharing the information with the public. Currently, there are two STOF traditional cultural properties listed on the National Register: the Red Barn (Brighton Reservation), listed in 2008, is significant for its position in the STOF cattle industry, and the Council Oak (Hollywood Reservation), known as the site of the 1957 STOF Constitution signing and the milestone celebrations of the twenty-fifth anniversary of the birthplace of gaming and the Tribe's fiftieth anniversary.

Case Studies

Four case studies will be explored to highlight how staff navigates at the interface between federal and Tribal rules and the cultural values that make the Seminole people unique. The STOF is composed of six reservations: Big Cypress in the Big Cypress Swamp, Immokalee (between Naples and Big Cypress), Hollywood (Tribal Headquarters on the East Coast), Brighton (on Lake Okeechobee to the north), Fort Pierce (east of Okeechobee), and Tampa. Two linguistic communities also compose the modern Tribe. These can be very simply understood as the Creek communities to the north at Brighton and Fort Pierce and the Miccosukee that encompass the southern tip of Florida, including the Big Cypress and Hollywood Reservations. As both Tribal and non-Tribal heritage managers, the THPO staff engages with cultural practitioners from both on-reservation and off-reservation contexts and who, as in any population, have a wide range of social and political viewpoints regarding their shared cultural heritage. As in any community, the Tribe constantly seeks to improve the quality of life for its members through the developments on each of its reservations.

Big Cypress: A Federal Water Management Project

A project was initiated on the Big Cypress Seminole Indian Reservation by a federal agency conducting a water improvement project within the reservation boundaries on a water treatment area. For perspective, the entire southern tip of Florida encompasses the Everglades, currently undergoing the largest restoration effort in the world. This project is one of hundreds being undertaken in areas identified by the STOF as ancestral and aboriginal lands both within the reservation and off-reservation. The project was initiated from the federal perspective to ensure that all regulatory requirements were met and that any legal authorities were addressed in the planning and execution of the project. However, there is a common misconception on the part of federal agencies that regulatory processes remain the same on the reservation as their counterparts undertaken off-reservation. During the preliminary project meeting, THPO staff explained the Tribal on-reservation review process, and other staff were on hand to address reservation protocols with attendees. The agency project manager was directed to coordinate with THPO staff for all ground-disturbing activities. If required, a THPO monitor could be scheduled forty-eight hours prior to commencement of work. However, the Tribal archaeologist had completed fieldwork on the project and prepared a buffer area in order to avoid impacting cultural resources. The agency was notified and provided the buffer area to complete engineering plans.

Once we established with the agency that Tribal lands were administered as federal trust land with applicable Tribal laws and a required Tribal review, it became apparent we needed to effect behavioral change so the agency could effectively work with Tribal government. The federal government is quite familiar with the off-reservation consultation process with Native American Tribes under Section 106 of the NHPA of 1966 (see Mueller, this volume). However, now that the agency was operating on Tribal lands, Tribal law is applied, requiring reviews for both cultural and environmental impacts. Tribal departments and agencies with regulatory authority over the project requests include the THPO and Environmental Resources Management Department, with additional oversight by the Tribal Land Use Commission, Tribal Water Commission, and Tribal Council to address water quality, endangered species, and cultural reviews. Coordination requires routing information to the correct department/agencies and adherence to the process flow for each entity. For instance, the Tribal clerk requires sign-off from the Tribal Legal Department before accepting a resolution in submission for an upcoming Tribal Council meeting. Strict protocols govern the resolution submission and presentation process.

A preliminary meeting was scheduled off-reservation with the federal agency to initiate discussion with Tribal departments about on-reservation protocols. Such meetings are conducted on a government-to-government basis and have inherent procedures and protocols (welcoming remarks, introductions, and meeting minutes) that accompany the formal nature of the meeting. In this case, the meeting took varying turns as staff discussed environmental issues, cultural concerns, and logistics of non-Tribal contractors working on the reservation.

While working on the Big Cypress Reservation, it is common to engage with Tribal members and their children, and this requires an understanding about reservation life. It is important to remember that it is an active community with a resident population including many young families. The nature of life on-reservation is not the same as that off-reservation, and we have found that agencies find this distinction difficult to fully understand or consider in their project planning. The Seminole Police Department was in attendance to reiterate the importance of contractors' compliance with on-reservation protocols, which include exhibiting culturally sensitive behavior, addressing speed limits, ATV use by Tribal members, and common wildlife issues within the Big Cypress Reservation. The THPO addressed the impact on cultural resources from ground disturbance throughout the project area. At one point, the THPO was asked if there were any additional cultural concerns within the project area—always a loaded question. This sensitive subject was navigated by staff explaining that if the contractors encountered any personal items, or items that raised concerns during the project implementation, they should contact the THPO immediately.

Although the THPO had completed a comprehensive survey prior to initiation of the project, there is always the potential to encounter unanticipated finds and new cultural uses of the Area of Potential Effect (APE) that have occurred after review completion. For instance, important medicinal plants might move into an area after it has been surveyed, or the APE may have been used for another purpose, requiring careful coordination with the community to identify the best path forward. The subject of cultural resources is culturally sensitive as it implies the possible presence of human remains. Even if human remains are not encountered, any archaeological materials are the result of now deceased ancestors and are to be respected and the correct cultural protocol followed.

The federal agency was represented at this meeting by approximately thirty staff from various departments, including engineering, planning, design, and construction. The agency staff responded with questions and uncertainty to the implication of potential cultural resources being encountered. The Seminole Police Department effectively reinforced the importance of notification in case any unusual items were encountered. It was concluded at the preconstruction meeting that the THPO staff would provide some ground rules prior to the initiation of construction through cultural sensitivity training to help better prepare the agency staff. Upon formal receipt of the project from the ERMD, the THPO began to address any cultural issues the project could encounter. In this case, there was a known cultural site adjacent to the proposed construction area. This required the TAS to establish a formal buffer without identifying the location of the actual site to maintain confidentiality of the sensitive cultural information. With the buffer established, staff coordinated with the federal agency to supply the Geographical Information Systems (GIS) shape files with the incorporated buffer area, allowing the project managers to finalize the engineered drawings. The THPO was then free to facilitate the project implementation while maintaining control of the sensitive information. Upon completion of the cultural resource survey and lab analysis, the Tribal archaeologist issued a report reviewed by the THPO. This report is submitted to the federal lead agency whether sponsoring the project, funding the project, or permitting the project. A concurrence of STOF THPO determination is requested and in this case was concurred by the federal agency leading the project on the reservation.

Once the federal agency had obtained the green light to move ahead with construction, the cultural sensitivity training was scheduled for agency staff to address cultural concerns. The THPO staff, represented by the Collections Manager and the Bioarchaeologist, facilitated the training. They provided field guidelines for the contractors and suggested any concerns be brought to the THPO for evaluation and possible consultation with Tribal cultural advisors. In this case, on the Big Cypress Reservation no known impacts were identified to plant-gathering areas or ceremonial grounds. The water containment construction was permitted to begin, and the TAS was able to monitor the project on an intermittent basis to ensure adherence to the CRO.

Even so, the project did not go without interruption. There have been two instances that construction work ceased within an area and cultural advisors have been called to investigate. Working with the cultural advisors provides an additional layer of logistics. A reasonable assumption would be that staff could just give the cultural advisors a call and request that an area be evaluated. However, due to the protocols within the Tribal community and internal hierarchy of cultural knowledge, only specific cultural advisors may evaluate specific areas of concern. This in turn requires time to coordinate behind the scenes with the specific cultural representatives for each reservation and potentially with cultural advisors outside the impacted community. In some cases, the cultural advisor may come from as far as Tampa, depending on the matter at hand. Thus, what may appear to be a simple project review to many federal agencies is actually much more intricate. This has required staff to learn patience and develop ongoing communication with Tribal cultural advisors to establish relationships and effective dialogue. As discussed previously, cultural reviews are required components of the permitting process. However, in a discovery situation when cultural material is encountered during a project, the cultural advisors will often complete a site visit to the area in question and make a formal determination.

Brighton: A Tale of Two Camps

The Brighton Reservation is home to the second case study. Here, the strong presence of the Tribal cattle business is represented by the Red Barn, the first Tribal property to be listed on the National Register (see Dilley and Gopher, this volume). There are many documented historic camps on this reservation that are considered through the on-reservation review process to evaluate impacts to cultural resources. These camps provide multiple opportunities for Tribal departments to coordinate in order to successfully navigate the permitting process. In this case study, I examine two different proposed home site projects.

The leased land is evaluated for impacts to cultural resources prior to assignment and construction. A housing development had been planned within the Brighton community years earlier, and some construction of home sites had been completed. Within this same parcel a Tribal member submitted a request for a home site lease to the Tribal Community Planning Department. The THPO was consulted as part of the standard on-reservation review process. Upon completion of the Tribal Archaeology review, it was clear that the land area selected for the home site development was within the known Billy Bowlegs III Camp, a significant historic campsite within the Brighton community. Based on this conclusion, the TAS consulted with Brighton community cultural advisors. The Tribal cultural advisors noted that previous issuances of home site leases had been prematurely assigned and already encroached on the camp, resulting in the installation of a mobile home and barn.

The cultural advisors recommended that the Billy Bowlegs III Camp and the land should be set aside from future development. The THPO contacted Tribal Community Planning and communicated the concerns of the cultural advisors. Tribal Community Planning noted that it had not been notified of this status and had previously prepared a housing development site plan for the area. It is common for cultural sites to be unknown by Tribal departments until a project is moved through the developmental review process. Tribal departments are primarily headquartered on the Hollywood Reservation, and the distance between reservations can lead to a lack of understanding about cultural issues that directly impact a reservation community that will ultimately be decided through the community decision-making process. A decision was made to preserve the Billy Bowlegs III Camp from future development through a land set-aside. Tribal Community Planning continued to work with the Tribal member in order to relocate the home site. The THPO proceeded to work with the Real Estate Division to prepare a set-aside for review by the Tribal Land Use Commission. The Tribal Council approved a set-aside, and the Billy Bowlegs III Camp will be preserved with a surrounding buffer. Ultimately, the site will be utilized by the Brighton Culture Department to educate the Tribal youth about camp life in Brighton.

This example emphasizes how the culture remains at the core of developmental decision making and also stresses interdepartmental communication and coordination in order to ensure the preservation of cultural areas when preparing future development plans. The collaboration between departments was further exhibited through the THPO working with Tribal Community Development to have other modern elements (mobile home and barn) removed from the historic camp at the request of the direct descendants and Brighton community. The request therefore resulted in positive community action that ultimately resulted in preservation of this important camp and also allowed the THPO to work with descendant family members on preservation and outreach objectives to allow the camp to play a part in the education of Tribal members learning culture through signage and school visits.

The second housing project was also a home site request from a Tribal member in Brighton. The Tribal member had been advised through family oral histories that the chosen home site location was his family's historic camp, and the Tribal member wanted to establish a presence at this location. In this case, what appeared to be routine investigation took a major change in direction. When the TAS completed the background research for the report, the Brighton cultural advisors notified staff that the proposed home site was located in the Naha Tiger Camp, another family's historic campsite. Initially, the

THPO asked Tribal Community Planning if the Tribal member would consider the relocation of the home site due to the cultural concerns. However, the Tribal member remained firm in his desire to locate his home site in the requested area and needed to understand the reasoning behind the cultural determination. The Brighton cultural advisors recommended a presentation at the monthly Brighton Community Meeting for both parties to present their cases.

This method of resolution is part of the community decision-making process and common on the reservations. The community meeting was the conduit for the dispute resolution. The Tribal member requesting the home site addressed the THPO staff, cultural advisors, Brighton community leaders, and several community members. The discussion surrounded the family association to the Naha Tiger Camp. It was determined through the community decision process that the home site in question was actually part of another family's historic camp. The proposed home site was denied, and THPO staff were asked to move forward and work with Tribal Community Planning to identify a new home site for the Tribal member and coordinate with real estate agents to establish a set-aside for the historic Naha Tiger camp. The importance of the community culture and family association to the camp is continually revisited as part of our process to review on-reservation projects on the Brighton Reservation.

Hollywood: Redefining Seminole Estates

A third case study visits the Hollywood Reservation on Florida's east coast. As the most urban of the reservation settings, Hollywood presents a less traditional and more contemporary cultural setting from the Brighton and Big Cypress Reservations. However, unlike the other reservations, there is a fast-paced atmosphere within this modern urban development that also focuses on maintaining the Seminole brand as it houses STOF headquarters, the Seminole Hard Rock Hotel, Classic Casino, Okalee Village, and other Tribal enterprises. Amid the contemporary setting, there still remains a deep cultural root system that is associated with the Creek and Miccosukee, represented by chickees dotting the landscape and the Council Oak tree, a significant cultural site listed on the National Register. This case study focuses on the redevelopment of a land parcel owned by the Tribe that housed Seminole Estates, a non-Tribal rental mobile home community. The parcel, located adjacent to Tribal headquarters at State Road 7 and Stirling Road in Hollywood, was the subject of an array of preliminary development proposals to include a water/

sewer treatment plant, the new Okalee Village, a sports entertainment facility, and a new housing development.

In contrast to the Big Cypress and Brighton Reservations, Hollywood is limited in its land acreage. The Hollywood Reservation is undergoing a resurgence of development that influenced the decision to convert the Seminole Estates rental parcel to provide housing, services, or commercial property opportunities for the Tribal community. While present at an interdepartmental meeting, THPO staff notified Tribal Community Planning that Seminole Estates would need to be evaluated for cultural resources due to its proximity to a Tribal cemetery. Due to historic inaccuracy of reservation parcels and surveying, the THPO would be evaluating the parcel during the demolition process of the removal of mobile homes and associated structures. The THPO evaluated the need to employ ground-penetrating radar (GPR) throughout the parcel to delineate and avoid impact on cultural resources, including the adjacent cemetery.

In this case, what seemed to be a straightforward project became rather complicated due to the use of outside contractors on the reservation for removal of structures. The contractors and project managers were ever-changing, creating a logistical nightmare. The new contractors were unaware and insensitive to Tribal culture. THPO staff were commonly not notified of the personnel changes and/or ground disturbance that were occurring on the parcel. The THPO staff continued to schedule dates for monitoring until the entire parcel was surveyed and further witnessed insensitive actions to include damage to the cemetery wall from poor operation of large construction equipment and unscheduled ground disturbance. THPO staff have come to expect this type of behavior from outside contractors due to a lack of understanding and education about cultural concerns. The project reinforced the need to coordinate with Tribal departments to schedule cultural sensitivity training prior to commencement of construction and demolition when adjacent to known sites and potentially sensitive areas on the reservations. Establishing a central point of contact (project manager) within Tribal departments throughout the life of the project will ensure clear communication and reduce potential adverse impacts to cultural resources.

Immokalee: A Cultural Community Boardwalk

Immokalee is home to the fourth case study, with its location west of the Big Cypress Reservation in Collier County. A smaller, more urban reservation than Big Cypress and Brighton, it houses a casino and will be home to a newly proposed hotel. Like the Hollywood Reservation, Immokalee is limited in its land holdings. A project proposal was presented to Tribal Community Planning to develop a circular boardwalk adjacent to the 4-H Program and existing cultural camp east of the casino to be solely for community and cultural use. The THPO was asked to attend an onsite meeting to discuss the location for the public restrooms and boardwalk adjacent to the cultural camp. The THPO noted the proximity of the roadway and the need to evaluate indirect effects from the installation of water and sewer lines. The review commenced to include the SSF, architectural history, and cultural review. This revealed a known site containing cultural material.

The Immokalee project coordinator was notified that the boardwalk configuration was in close proximity to the cultural site and would require a Tribal Archaeology monitor in order to minimize impacts. The THPO staff was deployed to complete fieldwork for the utility lines to rule out any direct impacts and determine a buffer. Ultimately, it was decided that a Tribal Archaeology monitor be assigned during the installation of the boardwalk posts to address potential cultural resources. Project location siting occurs within the community on each of the reservations prior to completion of the necessary cultural, site file, and architectural review. The boardwalk project provides an example of working closely with the Cultural Department, Tribal Community Planning, and the community to identify locations for large projects that may have many direct and indirect impacts. With this in mind, it is of the utmost importance to open the lines of communication between the STOF departments, Tribal community, and cultural advisors to proactively plan projects with minimal impacts.

Conclusion

The THPO plays an integral role in land use determinations and facilitation of the planning process for development across the STOF reservations. Three regulatory guidance documents are utilized daily to implement reviews for all on-reservation projects. Of these documents, only the STOF CRO outlines a legally enforceable process to protect the Tribe's cultural resources within reservation lands, areas where the STOF has customary usage rights, and land holdings that are owned by the STOF but not in trust. Both the STOF Historic Preservation Program Plan (THPO Plan) (National Park Service 2006) and the BIA/STOF/ACHP Programmatic Agreement still represent the paternalistic relationship that the Tribe has with the federal government.

As a division of a federally recognized tribe, the THPO is required to provide an annual report of its activities, to include surveys and determinations of eligibility for the National Register, to the National Park Service. The Programmatic Agreement requires the STOF to provide a determination of effect to the federal agency for each project that has been determined nonexempt (Bureau of Indian Affairs, Seminole Tribe of Florida, and Advisory Council on Historic Preservation 2012). All the while, the THPO has been responsible for protection of its cultural resources since the THPO was established in 2006. The ultimate goal through each of these is to reduce impacts to cultural resources across the reservation through compliance with Section 106 of the NHPA and compliance with the CRO. The early involvement by the THPO ensures that cultural resources will be taken into account at all stages of planning. Through the establishment of the SSF and Tribal Register, the THPO houses important cultural information and seeks to preserve the most significant Seminole sites.

The reservation communities of the STOF continue to exhibit cultural, temporal, and locational challenges. Cultural awareness, communication, and central points of contact throughout projects facilitate development on the reservations while maintaining cultural sensitivity. The Big Cypress and Hollywood Reservation case studies emphasize the importance of cultural sensitivity training for contractors and project managers prior to the implementation of construction. The coordination with cultural advisors throughout a project ensures there is reduced potential for adverse impacts to culturally sensitive areas and that site buffers are established to provide an extra layer of protection from construction activities. This early intervention allows appropriate communication channels to be set up and utilized throughout the project.

The community decision-making process remains at the center of Tribal development on both the Big Cypress and Brighton Reservations and requires staff to navigate and coordinate with cultural advisors. Including community members in the conversation ensures that cultural resources are considered as the reservations are developed. Each case study reiterated the importance of opening the lines of communication between cultural advisors and Tribal departments to incorporate cultural resources in the planning process at the earliest levels of project management.

Engagement with federal agencies on the reservation requires the THPO to continually assert the established on-reservation project review process as outlined in the adopted CRO. This process continues to be refined and streamlined in order for staff to efficiently and effectively review projects internally and address issues promptly. The Tribe continues advancement through technology and has invested in EnerGov permitting software recently implemented for the purpose of tracking review status by multiple Tribal departments. Tribal departments provided workflow processes to the EnerGov project team to incorporate into the database. This new software allows departments to know the review status and any issues that have been identified by reviewing departments during project development. The THPO will continue to strive to increase sovereignty for the STOF. By limiting the federal review process as the THPO seeks to establish agreements with federal agencies, the THPO assumes the responsibility for all cultural resource review on the reservations and follows the procedures adopted in the STOF CRO.

Figure 5.4. Anne Mullins. By permission of Kate Macuen, Collections Manager, Seminole Tribe of Florida Tribal Historic Preservation Office.

References Cited

Advisory Council on Historic Preservation. 2004. *Code of Federal Regulations* 36, part 800.

Bureau of Indian Affairs, Seminole Tribe of Florida, and Advisory Council on Historic Preservation. 2012. "Programmatic Agreement among the Bureau of Indian Affairs, Seminole Tribe of Florida, and Advisory Council on Historic Preservation." May 3.

National Park Service. 2006. Letter. October.

Seminole Tribe of Florida. 2013. Cultural Resource Ordinance (C-02-14).

Sturtevant, William C., and Jessica R. Cattelino. 2004. "Florida Seminole and Miccosukee." In *Handbook of North American Indians Southeast*, Vol. 14, edited by Raymond D. Fogelson, volume editor, and William C. Sturtevant, general editor, 429–449. Washington, D.C.: Smithsonian Institution.

Tribal Historic Preservation Office of the Seminole Tribe of Florida. 2006. "Tribal Historic Preservation Program Plan 30."

6

Tribal Archaeology

Changing Perceptions of Archaeology
within the Seminole Tribe of Florida

ERIC GRIFFIS, JEFFREY W. SEPANSKI, AND JACK CHALFANT

What is it like to complete archaeological research in an on-reservation setting? The answer is that it could be the same as anywhere else in the country as field crews work to excavate the requisite number of shovel tests or test units within a geographically specified area of potential effect. At the Seminole Tribe of Florida Tribal Historic Preservation Office (THPO), there is one significant difference between what we do and "typical" cultural resource management (CRM) based research. We remain in situ long after the project is complete. The philosophy of the THPO is that the long-term success of the on-reservation archaeology program revolves around the successful communication and engagement with the community in order to preserve and protect important elements of their collective heritage. The THPO is still fairly young as an organization, and the sight of people walking through pastures with shovels and trowels is novel to most, if not all, of the residents of any given reservation. The moments that archaeologists and community interact are therefore critical. This is definitely the case in this chapter, which begins with a particular incident that universally brings people of all cultures together—lunch.

Author Bios

Eric Griffis has a B.A. in anthropology and English from the University of Florida and an M.A. in southern studies from the University of Mississippi, where he concentrated in interdisciplinary cultural documentary studies. Originally from Florida, Griffis has worked as an archaeologist extensively within the state and has performed CRM fieldwork throughout the United

Figure 6.1. *Left to right*: Jack Chalfant, Eric Griffis, and Jeffrey Sepanski. By permission of Maureen Mahoney, Tribal Archaeologist, Seminole Tribe of Florida Tribal Historic Preservation Office.

States. His primary interest lies in utilizing digital media as a means to document the diverse and underrepresented cultures of the southeastern United States. Griffis worked in the Tribal Archaeology Section (TAS) of the THPO for two years before stepping into the role of the Oral History Coordinator at the Ah-Tah-Thi-Ki Museum.

Jeffrey W. Sepanski grew up in Naples, Florida. He obtained his B.A. in anthropology from Florida Gulf Coast University after serving eight years in the Army National Guard. He has worked with the Seminole Tribe of Florida for two years. His academic interests include ethnobotany and paleoclimatology.

Jack Chalfant was born on the Brighton Reservation on December 24, 1966; lived on the Brighton Reservation; and graduated from Okeechobee High School. He worked in the Department of Corrections in Desoto and Martin Correctional Institutions from May 1991 to April 2002, and as a police officer with the Seminole Police Department from November 2002 to December 2009. In May 2013, Chalfant received his A.S. degree in criminology from South Florida State College. He joined the Work Experience Program with the Seminole Tribe of Florida, started working with the THPO in September 2013, and was hired on as an Archaeological Field Technician in November 2013.

Introduction

As archaeologists who work on reservations, we see tangible changes in the perceptions Tribal members have of us. We believe the lessons we are learning on the front lines of interaction with the community members of the Seminole Tribe of Florida will aid in shaping and refining public policy and ethics regarding cultural preservation. When taking into account the whole of anthropological and archaeological thought, the practice of tribal archaeology is relatively new and still developing. In this chapter, we illustrate our experiences as field technicians communicating with the individuals for whom we work.

While researching this topic, we found that the perspective of the field technician working in the tribal reservation setting is missing from the canon of archaeological literature. We offer some anecdotes to illustrate the types of issues we often confront, couch them in historical context based on our research, and present some insights on how we are applying the lessons we are learning.

A Contentious Lunch Encounter

Archaeological field technician Jeffrey Sepanski recounts a run-in he had with a Tribal member while ordering lunch one day on the Brighton Reservation.

"Tribal Historic Preservation? What can a white man like you tell me about my culture?" I heard a man ask in an agitated tone behind me as I ordered lunch at the sandwich shop inside the Brighton Reservation Trading Post. I turned around to see who was talking and was shocked to realize the question was addressed to me.

I was wearing a work uniform shirt that displayed a large-size seal of the Seminole Tribe of Florida with the words "Tribal Historic Preservation Office" written around the outside. These shirts are an important tool in making us identifiable on the reservations. We routinely enter onto Tribal members' residential lots and agricultural pastures, so we want people to know we are employees, even at a distance. Lunch times at the trading posts are when we have the most interaction with people. Our THPO uniforms lead to a variety of responses from the community, from standoffishness to curiosity, and, on this day, to confrontation.

He was a tall Seminole man, about 6 feet 4 inches tall, in a T-shirt, jeans, and a baseball cap. Before I could say anything, he started in again, "Where did you get your education?"

I responded, "Florida Gulf Coast Uni—" before I was cut off.

"You never grew up here! I would trust my elders before anything you had to say!" At this point, all the patrons in the restaurant were looking over at us, and the room became all too quiet. "You know you called us savages and cannibals in one of your books. We are not like that! Why would we be cannibals when there are supermarkets and so many animals out here to hunt?"

"What book is that?" I responded.

"It was one of your archaeology books."

"There are books like that written a long time ago. We don't go by those books anymore."

Laurie, making my sandwich, interjected to ask what toppings I would like. "I'll have lettuce, tomato, and lots of jalapeños," I said. I was hoping this confrontation would quickly blow over now that it was time to order.

The Tribal member ordered his lunch and looked back at me, "Hello, I'm waiting for a response." He asked another question, "Can you tell me where the white man came from?"

Jack Chalfant, one of my coworkers who is also a Tribal member, interjected, "Europe!"

"Jack, be quiet. I'm talking to him. Why is it you dig up our bones and take them away? Why do you rob our graves? Why can't I go and dig up George Washington and put him in my museum? Why is that any different?"

I had been working at the THPO for only a few months, and I had never before had a confrontation like this. I was practicing good, responsible, ethical archaeology, the way I was taught in school, so was shocked at the accusations being directed at me from a Tribal member. I could not believe such a misconception of what we do as archaeologists exists. Then again, most people think we dig up gold and dinosaurs, chase Nazis, and are deathly afraid of snakes. To this Tribal member, I personally embodied the last 400 years of colonial history and outdated, yet pervasive, anthropological theory.

Overwhelmed with the number of questions, I said, "I would gladly sit down with you and go over all of your concerns if you'd like." He readily accepted the offer, and I found a seat at his table. It would take a few minutes to address all of his concerns. I told him we are archaeologists, but specifically Tribal archaeologists. We are employed by his Tribe (the Seminole Tribe of Florida), and we work for his benefit. I told him exactly what we do, such as what happens when we encounter human remains, and about the process of repatriation. It is truly unfortunate what has happened in the past, but we are working to mend the divide it has created. By the end of our conversation, the Tribal member said, "Thank you. You know, I wanted to see where you were coming from." We shook hands and parted ways.

The Saga of Tom Tiger

The Tribal member's concerns can be understood when considering the stories of the Seminoles' own conflicted history with outsiders. For example, at the end of the nineteenth century, a man named Micco Tustenuggee, or "Captain" Tom Tiger, was a well-known and well-liked Seminole man within his community and among many of the white settlers in South Florida. In 1897, a horse was stolen from him by a white man named Harmon Hull with the written intention of returning the horse within two months. However, after two months had passed, the horse had not been returned. Tiger questioned Hull about the matter, and Hull denied a horse was ever stolen (Jumper and West 2001, 20). The Friends of the Florida Seminoles, an organization composed entirely of white people, undertook litigation against Hull on Tiger's behalf, the first time such a court action was taken (McGown 1998, 91).

Even after his passing, Tom Tiger was at the center of another strange interaction involving the Seminoles, the Friends of the Florida Seminoles, the local settlers, and a mysterious man from out of state who claimed to be an archaeologist.

> Without setting to do so, Tom Tiger focused the nation's attention on the plight of Florida's Seminole Indians. . . . In life, he was the catalyst for the first non-Indian group dedicated to helping the Tribe. In death, he set off the nearest thing Florida has had to a 20th century uprising. (McGown 1998, 89)

In 1907, Tom Tiger died after being struck by lightning while building a dugout canoe. Family members buried his body on-site by using the canoe he built as a makeshift coffin and placed his personal belongings with him (Jumper and West 2001, 22). A year later, a man named John T. Flournoy went through the area looking for artifacts. Flournoy claimed that he was working for the Smithsonian Institution and exhumed Tom Tiger's body in the name of "science." This act outraged the Seminole community, and they demanded that the bones be returned or they would start the Fourth Seminole war. The Friends of the Florida Seminoles intervened again, and the bones were returned within three months. They were found not at the Smithsonian, but on display at a tourist attraction in Philadelphia. The Smithsonian, when contacted, claimed they had no affiliation with Flournoy (Jumper and West 2001, 23–25).

Stories such as these about Tom Tiger provide a vivid reminder to the Seminole people about their tumultuous history filled with outsiders coming in trying to "help" them. Some people have helped, some have taken advantage of them, and some have done both. These stories can harbor resentment from generations past. A healthy amount of skepticism and suspicion is understandable when it comes to looking out for their own best interests.

Resetting the Table

Jack Chalfant came to work with the Tribal Archaeology Section as part of the Work Experience Program within the Tribe. He leases pastureland on the Brighton Reservation to raise cattle. He explains what he thought archaeology was before he started training as an archaeological field technician.

> When I first saw some people in my pasture with a truck that said "Tribal Archaeology" on the side, my first thought was, "what are these grave robbers doing out here?" I asked them some questions about what they were looking for and they said they were looking for historical sites. I watched them for a while as they dug holes in the ground and put the dirt in a box with a screen bottom and sifted through all the dirt they pulled out of the hole. That first thought of what archaeologists were was conceived from what little knowledge I had of them from the movies and TV. I was under the assumption that they went around and robbed old graves, digging up the valuables and leaving the bodies exposed.

The acrimonious relationship between anthropologists and indigenous groups over the last 150 years is well documented (Thomas 2000; Deloria 1973). We know that in the mid-nineteenth century little separated antiquarians, treasure hunters, and archaeologists.

We can try to justify the past endeavors of archaeologists and their scientific research by acknowledging they were a product of their time. For example, consider the advent of the theory of evolution by Charles Darwin in the mid-nineteenth century. He explained, citing biological evidence, the idea of evolution as a process by which something changed while remaining partially the same. This process was quickly applied by others in an attempt to reconstruct the past. Lewis Henry Morgan's *Ethnical Periods*, written in 1877, expounds his ideas of unilineal evolution. He believed that culture was homogenous throughout humanity and could be divided into different stages of development: savagery, barbarism, and civilization (Erickson and Murphy 2008, 43–51). As a result, many archaeologists viewed other cultures as more primitive and therefore inferior and treated them as such. This justified archaeologists' assumptions of authority in their Eurocentric interpretation of history.

Vine Deloria Jr., a Native American, famously encapsulated the history of interaction between anthropologists and Native Americans up until the late 1960s in his book *Custer Died for Your Sins: An Indian Manifesto*. Deloria's *Manifesto* was at times wry, hyperbolic, and satirical, yet contained biting social commentary widely read and accepted at the time: "Indians have been cursed above all other people in history. Indians have anthropologists" (Deloria 1969, 83). And "it would be wise for anthropologists to get down from their thrones of authority and PURE research and begin helping Indian Tribes instead of preying on them" (Deloria 1969, 104).

In contrast to Deloria's outspoken pessimism about the benefits of Native Americans' interactions with anthropologists, the Seminoles have benefited greatly from anthropologists who did not just study them but became activists on their behalf. For instance, William L. Merrill recounts the impact that Smithsonian anthropologist William C. Sturtevant had in preserving the Seminoles' federal status as a tribe. In 1954, a "withdrawal" bill was proposed in Congress that would have ended federal supervision of the Seminoles. Most Tribal members opposed the bill, and Sturtevant submitted a statement to Congress, after which the bill was no longer pursued (Covington 1993, 237).

Between the abrasive interactions that Deloria illustrates and the relatively cordial relationships such as the one Sturtevant cultivated with the Seminoles, the field of anthropology went through a process of reevaluating itself. The intellectual flowering of ideas, such as postprocessual critiques and postcolonial thinking in the late twentieth century, has shaped the way many archaeologists think today. Archaeologists now employ more holistic methods and engage a plurality of interpretations of the archaeological record from individuals. A more conscious effort has been made to move away from the traditional idea of one expert, "the outsider," making the interpretations. The idea is to elevate the voice of indigenous people to that of equal status with academics in interpreting their own culture and history. While this is the goal toward which we are working, there is still progress to be made.

During the same time period, new legislative actions were also passed that required archaeologists to consult with tribal communities. The most notable laws were the American Indian Religious Freedom Act of 1978 (AIRFA), the

Archaeological Resources Protection Act of 1979 (ARPA), the National Historic Preservation Act of 1966 (NHPA), and the Native American Graves Protection and Repatriation Act of 1990 (NAGPRA).

These laws have provided much in the way of repairing relations; however, there are still contingents within the archaeological community who believe these laws are impeding research. Archaeologist and anthropologist Joe Watkins addresses the problem and implies the solution:

> Repatriation legislation . . . [has] . . . codified choices that were once voluntary—essentially legislating a great number of archaeologists' professional ethics. Legislation has been enacted that forces consultation with affected American Indian groups, thereby removing the opportunity for individuals to make an ethical choice rather than simply following the letter of the law. In spite of the legislation, however, it is still possible for an individual to circumvent the intent of the law. (Watkins 2000, xii)

Where some archaeologists only follow the letter of the law under duress, we are trying to create a voluntary archaeology ethic that works toward a greater understanding of the culture from within the culture, as well as from the outside. For example, some archaeologists are concerned that they are being prevented from studying ancient human remains (traditionally regarded by archaeologists as distinctly separate from, and therefore not traceable to, any specific historic tribe), thus limiting the potential for new understandings in the archaeological record. This common archaeological approach is insensitive to the concerns and beliefs of many Native Americans. Tribes do not always see the same clear-cut divisions of culture that were imposed upon them during the formative days of academic archaeological theory—divisions, such as "historic" and "prehistoric," that were influenced by Western colonial hegemonic thought. Such antiquated notions still linger today. Due to the complexities and hassles that can arise, many archaeologists continue to avoid involvement with tribal communities. This ultimately creates a Euro-American slant to the telling of the past. In other words, many archaeologists today study various aspects of Native American history without ever consulting with the current members of the tribes they are studying. This is unfortunate because the inclusion of Native American perspectives will only add to the holistic understanding of human history.

This kind of impasse between academics and tribal members can easily be remedied through communication. For instance, we incorporate traditional beliefs into our practice of archaeology. Since Seminole burials have been doctored by Medicine Men as a part of the funeral process, our work is overseen by traditional medicine practitioners. Our building has had medicine performed on it, and all artifacts brought in from the field are put into an isolation room, which is separate from the lab and collections areas, to undergo a process known only to Tribal members. A bioarchaeologist on staff examines any questionable artifacts in the field should we suspect that we have uncovered human remains. If she confirms that the bone is possibly human, it is immediately reinterred. In keeping with Seminole traditions, we have had medicine administered in the field on such remains. Archaeologists who have surveyed here in the past were once seen as looters. Our entire field of study was seen as taboo by most Tribal members. Now, we are building trust and mutual respect within the Tribe. Tribal member Jack Chalfant goes on to say how his perceptions have changed since working here a while:

> After working with the Tribal Historic Preservation Office for the past eight months, I have a whole new opinion on what they do. They are out there finding these sites and protecting them from destruction and preserving the past. If they do find human remains, they mark its location with a Trimble and that area is protected from development, the total opposite of what my opinion was. Working with the archaeologists, I look at archaeology as an investigation. I try to take the whole picture and see what it was like back in those times, how they had to work together to survive, what tools were available, how travel was limited to what vehicles, what means were available, and how abundant the food was back then. When we find a site, I can tell what kind of foods they ate by the remains that we find—turtle shells, fish bones, bird bones, and mammal bones (deer, hogs, small game animals). When I worked in the lab I learned that each animal has distinct markings that identify them even after being buried in the ground for hundreds of years. Some of the bones we find are from animals that I grew up eating—curlew, garfish, gopher turtles, water turtles, and rabbits. . . . Preserving the past for the future is what archaeology means to me, today, compared to what I used to think.

The Process

As Tribal archaeologists, we perform a variety of tasks—some similar to CRM, some academic-style research projects such as historical camp research, and some community-based or applied archaeology outreach. As far as compliance, we perform Phase I field surveys on a daily basis and occasional Phase II excavations just as every CRM firm does. We ensure due diligence is carried out to protect known sites and to discover previously unknown sites before construction projects begin. Chalfant goes on to explain why this process is important from a Tribal member's perspective:

> The Tribal Historical Preservation Office is an office that the Tribe needs to preserve the past and protect these historical places on the reservation. If there is an issue with a Tribal member wanting to build a house on one of these sites, it is brought to the attention of the community and discussed, and we let the community decide if he or she should be allowed to build on the site. That happened in Brighton, and I observed this process in action. That is one of the benefits of having a department like THPO—it keeps the Tribal community informed about what sites are protected and if new development is going to affect the historic site or camp.... Another benefit of having the Tribal Historical Preservation Office is that they created a Cultural Resource Ordinance that was adopted by the Tribal Council (governing body of the Tribe), which protects these historic places and campsites. Before any construction or clearing can be done, the THPO-TAS has to go out and survey the APE (Area of Potential Effect) to see if there are any historical sites, camps, or burials in the area. If none are found then construction/demolition may start. If some types of historic remnants are found to exist then we have to evaluate the site to see if it qualifies to be listed on the National Register of Historic Places (NRHP) or the Tribal Register of Historical Places. If the site qualifies for the NRHP, then the proper paper work is filed. But if it doesn't qualify for the National Register, it can still qualify for the Tribal Register and still be protected.

We evaluate sites for Section 106 compliance and the National Register nomination. We write reports to submit to our THPO director, or the Bureau of Indian Affairs (BIA), or to other relevant agencies depending on the project. But, as with most aspects of our job, there are different and additional considerations for us to be conscious of while performing our duties. A CRM archaeologist records sites for the Florida Master Site File (FMSF) and is concerned with the guidelines for meeting NRHP requirements. Inside the reservation, we do not report sites to the FMSF, but instead record them in our own Seminole Site File system. We standardize this process to coincide as much as possible with state and federal guidelines for obvious reasons

of simplification and to reduce redundancy in meeting compliance requirements.

The way we evaluate sites for the Tribal Register of Historic Places di-
verges greatly from the way we evaluate for the NRHP. Recently, for instance,
we performed a Phase I survey of 2 acres, which consisted of five shovel tests.
Our records research did not reveal any historic sites in or around the APE.
All of the shovel tests were negative, and there was no evidence of any structures. If we were doing standard CRM compliance archaeology, we would give
the property the "all clear" for development and that would be the end of the
story. However, all of our projects undergo a separate cultural review, which
is not the same as the archaeological review. The results of both are then considered in our THPO reports. Tribal members with special knowledge of a
particular area weigh in on whether a property holds significance. The Tribe
has preserved land or modified development plans for reasons pertaining to
historical, cultural, ceremonial, medicinal, and ecological importance. In the
instance of this project, a cultural advisor with in-depth knowledge of, and
experience in, the cattle industry in Brighton brought to our attention the location of a historic "camp kitchen" on the property. None of the usual artifacts
associated with Florida archaeological sites were found there, but nonetheless,
it is a place of special significance to the Tribe. No special steps needed to be
taken to preserve the area except for construction being offset slightly to accommodate the site. We at the Seminole Tribe of Florida THPO do not see
this consultation process as a burden or hindrance to the archaeological science we were trained in at the university. We view this process as enriching our
understanding of culture and serving the community in an immediate way.
We are very much performing "community-based" and "applied archaeology."

It is a goal of the THPO and a tenant of Tribal archaeology to improve
upon the values of archaeology to better represent the views of Tribal members. We actively seek to reach out through community-based archaeology
and have had Tribal members interested in, and even participating in, archaeological research. We have employed Tribal members in the TAS and have had
many high school students from the Big Cypress Reservation volunteer and
intern at the THPO and the Ah-Tah-Thi-Ki Museum. This is important on
many levels. First, working with members of such a close-knit community
allows them to see exactly what we do. Second, once misconceptions are dis-
pelled, Tribal members may discover they are interested in learning what we
have to offer, or even working in the field of archaeology. This is very important because, as Willie Johns explains it, Tribal members want to have a say

in their own cultural presentation. They do not want to be put on display, tell a creation myth for you to record, or let you sit in on their ceremonial practices so you can interpret and judge the meaning through the lens of your own establishmentarian methodology. Tribal members want to interpret their own culture through their own lens of understanding and have it hold equal value and weight when it comes to interpretation and presentation, and when it comes to creating regulations and policies. They want to be a part of the process, not the subject of it (Willie Johns, personal communication, August 13, 2013).

For example, Navajo Tribal member and archaeologist Richard Begay states that his tribe has no issues with the archaeologists employed to do compliance, but does have problems getting academic archaeologists to consider the Navajo people's stories of their own "history" and "prehistory." The Navajo Tribe has its own methods of preserving the estimated one million archaeological sites on its reservation lands and has been doing so for hundreds of years (Begay 1997, 162). We find the same sentiment to be true for the Seminole Tribe of Florida. Trust has grown between Seminole Tribal members and archaeologists to the extent that what we do today would be unfathomable just twenty years ago (Cypress 1997, 156). But trust is a fragile thing and must be nurtured by all involved.

In the not-too-distant past, professional archaeologists have come onto the Seminole reservations under the guise of doing historic preservation work and taken advantage of the information with which they were entrusted. There are a few ongoing instances of archaeologists excavating Seminole sites outside of the reservation boundaries in opposition to the Tribe's interests.

We hope that professional ethics within the discipline advance to the point when academics, CRM project managers, museum curators, and policy makers at least make an attempt to contact the Tribe. By opening the lines of communication, we have found much common ground with Tribal community members. Today, many Tribal members realize the importance of archaeology and how it can help preserve and improve upon Seminole cultural identity. Hopefully, archaeologists will reciprocate the sentiment.

Currently, the THPO is in a process of building relationships and repairing the damage done by those who came before us. We are making great strides. Community members are now interested in learning what we are finding out. Tribal members do fieldwork and lab work with us. The Ah-Tah-Thi-Ki Museum and THPO operations work in cooperation. The THPO wants to work together with outside archaeologists to do responsible research that benefits all involved. With our recently adopted Cultural Resource Ordinance (Appendix), we essentially created our own policy for how we will go forward with historic preservation. We hope to set an example of the way archaeology will serve the public in the future.

Our latest collaborative effort was a joint archaeological field school between the THPO and the Pemayetv Emahakv "Our Way" Charter School on the Brighton Reservation. The school consists of teaching sixth grade students, who live on the reservation, the basic concepts archaeologists use when conducting an excavation, from mapping to artifact cataloging. The site of the field school was an old homestead known to be occupied by non-Tribal members before the reservation was created. This gave students a unique opportunity to interpret a European-American site from their perspective. During the field school, Willie Johns spoke to the students, explaining his hopes for the future of the Tribe. "Growing up around this reservation, I never knew we had all these archaeological sites. . . . I'm glad to see y'all here and interested in what they're doing. Maybe one day y'all, when you're older, can take it a step higher. We need somebody to write our history" (Johns 2014). The THPO held this type of field school for the first time in 2014. We taught the students, and they taught us. Efforts like this, at the forefront of interaction with the community, create the most positive impact for all involved.

References Cited

Begay, Richard M. 1997. "The Role of Archaeology on Indian Lands: The Navajo Nation." In *Native Americans and Archaeologists: Stepping Stones to Common Ground*, edited by Nina Swindler, Kurt E. Dongoske, Roger Anyon, and Alan S. Downer, 162. Walnut Creek, Calif.: Altamira Press.

Covington, James W. 1993. *The Seminoles of Florida*. Gainesville: University Press of Florida.

Cypress, Billy L. 1997. "The Role of Archaeology in the Seminole Tribe of Florida." In *Native Americans and Archaeologists: Stepping Stones to Common Ground*, edited by Nina Swindler, Kurt E. Dongoske, Roger Anyon, and Alan S. Downer, 156. Walnut Creek, Calif.: Altamira Press.

Deloria, Vine, Jr. 1973. *Custer Died for Your Sins: An Indian Manifesto*. New York: Avon Books.

Erickson, Paul A., and Liam D. Murphy. 2008. *A History of Anthropological Theory*. North York, Ont.: University of Toronto Press.

Johns, Willie. 2014. Lecture to students at archaeology field school. Brighton Reservation, Fla.

Jumper, Betty Mae, and Patsy West. 2001. *A Seminole Legend: The Life of Betty Mae Jumper*. Gainesville: University Press of Florida.

McGown, William E. 1998. *Southwest Florida Pioneers: The Palm and Treasure Coasts*. Sarasota, Fla.: Pineapple Press.

Thomas, David H. 2000. *The Skull Wars: Kennewick Man, Archaeology, and the Battle for Native American Identity*. New York: Basic Books.

Watkins, Joe. 2000. *Indigenous Archaeology*. Walnut Creek, Calif.: Altamira Press.

7

"It's Every Day and It's a Lifestyle"

Seminole Culture and the Tribal Historic Preservation Office

MARY JENE KOENES

The Seminole Tribe of Florida has a population of about 4,000 people. It is perhaps not surprising then that not all Tribal members are directly involved in the Tribal Historic Preservation Office (THPO). Most only interact with its operations abstractly through presentations at community meetings or other outreach events. Many are likely only aware of the THPO through the clearance requirements necessary to get their future home sites cleared for development. The presented interview gives the perspective of someone who is deeply connected to their culture and history but who does not interact regularly with the THPO.

Author Bio

Mary Jene Koenes is a citizen of the Seminole Tribe of Florida and a member of the Panther Clan. Born in 1956 to a Seminole mother and white father, Koenes grew up in a traditional camp on the Big Cypress Seminole Indian Reservation. She is a fluent speaker of the Miccosukee language, only learning English after she was forced to attend the school on Big Cypress operated by the Bureau of Indian Affairs (BIA).

In 2007, Koenes began teaching the Miccosukee language at the Seminole Tribe of Florida's Ahfachkee School on the Big Cypress Reservation. Although she lives in a modern home, Koenes still lives in a traditional camp setting with her son and daughter and their families as her immediate neighbors.

On August 27, 2014, Koenes sat down with Ah-Tah-Thi-Ki Museum Oral Historian Stephen Bridenstine in the Culture Camp at the Ahfachkee School to discuss Seminole culture and her work teaching the Miccosukee language. In this revealing interview, Koenes shares her childhood experience growing

Figure 7.1. Mary Jene Koenes. Photo by author.

up in a traditional lifestyle, her thoughts about Seminole culture and language, and her feelings toward the work of the THPO.

STEPHEN BRIDENSTINE: I want to start off by asking you a few questions about your background. Could you describe the setting that you grew up in, both the physical surroundings and the family environment?

MARY JANE KOENES: Well, we grew up not too far behind the Ah-fachkee School on Albert Billie Drive.[1] The original camp that I grew up in is actually right across the street, east of the school. Then my uncle needed a place to stay so his dad and my grandfather, Albert Billie, built another camp a little bit down the road and we moved back there. I was raised in a camp with both of my maternal great-grand-parents, my maternal grandparents, and my parents, then also two of my uncles and my aunt.[2] So I grew up in a traditional camp with all the chickees with no walls and no windows and an extended family.[3]

SB: Did different family members have different roles in your upbringing?

MK: Yes, my mother worked in the fields so my grandparents did most of the raising of the children. We were constantly with our grandpar-ents and our great-grandparents since the younger family members worked. My mother worked and my aunt worked and both of my uncles worked in the fields. So the grandparents took care of us.

SB: What was the language of the household?

MK: Miccosukee. That's my first language. There wasn't any English spoken there. In fact, even my father, who is non-Indian, learned our language, and I didn't know that he was not even Seminole until years later. As I was growing up, the kids would tease me that my dad was a white man and I kept saying, "No he's not." (laughter) Because he speaks our language. But he knew we were going to have an uphill battle because we were half-breeds. So he made sure we were fluent and he spoke our language.

SB: Let me ask you about that. Do people still use the term "half-breed" within the Tribe today?

MK: I don't think they use so much the word "half-breed." They just go white or black. (laughs) So I don't know if that's less derogatory. But it doesn't bother me. I mean, it did when I was a kid because anything bothers you when you are a kid.

SB: So growing up with your grandparents and great-grandparents, would you say that you had a traditional Seminole education?

MK: Oh yes, definitely because that's all I knew. I didn't have formal education until the law actually came in and visited each camp saying, "You have to send your children to school." They told my grandparents through an interpreter that "you have to put them in school." And my grandmother did not want to send us to school. She said that she didn't believe in formal education and that we got enough education there, but I didn't speak English. Then they said, "Well if you don't send them to school, we'll have to arrest you." So we were literally forced to go to school.

SB: How old were you?

MK: I was around eight I think. I'm not sure because we didn't celebrate birthdays.

SB: Okay. So what happened? Did they haul you off to the school?

MK: Well, the school was actually right here on this ground we're sitting on. And like I said, we were back there maybe three blocks down the road. But there was one thing she [grandmother] told us our first day we had to go to school. She said, "Well, we don't speak any English so I'm sending you to school to learn a tool. And that is to learn English because we don't know if they're telling us the truth or if they're taking advantage of us. So I'm not sending you to become anybody else. I'm sending you to school to make sure that you learn a tool and that's to speak English."

SB: Who ran the school at that time?

MK: Mr. Jamieson. He was the teacher and the principal. Him and his wife, they actually had a little BIA house built for them and they lived here on campus.

SB: Okay, so this was a federally funded school through the BIA?

MK: Yes.

SB: What was the experience like then being a non-English speaker coming into the classroom?

MK: I sat first grade twice. (laughs)

SB: Really?

MK: Because all I needed to say was "banana" and I couldn't even say "banana." A whole year he had been teaching us but it was a different setting, different rules. I didn't understand them. The one thing I really didn't like was that he was really mean and adamant about not speaking your language. They actually had a bathroom which first was kind of weird because we didn't have bathrooms in our camp, but then if you got into trouble or you got caught speaking your language, you spent most of your time in the bathroom, on the toilet. So I guess that was to break us from speaking our language. But then when we got home, it was like, "No English spoken here. You speak your language."

SB: Did some of your peers at school have a better understanding of English? Had some of them maybe had more contact with English speakers?

MK: Some of them had already been to school because they went around every year approaching the age group that needed to start first grade. So some of the kids had already been to school. When I got there, they were speaking English, but I didn't understand what they were saying.

SB: So growing up then, did you know any non-Seminoles?

MK: Oh yeah.

SB: Specifically people your own age?

MK: No, not so much my own age because once I started school and started understanding English, I could do some interpreting for my grandparents. But other than that, I don't really remember playing with other non-Indian kids. I was always amongst my people.

SB: I understand the Seminole Tribe has a dedicated Culture Department, in addition to the culture classes taught here at Ahfachkee and up at the Brighton Charter School.[4] When people say "culture" in reference to the Seminole Tribe, what do they mean? What does that consist of?

MK: Well, to me it consists of my teachings, the way I was raised, traditions, things that we do every day that apply to us. It's not one component of your life. To me, it's a lifestyle and that's just the way you were raised. And the way I was raised was through my grandparents and my great-grandparents and the way they were taught. It doesn't mean that it is right or wrong but that's just the way my family was taught and the things they taught me. So my tradition just encompasses my whole life, it's not just one component. It's every day and it's a lifestyle.

SB: When people use the word "medicine" within a traditional Seminole context, can you define that in any way? Is that even possible?

MK: Even that, like I said, goes back to my teachings. That's part of my life. That's the lifestyle I was raised in. And a lot of non-Indians have a hard time because when they think of medicine, they're thinking about doctors. We do have medicine people that help us out with our illness or whatever the reason is that we would need to seek someone to make us medicine, but it's ingrained in me so I just can't really separate it. I think a lot of people don't understand it, not so much our people, but the non-Indians have a hard time understanding. "What do you mean by medicine?" There too it's a lifestyle because the medicine was handed down by the Creator for us to use, to survive, and to help each other for whatever reason, illness or broken bones or whatever it may be. So it starts back with the beginning of time and the Creator.

SB: Do certain people or clans have specific responsibilities or roles within the culture?[5]

MK: Well, the way it was explained to me and I understand it is that each clan carries their own bundle. Panther being the eldest, he carries the most important medicine bundle. But yeah, each clan has their different ways of doing things and different clans have different responsibilities of different areas. Anybody can be a medicine person, it's just how they follow each other and who helps each other and they have to understand what the order is and how they help each other. So that's just the way it was always taught to me.

SB: I understand you teach here at the Ahfachkee School. What classes do you teach?

MK: I teach the language, the Miccosukee language. And like even that, there's not a moment in the day when I'm teaching that something is not brought up within our teachings. There's always a teachable moment that you find yourself in where you're constantly reminding them that this is the way we were brought up. What I do and what we do here is that because most of us are Panthers here that teach, we share. We don't say that it is written in stone. We don't say ours is correct. We just share what we learn and what we've been taught to the kids because we all have different clans here in the school, so what we tell them is to make sure you go home and ask your grandmother how your clan does it. We're just sharing.

SB: I also understand that there are Creek-speaking people within the Tribe. Growing up, did you understand that there were these two languages spoken within the Tribe?[6]

MK: Yes, because my grandparents spoke both Miccosukee and Creek. When they went to Brighton, they could speak Creek to them, but the people there also could speak Miccosukee and Creek. The elders my grandparents' and my great-grandparents' age spoke both languages, and there are still a few that can do that, very few. I can understand enough to get into trouble with it—(laughs)—in the Creek language. And I can say some things and I can understand the gist of the conversation, but fluent I am not. I heard my grandparents speak it all the time, and I knew that there was a difference. I could understand both of them but I just didn't speak both of them. So like I said, my first language is Miccosukee, but because I was raised by my grandparents, I went everywhere they went and I was basically raised with their generation. So I knew there was a difference in the two languages.

SB: When the stories, the legends, the culture, or even just the knowledge within the Tribe is translated into English, what happens? What's lost? Does it change things?

MK: Yes, it really does change things. To me, I feel like there is no value or no weight to it when it's translated into English. I just feel like it doesn't have that strength that it's supposed to have when you're telling it in your own language because a lot of the stories and legends that you hear are teaching stories, so for some odd reason when you translate it into English, it doesn't have that same weight. I've been an interpreter for many years after I learned how to speak English and you try to do the best you can translating into English, but you really lose the weight and strength of that story.

SB: Has the use of Miccosukee by your community here in Big Cypress changed in your lifetime?

MK: Unfortunately, it's changed dramatically because my generation always spoke the language, even though we knew English. And then with more of the modernization of the reservation, like with television and radio, hearing more English, you can really see where it started to drift more into English. Now with the younger generation, it's their first language, not Miccosukee. That really saddens me because my grandmother always said, what makes you different from everybody else is the way you're brought up and then your language. Because, like I said, the language has weight to it and if you're speaking English, my elders feel like there is no weight to it. Even in my own household, I'm as guilty because I married a non-Indian but my kids understand me fluently, they just don't speak back to me in Miccosukee. Then my grandkids are the same way. They pretty much understand me fluently but they still talk back to me in English. So I'm just as guilty. (laughter)

SB: Do you know anything about the history of Ahfachkee, how the school got started and then also the language program?

MK: No, I'm not sure when the school actually started because I never really thought about it or looked into it. It just seemed like it's always been in existence. But the language program—I'm not sure how it got started, but I know a couple of missionaries, back in the day, were translating the Bible. It was funny, him and his wife, David West and his wife, Virginia, were around and they lived in a chickee behind the church.[7] I think that's the first time I ever saw an oven. She would make chocolate chip cookies and they would invite us to their house, but we didn't realize that's how they were paying us to translate. They would ask us how do you say this word or that word, and it wasn't until years later that I put two and two together that, "Oh okay, we were translators and didn't even know it." But we were having the best time eating chocolate chip cookies though. (laughs)

SB: Do the language classes here differ from any foreign language classes at a public school in Florida?

MK: Well, I think they're similar because we've been working with Jack Martin, the linguist, and he's been the one that's kind of guidelined it as if you were learning a second language.[8]

SB: And do you use total language immersion?

MK: No, we don't do total immersion. We do a lot of talking, but we don't do total immersion. We'd love to do total immersion but you'd have to have those students all day and teach math, history, and everything else in the language.

SB: What age or grade level do you start with?

MK: Here we start from pre-K all the way to twelfth grade.

SB: Does the language program here coordinate or have any cooperation with the Miccosukee Tribe or Independent Seminoles in terms of teaching the language?[9]

MK: Yes, we exchange material, and if they have a better idea, we don't reinvent the wheel which is constant, you know, because we're constantly building materials. If we see something that we don't have, maybe they already have it or Brighton might already have it. It might be in Creek but then we can take that same concept and just translate it into Miccosukee. So we're always helping each other.

SB: I understand that some people within the Seminole Tribe are Christian. Can you speak to what role Christianity has in the Tribe today?

MK: Christianity has been around for quite a while, you know, the missionaries coming down here and converting the savages into Christians—I've heard that so many times—but what they fail to realize is that we've always been one with the Creator.[10] We've always been following his rules. These are not our rules. We've always been one with the Creator because he's the one that provided everything for us and that's how we've always been taught.

My grandparents used to say the Bible is for the English-speaking people. They read things. We don't have books but these things have already been passed down to us by the Creator so I guess in a way we've always been Christians. I don't know if that's the right word but we've always followed what the Creator said. He set the laws down, like how you're supposed to treat each other. And during our ceremonies, that's what they do, give thanks back to the Lord that he had placed all this here for us. So they really weren't teaching anything different when the missionaries came.

SB: Have you ever participated in any cultural exchanges with other tribes or indigenous groups? What has that experience been like?

MK: I've had a few. I've been to New Mexico with the Navajos there. I've been to the Cherokee Tribe. I visited the Coushatta Tribe.[11] What's really neat is the first time I ever met the Coushatta Tribe, we were in Murfreesboro, Tennessee, with several different tribes. We met two Coushatta students the same age as us who had a lot of words that were similar to ours. Then we got to talking and the more I learned, I realized the southeastern tribes have some words that are the same as ours.

The way my grandparents explained it to me was that all the different tribes of the Southeast and seaboard, even all the way up to

Canada, used to come down here anyway, so that there were already some mixtures or some people left or who went with them. That's how I grew up but then as I got older, to actually be with these different tribes and see that. The only thing that I guess that was so totally different to me was the Navajo-speaking people. Their language is so totally different than anybody else's language it seems. So that was really interesting.

SB: Other than the Seminole Tribe of Florida, you have the Miccosukee Tribe of Indians of Florida, you've got a group of Independent Seminoles, and then you have the Seminole Nation out in Oklahoma.[12] Do you feel any sense of shared heritage with these other communities?

MK: Well, the Miccosukee Tribe, the only thing different there is the name of their tribe. We're the same genetic makeup. So we're the same people. They're my relatives. We have the same bloodline. The Independent members are the same way. They're the same genetic makeup. They're still my family. And then the Oklahoma Nation, I realize that at one time, they were part of us, and I'm sure they're genetically made up the same way I am. Now as to the feelings, I guess our elders, our grandparents, had placed some really strong feelings within us that they ran. And our ancestors stayed here to fight. That's why we're still here today. But that's just how I was raised and how that was imprinted on my brain.

SB: Growing up, did you hear many of the stories about the Seminole Wars and everything that the Tribe went through in the nineteenth century?[13] Did you learn that from family growing up?

MK: Pretty much. The one thing that my grandmother was really adamant about was that I was never to forget that we get to stand here on this earth today because of the sacrifices that our ancestors made. And I guess from a mother's point of view, the thing that she really stressed upon was to never forget how they had to sacrifice the children when they were hiding from the soldiers. They would place mud or cloth in their mouth and drown the babies and that was the ultimate sacrifice that a mother could make. So she would always say never to forget that. Because of that, of those sacrifices and of those babies, you're here today. So that was, I think, the most important thing that I could keep passing on.

And then the struggles that the Tribe went through and the things they did for fund-raising to get to Washington and establish where they wanted to go. How they would travel for miles and miles just to get to one place or another when there really weren't automobiles available to them. They would go in cattle trucks, in the rain, in the cold, whatever they needed to do to raise money. I think they were mighty resourceful. And I like to think that I have some of that in me. They were pretty resilient and tenacious. They just were a strong group of people and that's what she made sure I understood all the time. And when my grandparents were around, we were lucky if we had an automobile, if we had one and it would run that is. My grandpa walked a lot to Immokalee to buy canned goods. These are the different struggles that they had, and it was all leading up to signing for the Tribe. But she made sure we didn't forget any of that.

SB: Can you share what your experience has been like working with outsiders and sharing some of what you know about the Seminole Tribe and your community?

MK: Well, we do an orientation with the teachers here at Ahfachkee, and there have been several times where I've spoken to other people that are non-Tribal. They may but they may not know that the students have sort of a soul or nucleus to their family and that's really important to us. Like I said, it's not something that you just pick and choose what you want to do. And where they tend to categorize everything, that's hard for me to do with my tradition and with the medicine or with the way children are raised. Like I said earlier, it's my lifestyle, it's a whole globe of everything together and you just can't take it apart. They have a hard time understanding that because non-Indians tend to categorize everything, it's got to be in its little box, and we don't live in a box.

But there's a limit to what we can share and what our people, what our elders, have asked us not to tell. You can't give up all your secrets. But we share general stuff, how children are raised, what we do with our children at a certain time when they're born or after they're born, why they get their names, what the women's responsibilities are and what are the men's responsibilities, the uncles, and who does the discipline and everything else. And that was when you were raised in a traditional camp with all your grandparents and your uncles and everybody else there, but now because we are pretty much in single family dwellings, it kind of puts walls up.

Like in my setting, I have both of my children on either side of me so in my camp, my son is on one side of me and my daughter is on the other side of me. Since we live in a camp setting, the grandkids are always there. And even though my kids grew up in an extended family, they tend to still—my daughter sometimes has a hard time understanding that her brother's role is to discipline but that's part of my fault too so I explain to some of the visitors or the employees that I see barriers growing up and that makes a conflict with even our own teachings. But those are the kinds of things that we share and I in turn ask them, how do you get along without ever speaking to your mom maybe three or four times a year. I probably talk to my mom at least every day. That's what I would tell them, that I think we still have a lot of that here and the non-Indians really don't have that.

SB: I know I've had some really interesting conversations with Tribal members about what it's like when you're sitting in the casino in Hollywood and you overhear someone talking about, "Oh those Seminoles." You're sitting there and they're talking about you and your community. Or when I'm at the museum, visitors often ask me just the nosiest questions and I've sure you've heard them too, about the money, the culture, the Chairman.

MK: What amazes me is they don't look at us as human beings. We're all human beings. And they don't look at us as being very intelligent. They still think of us as savages. You know, "What would they know? How could they run a business?" And a lot of them don't even realize we exist. I get this odd feeling, "How could you not know that these people exist. Don't you live here? We're neighbors." I've heard all the stories and at first when I was younger it used to bother me, but I guess with age it helps you to understand that there is just ignorance and they're not educated about the Seminole people or the Indian people. They just know that there's cowboys and Indians.

I go to Ocala once a year, it's called the Ocali Days, and I have a little camp set up there and the Marion County school brings out between 900 and 1,200 students a day to come through there.[14] And they're like, "Indians! Where?" (laughter) So you're in all your regalia and your traditional clothing and they still don't realize that you're a Seminole. So we help educate the public through them, but some would just come flat out and say, "We don't like you." (laughs) And I said, "That's fine. Everybody has an opinion. That's okay. You know there are some people that I don't like. But you're entitled to your opinion, so that's okay." And some will say, "Where do you live?" I'm like, "Just six hours down the road from you." And they're like, "What is a reservation?" Those kinds of things. It's always amazing to me that they're just naive when it comes to Indian people.

SB: I've talked about this with other Seminoles and folks from other tribes, and it always comes up that in the public school curriculum, you talk about Indians from the very beginning of American history but somewhere around 1890 it just stops. And then when you look on Google maps, until recently, Indian reservations were outlined in a gray color but were never labeled as reservations. They were visible and yet invisible. So much of what I've learned in my own experience and everything I've studied is that this all has a lot to do with visibility.

MK: Exactly.

SB: And invisibility.

MK: What you don't see, don't bother you. What's not visible, you don't have to care about. And I always looked at it that way when I saw the maps. Like you said, it's grayed out but there are people that live there. They just kind of put a film over us.

SB: I actually went to school up in Canada, and there I feel Native people, First Nations, are slightly more visible. It's in the political discourse. And here in the U.S., it's different. It has a different feel to it.

MK: That's because they haven't come to terms.

SB: In the U.S.?

MK: In the U.S. You have to come to terms to accept somebody. You have to say, "Yes, we did this to Native people." If you haven't come to terms, you're not going to acknowledge that person. So that's how I feel. The United States is not going to accept it and say, "Yes, we came over and stole all this land. And yes, we killed thousands of people." That's like even the school shootings. They're horrible. The most horrible thing that you could do is massacre children, but yet when the colonists came over, they did the same thing to our children that were on this land, when we were here before they were. They did the same thing and they make it sound like right now it's so horrible. Yes it is horrible. But they don't stop and think what they did before. So until you acknowledge that, we're still invisible.

SB: And even when people think about what happened in the past, they think of it as in the past.

MK: Right.

SB: But it continues on through the generations. I mean, you heard stories about the Seminole Wars.

MK: Because try to imagine telling your child to breathe through a reed as you hold them under water because that's the only way we're going to survive. You can't hush a child because they're hungry, the mosquitoes are bad, an infant or a toddler is tired, hasn't had any sleep. And then you have to make the ultimate sacrifice. So when you can acknowledge something like that, and accept the fact that that's what my people went through, and we're still invisible. As a mother, I don't think I could do that to my children. But my ancestors' mothers made that ultimate sacrifice so that I could stand here today. And that was the one thing that my grandmother said, "Don't ever forget. If you ever get a chance to tell it, tell it." So I always do.

SB: Well thank you for sharing.

MK: You're welcome.

SB: I want to end with a few questions about the THPO. In your own words, and from your own experience, what does the THPO do? What is its role within the Tribe?

MK: At first, I thought they were invasive. (laughs) And I still kind of think that way a little bit. See the THPO people are basically all non-Seminoles. Their curiosity is heightened that, "Oh I could find an artifact that Seminole—." But we buried it for a reason and it's supposed to stay buried, so to me that's sort of disrespectful, but I guess with modern times, modern thinking, modern leaders, they feel like THPO is a necessity. And I guess it would help some of the younger people who don't know where some things are buried and why things are there, where they're supposed to be.

But I kind of have mixed emotions about THPO because I feel like they're invasive. I really don't think they should be knowing, but then, like I said, the modern newer Seminoles want to know and some of the leaders want to know. I guess it's the same way with our language, we feel like if we don't record it, it's going to be lost. So I can understand that part. Nobody will ever know that we ever existed if you don't have a live body telling you why these things exist and really know the true meaning of why they were really here. But I have mixed emotions about THPO.

SB: Have you had any direct experience with them, like for your own home site? Have they done any work for yourself or your family?

MK: No, because they didn't have THPO back then. When I found my home site, they didn't have anybody doing all that research and recording and everything. It was like, "Yeah, you can have this piece of land." And it is in a hammock so you know that at one point or another somebody would have lived there. But when we were clearing we didn't find anything. They used to take some of the belongings from the people that we've lost and put it out further west. But we know not to mess with it so we never messed with it until they were taking the relay tower down that used to be there. They found some stuff but we knew they were there. Other than that, I never had any dealings with them for my home site.

SB: One of the things that I know THPO has to be careful with and protective of are the areas with medicinal plants. Why is that? What's the importance of medicinal plants and having those areas off-limits?

MK: Well, the medicinal plants are very important to my people. That's what the Creator handed down for us to use for medicine so we don't want them destroyed because that's what helps our people. A lot of people don't understand that these were put on this earth by the Creator so you can't really transplant them and you can't really grow them. The Creator picked a particular plant to put in a particular soil. You just can't take one particular plant and decide, "Oh I'm going to go put it over here." It just doesn't work. And the Seminole people have always been stewards of the land anyway. We've always taken care of the land because they know that the land provides things for them, whether it's meat, the animals, the plants, or the water. That's what sustains our life. It's the earth. So they've always been protective of plants and animals and they've always been environmentalists.

SB: The THPO is also involved with identifying and protecting historic camps going back 50, 100, 200 years. Do you feel that that's something important or is it again mixed emotions?

MK: Well, sort of mixed emotions. But like I said, I can understand why they're recording that. At least you have a live person that you can ask and you can get the true meaning of why maybe this family camped here or why they camped there. And even that, our elders have always said, please don't record anything. But yet we've gotten to the point that we are recording because some of us do feel, I guess with mixed emotions since we're going against what our elders taught us, that if we don't record it, it's going to be totally lost.

And our teaching, it's evolution. It's supposed to take its course. Things are happening the way they're supposed to be happening. But when you intervene and start recording, then that's not the correct evolution, it's supposed to take its path. This is how it was explained to me. So, like I said, I have mixed emotions, and I understand what my people are saying and then I understand what the younger generation is doing and saying that if you don't record it, it is totally lost. I mean we do have the capability of recording it and that's a good thing, I guess. But I still hear my elders saying what they did say.

SB: This book project is aimed at a few audiences, THPOs at other tribes, state and federal agencies and officials, cultural resource contractors, museum professionals especially folks who work on NAGPRA [Native American Graves Protection and Repatriation Act] issues, and then academics. Is there anything you would want them to know or better understand so that when they're working with tribes they can do their jobs better? Any advice you can give them?

MK: I think don't be so pushy. They want to jump in there, especially the non-Indians because they feel like they have a time limit or they have to have a certain thing done at a certain time. That's where we don't work with time. We're told not to rush things or hurry things. Things will fall into the place where they're supposed to. So patience and getting to know your elders first. Don't just bombard them and start asking them questions. Go in there and be part of the community first and learn their ways. Be an observer, not someone who just bombards these people. Because we do have strong traditions about not accepting non-Indians. We still have our guard up.

So if you're working with THPO, the best thing to do is just learn the people first. Get to know them. Help them out. I'm not so much saying do everything for them, but if you get to know the elders and know their ways and understand where your boundaries are at, that's the most important thing. You just can't cross boundaries because this is your job. You just can't jump over there and say, "Well I'm going to ask you a bunch of questions." You need to really know the people. If they see that you're trying to learn them, they'll be more receptive because we've already got our guard up. Our doors are already shut. So you have to learn how to open it. And it's that simple. It's just like when you're a baby. When you're born you don't jump up and take off. You learn all these things as you're growing up so it's the same way. You just take baby steps and you just learn.

SB: Is there anything else you'd like to share about the Seminole Tribe or the THPO? Is there anything that you think would be important for folks to know?

MK: I've seen many, many struggles and like I said, our doors are still shut, but we've made leaps and bounds and major strides just to get up to the twenty-first century and just to have the things that we have today. But in a way, I kind of miss the old ways and I enjoy it here at the school because we have a fire going every day and that's the way I was raised, with a fire going every day. That's the heart and soul of your camp.

And always make sure that you're invited. Don't just walk in. A lot of people look at it as an open area even though it's a camp. There is still an imaginary line that you just don't cross. You always ask, "Can I come in?" We had a gentleman here one time, he would just walk into any chickee. The chickees here have specific duties. We have our cooking chickee which houses our fire and we have eating chickees and we have a chickee over there that belongs to just the women who are on their monthly. Then we have a sleeping chickee and a work chickee. They all have specific duties that they're housing and there are some places that you just don't walk into without asking. I mean I wouldn't walk into your bedroom without asking or just walk into your house without knocking and getting permission. So everybody thinks because it doesn't have walls and windows that they can just walk in.

And that's true with any area on the reservation. When you walk up to someone's camp, you try to either call ahead or get a hold of them to say, "I'd like to come by." And when you do come to the house, some of them may not let you in their home. So then you have to be satisfied with that, to stay on the outside and talk to them. It doesn't necessarily mean that you're going to get to go in just because you show up.

When they're doing medicine or ceremonies and stuff like that, don't overstep your boundaries. I know that they mean just to help but always be an observer and don't overstep your boundaries. It's just important that they learn all that. And it's not just my Tribe, most of the tribes are like that. You wouldn't go into any community and traipse around and think like you're part of that community. You have to learn your way in.

SB: One final question. Where do you see the Seminole Tribe heading in the future? Where do you think today's young generation is going to take the Tribe?

MK: That's really hard because all these wonderful children of my people all have individual minds. We have to get them together and constantly teach them that this is what you need to do for the Tribe and take care of the Tribe and make sure that we're still in existence. And they're very intelligent, so I don't know where they'll take us. But I hope in a good direction and I'm hoping that I've been part of that solution, being one of their teachers, helping to mold them. The main thing is to always be respectful and treat each other respectfully and make sure you're taking care of your elders because if it wasn't for your elders and if it wasn't for my elders, I don't know where I'd be, so hopefully I'm part of that solution that they'll take us in a good direction.

Notes

1. Big Cypress Seminole Indian Reservation is on the western periphery of the Everglades and is home to the primarily Miccosukee-speaking portion of the Tribe (Garbarino 1972).

2. Florida Seminoles traditionally practice matrilocal residence in which married couples and their children reside with the wife's parents (Spoehr 1940).

3. A chickee is an open-sided, palmetto-thatched-roof shelter supported on posts that served as the primary dwelling of Seminole people from the mid-nineteenth century through the mid to late twentieth century (Dilley 2015).

4. The Seminole Tribe of Florida has two schools, the Ahfachkee School on the Big Cypress Reservation, which serves students in pre-K through twelfth grade, and the Pemayetv Emahakv Charter School on the Brighton Reservation, which serves students in kindergarten through eighth grade.

5. The eight Seminole clans in Florida today are Wind, Otter, Bear, Snake, Panther, Toad/Big Town, Bird, and Deer.

6. Seminoles in Florida historically speak two related but distinct languages. Creek, or Mvskoke, is spoken primarily on the Brighton Reservation and areas north of Lake Okeechobee. Miccosukee is spoken on the Big Cypress Reservation and areas south of Lake Okeechobee. Seminoles from older generations were often fluent in both languages (Sturtevant and Cattelino 2004).

7. David West was a linguist and Christian missionary who with his wife, Virginia, lived and worked on the Big Cypress Indian Reservation during the 1960s in order to create a Miccosukee language dictionary (Smiley 1967; Howland 1967).

8. Jack B. Martin is a professor of English and linguistics at the College of William and Mary in Virginia. He has worked extensively with the Seminole Tribe of Florida developing teaching materials and dictionaries for both the Miccosukee and Creek languages.

9. The Miccosukee Tribe of Indians of Florida and a group of Independent Seminoles in Florida also teach the Miccosukee language in their respective communities.

10. Beginning in the late nineteenth century, a series of Christian missionaries of different faiths began to proselytize among the Florida Seminoles to varying degrees of success. One group that made early converts was Creek-speaking Indian Baptist missionaries from Oklahoma (Jumper and West 2001, 26–44). Thanks to these and other efforts, there are today Baptist churches with Seminole congregations on the Big Cypress, Hollywood, and Brighton Reservations.

11. The Coushatta (also called Koasati) were members of the historic Creek Confederacy, whose population today is split between three federally recognized tribes in Texas, Oklahoma, and Louisiana. They speak an Eastern Muscogean language related to both Creek and Miccosukee.

12. In Florida, there are two federally recognized groups of Native Americans: the Seminole Tribe of Florida and the Miccosukee Tribe of Indians of Florida. Additionally, there is a group of Independent Seminoles who do not wish to be federally recognized. In Oklahoma, there is the Seminole Nation, comprised mostly of descendants of the Seminole people forcibly relocated during the Seminole Wars (Covington 1993).

13. The Seminole Wars were a series of armed conflicts between the U.S. government and the Seminoles. They are generally split into three main conflicts: First Seminole War (1817–1819), Second Seminole War (1835–1842), and Third Seminole War (1855–1858). Citizens of the Seminole Tribe of Florida are descended from the few hundred Seminoles who escaped forced removal and remained in Florida at the end of the Third Seminole War (Sturtevant and Cattelino 2004).

14. Ocali Country Days Festival is a popular annual event in Ocala, Florida, that features music, storytelling, traditional crafts, and historical reenactments depicting north-central Florida in the 1800s.

References Cited

Covington, James W. 1993. *The Seminoles of Florida*. Gainesville: University Press of Florida.

Dilley, Carrie. 2015. *Thatched Roofs and Open Sides: The Architecture of Chickees and Their Changing Role in Seminole Society*. Gainesville: University Press of Florida.

Garbarino, Merwyn. 1972. *Big Cypress: A Changing Seminole Community*. New York: Holt, Rhinehart and Winston.

Howland, Brian. 1967. "Mikasuki Missionary." *All Florida Magazine*, 4–6. July 20.

Jumper, Betty Mae, and Patsy West. 2001. *A Seminole Legend: The Life of Betty Mae Tiger Jumper*. Gainesville: University Press of Florida.

Smiley, Nixon. 1967. "They're Writing Seminole Bible." *Miami Herald*, 20A. February 6.

Spoehr, Alexander. 1940. "Seminole Kinship." Ph.D. diss., University of Chicago.

Sturtevant, William C., and Jessica R. Cattelino. 2004. "Florida Seminole and Miccosukee." In *Handbook of North American Indians Southeast*, Vol. 14, edited by Raymond D. Fogelson, volume editor, and William C. Sturtevant, general editor, 429–449. Washington, D.C.: Smithsonian Institution.

8

Camp Life

Recording Historic Camps as Heritage

MATTHEW FENNO, KAREN BRUNSO, AND JESSICA FREEMAN

Oral histories concerning the clan camps of the early and mid-twentieth century are still abundant today, but it is feared much of this important history will be lost within a generation. Tribal schools realize the importance of teaching this recent history, as it was during these times that Seminole families were still entirely self-sufficient, growing and hunting the majority of their subsistence base. The self-sufficiency ethos is a key part of cultural identity and one that helps define who the Seminole people are. As the authors explain, the research undertaken by the Tribal Historic Preservation Office (THPO) to document these reservation-era camps is driven by a community need to actively manage and preserve this information for future generations of Tribal members. The importance of this work is driven home if you are lucky enough to witness a Tribal school group visiting a historic camp; armed with maps and plans showing where houses and gardens were located, students can immerse themselves in their own history. Archaeology adds to this story by providing not only the means to capture a picture of the camp that can be combined with oral histories but also providing a tangible tool by which students can actively participate in the learning process.

Author Bios

Matthew Fenno began his studies at Indian River State College in 2005, where he graduated with an Associates of Arts in history. His love for the outdoors and studying past cultures motivated him to transfer to the Department of Anthropology at Florida Atlantic University (FAU). While enrolled at FAU, Fenno began an internship with the West Palm Beach, Florida, county archaeologist and in addition volunteered with a nonprofit southern Florida cultural resources consulting firm. Fenno attended an FAU archaeological field school in Ecuador. During this field school, Fenno had the opportunity to interact with the local population of Rio Blanco, Ecuador, where he began to develop an understanding of their cultural values and heritage. After returning to Florida, Fenno was hired by the consulting firm he had been volunteering with while he continued his undergraduate studies. In 2011, Fenno was awarded a B.A. in anthropology, a B.A. Interdisciplinary Degree in social science, and a certificate of Latin American studies from FAU.

In order to pursue his interest in cultural preservation, Fenno applied for a position with the Seminole Tribe of Florida Tribal Historic Preservation Office (STOF THPO). He began working in the STOF THPO Tribal Archaeology Section (TAS). While at the THPO, Fenno has participated in Phase I and Phase II cultural resource investigations, conducted interviews with Tribal members about Seminole camps, prepared documents for the nomination of camps to the Tribal Register of Historic Places (TRHP), and coauthored reports of field investigations. In 2013, he continued his formal education and earned a Certificate of Geographical Information Systems (GIS) from FAU.

Although many of the Seminole camps that TAS investigates may not be eligible for the National Register of Historic Places, they are still important to the Tribe and Tribal members, and Fenno strongly believes by investigating and recording camp life he assists the Tribe in preserving their history.

Karen Brunso is a citizen of the Chickasaw Nation and a field technician with the STOF THPO. She received her B.A. in anthropology from the University of Iowa. Growing up, she lived throughout the United States, seeing most of the country and its people. Her favorite places to visit were the historical museums and the various prehistoric and historic sites. That childhood love of history led Brunso to study archaeology in college. While in college, her passion for archaeology and Native American history led a classmate to predict that Brunso would end up working for a THPO. In 2012, that prediction came true when Brunso was hired by the STOF THPO. Researching historic Seminole camps allows Brunso to combine all the lessons learned from her past in involving the community in the archaeological process preserving the camps' legacy.

Jessica Freeman has been working with the STOF THPO since August 2013 as an archaeological field technician with the TAS. Freeman initially attended Augusta State University in Augusta, Georgia, where she began to recognize her interest in historic archaeology and public engagement. She later transferred to the University of Georgia, where she graduated with a

B.A. in anthropology and a Certificate in Archaeological Sciences. Fresh out of college, Freeman came to work for the STOF THPO. Since working with the THPO, she has participated in Phase I and Phase II cultural resource investigations on the various Seminole Tribe of Florida reservations. Freeman's involvement in these investigations includes conducting background research, performing fieldwork, and preparing final reports. Often these projects can lead to the discovery of historic Seminole camps, which provides an opportunity for Freeman to undertake more extensive archival research and to conduct interviews with Tribal members. Working with the THPO has been an incredibly enriching experience for Freeman. It has allowed her to pursue her interests in historic archaeology and to be actively engaged with the Seminole Tribe of Florida community not only through interviews with Tribal members but also through her participation in on-reservation special events.

Introduction

One of the primary goals of the STOF THPO is to protect important cultural resources on Tribal land and to help preserve Seminole cultural traditions through involvement with the community. To help achieve this goal, the STOF THPO TAS plays a key role in researching and recording historic twentieth-century Seminole camps—which are very significant to Tribal heritage. This research is performed with intense consultation with Tribal members to gain better insight into life within these historic period sites. The continuous relationship between Tribal members and the TAS is unique to tribal archaeology and critical to the research process. With the majority of the TAS being non-Tribal members, without Tribal member input, research would be solely based on historic documentation and previous archaeological records. By doing this research, we also offer a vehicle for Tribal members to converse about their life and recent family histories within these historic Seminole camps. The STOF THPO can help preserve these sites by creating a lasting record for future generations, and potentially allowing for culturally significant camps to be listed on the TRHP. In identifying and recording Seminole cultural sites, the TAS combines traditional methods of archaeology, background archival research, and Tribal member contributions in the form of detailed interviews to paint a complete picture of the Seminole way of life. The Johns camp and the Tom Smith camp highlight the results of this process and will demonstrate the great influence Tribal members have in every step to help create a record for their descendants, as well as how community involvement allows for a more complete understanding into these historic period sites.

What Is a Camp?

Camps hold a significant role in Seminole heritage. According to Alexander Spoehr, the everyday life of Seminoles was based around the campsite (Spoehr 1941, 10). Sites were located in the higher elevation pine flatwoods and tree island hammocks, which provide tree cover with large oaks, sabal palms, and pines offering shade from the intense sun (Spoehr 1944, 124). The higher elevation also makes these areas less prone to flooding than the wetlands surrounding them, creating a more suitable setting for habitation. Historic Seminole camps consisted of varying "number of palm thatched, open-sided" structures—known as chickees—that had various functions, including sleeping quarters, cooking, and storage (Spoehr 1941, 10) (Figure 8.1). The placement of chickees tends to follow a similar layout, in which the cooking chickee is in the center with all other structures surrounding it (Spoehr 1941, 10). In an individual site, the number of occupants varies with "each family in the camp [having] its own dwelling" (Covington 1993, 205).

While camps can be defined in terms of physical location and layout, it is important to know that they are also identified by the family unit itself (Spoehr 1941, 10). Traditionally, residency of these historic sites was matrilineal; camp membership revolved around the matrilineal clan that was assigned to the women of the camp (Spoehr 1941, 15). Seminoles could not marry within their own clan, and after a man married into another clan he would then move to his wife's camp and help provide for her family (Covington 1993, 7; MacCauley 2000, 496). With many families living in a single location, life is very close and intimate. Joe Lester John of the Happy Jones camp described that in a camp, "You have comradery. You all suffer the same things, you all enjoy the same things, you all share the same pain, [and] you all share the same joy. That's one good thing [about camps], you are all close" (Seminole Media Productions 2010). This closeness among group members is what helps make each site unique, producing stories and memorable moments in the life of each individual person.

Precontact versus Contact

On the reservations, particularly in higher elevation areas that are most appropriate for inhabitation, many of the twentieth-century historic camps overlap with precontact sites. Today, our research efforts here at the THPO focus primarily on the postcontact Seminole sites that are spread out among the reservations. However, in previous years the THPO mainly researched the precontact sites—with little attention given to the Seminole cultural sites. The interest in researching postcontact sites was sparked out of the emergence of the TRHP in 2011; during this time, culturally significant Seminole camps and sites began to be researched more in depth (Seminole Tribe of Florida Tribal Historic Preservation Office 2014). A shift from investigating precontact sites to focusing on aspects of more recent Seminole heritage was an important step to become more actively involved in the Tribal community, as well as to study topics the Seminole people are able to connect with and care the most about (Paul Backhouse, personal communication, 2014). "The historic camps are the most immediate history of current clans and families," and these campsites are the focal point that helped form the Seminole Tribe of Florida as it is today (Paul Backhouse, personal communication, 2014).

When the Creeks began moving into Florida in the 1700s, they encountered remnants of precontact tribes, including the Calusa (Sturtevant 1971). While the populations of these prehistoric tribes were greatly reduced, the Seminoles uphold that it is unlikely that these tribes were completely wiped out. There are many Calusa words that have been absorbed into the Creek language of the Seminoles; likewise, Medicine Men still sing Calusa songs (Densmore 1956). Tribal members believe that the remnants of the precontact tribes with the Creeks have formed the Seminoles today (WGCU Public Media 2012). Among the Seminoles, interest in precontact sites is on an individual basis. Sometimes Tribal members do not particularly care for the prehistoric components, while there are some cases in which people show a genuine curiosity and would like to see prehistoric artifacts that we have collected from surveys that are being conducted on their property. This is not to say that the Seminole community is uninterested in the precontact components in the slightest; it is just that the precontact sites are slightly removed from the current family histories that survive today. This inevitably creates a lower level of interest in the community because they simply prefer to have their most direct history recorded. Thus documentation of the twentieth-century campsites is critical in helping to preserve the Seminole Tribe of Florida heritage and community.

Camp Research Process

Camp Identification

As mentioned, the historic Seminole camp research is a fairly recent endeavor; therefore it is important to understand that there is no set way to go about investigating these sites. The following steps we are about to outline for the research process are performed in various orders, with the order strongly depending on the circumstances of camp identification. These sites are brought to our attention in a couple of different ways. The TAS may want to pursue research of a historic campsite if a prominent figure in Seminole history resided there or if it was the setting of a culturally significant event. Several texts—which will be mentioned later in this chapter—call attention to numerous prominent individuals, including cattle foremen and government officials, who have helped to shape the Seminole Tribe as it is today. A cultural advisor may also inform us of an important member of the Tribe and likewise if a special event worth recording occurred at a certain camp. Tribal members may also reach out to the TAS and request research be completed on a site that they would like to have investigated and recorded. In addition, the TAS discovers historic sites while conducting archaeological field surveys for projects that are assigned to be cleared before any construction and ground-disturbing activity occurs on the reservations. When on-reservation projects are proposed, this triggers a cultural resource survey and assessment as mandated in the Seminole Tribe of Florida Cultural Resource Ordinance (C-01-16) (CRO) (Appendix) and Section 106 of the National Historic Preservation Act (NHPA) (see Mullins, this volume). Upon discovering a camp in the field, we make attempts to contact Tribal elders and descendants, particularly individuals who may have once lived there, who can provide us with valuable information concerning the site and the people who inhabited it. Tribal members are more than willing to make suggestions and direct us to the appropriate people within the community to speak with concerning certain camps; the TAS normally interviews about one or two individuals for each specific camp. In many cases, Tribal members will arrange a meeting with the TAS in the field; during these engagements, Tribal members provide detailed descriptions of the camp layout and function, while inviting tales from the camp come alive. Involvement from the Tribal community is the important link between the different ways that these sites are identified. The TAS would not know who lived in each of the camps we investigate or their cultural importance if it were not for their input. Ultimately, the Tribal community provides the direction from which we conduct research.

Background Archival Research

A critical step in the research process involves the investigation of historical documents and photographs for information about camps and associated members. The Ah-Tah-Thi-Ki Museum Seminole Library and Archives has many resources that are useful in this process, including videos, audio recordings, newspaper clippings, and photographs that shed light on people living within the camps. One especially helpful source is the Boehmer Photograph Collection. These 2,000 photographs were taken by Edith and William D.

Figure 8.1. Camp on the Brighton Reservation ca. 1940, showing traditional chickee structures. By permission of the Ah-Tah-Thi-Ki Museum. (ATTK catalog no. 2009.34.1401, original repository: Smithsonian Institution National Anthropological Archives)

Boehmer, who ran the school on the Brighton Reservation from the 1930s to the 1960s (Ah-Tah-Thi-Ki Museum 2012). The Boehmers took very detailed notes about the photographs, documenting important events on the Brighton Reservation that happened during this time. The museum archive is particularly valuable because it is continuously updated and supplemented with information from Tribal members, including identifications of individuals and descriptions of events in photographs. Supplementary photographs and recordings of Tribal members have also been found through the Florida Memory Project, which offers access to the collections of the State Library and Archives of Florida. Furthermore, a collection of photos were found in the archives at the George A. Smathers Libraries of the University of Florida, Louis Bishop Capron Papers 1891–1971. Through these photographs, the people and daily camp activities come to life. In addition, the TAS uses historic and modern aerial photographs of the reservations to aid in observing the environmental setting, as well as changes in site layout and size over extended periods of time from the 1940s to the present.

The Ah-Tah-Thi-Ki Museum holds a copy of the Indian Census records for the Seminole Tribe of Florida (Ah-Tah-Thi-Ki Museum 2012). The Indian Census was performed by the Bureau of Indian Affairs (BIA) and submitted to the federal government every year under the act of July 4, 1884 (23 Stat. L, 98 National Archives 2008). These census records identify people with their approximate birth and death dates along with estimated time frames for important events such as marriages. However, upon consultation with Tribal members, these records have been found to be somewhat inaccurate, containing incorrect names and familial associations assigned to certain individuals. The Seminoles were very untrusting of the U.S. government, due to constant fear of conflict and deportation; thus many were reluctant to provide certain information to the census takers (Jack Chalfant, personal communication, 2014). There are also many misinterpretations of names (Jack Chalfant, personal communication, 2014). The Seminole people would provide their Indian name to the census takers, which would get misinterpreted as something different; some individuals were also assigned an English name by the census takers (Jack Chalfant, personal communication, 2014). To check the accuracy of the historic census information, the TAS consults with the Tribal genealogist, Geneva Shore. Shore helps to identify correct clan membership, names, and birth and death years of Tribal members, as well as identifying people who were members of particular camps. The data gathered from the Tribal genealogist is an immense help to the research process, allowing a way for information to be verified and corrected if needed.

The ethnographic work of Clay MacCauley and Alexander Spoehr offers great insight into camp structure and lifeways of the historic Seminoles. MacCauley's "The Seminole Indians of Florida" was published in 1887 in the Smithsonian Institution's Bureau of Ethnology Fifth Annual Report (Sturtevant 2000, vii). MacCauley outlines important details, including camp life, social norms, familial ties, and camp structures, about the Seminoles living in an area surrounding the Big Cypress Reservation after the Seminole Wars; Spoehr researched the Cow Creek Seminole Band (later the Brighton Reservation) in 1939 and wrote two articles detailing what he observed, "Camp, Clan, and Kin among the Cow Creek Seminole of Florida" and "The Florida Seminole Camp" (Spoehr 1941, 1944). Spoehr's articles discuss family structure for certain camps along with details of how they were organized and their environmental setting. The dates of Spoehr's research overlap with some of the camps the TAS has researched, providing a great source of information. There are several other earlier ethnographic papers about the Seminoles in Florida; however, these sources are not used in our research because they do not directly refer to the camps. Rather, the articles refer to other aspects of Seminole culture, such as housing assessments, subsistence, or clothing, but contain little about the layout and function of the campsites.

Additional information concerning camps and influential individuals within the Seminole community can be found through several other secondary sources. Harry A. Kersey's *The Florida Seminoles and the New Deal* (1989) contains details pertaining to the government aid and employment programs that were established for the Seminole Tribe from 1933 to 1942, as well as prominent figures of the time that helped shape the Tribe as it is today. Kersey has also written *An Assumption of Sovereignty* (1996); this text covers the major political and social changes that the Seminole Tribe went through from 1953 to 1979. James Covington's *The Seminoles of Florida* (1993) is an excellent overview of Seminole culture and history, while highlighting important Seminole individuals throughout their history as well. Texts can also lead to unexpected valuable information. For example, in Theda Perdue's contribution, "Indians in Southern History" (1998), for *Indians in American History: An Introduction*, she used a photograph of Seminole women in a camp. The photograph's citation led back to the Chicago Field Museum, and it was discovered that the museum had five other photographs. Though these photographs did not contain anyone from the camps currently being researched, they may prove to be a great resource later.

Field Survey

If the location of a camp is known prior to an archaeological survey, the TAS will utilize background research and Tribal member interviews in determining the appropriate level of field survey to be performed. Primarily, the TAS conducts a Phase I survey on each site, which can include pedestrian survey, subsurface shovel testing, and/or metal detecting. The purpose of these survey methods is to aid in estimating the site boundary and examining the current condition of the camp, as well as to identify and document associated artifacts. During this process, we take detailed notes and several photographs to document the environmental setting, previous disturbances, and any historic or modern structures that may be located within the site boundaries. Some Tribal members have requested that artifacts not be collected during the field survey. The TAS will honor this request by only performing a pedestrian survey—with no ground-disturbing activity—leaving the artifacts in place; however, we will take photographs and make note of the artifact locations. If artifacts are collected, they are transported to the THPO Archaeological Laboratory on the Big Cypress Reservation where they are cleaned and analyzed, and then stored securely in the Seminole Tribe of Florida Curatorial Facility vault.

Tribal Member Interviews

Undoubtedly, the most important source of information comes from personal interviews with Tribal members who once lived within the camps. Even though these sites are described in other archival sources, the interviews with Tribal members add their perspective, which is missing from a non-Tribal member's account, resulting in inaccuracy. For instance, Mollie Jolly told the TAS that when Alexander Spoehr would come to the Tom Smith camp, the children were told to hide—thus Spoehr did not accurately record the site (Mollie Jolly, personal communication, 2013). The interviews help provide context to the information that TAS records during the various steps of the research process. Interviews allow for detailed firsthand accounts on site layouts, including the location and functions of the various structures, along with personalized stories making each camp unique. If the Tribal member is willing, he or she may draw a map showing the layout of structures and their purposes as well as a diagram of the family lineage within the camp. These accounts transform the historic sites from a location on a map to a place where people lived and grew up.

Interviews are not solely to obtain information for research; they are also a way to get involved with the community and to create strong social ties. Engaging with the Tribal community in this way helps to break down barriers and misunderstandings from both the Tribal and non-Tribal standpoint. These interviews offer Tribal elders an opportunity to memorialize their experiences in camps and help create a concrete record for their descendants, ultimately preserving their cultural heritage. We often bring photographs that were uncovered during the archival research portion to the Tribal member interviews. Tribal members are happy to identify people or correct any misidentifications in the photographs. More important, they are able to see people that they grew up with, and in some instances they are able to look at photographs that they have never seen. We are more than willing to offer copies of photographs. For example, during an interview, a Tribal member mentioned that she was an extra in the 1966 film *Johnny Tiger* and expressed how she always wanted a copy of the film but could never find it. After the interview, the TAS promptly began searching for the film and discovered a copy on file with the Ah-Tah-Thi-Ki Museum—a copy was made and taken to the Tribal member. She was so delighted to see so many people that she knew and grew up with— she even shared it with her children and relatives.

During this process, the TAS will ask Tribal members if they want to pursue preservation of their camp; there are a variety of preservation options. Tribal members can choose to preserve the land that their camp was on and ensure that no construction is completed in this area; they may also choose to preserve it by rebuilding chickees and other structures as they once stood. Some of these sites may also be eligible for the TRHP; thus upon completion of the research process, a Tribal Register nomination may be completed. Additionally, camp members may request a land set-aside. The process starts with the camp members and their descendants, or the community as a whole, requesting a set-aside to preserve an area from development. Then the set-aside is sent for approval by the reservation community at the community meeting; after approval from the community, the set-aside is sent to the Land Use Committee. Following approval from the Land Use Committee, the set-aside is sent to the Tribal Council for the final say, and the process is complete (Kate Macuen, personal communication, 2014). If Tribal members do not wish to fully preserve the site, the area where the camp was once located can be reused for the construction of housing or business developments. Tribal members affiliated with the camp are ultimately the ones who decide who can build on the site location; they can also set limitations on who they wish to live on the land based on clan membership or other familial relations. The interaction with the community is critical in determining which method is most appropriate for each camp; it is essential to understand the Tribal member's wishes and to make every attempt to follow through with his or her requests.

Camp Research Results: The Johns Camp and the Tom Smith Camp

The Johns camp and Tom Smith camp are two camps on the Brighton Reservation that have recently been investigated by TAS. These camps will be used as examples to help emphasize the steps of the camp research process. The Johns camp was located during a project proposed for a future home site in 2007, and it was investigated again in 2013. The Johns family is very prominent in the Tribal cattle industry, and some family members have also been Tribal Representatives. After subsequent research and interviews, the camp was recorded in detail; however, it was not listed on the TRHP due to the great amount of disturbance at the site. In contrast, Tribal member Willie Johns was asked in 2012 by the TAS which camps to research on the Brighton Reservation; one of the sites he suggested to record was the Tom Smith camp. Tom Smith was a popular Medicine Man on the Brighton Reservation; as a Councilman, he was also a part of the governing body that presided over the Green Corn Dance ceremony. The Tom Smith camp had a recommendation of eligibility for the TRHP due to the important role that Tom Smith played in the Tribe as a Medicine Man and Councilman. The Johns camp and Tom Smith camp research shows the extensive amount of work the TAS performs in consultation with Tribal members to accurately record each camp's legacy.

The Johns Camp

The Johns family established several camps in the Okeechobee Basin area; we will be discussing the fourth Johns camp, which is located in the central portion of the Brighton Reservation. This camp was located in a mixed oak and palm hammock environment that consisted of live oak, sabal palms, palmetto, air potato, and beautyberry. Based on the historic aerials, the camp was surrounded by wet prairie with a pond directly to the east. Today, however, the area has been developed and largely disturbed due to the construction of a home site.

The Johns Family History

The Johns family understands they are descended from the Oconee (see Willie Johns and Stephen Bridenstine, this volume). The Creek Indians, who were known as the Oconee, lived in an area along the Oconee River in the state of Georgia (Covington 1993, 12). They struggled from tensions between competing groups of people, including other tribes, as increasing numbers of Euro-Americans moved into their traditional Oconee territory; as a result, the Creek Oconee moved across the border into Florida (Wright 1990, 109; Covington 1993, 12). One Oconee leader was Cowkeeper, who migrated down to Florida (south of Gainesville) in the mid-eighteenth century with his people. Cowkeeper founded a town that was called Cuscowilla near the Alachua Prairie in Central Florida. Here they thrived on the stray Spanish cattle that roamed over the prairies (Ah Tah Thi Ki Museum 2008, 7).

The Johns camp was investigated twice during previous archaeological projects—once in 2007 and again in 2013. Willie Johns, resident of the Brighton Reservation and former inhabitant of the Johns camp, was our chief cultural advisor for this project. He explained that from the 1930s into the 1940s, the Johns family lived in the Bluefields area of St. Lucie County, which is approximately 18 miles west of Fort Pierce. In the 1940s, the family moved to the town of Okeechobee and then to the Brighton Reservation. They established several

Figure 8.2. Dolly Johns, ca. 1960, matriarch of the Johns camp, aunt of Willie Johns (see chapter 1). By permission of the Ah-Tah-Thi-Ki Museum. (ATTK catalog no. 2009.34.1862, original repository: Smithsonian Institution National Anthropological Archives)

camps on the reservation and moved back and forth to Okeechobee as work became available. This was a matrilineal camp with Dolly Johns, Willie Johns's aunt, being the matriarch (Figure 8.2). Everyone called her "Mama." The Johns family were members of the Wildcat (Panther) Clan. The first camp inhabited was north of North Tucker Ridge Road and west of Billy Bowlegs Road in the northern portion of the Brighton Reservation. However, they did not live here long due to continuous flooding. The second camp was located in the northwest portion of the Brighton Reservation next to the school and BIA headquarters. This camp was inhabited for only a short time. The third location the Johns family moved to was a place near Red Barn located in the western portion of the Brighton Reservation on Harney Pond Road. Soon after, they moved to a hammock in the central portion of the Brighton Reservation, where they established their fourth and final camp. The fourth camp will be discussed in this chapter (Willie Johns, personal communication, 2014).

Field Examination of the Johns Camp

The hammock containing the Johns camp measures roughly 330 meters (1,083 feet) north to south by 236 meters east to west (774 feet), with an approximate area of 4 hectares (9.8 acres). The THPO identified two archaeological components within the hammock during the previous field surveys, one a historic Seminole camp and the other a precontact period midden. The precontact component located in the northwestern portion of the hammock contained solely faunal remains. The historic camp covered the full extent of the hammock and consisted of diagnostic glass bottles and whiteware (Fenno 2013a).

Life at the Johns Camp

The fourth Johns camp had nine permanent structures and a few temporary ones. Willie Johns explained that six of the structures were living quarters. These structures were chickees with pine posts and palm thatch roofing, but were not open on all sides as are traditional Seminole dwellings. Instead, they were enclosed on all sides with 2 × 4 studs and plywood. There were no windows, but they had an opening at the top for light and circulation. The Big-house, which was located in the southern portion of the camp, was built by Barfield Johns, Dolly's brother. It included a refrigerator (after 1957 when electricity came to the camp), a stove, and sleeping quarters. Behind the Bighouse were a few chickees used only by pregnant women and new mothers who were separated for medicinal purposes. Patty and Connie, Willie's cousins, lived at this camp and had another chickee northwest of the Bighouse. Their mother was Emma Johns, who was one of Dolly's five sisters; Emma died at a previous camp in the Bluefields area, so the girls began living with Dolly. Two of Dolly's sisters, Lillian Johns and Lois Micco, were living at this camp. A third structure, located to the north of the Bighouse, was used by Lillian and her five children. Lois Micco had a house to the north of the camp with her husband, Howard Micco, and their daughter, Leah. Near Howard and Lois's house was a lean-to for relaxing and socializing. The young men had a separate bachelor chickee located in the southern central portion of the camp; this is where Willie Johns and his other unmarried male cousins slept (Willie Johns, personal communication, 2014).

Barfield Johns is one of the three brothers of Dolly Johns, and he was the only brother who lived at this Johns camp. He had a house and lived in the southern part of the hammock with his wife. In between his house and the Johns camp, Barfield had a large hog pen that was located in a pond bordering the eastern portion of the hammock (Willie Johns, personal communication, 2014).

An outhouse was located in the northeastern portion of the camp. In 1957, the camp received electricity, which allowed for new innovations. Before electricity, the camp only contained a hand pump, but once electricity was installed, the inhabitants were able to build a shower with an electric water pump. Showers for the camp were located on the western portion of the hammock. There was also a flower garden that had a variety of hibiscus bushes. The camp also contained a basketball hoop made out of a bicycle tire on a cabbage palm tree where children would play basketball. After the basketball games they would sometimes play baseball next to the camp. Under the water tower near their camp, football games were also played with no equipment other than a football; this area would frequently flood, and they would play in the mud. Many of the boys from around the reservation would play, and some games would be rough. Willie said: "Everyone wanted to challenge the Johns boys" (Willie Johns, personal communication, 2014).

A vegetable garden was located in another hammock to the east of the camp, where corn, beans, pumpkins, and squash were grown. The pumpkins were grown in a unique manner. A palm tree would be burned and allowed to fall; pumpkin seeds were then planted and allowed to grow along the fallen palm. Mulberry bushes surrounding the camp were also used as a food source. Bananas were grown behind a few of the houses, along with citrus in neighboring hammocks. Hunting was also a daily occurrence to provide sustenance. The Johns fished in the pond across Reservation Road to the east of the camp.

Harney Pond Canal was another fishing hole; Willie Johns evoked that it was beautiful before it was straightened and dredged (Willie Johns, personal communication, 2014).

When the THPO recorded the site in 2007, it was not researched immediately, and as of 2013 the area currently has a house overlapping the Johns campsite boundary. This historic camp is not being preserved or nominated for the Tribal Register at this time due to the high level of disturbance in the area from the construction of the home site. However, the person who owns this house is a member of the early camp itself—evidence of the continuous occupation through clan affiliation and camp membership. Without this oral history from Willie Johns there would be no recorded information about this camp, and the Johns camp could have eventually been lost to history. With this combined effort from both the TAS and Tribal members, we were able to document a firsthand account of what life was like within this camp.

The Tom Smith Camp

Tom Smith's camp is located in the northeastern portion of the Brighton Reservation. The campsite is located within a mixed hardwood hammock environment that consists of citrus, live oak, wild coffee, beautyberry, sabal palm, palmetto, guava tree, and Caesar's weed (Fenno 2013b). Based on the historic aerials, a wet prairie bounded the hammock, although today it is surrounded by improved pasture (Fenno 2013b). Underbrush was cleared from the center of the hammock, leaving only the canopy for shade (Fenno 2013b). In this clearing Mollie Jolly, the granddaughter of Tom Smith and a teacher at the Brighton Elementary/Middle School (Pemayetv Emahakv), set up benches and a fire pit to act as cultural and educational teaching tools (Mollie Jolly, personal communication, 2013).

Tom Smith Family History

Tom Smith was born in 1888 to Billy Smith (Wildcat Clan) and Sally Parker (Bird Clan) (Mollie Jolly, personal communication, 2013). Billy Smith was a Medicine Man known as Little Chief who is descended from Wildcat, an important Seminole leader during the Second Seminole War (Mollie Jolly, personal communication, 2013). Prior to the formation of the Tribe, Medicine Men represented a political and judicial council for the Tribe during their traditional Green Corn Dance ceremony (Covington 1993, 150). Each Green Corn Dance had a council of Medicine Men who were in charge of the medicinal practices and judicial functions during the ceremony (Covington 1993, 150). In 1934, Billy Smith led the Green Corn Dance with two assistants

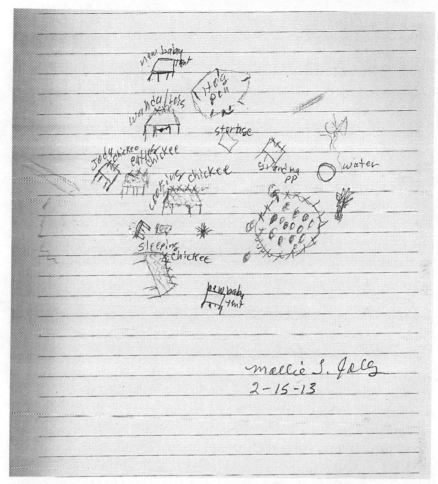

Figure 8.3. Hand-drawn map of the Tom Smith camp by Mollie Jolly, showing the placement of chickees in the camp. By permission of Mollie Jolly, February 15, 2013.

(Covington 1993, 258). By 1940, Tom Smith, Naha Tiger, and Charlie Micco were listed as Council members (Covington 1993, 258). Based on Roy Nash's 1930 map (Nash 1931), Billy Smith's camp was located approximately 15 miles west of Fort Pierce around the Bluefields area. Tom's mother, Sally Parker, is a noteworthy member of the Seminole community, as she was a daughter of Polly Parker. In 1858, during the Third Seminole War, Polly was captured in the Istokpoga area of Highlands County and forcefully transported to Egmont Key, which is an island on the west coast of Florida at the mouth of Tampa Bay where Seminoles were held to await removal to Indian Territory (Devane 1963). At the end of her incarceration at Egmont Key, she and other

Seminoles were marched aboard a steamship (Devane 1963). While the ship refueled at St. Marks, Florida, Polly, with a small group of others, talked the guards into letting them go ashore to collect herbs for medicine (Devane 1963; Montgomery 2013). The group made their move, and some of them escaped, hiding during the day and traveling by night; they eventually made their way back to the Okeechobee area to live with the Cow Creek Band (Devane 1963; Montgomery 2013). With this brave act, Polly Parker's legacy has lived on in her descendants, who include many prominent members of the Seminole Tribe of Florida.

Tom Smith had two brothers, Morgan Smith and Dick Smith, and three sisters, Mercy Smith Jones, Dollie Smith, and Gully Smith. Morgan Smith was one of the first trustees for the Big Cypress Reservation Cattle Program, and Dick Smith raised cattle on the Brighton Reservation. Mercy Smith Jones lived with her husband in another camp, and Gully Smith died from an illness (Mollie Jolly, personal communication, 2013).

In the early twentieth century, Tom Smith married Stella Jumper. This marriage probably occurred after 1920, as the 1920 Indian census records lists Stella as being single (U.S. Census Bureau 1920). Stella was born in 1900, presumably in the Bluefields area of St. Lucie County. She was a member of the Deer Clan and had a brother named John Josh who was one of the first trustees of the Brighton Cattle Program and a member of the Seminole Tribal Council. Tom and Stella had five children together: Ada Smith Bowers, Juanita Smith Tommie, Lois Smith, Wanda Smith, and Jodi Smith. However, only Tom, Stella, Wanda, and Lois, along with Juanita Tommie, her husband (Billie Tommie), and their children lived in the Tom Smith camp. Mollie Jolly's mother, Juanita Smith Tommie, had to move for work, leaving Mollie to live at the Tom Smith camp when she was two. Creek was the primary language in the camp, although Mollie Jolly also spoke her father's language, Miccosukee (Mollie Jolly, personal communication, 2013).

Field Examination of the Tom Smith Camp

According to the modern aerial photography, the hammock containing the Tom Smith camp is approximately 148 meters (486 feet) north to south by 260 meters (863 feet) east to west. During the Phase I investigation, the THPO identified two archaeological components within the hammock: a twentieth-century historic camp and a precontact midden. The precontact component located in the central northwestern portion of the hammock contained Belle Glade Plain pottery fragments and faunal bone. Its approximate boundaries are 17 meters (56 feet) north to south by 29 meters (95 feet) east to west. Faunal bone was also recorded in the southwestern portion of the hammock, but it is unclear if these artifacts are related to the precontact or historic period. The historic component encompasses the precontact site and measures 61 meters (200 feet) north to south by 105 meters (344 feet) east to west. Artifacts identified in the historic component included a lead ingot, copper fragments, glass bottles, and one white ware sherd (Fenno 2013b).

Life at the Tom Smith Camp

The Tom Smith camp consisted of six permanent and two temporary structures (Figure 8.3). Frequent visitors or extended family used the northernmost sleeping chickee as a guesthouse. Jodi Smith, Tom's son, occupied the eastern sleeping chickee when he was younger. Later, Jodi moved to Hollywood, Florida, with his wife, Alice Doctor, and the structure was demolished. The Smiths' twin daughters, Wanda and Lois, shared the southern chickee. The western chickee was for Tom and Stella. Other structures within the camp included a cooking chickee in the center of the camp and an eating chickee to the southeast of the cooking chickee. To the north of the cooking chickee was a piece of plywood over two posts, used for curing beef. A storage structure was located in the southern portion of the camp. The two temporary structures were tents (one in the north and one in the south) that women would use when a baby was being born. Women would be separated from the camp for medicinal purposes six weeks prior to the birth and six weeks after (Mollie Jolly, personal communication, 2013).

A scratch pond was located in the western portion of the camp. A scratch pond is a hole dug in the ground to collect water, which varied in size depending on the size of the camp. The water would settle in the scratch pond and be scooped out with a bucket as needed. In addition to the scratch pond, Mollie Jolly remembers that a watering hole was near a papaya tree in the eastern portion of the hammock. Tom eventually created a well by digging a hole and removing the murky water until clear water remained. Upon encountering clear water, plywood was used to add support to the well walls, and palmetto fronds were used to cover the well (Mollie Jolly, personal communication, 2013).

Other components of the camp focused on providing subsistence for the inhabitants. One of the main portions of the camp was a garden, in which Mollie Jolly remembers her family growing corn, peas, sweet potatoes, pumpkins, and peanuts. Seeds were planted within small mounds in the soil. Tom Smith created a barrier to protect the garden from animals by stringing barbed wire around the trees surrounding the garden. A hog pen was also located in the southern portion of the camp. Mollie Jolly stated that the family had four hogs. She was responsible for catching the hogs by their hind legs, whereupon Tom would strike the hog in the head with a hatchet, and the hog would be dressed out for consumption. There was a gopher tortoise cage, which was a square plywood pen. The camp's inhabitants hunted gopher tortoises by poking a long rod into animal burrows until they found a tortoise; the tortoise was then extracted and caged to cook later. Tom Smith had two horses, James and Stelba, which were kept in the northeastern portion of the camp near Tom's driveway. Tom shoed and trimmed the horses' hooves himself. Other animals in the camp included chickens, two dogs (Blackie and Ketchup), and a cow for milking. The family kept the milk and butter in a posthole located in the hammock. This hole was dug into the bedrock and piece of plywood covered it, keeping the interior cool (Mollie Jolly, personal communication, 2013).

The main source of food and income for the Tom Smith camp was hunting. Tom Smith would sit in a half-moon-shaped work area with his blanket and tools casting his own bullets for hunting. Tom hunted regularly, occasionally accompanied by his younger brother, Dick Smith. He would leave early in the morning and not return until sundown. Every morning that he went hunting, Tom would gather the wood for his wife to start the fire. She would then make *sofkee* (corn drink or soup) and put it in a Mason jar. Stella packed the jar full of *sofkee* and other food for Tom to eat while he was out hunting and placed it in a drawstring bag she made herself. The children were responsible for giving the horses water before Tom left for the day and after he returned. Toward the end of the day, if Tom had not returned, Mollie Jolly explained that Stella would have Mollie run out to the trail behind the hammock to see if Tom was returning (Mollie Jolly, personal communication, 2013).

While out hunting, if Tom came across sweet oranges, he would bring them back to the camp. Tom distributed whatever he caught among the other families in camps around area. These included the Billy Bowlegs III, Jones, Hall, and Buster Twins camps. Tom and his brother, Dick, would also take the furs of the animals that they killed while hunting to Okeechobee to get money to purchase supplies.

Another major source of food was fishing. Children were responsible for collecting tree frogs as bait. The camp's inhabitants (sometimes with Jodi Smith, Dick Smith, and Oscar Hall) would go fishing in the pond to the south of the Buster Twins camp (Mollie Jolly, personal communication, 2013).

When Tom Smith died in 1961, Stella Smith, with eight grandchildren, moved to what would be known as the Stella Smith camp in the northwestern portion of the Brighton Reservation; this location was closer to the school, which made it easier for the kids to attend. However, Stella and the children would regularly go back to the Tom Smith camp to visit. Mollie Jolly stated it felt like home (Mollie Jolly, personal communication, 2013).

Following the in-depth research process, due to the limited amount of disturbance within the camp boundaries and the important role Tom Smith played within the Tribe, it has been determined that the Tom Smith camp is eligible for the Tribal Register. Currently, the THPO is consulting with Mollie Jolly in creating a set-aside for the Tom Smith camp. Plans include adding signs within the camp to help the Culture Department educate students about camp life. Through the research and survey process, stories are uncovered and preserved, allowing future generations to learn about their heritage and carry on the Seminole legacy.

Conclusion

This process encourages Tribal members to collaborate with the THPO. The interviews and hand-drawn maps provide the vehicle for Native voices to be heard. Without their input, research would only be secondhand. In this manner the THPO, in collaboration with the Seminole community, studies their past; having the Tribal member's viewpoint is critical in order to fully understand the way of life in these historic camps. By Tribal members helping to locate sites and allowing us to document unique stories, we are able to help preserve the heritage of the Seminole Tribe of Florida and record valuable information for future generations.

Figure 8.4. *Left to right*: Jessica Freeman, Karen Brunso, Matthew Fenno. By permission of Maureen Mahoney, Tribal Archaeologist, Seminole Tribe of Florida Tribal Historic Preservation Office.

References Cited

Ah-Tah-Thi-Ki Museum. 2008. *Cattle Keepers: The Heritage of the Seminole Cattle Ranching*. Clewiston, Fla.: Ah-Tah-Thi-Ki Museum.

———. 2012. Seminole Library and Archives. http://www.ahtahthiki.com/LibraryArchives-Collections-Seminole-Tribe-Florida. Ah-Tah-Thi-Ki-Museum.html.

Covington, James. 1993. *The Seminoles of Florida*. Gainesville: University Press of Florida.

Densmore, Frances. 1956. *Seminole Music*. Bureau of Ethnology Bulletin 161. Washington, D.C.: Smithsonian Institution.

Devane, Albert. 1963. "History of Old Fort Drum." *Okeechobee News*, November 8. http://www.rootsweb.ancestry.com/~flokeech/newspaper/historyoldftdrum.html.

Fenno, Matthew G. 2013a. *A Phase I Cultural Resource Survey and Assessment of the Connie Whidden Lease Modification, Brighton Reservation, Florida*. Clewiston, Fla.: Seminole Tribe of Florida.

———. 2013b. *Tribal Register Narrative Form and Narrative Statement: Tom Smith Camp*. Clewiston, Fla.: Seminole Tribe of Florida.

Kersey, Harry. 1989. *The Florida Seminoles and the New Deal*. Boca Raton: Florida Atlantic University Press.

———. 1996. *An Assumption of Sovereignty*. Lincoln: University of Nebraska Press.

MacCauley, Clay. 2000. *The Seminole Indians of Florida*. Gainesville: University Press of Florida.

Montgomery, Ben. 2013. "Polly Parker's Escape Gave Life to Florida's Seminole Tribe." *Tampa Bay Times*, December 7.

Nash, Roy. 1931. "Report to the Commissioner of Indian Affairs Concerning Conditions among the Seminole Indians of Florida." In *Seminole Indians, Survey of the Seminole Indians of Florida, Presented by Mr. Fletcher*. 1931. Sen. 71:3rd. doc. 314. Exh. 41.

National Archives. 2008. Indian Census Rolls, 1885–1940. http://www.archives.gov/research/census/native-americans/1885-1940.html.

Perdue, Theda. 1998. "Indians in Southern History." In *Indians in American History: An Introduction*, edited by Frederick E. Hoxie and Peter Iverson, 121–139. Wheeling, Ill.: Harland Davidson.

Seminole Media Productions. 2010. *Remembering the Seminole Camp Way of Life*. 76 min. Seminole Media Productions.

Seminole Tribe of Florida Tribal Historic Preservation Office. 2014. Tribal Register of Historic Places. http://www.stofthpo.com/Register-Historic-Places-Seminole-Tribe-FL-Tribal-Historic-Preservation-Office.html.

Spoehr, Alexander. 1941. "Camp, Clan, and Kin among the Cow Creek Seminole of Florida." *Florida Anthropological Series,* 33(1). Florida Museum of Natural History.

————. 1944. "The Florida Seminole Camp." *Florida Anthropological Series* 33(3). Florida Museum of Natural History.

Sturtevant, William C. 1971. "Creek into Seminole." In *North American Indians in Historical Perspective,* edited by Eleanor Burke Leacock and Nancy Oestrich Lune, 92–128. New York: Random House.

————. 2000. "Introduction." In *The Seminole Indians of Florida,* by Clay MacCauley, vii. Gainesville: University of Florida Press.

U.S. Census Bureau. 1920. Bureau of Indian Affairs. Seminole Agency, Dania, Florida. https://www.censusrecords.com/content/1920_Census.

WGCU Public Media. 2012. "Untold Stories: The Unconquered Seminoles." WGCU Public Media, Florida.

Wright, Leitch J. 1990. *Creeks and Seminoles.* Lincoln: University of Nebraska Press.

9

Everything You Know Is Wrong!

Community Archaeology at Fort Shackelford

ANNETTE L. SNAPP

It is often stated that the so-called Seminole Wars that stretched for a large part of the early and mid-nineteenth century were the most financially costly campaign undertaken by the U.S. government against the indigenous inhabitants of the North American continent. Despite suffering greatly throughout these engagements, the Seminoles never signed a peace treaty or surrendered to their aggressors. Their indomitable resistance to their oppressors remains a core facet of the Seminole worldview.

The construction and reuse of strategic military forts throughout Florida was part of a U.S. tactic to keep an army supplied in a vast theater of war. The forts also had another purpose: to keep a close watch on the enemy. Fort Shackelford is particularly important in this regard, as it was placed in the heart of the Seminole community in the Big Cypress swamp. The placement of the fort was, in fact, at the center of events that led to the Third Seminole War. Today, the location of the fort is believed to be on the Big Cypress Reservation. Conventional means of finding the fort, through historic research and archaeological investigation, appear to have pinpointed its location. In any other context, the project would have been written up, published, and otherwise filed away. In hindsight, and as this chapter clearly demonstrates, this outcome would not have told anywhere near the full story. The actual history of the fort is a human story that can only be told with time and a strong relationship with the community.

Author Bio

Annette Snapp earned an M.A. in applied anthropology with a concentration in public archaeology from the University of South Florida as well as a

Master of Studies and Ph.D. in ethnology and museum ethnography from the University of Oxford. She has served as a professional archaeologist for over twenty years in Florida and the southeastern United States, and is also certified by the Register of Professional Archaeologists. In 2009 and 2011, Snapp codirected archaeological field schools at Florida Gulf Coast University in conjunction with Paul Backhouse of the Seminole Tribe of Florida Tribal Historic Preservation Office (STOF THPO). From 2013 to 2016, she served as the Ah-Tah-Thi-Ki's Operations Manager.

Introduction

Third Seminole War–era Fort Shackelford was built, abandoned, and burned in 1855. One hundred and fifty-four years later, in 2009, the exact location of this fort became the subject of an archaeological field school. Given the amount of time that had passed and the brevity of the fort's life, we expected that confirming the fort's location might be somewhat challenging, but we did not know when we began how critical Seminole Tribal input would be to understanding our results. In fact, knowledge gained through Tribal oral histories was very important to strengthening our archaeological understanding of Fort Shackelford.

One historic account of a past event on the Big Cypress Seminole Indian Reservation is important for setting the backdrop for the archaeological field school. This story serves as a cautionary tale for the Seminole Tribe about revealing important cultural information to outsiders. This account, by Josie Billie, has served the community for decades and directly involves Fort Shackelford, the subject of the 2009 archaeological field school. Through time, in our efforts to interpret the results of the field school investigations, we found ourselves repeatedly coming back to this story and the results of its influence over the years.

Josie Billie and the Cautionary Tale

Josie Billie (see Figure 9.1) was an important figure in the Seminole Tribe. During his lifetime, he served as a doctor, member of Council, Medicine Man, and Christian minister. William Straight, in an article summarizing the accomplishments of Josie Billie, noted that "throughout the years [Josie] has been an innovator who early recognized that the Seminole could not continue to live in isolation. He has attempted to bring to his people the best of the white man's way of life while retaining the best of the Indian's culture" (1970,

Figure 9.1. Josie Billie, Seminole Medicine Man, in 1963. Image by Tolle. By permission of the State Archives of Florida.

40). It is worth noting that Josie Billie's father, Littly (Little) Billie (also known as Little Billie Fewell, Billie Conepatchie, and Billy Koniphadjo), was the first Seminole to attend a white school, which he did for three years. His actions were considered a severe breach of Seminole tradition and only due to the intervention of his father's family members was he able to escape severe punishment (Straight 1970, 37–38). Perhaps as a result of his father's interest in education with the white settlers, Josie Billie may have been more trusting of outsiders than other Tribal members. But the following incident taught him a lesson about that trust and his culture.

In 1964 or 1965, Josie Billie told of his own personal mishap with outsiders in an event involving the location of Fort Shackelford. Josie Billie explained that after burning Fort Shackelford in 1855, fighting a battle, and running off soldiers, the Seminoles discovered inside the fort at the captain's quarters gold coinage—perhaps $20 gold pieces—which was used to pay the soldiers. Since the battle resulted in the death of soldiers and the Seminoles do not take from the dead, they decided the best approach was to bury the gold coins and not tell anyone. According to Josie Billie, in the mid to late 1930s, after studying military archives, professional archaeologists from either the University of Miami or the University of Florida approached him about the location of Fort Shackelford. They asked him to show them the location of the fort and assured him that they would not take anything from the location without his approval. He felt comfortable with these assurances and showed them where the fort once stood. These people whom Josie Billie believed to be archaeologists then took him back to his home and thanked him, telling him they were leaving (Manuel Tiger, personal communication, August 21, 2014).

The next morning Josie Billie became suspicious. He realized that his trust might have been violated. He returned to the fort location he shared with the archaeologists just the day before and found he had been deceived. Instead of leaving as they had told him, the archaeologists had circled back to the site and dug at the spot he identified as the fort's location. Upon arriving at the fort site, he discovered a tripod with a hoist and tackle block left behind by the archaeologists and thought to have been used to remove the chest of gold buried by the Seminoles earlier. He realized it had been a mistake to tell the archaeologists where the site actually was located. The deceit was never forgotten, and Josie Billie warned the Seminole community to be wary of outsiders—a warning that has never been forgotten (Manuel Tiger, personal communication, August 21, 2014).

Using his own unfortunate experience with the site of Fort Shackelford as an example of what can happen, Josie Billie urged the community to not reveal important cultural information with outsiders because they are liable to take the cultural resources away (Manuel Tiger, personal communication, August 21, 2014). This message resonated with Councilman Tiger later when he remembered Josie Billie's prediction that one day the Tribe would not exist. When he first heard this message, he believed that it was about the extinction of Tribal people. But today he sees the message as a warning about the loss of culture leading to the loss of the Tribe (Manuel Tiger, personal communication, August 21, 2014). In this light, the protection of all cultural resources is vital to the survival of the Tribe. Protecting the location of Fort Shackelford, then, is a component of cultural preservation.

Archaeological Field School

Josie Billie's cautionary tale is one that promotes a wariness of outsiders. In 2009, when we initiated an archaeological field school project to determine the accuracy of a concrete marker originally placed at the site believed to be

a

b

Figure 9.2. Fort Shackelford concrete marker (*a*) and brass plaque (*b*) produced and delivered in 1941 to the Big Cypress Reservation by D. Graham Copeland. 2009. By permission of the Ah Tah Thi Ki Museum.

that of Fort Shackelford, we were unaware of this oral history and of the events that had transpired at the very spot we hoped to relocate.

So we forged ahead. The STOF THPO collaborated with Florida Gulf Coast University on an archaeological field school. Students from the university traveled to and stayed on the Big Cypress Seminole Indian Reservation to learn and practice archaeological investigative techniques at a location believed to be the site of Fort Shackelford. It provided an opportunity to explore the heritage and memory of Fort Shackelford for its historical context as well as for its relevance to the modern lives of the Tribal and non-Tribal residents of South Florida (sensu Orser 2010). Practically, the project offered a unique opportunity for the involvement of members of the Tribal community, the STOF THPO, and Florida Gulf Coast University in the investigation of a historically contested site within the heart of the Big Cypress Seminole Indian Reservation.

Community Archaeology

The relocation of what are often ephemeral Seminole War–era military installations is a notoriously difficult archaeological proposition (Olsen 1965; Jennings 2001; Bell 2004). The main question for the fieldwork was to test the validity of an extant concrete marker that was placed in 1941 under the direction of D. Graham Copeland, surveyor for Collier County and architect for the Tamiami Trail. The marker, which stands today in an open pasture on the Big Cypress Seminole Indian Reservation (Figure 9.2), is capped with a brass disc that reads: "This is the site of Fort Shackleford [sic], Base for Federal Troops in Second and Third Seminole Wars. Please do not remove this plate." No aboveground features remain visible to suggest that this was the location of the fort, and the pasture has clearly been heavily modified by agricultural practices. A secondary research goal was therefore to determine the integrity and spatial extent of any culturally significant deposits recorded at this location.

Copeland's marker is a fixed point in the landscape and was expected to require a limited amount of excavation work to confirm (or not) its accuracy in marking the site of Fort Shackelford. This target was ideal for the investigations of an archaeological field school. It became the starting point of a journey. This passage would eventually show us that locating an old fort can be difficult for many reasons, and that some of those reasons may be the result of community actions to preserve precious cultural resources.

Brief Background of the Seminole People

The history and ethnogenesis of the people today identified as the Seminole Tribe of Florida are socially, politically, and geographically complex (e.g., Fairbanks 1974; Wright 1986; Sturtevant 1971; Weisman, 1989, 1999; Covington 1993; MacCauley 2000). Continued pressure from colonial expansion in the southeastern United States destabilized and displaced indigenous groups, pushing them unceasingly toward the periphery of habitable land (Hahn 2004). By the end of the Second Seminole War in 1842, the Seminoles were living within the interior of South Florida. It was not long, however, before the 1850 Swamp and Overflowed Land Act granted federal swamplands to the states, catalyzing an interest in Seminole Reserve lands (Missall and Missall 2004, 211–212). Land speculation, in tandem with the fear of Seminole guerrilla attacks on settlers, led to a renewed effort to move the Seminoles farther into the Everglades and ultimately force their removal to the western Indian lands.

Fort Shackelford was but one of a group of federal forts built on dry patches of land at the western edge of the Everglades. These forts were intended to exert pressure on the Seminoles in an effort to encourage emigration to Indian lands west of the Mississippi, modern-day Oklahoma (Jennings 2001, 24–25). Fort Shackelford was a U.S. military outpost constructed on Seminole Indian Reservation lands on the cusp of the Third Seminole War in early 1855. Its location proved to be a U.S. military invasion of the lands set aside for the Seminoles after the Second Seminole War. By December 1855, the fort was burned down, and it was never rebuilt. Instead, what remained of the fort melted into the watery landscape.

What Do We Know of the Fort from Historic Documents?

Activities associated with the building of Fort Shackelford began early in 1855 when on February 23, 1855, Companies C and E of the Second Artillery, under the command of Captain Elzey, marched, under orders, toward Waxy Hadjo's Landing in order to survey an appropriate location for a blockhouse fortification. Having found a suitable site, the construction of the blockhouse commenced on February 27, 1855 (Eck 2002, 92). After erecting the blockhouse, Captain Elzey continued to Fort Simon Drum, where he was relieved by Brevet Major Hays. According to James Hammond (2008:75), the area of Fort Shackelford may have previously been reconnoitered as early as October 1841, when five detachments including 200 soldiers were sent to hunt for the Seminole leader Abiaka (also known as Sam Jones).

The naming of this fort was probably in memory of a fellow soldier named Muscoe Livingston Shackleford, who served as a first lieutenant in the Second Artillery—the same group that built Fort Shackelford. After graduating from West Point in 1832, Muscoe Shackleford fought in the Second Seminole War and was present at the Battle of Wahoo Swamp on November 21, 1836. Subsequently, he served in the Mexican-American War, where he was mortally wounded in the Battle of Molino del Rey on September 8, 1847, dying in early October in Mexico City (Cullum 1891, 648). Naming forts after fallen comrades was common during the Seminole Wars (John Missall and Mary Lou Missall, personal communication, 2010).

As far as the fort's appearance, Third Seminole War forts were typically not substantial structures and for the most part comprised only a single blockhouse and several ancillary thatched huts (Jennings 2001, 25). Few documents contain any descriptive information on the location or structures that comprise Fort Shackelford. In a letter dated July 1, 1855, Brevet Colonel Munroe reports that Captain Elzey of the Second Artillery near Waxy Hadjo's Landing, "having selected the most eligible position for a blockhouse in that vicinity, he commenced its erection on the 27th [of February]. The point selected is the most Southern (near the Everglades) that it is practicable for wagons to reach" (Eck 2002, 92). In addition, Ives (1856, 26) also stated, "The blockhouse is situated upon a pine island one mile from Waxy Hadjo's landing, near the edge of the Everglades, and just within the swamp."

Fort Shackelford, then, was a blockhouse, possibly with picketing. Contemporary hand-drawn maps of Fort Denaud (of which Fort Shackelford was a subsidiary) indicate around ten smaller structures in addition to the main blockhouse, with no evidence for picketing at this location (Webb 1909, 411). In 1862, Dennis Hart Mahan, a military engineer at West Point and the contemporary authority on American fortifications, described the typical structural components of a fort, which included picketing and a two-story blockhouse usually constructed of the same material as the picketing (Mahan 1862, 63). Pine is believed to have been used because of the relative uniformity of the wood. However, in a description of the erection of Fort Simon Drum (Collier County), cypress was used for the fortification (Wickman 1985, 311). At the location of Fort Shackelford, both types of wood were available and could have been used.

An April 20, 1855, letter from Lieutenant and Acting Assistant Adjutant-General Thomas J. Haines to Captain Bennett H. Hill states that the men stationed at the fort were "soon to be withdrawn" for the summer/wet season and that any company being sent across the region should be equipped with adequate provisions for the return to Fort Dallas (modern Miami) (Eck 2002, 86). By June, the soldiers at Fort Shackelford had abandoned the blockhouse due to flooding. Later that year, on December 7, 1855, Lieutenant George L. Hartsuff, in command of an exploring party headed toward the Big Cypress to survey the area, found that Fort Shackelford had been burned (Eck 2002, 92). While returning from Big Cypress, the party was ambushed by Seminoles near Billy Bowleg's camp on December 20—an incident that marks the beginning of the Third Seminole War (Covington 1982; Missall and Missall 2004, 213). The site location, construction, and naming of this military outpost are only the beginning of this fort's long journey through time.

History of Big Cypress and Copeland's Marker

By the end of the Third Seminole War in 1858, a few hundred Seminoles remained in their South Florida home despite efforts by the federal government to force them to move to Indian lands out west. Those who stayed in their Florida homeland entered a period of very limited contact with outsiders (Sturtevant 1971). Until the late nineteenth and early twentieth centuries, the Seminole people restricted any regular interactions with others to traders at trading posts and few others. By 1899, the main parcels of the Big Cypress Seminole Indian Reservation, totaling 14,000 acres, had been set aside for the Seminoles. The Big Cypress Reservation included the location of Fort Shackelford.

Unfortunately, the burning of Fort Shackelford soon after it was built in 1855 left little of its existence for people coming later to find in the landscape. Nonetheless, in the 1940s, D. Graham Copeland (surveyor for Collier County) sought to mark the location of Fort Shackelford and other locations associated with the Seminole Wars in South Florida. He did this "by using military maps that started being drawn in the year 1839. He used these maps to not only record the trails and routes, of the Second and Third Seminole Wars used by the U.S. Army, but he also used letters, archives, and interviews of the older pioneers in the area, including many of the Seminole leaders" (Hammond 2008, 73).

By this time, nearly ninety years had passed since the burning of Fort Shackelford, and this military installation had already garnered a reputation for being "elusive" (Goggin 1948, 354). Close examination of Copeland's efforts to mark the location of Fort Shackelford introduced more questions than answers.

Despite the careful records kept by Copeland, the placement of the concrete marker for Fort Shackelford remains today somewhat shrouded in mystery. We discovered this recently when we became aware of a letter written by Copeland to W. Stanley Hanson that adds more fog to the Shackelford location mystery. The Hanson Collection contains a letter dated June 19, 1941, from D. Graham Copeland to Hanson, who was a Fort Myers tax collector and a Lee County commissioner who advocated for the Seminole people and was known as the "White Medicine Man." In the letter, Copeland states that

we headed for the Indian Reservation where we hoped to see you and get you to point out to us the location of old Fort Shackleford [sic] so that it could be monumented. Unfortunately, we did not get there.

I gave Mr. Faire a concrete monument and a specially prepared brass circle, giving the details, to be mounted on top of the monument on the site of the old Fort.

I will greatly appreciate you and Mr. Faire and your associates planting this monument on the site of old Fort Shackleford [sic] as soon as it can be conveniently done.

When the monument has been planted, will you kindly refer it by bearing and distance to the *nearest* Government Section corner and advise me as to these data, so that I may have a record thereof. (Hanson Collection)

Clearly, Copeland did not personally set the concrete monument with a brass disk atop at the site of Fort Shackelford. Instead, he entrusted the positioning of the marker to Hanson and Faire, who presumably did so later in response to Copeland's request.

But the question of whether the correct site was originally marked is raised by Copeland himself, who writes later in the same letter to Hanson:

Sam Thompson also told me yesterday that the site of old Fort Shackleford [sic] was outside of the original Indian Reservation. . . . This is extremely at variance with all previous information I have been able to gather on the subject. . . .

Will you kindly check this and advise me as to your findings? I feel sure that you will know definitely the location of old Fort Shackleford [sic]. (Hanson Collection)

Was Sam Thompson's memory faulty regarding another location for the fort? And did Hanson "know definitely the location" of Fort Shackelford?

Our initial efforts followed a traditional archaeological field school trajectory of background research prior to fieldwork. We knew a little about the environment, the types of fortifications typically constructed in South Florida during this conflict, and the soldier for whom the fort was named. We also discovered that while Copeland did not personally place the concrete marker for Fort Shackelford, he appears instead to have directed its placement by someone he thought would know its location. The archaeologists who had deceived Jose Billie had come and gone by 1941 when the concrete marker was positioned to mark the location of Fort Shackelford. In the background, Josie Billie's cautionary tale played on.

What Do We Know of the Environment?

This historical context provided us with a backdrop for the events that transpired during the Seminole Wars as well as Copeland's effort to mark the fort's location in 1941. We utilized additional traditional archaeological lines of evidence to add depth to our understanding of this location.

Local Setting

The concrete marker placed under the direction of Copeland in 1941 is in an area of low topographic relief as compared to the slightly higher landforms located to the north and west. It is characterized by low, flat topography. The general soils consist of sand, limestone, and organic deposits supporting a myriad of features such as wet prairies, cypress heads, hammocks, and so forth. Slash pine (*Pinus elliottii*) is the dominant pine species (Abrahamson and Hartnett 1992, 103–107, 114).

During six months of the year, the water table is within 30 centimeters of the surface and the depth to bedrock is shallow. Today, the area is a pastureland that has been transformed for agricultural use by clearing the natural vegetation, leveling the land surface, and excavating a series of drainage ditches. Directly to the west of the suspected Fort Shackelford site is a wetland that is typical for marshes found at the edge of the Everglades (Belz et al. 1990, 54). This area is ponded six to nine months of the year and supports both cypress (genus *Taxodium* in the cypress family, *Cupressaceae*) and pond-apple (*Annona glabra*).

One of the most influential factors in this ecosystem are the seasonal changes in precipitation, with a pronounced wet season during the summer months when flooding often occurs. Standing water can be expected during the rainy season (Abrahamson and Hartnett 1992, 107).

Numerous early narratives describe the difficulty of traversing the southern Florida landscape. For instance, the military road leading from Fort Simon Drum to Fort Shackelford "can be traversed by wagons as far as Fort

Shackelford, during the dry season; places being occasionally met with that are boggy and somewhat difficult to cross. Oak and pine islands are seen about six miles to the north of the road; often appearing in the distance like an unbroken line of forest" (Ives 1856, 26). Because of these environmental conditions, U.S. military strategy had to address the seasonal difficulties associated with operating a field campaign in a landscape that, for six months of the year, was inundated.

In a July 15, 1855, letter from Brevet Colonel John Munroe to Colonel Samuel Cooper and Colonel Lorenzo Thomas, Munroe writes: "Sir, As the season for active operations in this Peninsula has closed, and the troops have been withdrawn from the field," suggesting seasonal military operations (Eck 2002, 89). Military operations in the interior areas of the southern peninsula of Florida, then, were limited to the dry season. In fact, in the same letter, Munroe reports that Fort Thompson was abandoned in favor of Fort Denaud as it was less likely to flood. Munroe's letter report ends with an overview of the landscape, stating that "the Country examined South of the Caloosa-Hatchee so reported as entirely worthless for agricultural purposes with the exception of a few small scattered Hammocks, and in the summer season, nearly the whole of it is under water" (Eck 2002, 94). It is important to underscore this implication as counterintuitive to our modern heritage management concepts, which tend to focus on the permanence of important places. Military installations such as Fort Shackelford were always intended, then, to be temporary. Minimal investment and seasonal occupation of forts was normal practice for a conflict that had shifted geographic focus for more than half a century.

Results of Archaeological Investigations

Preliminary efforts to understand the project area provided a good foundation for moving forward, and all results appeared to support the accuracy of the marker. For example, Geographic Information System (GIS) research showed that the projected location of Fort Shackelford was probably in the general vicinity of the Copeland marker, although thought to be up to 250 meters to the west.

Examination of early aerials of the area reveals that between 1940 and the late 1960s, the project area shows massive changes to the landscape. An east–west canal was constructed south of the concrete marker, with drainage ditches crisscrossing the pastures. Push-up piles were also present in the 1960s as a result of the land-clearing process and can be seen in the vicinity of the concrete marker.

Ground-penetrating radar (GPR) was conducted over 13,750 square meters, with 10,000 square meters centered on Copeland's concrete marker. No distinct linear features were noted in the resultant GPR renders. However, a very interesting circular feature was noted to the southeast of Copeland's marker. Ground inspection gave few clues as to whether the feature was caused by plant growth, a raised surface, subsurface archaeological features, or a mixture of all of these. Other anomalies were also noted.

Three separate metal-detecting surveys were conducted prior to the field school. A historic musket ball, two historic buckshot, one historic lead bullet, one button cover with anchor and rope design, an unknown metal in a "u" or "v" shape, and a modern pull tab were found in the vicinity of the Copeland marker. These results continued to support the concrete marker's potential accuracy.

A series of six 2 × 2 meter test units were set out to investigate GPR anomalies and the area around the concrete marker. Highly corroded ferrous metal fragments, charcoal fragments, two cut nails, and a buckshot ball were recovered from the unit placed northeast of the marker. More metal fragments, buckshot, a possible rivet, and a badly corroded container, along with charcoal fragments, were recovered to the southwest of the marker. The unit placed to explore the circular anomaly discovered during the GPR survey revealed a dark gray linear east–west-aligned anomaly that appears to be associated with agricultural activities. The remaining two units similarly contained dark gray linear east–west-aligned anomalies that appear to be associated with agricultural practices. A total of three shovel tests were dug in the nearby push-piles that resulted from land clearing. A significant amount of historic artifacts were recovered in these tests, including glass, ceramic fragments, and metal fragments—all dating from the late nineteenth/early twentieth century and likely associated with historic Seminole camps.

Analysis

A total of 260 artifacts were recovered from the 2008–2009 field seasons (Table 9.1). The majority of these artifacts were nondiagnostic metal fragments. There was nothing that would point definitively to our having found the location of the fort, although one metal artifact in particular initially appeared to have a clear connection to military activity. Recovered during a preliminary metal detector survey was a metal button with a fouled anchor design on it (see Figure 9.3). The button was of interest since the U.S. Navy was involved during the Seminole War actions that took place in the Everglades. Therefore,

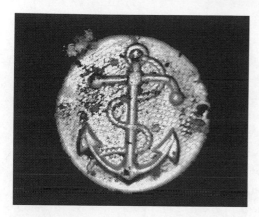

Figure 9.3. Fouled anchor design on lead button cover discovered during metal detecting surveys prior to the 2009 Archaeological Field School. By permission of the Ah-Tah-Thi-Ki Museum. (ATTK Catalog No. 2008.9.3)

early on we believed that this location may, in fact, reveal itself as the site of the fort.

Research into historical military buttons revealed similar designs, but none seemed to match the distinctive and clear design from this item. Vertical fouled anchor designs (like the one found on this button cover) are somewhat common in navy junior officer buttons. But the design present on this button cover is different from these genuine designs in that it lacks a border and also has diagonal stippling in the field. Historical examples resembling our artifact include a fouled vertical anchor with a border and horizontal striping in the field (see Plate 35, Examples 329-A–329-L in Johnson 1959; and Plate D-20 Navy Buttons Used during the Late 1840s–1865 Period Example 10-NA236A1 in Tice 1997). Ultimately, there were no matches to the design of this button piece with actual historic military buttons.

The possibility of the button fragment being from a modern-era button has been confirmed by experts familiar with material culture from the Seminole Wars and military accoutrements. Gary Ellis notes that "on its face it most closely resembles a style popular in the 1950 and 60s for pseudo and mod-style navy jackets. The buttons were foreign-made with pot-metal cores and cheap stamped iron sheet-metal outers" (Gary Ellis, personal communication, January 3, 2011). Jonathan Leader agreed with Ellis's suspicions that it is modern and pointed to the composition of nearly 100 percent lead as similar to that of tire balancing weights (Jonathan Leader, personal communication, January 4, 2011). Ellis also noted that the field of dappling or dimpling is uncommon for military designs, as he believes it would be too hard to polish and iron (Gary Ellis, personal communication, January 3, 2011), further supporting the conclusion that this item is from the modern era.

But there was more information to be mined from this artifact that came from the community. Moses Jumper Jr., current manager of the pastures under investigation, shared crucial information that yielded a likely explanation for this artifact. His father, Moses Jumper Sr., managed the property from 1963 to 1993 and was known to have owned and worn replica uniform jackets (Moses Jumper Jr., personal communication, 2009). We eventually concluded that this button piece belonged to a replica pea jacket (a common fashion in the 1950s and 1960s) possibly belonging to Moses Jumper Sr. Without this valuable community information and participation, our conclusions would not have been so clear, nor would we ever have been able to potentially connect this unique artifact to an actual person. Community insights drove our conclusions forward significantly. While we still believed that nondiagnostic metal artifacts may have come from the fort, we found there was more to learn from the community.

Community Knowledge

Additional lines of information from the Tribal community emerged during and following the field school that suggest we may not have been exactly where we originally believed—at the precise site of Fort Shackelford. Only through the participation of the Tribal members were we able to gain a deeper understanding of our results and the meaning of those results within a physical and cultural landscape.

* * *

In building a framework for traditional archaeological research, we did not know in what way community involvement would impact our efforts and conclusions about what we discovered. The information provided by Moses Jumper Jr. about the fouled anchor button cover potentially links the artifact with a specific Tribal member, his father, Moses Jumper Sr. We did not have the knowledge to be able to make that connection, and without community input, that connection would likely have been lost entirely.

But perhaps the most compelling and illuminating information provided by the community arises from Josie Billie's cautionary tale. A wariness of outsiders has led to a campaign of disinformation that confuses rather than reveals the knowledge being sought by outsiders.

Moving the Concrete Marker

In speaking with Councilman Manuel Tiger about Fort Shackelford, he also indicated that following Josie Billie's incident with the archaeologists in the 1930s, Tribal members moved Copeland's concrete marker away from the actual site of Fort Shackelford. The monument was not destroyed, as he explained, because it is important to retain the memory of the campaign or battle that took place there and at which the Seminoles prevailed (Manuel Tiger, personal communication, August 21, 2014). But by moving it away from the original location, the risk of disturbance of the site by outsiders was reduced. This community knowledge is priceless in better understanding our results. With no diagnostic artifacts to absolutely confirm that the concrete marker does denote the location of Fort Shackelford, further investigations are required to understand the location of the marker in relationship to more certain evidence of the fort. As a result of this information, we began to view the location of the concrete marker with more caution. The efforts of the community to obscure the location of the fort to prying outside eyes may come directly as a result of the deception experienced by Josie Billie and his cautionary tale.

Metal Detectorists

As we worked to write up a draft report on our results and conclusions from our field school, we thought we had all the information possible on the fort's location, and we shared our thoughts with community members who had still more to add to this story. One report from the community involved metal detectorists visiting the Fort Shackelford site on the Big Cypress Reservation. The account is that the Seminole Tribe was once asked in the 1970s by metal detector enthusiasts to go to the Fort Shackelford site and search for historic metal artifacts. In order that their efforts might be fruitful, Tribal members scattered various metal fragments in an area they identified to the metal detectorist group as Fort Shackelford. In the archaeological field, this is referred to as "salting" the site. Unaware of the intentional addition of materials to a site, investigators frequently mistake them as genuine and originating from the activities under investigation. For us, it presented another fly in the ointment as far as interpreting the materials recovered.

Questions arose, then, about whether the precise location of the fort was used during this metal detecting party. Were some or all of the metal fragments found during archaeological fieldwork part of the remnant materials left behind after this event? Were these metal fragments added to the landscape in another effort to protect an important cultural site from interfering outside eyes? Our own eyes opened to the possibility that all or some of the materials collected during our archaeological field school were a result of this "salting" event rather than actual military activity. This may be another chapter in Josie Billie's cautionary tale.

THPO History and Function

Knowing about this past event involving people who were believed to have been archaeologists and who betrayed this important Tribal member, Josie Billie, also helps explain a related story of community efforts to hamper unwanted archaeological investigations. The first Tribal Historic Preservation Officer, William Steele, reportedly attempted to undertake archaeological fieldwork only to find his shovels missing from his field vehicle. No other equipment was disturbed (see Backhouse, this volume). By taking his shovels, they were able to hinder his digging without disturbing anything else. Archaeology is a science that handles materials that once belonged to those who have gone before—an area traditionally left untouched by the Seminole people. The betrayal of Josie Billie continues to serve as a cautionary tale about protecting Seminole culture and, to Tribal members, about archaeologists as well.

Conclusion

Community participation has been vital to understanding the role of Fort Shackelford in the community as well as the landscape where it was positioned. Josie Billie's cautionary tale about protecting culture for future generations can be seen weaving throughout the various histories associated with Fort Shackelford.

There is also no doubt that the establishment of collaborative relationships and the fundamental commitment to an indigenous perspective were extremely important outcomes of the archaeological field school. Tribal members were able to either visit the site or to watch two video broadcasts as excavations got under way. The first, "Fort Shackelford a Learning Journey with the THPO Field School on Big Cypress" (Seminole Media Productions 2009), was shot prior to the beginning of the fieldwork as students were arriving and setting up camp. The second, "Fort Shackelford Rediscovered" (Seminole Media Productions 2009), followed a documentary-style format at the site, highlighting the excavations with some interpretative content placing the

Table 9.1. Artifacts recovered by context during the 2008–2009 field season

Context	Surface Collection	Metal Detector Survey	Shovel Testing	Test Unit
Lead Shot	0	4	0	1
Metal Button Cover	0	1	0	0
Solder	0	0	0	2
Historic Nail	0	0	2	2
Unidentified Metal	31	0	29	160
Historic Glass	0	0	3	0
Unidentified Glass	1	0	14	0
Nottingham StonewareStoneware	6	0	1	0
Unidentified Prehistoric Ceramic	3	0	0	0
Total	41	5	49	165

evidence in the context of the history of the Big Cypress Reservation. We did not formally survey Tribal members who watched the broadcasts but understand that both were favorably received.

Students were able to critically examine the concept of "Tribal Archaeology" and to assess its application in relation to academic and cultural resource management (CRM) models typically taught in the classroom. This exercise was powerfully reinforced by the context of working and living with the local community. An additional and unanticipated consequence of the project was the self-reflective outcome for the staff of the THPO. The THPO is a young organization (authorized by the National Park Service in 2006) with no institutional memory of running a major field campaign. The ability therefore to explore various functions of the office during the afternoon symposia allowed staff to critically reflect on the core concepts and workflows that they have been working so hard to create.

The outcomes of this process were consistently positive, formalizing relationships and facilitating contemplation by both staff and students of the broader context of historic preservation and the role of indigenous perspectives in current archaeological practice. The knowledge shared by the Tribal community added great depth of understanding to this project and to the role of the community in protecting important cultural resources.

Looking for the precise location of Fort Shackelford continues to be an interest of the THPO. As historic maps and documents are discovered by staff, they are studied and analyzed for any clues that may emerge concerning the location of this still elusive fort. Plans for returning to the field to expand archaeological investigations remain on the table for consideration. Meanwhile, the Tribal community shares an interest in the location of the fort and activities associated with it.

In our efforts to confirm the site under investigation as that of Fort Shackelford, we discovered a deeper understanding of the fort that revealed it to be more than a location. It is a process, a dialogue, and a journey—one that has not ended and one whose importance is not so much in the destination but in the histories learned along the way, the building of relationships between researchers and the community, and understanding new ways of exploring historic events and their impacts on the affected communities. Locations of cultural significance to the Seminole Tribe, including Fort Shackelford, have for many generations been recognized as places to be guarded from outsiders. By protecting these sites, the community can hold on to their culture so the Tribe can flourish for years to come. In our interactions with the Seminole community, we discovered that they have been active in protecting their past and their culture so that the Tribe may continue to thrive.

Figure 9.4. Annette Snapp. By permission of Gene Davis, Facilities Manager, Ah-Tah-Thi-Ki Museum.

References Cited

Abrahamson, Warren G., and David C. Hartnett. 1992. "Pine Flatwoods and Dry Prairies." In *Ecosystems of Florida*, edited by Ronald L. Myers and John J. Ewel, 103–149. Orlando: University of Central Florida Press.

Bell, Christine. 2004. "Investigating Second Seminole War Sites in Florida: Identification through Limited Testing." Master's thesis, University of South Florida.

Belz, David J., Lewis J. Carter, David A. Dearstyne, and John D. Overing. 1990. *Soil Survey of Hendry County, Florida*. Washington, D.C.: U.S. Department of Agriculture, Soil Conservation Service.

Covington, James W. 1982. *The Billy Bowlegs Wars*. Chuluota, Fla.: Mickler Press.

———. 1993. *The Seminoles of Florida*. Gainesville: University Press of Florida.

Cullum, George W. 1891. *Biographical Register of Officers and Graduates of the U.S. Military Academy at West Point*, Vol. 1. 3rd ed. New York: Houghton, Mifflin.

Eck, Christopher R. 2002. "South Florida's Prelude to War: Army Correspondence Concerning Miami, Fort Dallas, and the Everglades Prior to the Outbreak of the Third Seminole War, 1850–1855." *Tequesta* 62:68–113.

Fairbanks, Charles H. 1974. *Ethnohistorical Report on the Florida Indians*. New York: Garland.

Goggin, John M. 1948. "A New Collier County Map." *Florida Historical Quarterly* 26(4):353–355.

Hahn, Steven C. 2004. *The Invention of the Creek Nation, 1670–1763*. Lincoln: University of Nebraska Press.

Hammond, James. 2008. *Florida's Vanishing Trail*. South Florida: self-published.

Hanson Collection. Letter from D. Graham Copeland to W. Stanley Hanson, June 19, 1941. On file, Ah-Tah-Thi-Ki Museum.

Ives, Lieutenant J. C. 1856. *Memoir to Accompany a Military Map of the Peninsula of Florida, South of Tampa Bay*. New York: M. B. Wynkoop, Book & Job Printer.

Jennings, Jay. 2001. "Fort Denaud: Logistics Hub of the Third Seminole War." *Florida Historical Quarterly* 80(1):24–42.

Johnson, David Funston 1959. *Uniform Buttons: American Armed Forces 1784-1948*. Watkins Glen, N.Y.: Century House.

MacCauley, Clay. 2000. *The Seminole Indians of Florida*. Gainesville: University Press of Florida.

Mahan, D. H. 1862. *A Treatise On Field Fortification. Containing Instructions On The Methods Of Laying Out, Constructing, Defending And Attacking Intrenchments, With The General Outlines Also Of The Arrangement, The Attack And Defense Of Permanent Fortifications*. New York: John Wiley.

Missall, John, and Mary Lou Missall. 2004. *The Seminole Wars: America's Longest Indian Conflict*. Gainesville: University Press of Florida.

Olsen, Stanley J. 1965. "A Seminole War Fort Site in Northern Florida." *American Antiquity* 30(4):491–494.

Orser, Charles E., Jr. 2010. "Twenty-First-Century Historical Archaeology." *Journal of Archaeological Research* 18:111–150.

Straight, William M. 1970. "Josie Billie, Seminole Doctor, Medicine Man and Baptist Preacher." *Journal of the Florida Medical Association* 57(8):33–40.

Sturtevant, William C., ed. 1971. *A Seminole Sourcebook.* London: Taylor and Francis.

Tice, Warren K. 1997. *Uniform Buttons of the United States 1776–1865.* Gettysburg, Pa.: Thomas Publications.

Webb, Alexander Stuart. 1909. "Campaigning in Florida in 1855." *Journal of the Military Service Institution of the United States* 45:397–429

Weisman, Brent Richards. 1989. *Like Beads on a String: A Culture History of the Seminole Indians in Northern Peninsular Florida.* Tuscaloosa: University of Alabama Press.

———. 1999. *Unconquered People: Florida's Seminole and Miccosukee Indians.* Gainesville: University Press of Florida.

Wickman, Patricia. 1985. "A Trifling Affair": Loomis Lyman Langdon and the Third Seminole War. *Florida Historical Quarterly* 63:303–317.

Wright, J. Leitch, Jr. 1986. *Creeks and Seminoles: The Destruction and Regeneration of the Muscogulge People.* Lincoln: University of Nebraska Press.

10

Tarakkvlkv (Land of Palms)

Bridging the Gap between Archaeology and Tribal Perspectives

MAUREEN MAHONEY

The most recent history of the Seminole Tribe of Florida (STOF), and its settlement on defined reservations, represents the tumultuous conclusion of a process that began with the European exploration of the North American continent more than 500 years earlier. The oftentimes harrowing history leading up to this point is well documented, but less so is the evolution of the communities Tribal members identify today as home. The recent history of the Brighton Reservation is contained in the settlement patterns of the camps established by the various groups moving onto lands of a hostile government—a government that had attempted, as recently as a generation prior, to forcibly remove them to Indian Territory. Collective memory is transferred through oral histories, but the patterns that emerge can be viewed through a broad temporal lens to reveal the sociocultural motivations of the broader population. The location of camps near the periphery of the reservation in the early years speaks to the mistrust of the families concerned about the ease of escape should they find themselves in peril from the U.S. government. Two decades later, the clustering of camps near schools, roads, and trading stores demonstrates a transition and connectedness to the non-Seminole world. These years were certainly formative in the history of the Tribe. The Tribal Historic Preservation Office (THPO) uses Geographical Information System (GIS) as the tool to draw together oral history and archaeological information in the telling of these important stories.

Author Bio

Maureen Mahoney has been working with the THPO since 2009, first as a Field Technician and moving into the role of Tribal Archaeologist in 2011.

Prior to working at the THPO, Mahoney graduated from Florida State University with an M.A. in anthropology and worked for the National Park Service and private cultural resource management (CRM) firms throughout the Southeast. As Tribal Archaeologist, Maureen advocates for collaboration with Tribal members in order to reflexively incorporate indigenous perspectives into heritage management and decision making.

Introduction

Seminole families who survived the brutal conflicts that characterized the nineteenth century faced new challenges in the twentieth century. The Seminoles were adapting to massive social, economic, and ecological changes (Covington 1993; Spoehr 1941). To date, only a small amount of research has focused on their physical occupation of distinct camps and their choices of settlement locations in the early to mid-twentieth century. This chapter (in combination with Fenno et al., this volume) furthers this research by using Tribal archaeological tenets combining archaeological fieldwork results with collaborations by Tribal members to complete an examination of settlement patterns for the Seminole Tribe of Florida's Brighton Reservation, situated on the northwestern corner of Lake Okeechobee. Although it is possible to undertake these analyses with only one line of evidence (that is, the archaeological record *or* oral histories *or* the use of GIS), combining all available lines of appropriate information provides a fuller understanding of the cultural history of Seminoles moving onto the reservation at this critical time. This examination also highlights an example of a project where both the analyses and the interpretations are undertaken by collaborating with community members, allowing for many voices to be heard.

There are two primary goals for completing this analysis. First, it will be useful for archaeologists working in South Florida unfamiliar with settlement patterns of mid-twentieth-century Seminole camps. The documentation of these sites is important so they are not overlooked during development projects. Since the archaeological record for this type of site is often only composed of generic glass, ceramic, or faunal remains, it may be difficult for archaeologists to note it accurately. While these artifacts provide information about a portion of the camp's makeup (as detailed in Fenno et al., this volume), this chapter broadens these interpretations by working with Tribal members to determine why people chose to settle camps in specific areas. This information will allow archaeologists to recognize and assign these sites as camps and to understand the social, historical, and economic context of the people that lived (and still live) in them. We hope that by humanizing the recent past in this way, heritage planners will have a broader understanding of Seminole culture and history and the importance of engaging the Tribe in heritage management decisions regarding their preservation and interpretation.

A secondary, but just as important, goal for this chapter is to provide THPOs a case study for an applicable project in which heritage management and Tribal wishes are in concert. As explained in the Fenno et al. chapter in this volume, the STOF THPO's focus was once the prehistoric sites on the reservations, which ultimately led to a disconnect between the THPO and the community. The camp research that is highlighted in this chapter illustrates one project undertaken in order to bridge the gap between archaeology (and other heritage management concepts) and the community so that archaeology is combined with Tribal wishes. These camps hold special meaning to community members because they are the camps of their grandparents and parents. Working with Tribal members on sites relevant to them has greatly strengthened our THPO program; has allowed us as archaeologists to work with community members to determine the methodology, interpretations, and preservation options for each project; and has placed the heritage management decisions in the hands of the community. Our hope is that THPOs across the country will find this information useful when they document their recent history and introduce archaeology to their Tribes.

The Land of Palms

The study area for this chapter is the Brighton Reservation. The majority of the inhabitants of the reservation are descended from Muskogee-speaking Creeks who arrived in Florida from Alabama and Georgia in the early eighteenth century (Covington 1993). However, many Tribal members also explain that they have always been in Florida, an interpretation that should not be overlooked (Jack Chalfant, personal communication, July 2015; Bowers, this volume).

The settlement pattern of the Creeks and early Seminoles in Florida was the (Creek) *talwa*-type settlement of a square ground located near a major river (Weisman 1989). Around this central area were individual frame houses, constructed around their own smaller square ground (McReynolds 1957; Blakney-Bailey 2007). Toward the end of the eighteenth century and the beginning of the nineteenth century, settlement patterns changed to better suit an agropastoralist subsistence lifestyle. The new pattern consisted of domiciles more widely dispersed and not centered on a square ground, situated on well-drained upland soils best for crops such as maize (Covington 1993; McReynolds 1957; Milanich 1995, 1998; Weisman 1989, 1999, 2000a, 2000b).

With the occurrence of the Seminole Wars, Seminoles from central and north Florida began pushing south into the denser swamps around Lake Okeechobee and the Big Cypress region. During and after the wars, the Seminoles in Florida began settling in clan camps, similar to the matrilocal residences that once made up the *talwa* (Weisman 1989, 1999, 2000a). These clan camps served as the permanent camps of the inhabitants and contained not only the domestic structures but also small garden plots. Residence at the camp was based on matrilineal descent, which meant that the camps contained the woman and her daughters and their children and husbands, as well as any unmarried brothers (Covington 1976).

The Cow Creek Settlements

Those Seminoles who settled around Lake Okeechobee during and after the Seminole Wars were known as the Cow Creek Seminoles. Camps of the Cow Creeks were mostly situated in St. Lucie County or Martin County or near Fish Eating Creek, which flows northwest from Lake Okeechobee. In 1884, Clay MacCauley noted two settlements—the Fish Eating Creek camp and the Cow Creek camp—that were associated with Cow Creek Seminoles (Figure 10.1). The Cow Creek settlement had twelve inhabitants and the Fish Eating Creek settlement thirty-two (MacCauley 2000, 478). According to MacCauley (2000, 478), each settlement consisted of an unknown number of camps that were approximately .5 mile (805 meters) to 2 or more miles (3,218 meters) apart, while the settlements were 40 to 60 miles (64–97 kilometers) apart. Each camp was situated on upland tree islands that were higher than the surrounding wet prairie and generally near deep-water sources, such as creeks or ponds. These tree islands would remain dry during the summer months, which typically contain periods of flooding. The hammocks were also used for gardens in which the Seminoles grew pumpkins, corn, beans, and squash (Lorene Gopher, personal communication, August 2012). While MacCauley's work is invaluable, later documents (Nash 1931; Spoehr 1941) reveal the presence of more than the two settlements recorded by MacCauley, meaning that other Cow Creek settlements probably existed in the late nineteenth century.

While MacCauley was able to record the general makeup of these camps, his temporally fixed view does not bring attention to the locational changes of the Cow Creek camps. For example, former chairwoman of the Tribe Betty Mae Jumper remembers that the Fish Eating Creek settlement mentioned by MacCauley moved four times in a thirty-year period (Jumper and West 2001).

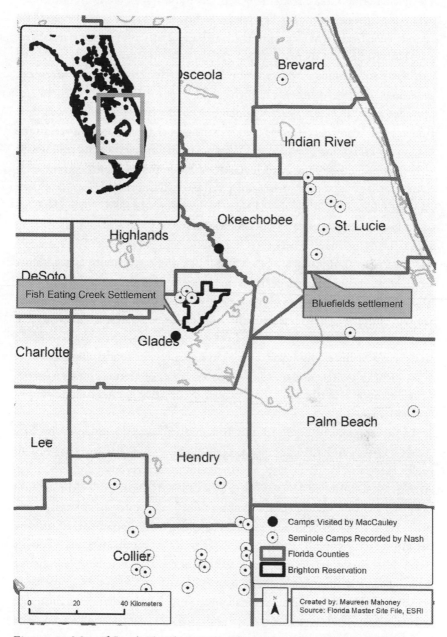

Figure 10.1. Map of South Florida counties, the Brighton Reservation, and sites mentioned by Clay MacCauley (1884) and Roy Nash (1931). Created by Maureen Mahoney, Tribal Archaeologist, Seminole Tribe of Florida Tribal Historic Preservation Office.

The Fish Eating Creek settlement was led by Jumper's great-grandmother, who was a member of the Snake Clan and whose family had moved from Wild Island (near Sebring, Florida) to this settlement in 1868 (Jumper and West 2001). According to Ober (1875, 142, 171), the settlement contained thirty-two chickees and included a square ground. In 1878, due to cattle operations encroaching onto the Seminole camp, the settlement moved to the Bluefield area (Jumper and West 2001, 11). One member of this later settlement was Billy Bowlegs III, who was raised as a child with this clan and later moved to the Brighton Reservation (Jumper and West 2001, 3). During this time, numerous clan camps could be found at Bluefield. Willie Johns (personal communication, August 2014) remembers seeing pictures of his mother and aunts at their Panther Clan camp in Bluefield before he was born. In 1889, the Snake Clan camp became tainted due to the Bluefield massacre and was relocated to an area along State Road 70 between Okeechobee and Fort Pierce. This massacre occurred when Jim Jumper, a black Seminole, murdered multiple Seminoles when he was refused marriage to a Seminole woman (Jumper and West 2001, 6). Later, like many families in the area, the Snake Clan camp moved to Indiantown (Jumper and West 2001, 29). These camps were strategically placed in order to access the Bowers Trading Post in Indiantown, where families could trade alligator hides and huckleberries in exchange for foodstuffs or hunting equipment (Covington 1976, 55). In this instance, economic and subsistence considerations as well as logistical proximity greatly affected the location of the settlements.

Later camps near Bluefield and Indiantown were documented by Roy Nash, who was an Indian agent tasked with determining the number of Seminoles living in Florida in 1930. In his report to the commissioner of Indian Affairs, Nash included a map that shows the location of camps throughout South Florida. Although Nash was able to document a number of camps, it is probable that not all Seminole camps were recorded since most were "hidden" behind dense vegetation, purposefully done to keep outsiders out (Spoehr 1941). It is also possible that the inhabitants were at temporary camps for hunting or gathering. According to Kersey (1989), one such temporary camp was occupied by Naha Tiger and his family in 1934 when they were gathering huckleberries. The map produced by Nash suggests that the camps associated with the Cow Creeks were located mostly in St. Lucie County, though a small number also occurred in Martin, Palm Beach, and Glades Counties. The three camps in Glades County (Billy Stewart camp, Charlie Micco camp, and Billy Bowlegs III camp) indicate the use of this area prior to the formation of the reservation in 1935.

The Creation and Organization of the Brighton Reservation

Before the development of the Brighton Reservation, the camps inhabited by the Seminoles were scattered on the state of Florida, U.S. government, or private property lands (Covington 1976). In January 1934, it was agreed that the scattered reservation lands should be consolidated and new tracts should be purchased. The lands for the Brighton Reservation were set aside between 1935 and 1938 and consisted of 35,279 acres (14,276 hectares) of land. Officially, the reservation opened on June 13, 1935, though not all Seminoles immediately moved to the reservation (Kersey 1989, 96). This land initially looked promising for the Seminoles. It had the high, dry tree islands they used for habitation and raising a garden and hogs; however, it proved to contain some deficiencies. First, the reservation was, and continues to be, broken up with off-reservation parcels that belong to an agricultural company. Furthermore, ranchers surrounding the reservation prior to its establishment constructed multiple ditches and canals in order to drain their land, though this gave way to water flowing onto the reservation land, making it easily flooded (Covington 1976, 60).

The formation of the reservation brought newly developed areas and programs designed to enrich the lives of the Seminoles. Alexander Spoehr, an ethnologist working on his dissertation, which detailed the kinship and makeup of camps, documented these new programs and developed areas when he visited the reservation in 1939. One important newly formed program at that time was the cattle industry. The cattle industry had a slow start, but with the motivation of Tribal members and U.S. government officials, by 1937 it became an economic success as a self-sufficient Tribal program. In 1939, three cattle trustees were elected by the Brighton community to help run the cattle industry. The first three trustees were Charlie Micco, John Josh, and Willy Gopher (Covington 1980, 33). An additional federal program, the Civilian Conservation Corps–Indian Division (CCC-ID), also helped with the formation of the cattle industry. This program began employing Tribal members in January 1934. The CCC-ID was responsible for erecting and repairing fences, improving the trees and shrubs, digging wells, installing windmills and trails, planting Bahia grass for cattle, erecting a telephone line, and building a garage and bridge (Covington 1976, 62). In 1941, the CCC-ID was also responsible for constructing the Red Barn, which housed the horses of the cowboys who worked the cattle around the reservation (Dilley and Gopher, this volume).

An important newly developed area that emerged at approximately the same time as the cattle industry was the administration complex. The complex was situated in the northern part of the reservation and consisted of a school, a community workroom for crafts, a shop, men's and women's showers, a laundry room, quarters for the teacher's family, a playground, and a group of chickees for transient Seminoles (Covington 1993). A small cattle pen was once situated on the western side of this complex (Willie Johns, personal communication, October 2014), and a clinic was in the northern part (Jack Chalfant, personal communication, October 2014). This administration complex was also the location where food commodities were held when they were brought in from Hollywood, Florida, and before they were delivered to each of the camps on Brighton (Willie Johns, personal communication, October 2014). Another important portion of the complex was the school, which opened in 1939. According to Kersey (1989, 104), this school became the "hub of community life at the Brighton Reservation before the wholesale conversions to Christianity brought by Baptist churches." In the initial days of the school, the students were picked up at their camp by their teachers, William Boehmer and his wife, Edith. Approximately 30 percent of school-age students attended the school in its early days, though this number increased in the 1940s (Covington 1976, 63). In the 1960s, the administration complex was moved to the central portion of the reservation near newly constructed Housing and Urban Development (HUD) housing. Many Tribal members moved away from their camps with the construction of these HUD houses. The camps may have also moved closer to the electrical lines, which were established along major roadways in the 1930s (Jack Chalfant, personal communication, July 2014).

Beginning in the 1950s, Baptist churches came to play a large role in the life of many of the Seminoles living on the reservation. Missionaries, such as Willie King and Stanley Smith, had been contacting the Cow Creek Seminoles since the early 1930s and would go to the various camps to preach (Onnie Osceola, personal communication, September 2014). In 1951, Billy Osceola began a small church at the Huff camp, where people from all over Brighton, as well as Immokalee and Big Cypress, would come and listen to his sermons (John Huff, personal communication, August 2014). In 1959, many notable Seminoles organized the Southern Baptist church directly to the north of the reservation boundary. In order to keep Christianity from entering Brighton, no church was permitted on the reservation until later in time (Onnie Osceola, personal communication, September 2014).

Despite the hurdles of the early days, the Brighton Reservation has thrived to become what it is today. Remnants of the early reservation–period structures and sites still exist, but the reservation has dramatically changed. The Red Barn still stands and is celebrated as a monument to Brighton's early cattle days. Furthermore, archaeological work in the administration building complex found remnants of the old cattle pen that was once used. Today, approximately 31,822 acres (12,878 hectares) are identified as agricultural land split between pastures for cattle and sugarcane fields. Environmentally, the Brighton Reservation has drastically changed since it was formed in 1935. Multiple canals and ditches have since been constructed to help drain pastures of excess water. Although many of the high, dry tree islands still exist, many others have been cleared of vegetation for various types of development. As mentioned previously, the administration hub of the reservation is no longer situated in the northern portion of the reservation but is now in the central portion. Home sites of the approximately 637 people now living on the reservation are spread throughout Brighton, though many cluster where their family camps were once situated.

Methodology

Each camp documented by the THPO is investigated by working with Tribal members to determine the appropriate level of archaeological survey and what information should be included in the full written analysis (see Fenno et al., this volume, for an explanation on how and why the THPO documents camps). Archaeological investigations are supplemented by collaborating with Tribal members who explain how a camp was composed while it was in use, including who lived there as well as information about the occupants' daily lives. All the above-mentioned forms of investigation are part of the routine Tribal Archaeology Section's examination of camps. The outcomes of these examinations not only highlight the positive contributions of collaborative projects but also show that these types of projects make the interpretation of the archaeological record richer. The THPO has been able to document a number of camps, and we strive to continue to make this documentation a collaborative learning process. The community members and archaeologists work together in order to record, preserve, and interpret camps in ways appropriate to the Tribal government, the federal government, and, most important, the communities that make up the Seminole Tribe of Florida.

Camp Site Analysis

For this study, I examined the thirty-three permanent camp sites on the Brighton Reservation that were listed on the THPO's Seminole Site File by July 2014 (Table 10.1; Figure 10.2). A thirty-fourth camp has been documented by the THPO, though because no known dates for its occupancy have been determined, I did not use this camp for the analysis. I also did not use the temporary camp locations for this examination since their locations are much harder to note, as they may have only been settled for a few days. Camps examined in this chapter are listed by either the name of a male inhabitant of the camp or the matriarch's name, as both names have been used by Tribal members to explain the camp to the THPO. Many of the camps examined moved many times during the decades analyzed. For example, inhabitants of the Johns camp moved four times from 1940 to 1960 while they were on the reservation. For these instances, the camp is listed by the sequence in which it was settled (for example, first Johns camp, second Johns camp). The camps that I analyzed were settled on the reservation between 1900 and 1960, though most camps were occupied between 1935 and 1959. Data for each of the camps was at times gathered through participatory mapping (Cancel, this volume), while at other times it was obtained through recording a single camp for listing on the Tribal Register of Historic Places (Mullins, this volume) or when encountering remnants of a camp while surveying for development projects. While many dates were obtained through working with Tribal members, by analyzing the location of the camps on historic aerials, or with diagnostic artifacts, the dates are often broad and not specific. I chose 1960 camps as the end date for the analysis because, at this point, many Tribal members were moving into the HUD houses being constructed in the central portion of the reservation. In order to note the changes of the settlement patterns over sixty years, I examined the location of camps per decade. This allowed me to analyze the camp locations for a small window of time and permitted a comparison between their locations and what was occurring historically on the reservation.

Archaeological data for each of the camps is not provided in this chapter but can be found for the Tom Smith and fourth Johns camps in Fenno et al. (this volume). Although it is not provided, the archaeological fieldwork completed to examine these camps aided in developing this chapter since many of the camps were first documented by the THPO through the artifacts found at the sites. The archaeological data was not incorporated into the analysis since many of the artifacts were generic glass or ceramic artifacts that helped to determine an approximate date and allowed us to note the site as a camp, but did not readily provide patterns that might hint at the reason why specific locations were chosen for settlement. Although the archaeological data did not add as much to this chapter as traditional archaeology settlement pattern studies might warrant, it highlights how collaborating with Tribal members can result in a greater understanding of these historic lifeways. However, future examinations of these artifacts and their distribution might clarify historic camp

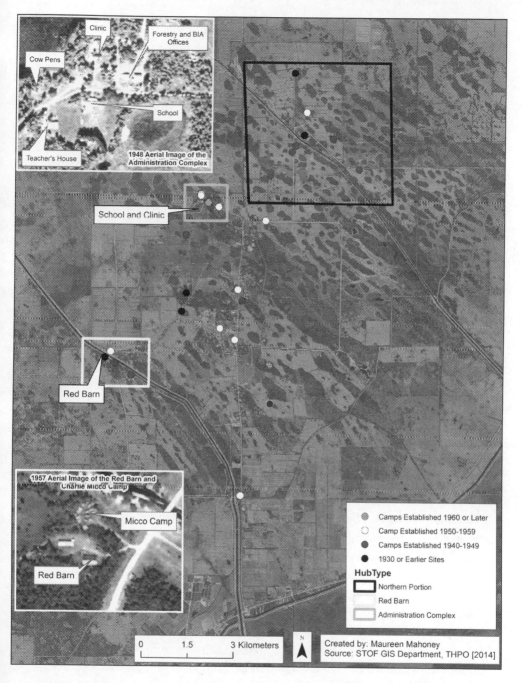

Figure 10.2. Map showing the various camps mentioned in the text and their date of establishment. Two call-outs—one near the administration complex and one near the Red Barn—show the makeup of these areas. Created by Maureen Mahoney, Tribal Archaeologist, Seminole Tribe of Florida Tribal Historic Preservation Office.

locations even more than what is presented here. Furthermore, interpretations presented in this chapter were not solely determined by THPO archaeologists; rather, we worked with community members to document these camp locations and settlement patterns.

Historic Camp Settlement Patterns Over Time

Based on the background research, each time period analyzed for this chapter corresponds with a major occurrence or cultural influence of the time. The first time period (1930s and earlier) correlates to the formation of the reservation in 1935. During this period, there were only a small number of families living on and using the reservation land. Programs such as the cattle industry and the school had just started to form and had not yet become immensely popular. The 1940s correspond most directly with the rise of the cattle industry and the use of the administration complex. The last two decades (1950s and 1960s) are associated with the administration complex as well as a new settlement pattern in which the camps were settled along major roadways.

The 1930s and Earlier Camp: The Reservation Formation Period

By separating the camps by decade, I was able to discern seven camps found in the reservation or slightly off the reservation (Billy Bowlegs first camp, Charlie Micco's off-reservation camp) that were established in the 1930s or earlier (Figure 10.3). Three camps—the John Jimmie camp, the Bowlegs first camp, and the Charlie Micco off-reservation camp—were established prior to the formation of the reservation. After the reservation's creation in 1935, Bowlegs and Micco moved to on-reservation camps, Eli Morgan and Jake Morgan established new camps, and John Jimmie remained at his first camp. The camps that were established both on and off the reservation were located on high, dry tree islands that deterred water in the wet season.

In comparison to the five camps that the THPO recorded as forming between 1935 and 1939, Spoehr (1941) recorded the existence of thirteen camps during this time period. Spoehr's map (1941, 11), while somewhat skewed in shape, shows that the camps on the Brighton Reservation were organized so that they fell near other similar clan camps. According to Spoehr, Bird Clan camps were situated in the northern part of the reservation, Talahasee (later combined with Bird) Clan camps were located in the western portion of the reservation, Panther Clan camps were found in the northern and eastern sections of the reservation, and Deer and Snake Clan camps were in the southern part of the reservation. There are some similarities noted between the THPO

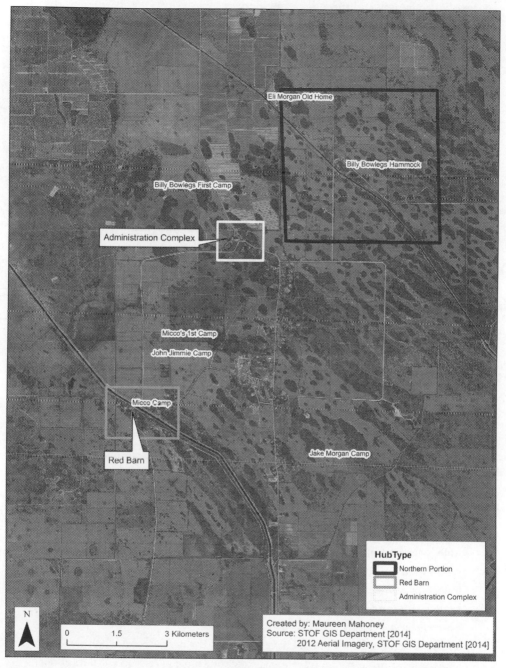

Figure 10.3. Map displaying the location of camps established in the 1930s or earlier and what hubs they were settled in or near. Created by Maureen Mahoney, Tribal Archaeologist, Seminole Tribe of Florida Tribal Historic Preservation Office.

recorded camps and those noted by Spoehr (Figure 10.4). According to the THPO data, the Panther and Bird Clan camps were situated similarly to where Spoehr found them. In contrast to Spoehr's map, no Deer or Snake Clan camps are known to exist in the southern portion of the reservation during this time or even later (Geneva Shore, personal communication, October 2014). Since Tribal elders, such as Geneva Shore, do not remember Snake or Deer Clan camps in this area, it is possible that Spoehr did not accurately record them. However, it is clear that not all camps mentioned by Spoehr have been recorded by the THPO.

While all of the earliest known camps were spread throughout the reservation and slightly off the reservation, many were settled to be near a work site. Generally, these work sites were areas used to work cattle, such as the Red Barn. Camps were also located near roads that led individuals to fields where they picked crops that were important since they allowed Seminoles to make a living. For example, Charlie Micco and his family inhabited one of their first camps near Brighton in order to be near an off-reservation company that worked cattle. When cattle were introduced to Brighton in the 1930s, Micco moved his camp near the Red Barn, which was once one of the main hubs for working cattle. Micco and his family continued to live in this area throughout the Red Barn's use as the main cattle complex (Coleman Josh, personal communication, April 2012). The location of this camp highlights the important role that Micco played in the cattle industry, which led to him being selected as one of the first cattle trustees for the Brighton Reservation (Covington 1993).

As mentioned previously, Billy Bowlegs III lived in numerous areas throughout his life, including Bluefields, Indiantown, a camp slightly outside of the reservation boundary, and a camp in the northern portion of the reservation boundary. Like Micco, Bowlegs might have settled his camp for work-related reasons, though Bowlegs also settled at his on-reservation camp since it had been previously cleared and used as a garden by another Seminole (Martha Jones, personal communication, December 2012). Both the off-reservation and on-reservation camps were located near main roads that allowed for easy traveling. These access roads especially helped Bowlegs's sister Lucy Pearce and her daughter Ada (both of whom lived with Bowlegs in his on-reservation camp) travel to their work sites, where they picked tomatoes and other crops. Bowlegs may have also used the access road when working as a guide for hunters and traveling throughout Florida to teach settlers about the Seminoles (Moore-Wilson 1910). Bowlegs's son, Eli Morgan, established his first camp a short distance from Bowlegs's on-reservation camp. This is slightly different than most existing camps because traditionally the children

Figure 10.4. Map showing the clans of the five camps established in the 1930s or earlier. The location of these clans can be compared to what Nash recorded for clan camp locations in 1930. Map created by Maureen Mahoney, Tribal Archaeologist, Seminole Tribe of Florida Tribal Historic Preservation Office.

lived near a related clan camp associated with the mother rather than the father. Although it is not clear why Eli Morgan disregarded this convention, it is a pattern noted with a small number of on-reservation-period camps.

Unlike the Micco and the Bowlegs III camps, the outlying Jake Morgan camp was not situated near a road or a work site. Willie Johns (personal communication, June 2013) remembers that in the mid-to-late 1950s, Jake Morgan was a loner, which could explain his solitary camp location. Spoehr (1944, 140–141) related that Jake Morgan lived with his sister and other family members. It appears that over time, Jake Morgan left an established family camp and went to live by himself. Spoehr (1944, 143) noted three individuals, all male, living alone when he met with the Cow Creeks in 1939, so it was not an unprecedented occurrence.

In summary, camps on the Brighton Reservation founded by 1939 highlight several features relating to the formation and beginning of the reservation. Two camps, Billy Bowlegs III's camp in the northern portion of the reservation and Charlie Micco's camp near the Red Barn, were settled in locations that would become two centers for later settlement on the reservation. The camps near Red Barn, including the Micco camp, were settled to help the cattle industry. Although Bowlegs's camp was presumably settled as it had been previously cleared, roads situated near the camp allowed those living in the camp to easily access work sites. Both settlement patterns highlight that economic reasons determined camp locations.

The 1940–1949 Camps: The Cattle Industry and Distrust of the Government

Based on the mapping completed by the THPO, the number of camps greatly increased in the 1940s (Figure 10.5). During this decade, approximately seventeen camps were established throughout the reservation, and all were settled on upland hammocks. There appears to be three main groupings for camp location for the time period: camps in the northern portion of the reservation, camps near the Red Barn, and camps near the administration complex.

The first grouping consists of five camps (First Johns camp, Tom Smith camp, Naha Tiger Second camp, Naha Tiger Third camp, Buster Twins camp) that were located in the northern part of the reservation surrounding the Billy Bowlegs III camp. Presumably, there are multiple reasons for this grouping. First, many of the occupants of the camps may have moved to this location to be near the already occupied Bowlegs camp and the established roads in this area. We know these occupants interacted regularly, as Billy Bowlegs III borrowed Tom Smith's horse, and Tom Smith routinely dropped off extra meat

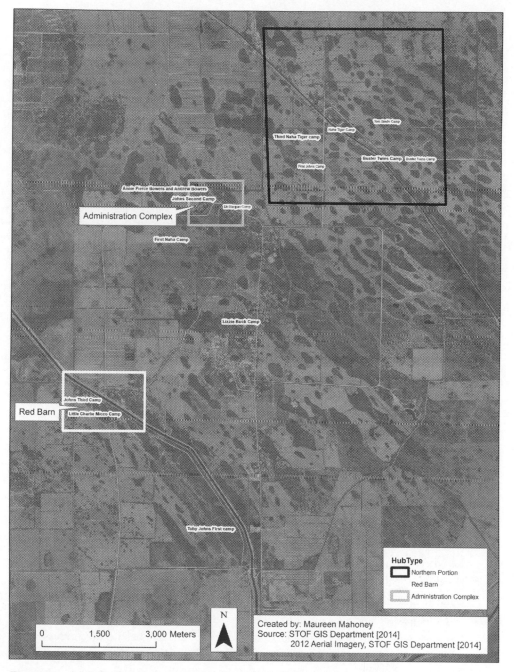

Figure 10.5. Map displaying the location of camps established in the 1940s and what hubs they were settled in or near. Created by Maureen Mahoney, Tribal Archaeologist, Seminole Tribe of Florida Tribal Historic Preservation Office.

he hunted to Bowlegs and the Buster Twins (Mollie Jolly, personal communication, March and April 2013). The sharing of resources suggests a close sociocultural framework among this camp cluster. People may have also settled near the Bowlegs III camp since he was a highly significant member of the Tribe and many Tribal children would spend time at his camp in order to learn from him (Willie Johns, personal communication, November 2011).

Camps may have also been settled in the northern portion of the reservation because Tribal members did not trust the U.S. government, and this location allowed for the easiest and quickest escape route if the army came to force migration as it did less than 100 years earlier (Covington 1993). Many of these early reservation camps were hidden from view in the hammock (Spoehr 1941), and several Tribal members remember their parents making the children go hide in the woods if an unknown non-Seminole person came near the camp (Mollie Jolly, personal communication, March and April 2013). Tribal members like the Buster Twins did not trust any non-Seminoles and may have only been comfortable living in an area with an easy escape route (Lorene Gopher, personal communication, August 2012).

Like the earlier Charlie Micco camp, the second core area for camps was established near the Red Barn. These camps consisted of the John Josh camp, the Little Charlie Micco camp, and the third Johns camp. For the inhabitants of the John Josh camp and the Little Charlie Micco camp, the original location of habitation was the Charlie Micco camp, which also continued to be inhabited during this time. All four camps in the area were settled at this location in order to be close to the Red Barn, the main focus of work for the men of the camp. Like Charlie Micco, John Josh was heavily involved in the cattle program and was one of the three original cattle trustees with Micco (Coleman Josh, personal communication, April 2012). The John Josh camp followed the usual matrilocal settlement pattern. Henly Josh, John Josh's wife, was a member of the Bird Clan, which was the clan associated with the Charlie Micco camp. Conversely, neither the Little Charlie Micco camp nor the third Johns camp followed the traditional matrilocal settlement pattern. Little Charlie and his family continued to live near Bird Clan camps and the Red Barn instead of Otter Clan camps, which was the clan associated with Little Charlie's wife, Minnie. In this instance, it appears to have been more important to settle the camp near a work area than to follow the matrilocal tradition. This settlement pattern was also found with the third Johns camp, which was a Panther Clan camp but whose inhabitants were greatly involved in the cattle industry. Although neither camp location was matrilocal, those in the camps were generally of one clan. In the Little Charlie Micco camp, inhabitants of the camp also included members of Minnie's clan, who settled at the camp due to this relationship. In the third Johns camp, the occupants primarily included family members who all belonged to the same clan.

The third hub that grew in the 1940s formed near the administration complex. This hub included the Annie Pearce and Andrew Bowers camp, the Jack Smith camp, the second Johns camp, and the Eli Morgan house. The presence of the camps near these institutional centers attests to the utilization of the facilities, such as the school and clinic. Like the camps near the Red Barn, many of the camps may also have been settled at this location to work cattle since the complex also contained cow pens.

Although the majority of the camps fit the patterns described, three camps—the Lizzie Buck camp, the Toby Johns camp, and the Naha Tiger First camp—were located away from the central hubs of this period. Each of these camps was settled along roadways, which is a pattern originally noted for the 1930 camps, such as the Bowlegs III camp. These later camps may have been settled near roads so that the inhabitants could easily travel on them. For the Toby Johns camp, Willie Johns (personal communication, July 2014) explained that Toby Johns did not stay at the camp regularly, meaning it could have been settled to take advantage of the natural resources in that area and used as a hunting camp.

The years between 1940 and 1949 saw most camps focusing on three areas for settlements: in the northern portion of the reservation, near the Red Barn, and near the administration complex. Camps around the Red Barn were established in order to use the barn, the main form of work for many of the men who lived on the reservation. Those camps in the northern portion of the reservation may have settled around the camp previously established by Billy Bowlegs III since many of the occupants of the camps worked together for socioeconomic reasons. However, these camps may have also been settled since many Seminoles were distrustful of the U.S. government, and this area served as an easy escape route. The third settlement pattern to emerge during this decade was the establishment of camps near the administration complex, which provided a school and a government office and highlights the increased use of these facilities in the 1940s.

The 1950–1969 Camps: Opening up to Non-Seminoles

The ten camps settled in the 1950s and 1960s continued to be established in the northern portion of the reservation, near the Red Barn, or near the administration complex (Figure 10.6); however, a new pattern emerged of camps being organized near major roads on the reservation. This pattern is slightly different than what was seen in the 1930s since the roads during the earlier decade had not been completely developed by that time. Based on historic aerials, all camps continued to be established in upland tree islands. Camps settled in the 1950s include the Jack Smith camp, the Snow camp, the Ada Pearce camp, both of the Robert and Alice Osceola camps, the fourth Johns camp, the Frank Shore camp, the Huff camp, the Happy Jones second camp, and the Sampson Snow camp. The only camp that the THPO has documented as being established in the 1960s was the Stella Smith camp. Only the Sampson Snow camp was settled in the northern portion of the reservation, though the earlier camps in this area were still inhabited during this time period. Three camps—the Snow camp, the Jack Smith camp, and the Ada Pearce camp—were established near the administration complex, replacing the earlier camps after many of the previous inhabitants moved to new locations. In the early 1960s, Stella Smith's camp was also established near these institutions. One camp, the Frank Shore camp, was permanently settled near the Red Barn in the late 1950s in order to be located near the main hub of the cattle industry. Although this camp had earlier been used temporarily, it was not until this year that the family permanently moved to this location (Geneva Shore, personal communication, July 2012).

The single new pattern that emerged during these decades is the location of camps settled near major roadways. During the 1950s, approximately 50 percent of the recorded settled camps were located adjacent to a main road. According to Jack Chalfant (personal communication, July 2014), electricity was brought to these roads in the 1930s and attracted many camps to these areas, but many of the camps were also settled because these roads were main thoroughfares. The fourth Johns camp and the Ada Pearce camp were settled along Reservation Road since the school bus traveled that route and picked up children to go to school (Willie Johns, personal communication, January 2014; Lorene Gopher, personal communication, August 2012). The Huff camp, which was settled in the central portion of the reservation and adjacent to Reservation Road, may have been settled at this location in order to draw in tourists traveling along the road (John Huff, personal communication, 2014). This camp included a tourist shop at which Seminole handcrafts were sold.

Although camp locations in the 1950s highlight that the Seminoles on the Brighton Reservation still focused on the cattle industry, using the administration complex, and settling in the northern portion of the reservation, it also shows a time when camps were settling in more public areas. Positioning camps along the major roadways suggests that the inhabitants may have been

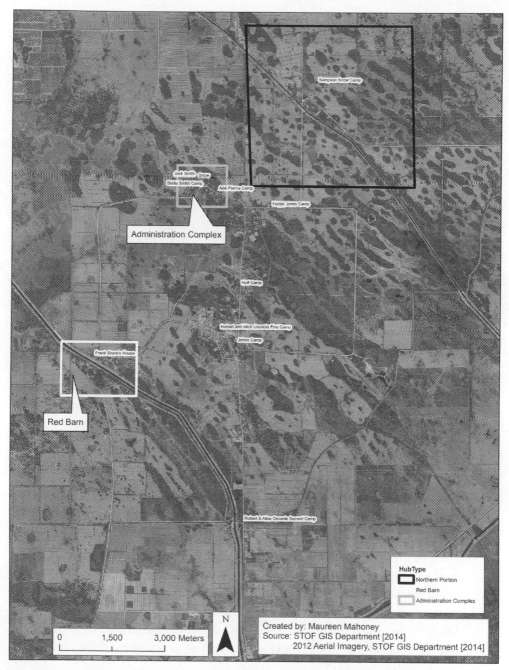

Figure 10.6. Map displaying the location of camps established in the 1950s and 1960s and what hubs they were settled in or near. Created by Maureen Mahoney, Tribal Archaeologist, Seminole Tribe of Florida Tribal Historic Preservation Office.

less fearful of non-Seminoles and felt more comfortable on the reservation land. This is clearly seen with those camps whose children went to school and with the opening of the tourist gift shop at the Huff camp, which invited the public in to see the crafts.

Results

Based on working with the community and the archaeological fieldwork, Seminole camps on the Brighton Reservation in the historic period were generally clustered in groupings to take advantage of social or economic features. The decades examined for this analysis can also be divided into three distinct groupings that correlate to the history of the reservation. The importance of these hubs changed over time with the shifting of what the community deemed significant. Camps settled from 1900 to 1939 correspond to the formation of the reservation and the emergence of many enterprises. From 1940 to 1949, camps were primarily located near the Red Barn, near the administration complex, or in the northern portion of the reservation. The placement of these camps highlights two important features in the history of the Brighton Reservation. First, the emergence of camps near the Red Barn shows the important role that the cattle industry played for many Tribal members. The settlements in the northern part of the reservation and those near the administrative complex indicate that the Cow Creeks differed in their opinion regarding the U.S. government. Inhabitants in camps in the northern part of the reservation may have knowingly established their camps in an area that allowed for an easy escape since they feared that the U.S. government might force migration to the west. Those camps near the administration complex imply a slightly more trustful attitude toward the government since these inhabitants used the services provided at this complex. The 1950–1969 period saw the rise of camps settling near this complex and using the resources provided by the U.S. government, as well as camps being established along major roadways. This shift in camp location may suggest a tolerance and acceptance of government institutions and other non-Seminoles; however, it is clear that many still held tightly to tradition. For example, when the government built HUD houses at the Buster Twins camp, the twins refused to live in them and continued to use their chickees (Lorene Gopher, personal communication, August 2012).

Discussion

It is my hope that the results and interpretations presented are simple and logical so that all audiences can easily piece the results together and use them for their own analyses. Many of the conclusions introduced above may aid those archaeologists working in South Florida to document these mid-twentieth-century camps appropriately during any development projects. Although the archaeological fieldwork results may not have been defined like traditional archaeological studies, it has been an important component in these analyses. For example, at the fourth Johns camp (see Fenno et al., this volume), we first noted the site when the Tribal Archaeology Section was completing a Phase I survey of the area for the development of a potential home site. Finding the glass bottles and small amounts of whiteware led us to engage with the community to further learn and ultimately document the camp. For those archaeologists working on development projects off-reservation, this chapter should at least minimally help document Seminole camps. Because certain entities, such as the administrative complex and the cattle program, were only found on the reservation, similar settlement patterns may not have occurred off the reservations. Other settlement patterns, such as Seminoles establishing camps in locations for economic reasons, certainly existed for off-reservation camps. Because these areas were dispersed throughout South Florida and may not have been near traditional camp areas, it is possible that certain settlements disregarded matrilocal conventions. For this reason, archaeologists in South Florida should be aware of possible economic features (such as access roads) within and around Seminole camps so they are recorded accurately. In this, I hope these camps may be preserved and protected and that the Tribe will be consulted in projects relating to their documentation.

Furthermore, other THPOs could use this project as an example to document their own tribe's recent history. For the STOF THPO, we found that the examination of these camps resonates with the community since many of the living elders resided at them, and it is a way for them to share their memories. It is important to note that we do not just take these memories and stick them on a shelf; instead, we write up everything (including the archaeological fieldwork results) and give that to the Tribal school. In this way, the information is shared with the community, who can use it to determine the appropriate level of a site's preservation. It is not up to us as archaeologists as to what camp is preserved. Rather, the family and community make that decision. Our goal for these projects as Tribal archaeologists is to help add to the stories of these camps by providing what we can (fieldwork, examining historic

Table 10.1. Dates when camps were established

Camp	Date Established
John Jimmie	Possibly from 1900
Billy Bowlegs First Camp	Prior to 1936
Billy Bowlegs III Camp	After 1936
Jake Morgan	Prior to 1939
Eli Morgan Old Home (near northern part of reservation)	Late 1930s
Charlie Micco Off-Reservation Camp	1939 or earlier
Charlie Micco Camp (near Red Barn) (second camp in area)	1939 or earlier
Little Charlie Micco Camp	1940s
Toby Johns First Camp	1940s
Eli Morgan Camp	1940s
Naha Tiger First On-Reservation Camp	Prior to 1941
Naha Tiger Second On-Reservation Camp	1945–1947
Naha Tiger Third On-Reservation Camp	1949–1957
John Josh Camp	1947 or 1948
Tom Smith Camp	Prior to 1949
Buster Twins Camp	1949–1957
Annie Pierce and Andrew Bowers	1940s
Happy Jones First Camp	1940s
Lizzie Buck Camp	1948–1957
First Johns Camp	Early 1940s
Second Johns Camp (near school)	Mid-1940s
Third Johns Camp (near Red Barn)	Late 1940s
Johns Camp (near water tower)	1950s
Sampson Snow Camp	1950s
Happy Jones Second Camp	1950s
Huff Camp	1950s
Ada Smith Camp	1953
Frank Shore Camp	Late 1950s
Snow Camp (near old school)	1950s
Jack Smith Camp (near old school)	1950s
Alice and Robert Osceola First Camp	Early 1950s
Alice and Robert Osceola Second Camp	Late 1950s
Stella Smith Camp	1961

aerials, library searches) so the community has all of the resources available to them for the management of Seminole sites. Both the individual camp chapter (Fenno et al., this volume) and this chapter can hopefully be used by other THPOs as an example of bridging the gap between various heritage management activities, such as archaeology, and tribal wishes so that these important sites are documented and protected according to tribal requests.

Conclusion

This chapter has highlighted one project that combined the results of archaeological fieldwork and Tribal member input in order to determine mid-twentieth-century settlement patterns on the Brighton Seminole Indian Reservation. This historic synthesis has become an important project for the STOF THPO, since it has allowed us to document important Seminole sites according to the wishes of the community and in the process has placed heritage management decisions in the hands of Tribal members. This chapter can be used by two types of audiences: by archaeologists to accurately document and work with the Tribe regarding these mid-twentieth-century camps and by other THPOs who incorporate their community's wishes in regards to site management. Although each community is unique, the ultimate goal behind this project, as well as any project undertaken by the STOF THPO, is to engage the community in order to make them a part of the heritage management process and decision making.

Figure 10.7. Maureen Mahoney. By permission of Jack Chalfant, Field Technician, Seminole Tribe of Florida Tribal Historic Preservation Office.

References Cited

Blakney-Bailey, Jane Anne. 2007. "Analysis of Historic Creek and Seminole Settlement Patterns, Town Design, and Architecture: The Paynes Town Seminole Site (8AL366), a Case Study." Ph.D. diss., University of Florida.

Covington, James W. 1976. "Brighton Reservation Florida, 1935–1938." *Tequesta* 36: 54–65.

———. 1980. "Seminole Leadership: Changing Substance, 1858–1958." *Tequesta* 40:31–38.

———. 1982. *The Billy Bowlegs War 1855–1858: The Final Stand of the Seminoles against the Whites*. Chuluota, Fla.: Mickler House Publishers.

———. 1993. *The Seminoles of Florida*. Gainesville: University Press of Florida.

Jumper, Betty Mae, and Patsy West. 2001. *A Seminole Legend: The Life of Betty Mae Tiger Jumper*. Gainesville: University Press of Florida.

Kersey, Harry. 1989. *The Florida Seminoles and the New Deal 1933–1942*. Boca Raton: Florida Atlantic University Press.

MacCauley, Clay. 2000 (1887). *The Seminole Indians of Florida*. Gainesville: University Press of Florida.

McReynolds, Edwin. 1957. *Seminoles*. Norman: University of Oklahoma Press.

Milanich, Jerald T. 1995. *Florida Indians and the Invasion from Europe*. Gainesville: University Press of Florida.

———. 1998. *Florida's Indians from Ancient Times to the Present*. Gainesville: University Press of Florida.

Moore-Wilson, Minnie. 1910. *The Seminoles of Florida*. New York: Moffat, Yard.

Nash, Roy. 1931. "Report to the Commissioner of Indian Affairs Concerning Conditions among the Seminole Indians of Florida." In *Seminole Indians, Survey of the Seminole Indians of Florida, Presented by Mr. Fletcher*. Sen. 71:3rd. doc. 314. Exh. 41.

Ober, Frederick A. 1875. "Ten Days with the Seminoles." *Appleton's Journal of Literature, Science, and Art* 14 (July–December): 142-173.

Spoehr, Alexander. 1941. "Camp, Clan, and Kin among the Cow Creek Seminole of Florida." *Florida Anthropological Series* 33(1). Florida Museum of Natural History.

———. 1944. "The Florida Seminole Camp." *Florida Anthropological Series* 33(3). Florida Museum of Natural History.

Weisman, Brent Richards. 1989. *Like Beads on a String: A Culture History of the Seminole Indians in Northern Peninsular Florida*. Tuscaloosa: University of Alabama Press.

———. 1999. *Unconquered People: Florida's Seminole and Miccosukee Indians*. Gainesville: University Press of Florida.

———. 2000a. "Archaeological Perspectives on Florida Seminole Ethnogenesis." In *Indians of the Greater Southeast: Historical Archaeology and Ethnohistory*, edited by Bonnie G. McEwan, 299–317. Gainesville: University Press of Florida.

———. 2000b. "The Origins of the Seminole Plantation System and Its Role in Florida's Colonial Economy." In *Colonial Plantations and Economy of Florida*, edited by Jane Landers. Gainesville: University Press of Florida.

11

Archaeometry

Where GIS Meets the People

JUAN J. CANCEL AND PAUL N. BACKHOUSE

The Archaeometry Section of the Tribal Historic Preservation Office (THPO) is crucial to the operation of all the THPO areas. The philosophy of the section is for technological inclusivity—providing the tools and support for applications like GIS Portal and the hardware to enable mobile mapping. These solutions can be operationalized both by staff and the Tribal community. This inclusivity has resulted in some dynamic projects that have been the calling card of the THPO within the community and have forged connections that transcend cultural differences. The ability to generate maps and other digital and physical media promotes collaborative dialogue and active engagement between the community and the THPO, allowing active participation by all constituents and informed cultural heritage decision making. This is perhaps exemplified by the concept of participatory mapping, in which stakeholder groups within the Tribal communities actively work together to provide the information that is then geographically realized. The resultant maps oftentimes allow Tribal elders the ability to visually communicate cultural information with younger generations accustomed to receiving information in a geographic format.

Author Bios

Juan J. Cancel has been working in the THPO since 2007, beginning as the Geographical Information System (GIS) Specialist and then in 2009 moving into the role of Chief Data Analyst managing the Archaeometry Section. Cancel began with the THPO after working in the Lionel Pincus and Princess Firyal Map Division at the New York Public Library for approximately two years and graduating from Hunter College–City University of New

York. He applies GIS techniques to analyze the spatial relevance of cultural resources. Cancel is introducing current and new technologies to improve the level of work conducted at the THPO. This has led him to work closely with the community to understand the Tribe's view of the cultural landscape.

For Paul Backhouse, see chapter 3.

Introduction

Archaeometry at the Seminole Tribe of Florida Tribal Historic Preservation Office (STOF THPO) promotes inclusive heritage thinking by providing the technical support and education to connect people to their heritage through advanced software and hardware solutions. We achieve this goal by adhering to a philosophy of technology for all. This means that when someone wants to create a map or carry out a geophysical survey, they then have the tools, or have access to specialists with the tools, to complete the job. The philosophy of empowering multiple stakeholders and communities as opposed to relying on power-users has been central to the development of the THPO. This was a conscious decision we made collectively early in the development of the department.

For the purposes of this chapter, we explore the implementation of GIS at the THPO. Federally recognized Indian tribes have access to the full package of ESRI GIS products through a long-standing enterprise licensing agreement administered by the Bureau of Indian Affairs Branch of Geospatial Support (http://tinyurl.com/7b7fdrq). In 2007, the newly recognized THPO had access to powerful software but lacked an implementation strategy that would allow for systemic, rather than specialist, application to harness its potential. Put simply, we wanted to find ways in which archaeometric solutions (including GIS) could be built into the everyday workflow of the office. By empowering creativity and ownership of projects across the staff of the THPO, we established an approach that has been the epistemological backbone of Archaeometry at the STOF THPO. This approach has, in turn, allowed Archaeometry staff the latitude to engage in the types of participatory programs that have become our focus.

What Is Archaeometry?

Archaeometry is a broad holistic term used to describe archaeological science (Darvill 2009). Some see it as a concept that conveniently describes the scientific-based technologies utilized by modern archaeologists and heritage managers. At the STOF THPO, Archaeometry deals with the implementation and support of GIS, remote sensing, geophysical survey (primarily ground-penetrating radar [GPR]), and absolute dating. In addition, the Archaeometry Section is responsible for designing the digital data storage and retrieval schema for the office.

We began in 2007 as a team of two: a Chief Data Analyst and a GIS Specialist. The former designed, developed, and managed the initial archaeological databases, and the latter introduced GIS as a platform to capture that same archaeological data in a spatial format. By providing technical support for other areas of the THPO, the Archaeometry Section laid the groundwork for the integrated systems that are central to its current incarnation. Quick access to powerful visualizations of the data through GIS allowed Tribal leadership to see the potential of this endeavor, and soon the THPO found itself working with sister departments and Tribal community interest groups. Involvement in the arenas of Tribal government and the community at large soon followed.

Eight years after implementation, the staff still consists of only two people, although today we are greatly assisted by Tribal Work Experience Program placements, interns from local university programs, and volunteers. The Chief Data Analyst continues the work of database management, but now instills a far greater cultural aesthetic into the direction of the section. The Geospatial Analyst manages the GIS and daily data needs of the THPO, capturing the latest archaeological data and serving it out to users through both remote and mobile applications. The evolution of roles and constant goal-oriented innovation have transformed the office. We recognize in working for the Tribe that cultural identity, cultural beliefs, and cultural understanding have to play a role in the work we do. We have consistently found that scientific and cultural goals are not mutually exclusive. The most successful projects we have worked on are those that utilize archaeometric concepts to engage diverse community groups. We have found the visual platform provided by mapping to be a great place to begin a dialogue.

Building a THPO GIS

Many people don't realize they use GIS every day when they use software on their computer like Google Maps to see where things are, get directions from one place to another using mapping apps, or drive their car built with a navigation system to help the average person get around. GIS has become fundamental and almost second nature to use. Participant, rather than specialist, user profiles are clearly central to a paradigm that seeks to empower people in collaborative problem solving through simple to adopt and use mapping technologies (Dangermond 2013). The role of Archaeometry within this paradigm is to create systems for interacting with data that appear seamless and mirror the intuitive sensibilities used in the broader electronic world. Once the framework is in place, Archaeometry works largely behind the scenes to maintain infrastructure and keep pace with data ingestion.

In less than a decade, we have evolved our workflow from physical files and folders to complex relational database models that facilitate multiple users working concurrently with the same data, often in very different geographic locations. Without a common framework of record-keeping, the Tribe was employing multiple contractors to survey, and oftentimes resurvey, parcels of land already subjected to a cultural resources assessment. This practice was not only economically wasteful, it also had the potential to subject cultural resources to multiple invasive surveys. Most important, the lack of manageable internal systems meant the Tribe had very little control over the decisions made regarding its own cultural resources. The development of the THPO not only fundamentally altered this dynamic, it also created a pressing need to build systems that could cope with the development across the Tribe's six reservations.

The database schema that we have created is one response to the preceding problem. Many of the databases have common fields, which allows for them to have relationships with one another and to "talk" to each other. This creates multiple ways to view similar data. Because we share the philosophy that everyone within our organization should be able to access data and explore it within a common framework, much planning was necessary to develop the database(s) structure. The relatively small size of the office staff and accessibility of key members of the team allowed us to implement consistent data schema across all THPO projects early on. The benefits of such an approach are enormous and allow staff access to a large amount of information quickly and easily. The success in staff adoption of a unified GIS perspective came from the early adoption of mobile GIS for data collection.

Mobile GIS

The mobile GIS program began in 2008 directly following the ESRI International GIS User Conference in San Diego, California. That year, support for mobile GIS integration was one of the key themes of the conference, indicating an increasingly integrated architecture by which to capture and access spatial data (ESRI 2008). The benefits for adoption by the THPO were potentially enormous, so we began looking into the types of devices practical in the hot and humid subtropical South Florida environment. Concurrently, we began to work on a geodatabase schema that could be served out to multiple crews working simultaneously on different reservations. The system specifications needed to present field crews with known cultural information relevant to their project boundaries (for example, location of nearby resources) and also to capture information relevant to an archaeological investigation. The database had to be simple enough so that information requirements were not overly burdensome in the field. It also needed to capture the resolution necessary to allow future analysis and facilitate heritage management decision making. Because of the geomorphological realities of working in an aggrading environment, pedestrian survey methodologies have low artifact return rates; the geodatabases for shovel testing and site delineation therefore became the two central workhorses with which to test mobile GIS use by our field crews.

The shovel test layer(s) incorporates both arbitrary shovel-test locations and a reference virtual 100 meter sampling grid across the areal extent of the reservation. This approach allows us to sample different environments, soil types, hydrological conditions, and topographic variations in order to develop a comprehensive understanding of the reservation's potential for buried cultural sites. The methodology takes a long-term perspective on data collection, with each individual project slowly filling in a small portion of the overall reservation. We have stuck to these schemas, with some refinements along the way, over the course of eight years, and today the field staff routinely employs multiple smart GPS devices. Although most projects are geographically small, with 17,546 shovel tests completed as of December 2014, we have now pieced together data on more than 25 percent of each of our two largest reservations (Tribal Historic Preservation Office 2014)

Community Archaeometry

None of the preceding development of the Archaeometry Section explicitly involved the community. Much of what the technology facilitated (for example, digging in the ground) conflicted with Tribal cultural beliefs. At various Tribal planning meetings, it quickly became obvious that GIS provided a robust tool for people to communicate visually that transcended cultural differences. We thus began to consciously infuse the ideals of community participation with our daily workflows. The purchase of GPR helped to demonstrate the positive application of archaeometric techniques to the community. Because the equipment is physically noninvasive, we look at sensitive areas differently and maintain the respect of the Tribal communities' beliefs.

One example of the use of this equipment has been in managing the Tribal cemeteries on the reservations. Because of the cultural sensitivity of the subject matter, we cannot provide great detail; however, it will perhaps be instructive to see how this technology has been applied and how that has built a stronger relationship between the THPO and the communities we serve. Mortality is a subject spoken of with much caution in Seminole culture; indeed, Tribal members do not traditionally pick a location to be interred, as doing so could trigger the reality to be made manifest (Sturtevant 1954). For a number of cultural and historical reasons, the early grave locations were typically not marked. Placement of a recently passed loved one is both culturally delicate and time sensitive.

The THPO began systematically surveying the Tribal cemeteries using traditional surveying tools as well as the aforementioned GPR equipment. Our goal was to find unmarked areas that had a high likelihood of a prior burial. Areas that were not intruding on past individuals helped families perform appropriate burial ceremonies for the more recently deceased. The past and present come into sharp focus at such times. It has been very important that the THPO has maintained itself as a community resource that can provide a bridge to the highly culturally uncomfortable traditions of a non-Seminole world. This experience has helped shape our relationship with the communities. We realized that in order to improve our work, we needed to start asking questions and engage directly in a dialogue with as many community members as possible. The Yes or No questions: Should we as outsiders know about this? Should we as outsiders be involved? Should we get someone with more intimate cultural knowledge to take care of this? These basic Yes or No questions have allowed us to be involved. To be sure, people will quickly let you know when a question is poorly timed or is inappropriate, but, regardless, it is important to ask.

Participatory Mapping

In the last decade, as GIS has become more accessible, the resulting applications have broadened significantly, and a strong focus on the integration of people has emerged (e.g., Bodenhamer et al. 2010). A paper presented at the 2009 ESRI International User Conference was foundational in changing the way we thought about the implementation of GIS at the STOF THPO. Jeoren Verplanke (2009) discussed a project in which he worked with indigenous communities to help them map their traditional landscape using mobile GIS. The project was fully participatory in that it required significant input and interaction with the communities to be successful. A shared sense of purpose generated by the very real threat of the indigenous groups losing their lands to expanding logging and mineral mining concerns catalyzed the author and the communities to work closely. Data collection was not in the traditional mode of researcher and informant but fully participatory. The balance of intellectual ownership and investment in the outcome firmly sided with the community rather than the originating author (Verplanke 2009). Subsequent correspondence with Verplanke and additional research demonstrated to us the potential of such an approach, and that approach became the blueprint for our application of GIS at the STOF THPO.

Six years on, this core participatory philosophy remains central to our approach. The direction of our research is now often community driven. We realize that GIS can be used in a great number of situations to bring stakeholders to the table and drive participatory engagement, crossing many arbitrary boundaries that otherwise serve to decrease communication. Tribal elders and youth can engage with one another over a visual medium such as a map. Sometimes participatory projects are as simple as printing a large-format historic map of a particular reservation and taking it to a forum where community members can share their knowledge and experiences with one another. Oftentimes this exercise results in information they would like protected or recorded, by marking up the map, recording an oral history, or making notes. Discussion at such participatory sessions is often in Miccosukee (one of two languages spoken by the Seminole Tribe of Florida). Because Miccosukee is not spoken by many researchers outside of the Tribe, the language allows participants to discuss culturally sensitive information privately before deciding what should and should not be shared or entered into a permanent record.

Case Study 1—Cattleman's Association–Heritage Trails Project

The history of the Tribal Cattleman's Association underscores the importance of this community organization as the traditional economic backbone of the Seminole Tribe of Florida (Dilley and Gopher, this volume). Cattlemen are by definition busy working people who spend much of their day outdoors tending cattle and working in their pastures. Opportunities to interact with the THPO are typically very limited, as days are often long and geographically oriented to more remote parts of the reservations (Dilley and Gopher, this volume). Nevertheless, they do frequently observe field crews making their way through their pastures or encounter them at lunch when both cattlemen and cattlewomen and archaeological field crew converge to eat (Griffis et al., this volume).

Work on a participatory mapping project provided an opportunity to engage with this community and celebrate the rich heritage of cattlemen and cattlewomen on the Big Cypress Reservation (for an academic overview, see Garbarino 1986). The engagement began with the Seminole Tribe of Florida, Inc. and their Big Cypress Board Representative, who was interested in recording the original historic trails that extended from the Big Cypress Reservation to the market town of Immokalee, approximately 30 miles to the west. The Big Cypress Reservation sits on the western margin of the Everglades, and the trails into and out of this area were notoriously difficult to traverse, especially during the summer wet season. The locations of early to mid-twentieth-century corrals, cattle dips, and pasture leases were also of much interest to the cattlemen and cattlewomen. The Archaeometry team (including Tribal youth working with the department as part of the Tribe's Work Experience Program) met regularly with the Tribal members who have been or continue to be involved with cattle to explore modern and historic maps. They began to piece together the old trails and landscape features that comprise the early to mid-twentieth-century ranching heritage of Big Cypress. Modern names for trails, such as the Deer Tick Fenceline (Joe Frank, personal communication, 2014), brought out additional stories contextualizing the cattle industry on the reservation with broader developments within Florida and the United States. Although the context of this history is well known, it has not to date been approached from a Tribal perspective.

The annotated maps that resulted from the various participatory sessions were a source of pride for the Cattlemen's Association. It was requested that they be displayed along the route of the annual 2015 Big Cypress Cattle Drive. The maps were set up in a traditional chickee (Figure 11.1) along the route junctures where the cattlemen and cattlewomen stopped to rest and eat meals. The display was a great success and engaged many of the drive's participants in looking at the maps, sharing stories with one another, and invariably adding more information to the already rich heritage. The project also opened the door to many other historical and cultural events the participants wanted to share and memorialize.

The Heritage Trails project was very successful and created an opportunity for relevant engagement with the community. The cattlemen and cattlewomen would at times purposefully hold back information, but we respected those decisions as a way to protect certain aspects of their cultural identity. We understood that the cattlemen and cattlewomen had a great respect for those who came before them and paved the way for the future success of the cattle

Figure 11.1. Quenton Cypress displays maps generated by the Cattleman's Association Heritage Trails Project during the 2015 Big Cypress cattle drive. By permission of Juan J. Cancel, Chief Data Analyst, Seminole Tribe of Florida Tribal Historic Preservation Office.

industry. Like many other significant matters to the Tribe, it was equally as important to recognize that the cattle business centered on the family unit and was passed on to subsequent generations as a thing of pride. We learned that the cattle trails were much more than routes for livestock (often with multiple purposes for other industries). By socializing the trails and landscape in this way, the stories surrounding the journeys the cattlemen and cattlewomen took became a tangible mechanism by which they could explore, celebrate, and promote a common heritage using their own voices.

Case Study 2—Youth Education–LEGO project

The discipline of GIS demands a special skill set. Through collaboration with our Tribal Education Department, the THPO works to identify career entry opportunities for Tribal members and teach the technical skills necessary for employment in the heritage sector. This program is working remarkably well, and 2015 saw a record influx of participants in the program as part of the Work Experience Program for adults and the Summer Work Experience Program for Tribal youth. Beyond these two avenues for workplace experience, the Archaeometry Section of the THPO partnered with the Education Division of the Ah-Tah-Thi-Ki Museum to engage younger (fourth and fifth grade) Tribal youth in core geographic concepts.

The plan for the program was to develop a fun and immersive participatory experience that would engage the students in visualizing their physical environment. Inspired by a news article in which an avid LEGO builder had recreated a scale version of the ill-fated Italian town of Pompeii (Barker 2015), the premise became to build a scale model of the Big Cypress Reservation in LEGO bricks.

During the summer of 2015, we began a pilot program and worked directly with the Big Cypress Reservation's Ahfachkee School's summer program and the Recreation Department. A small group of excited Tribal children participated in the project. The experience was as educational for the instructors as it was for the kids. Core concepts such as scale and awareness of physical surroundings were infused into the class environment. Practical considerations of how big a doorway needed to be to allow a LEGO figure to traverse into a building allowed for practical learning opportunities, such as using a laser rangefinder to measure heights of buildings. Scale was a core concept, and the necessity of math became part of the learning experience for the participants rather than being something applied only to abstract problems.

From this pilot project, we learned we needed a lesson in logistics and planning ourselves. We had to come up with lesson plans that connected LEGO bricks with the spatial concepts of fractions and scale. The classroom was an integral component for setting up foundational math concepts some students found difficult. Once key spatial concepts were understood, we began building. We soon discovered the number of LEGO bricks necessary, and the number the kids utilized in any one session was staggering. We quickly decided that given the dual constraints of time and resources, the program should concentrate on one small location within the reservation. The location should also be somewhere familiar to the participants as they come to grips with the class concepts. The kids' classroom trailer at the Ahfachkee School was ideal for this purpose.

The results of the program were remarkable (Figure 11.2). The student-instructor environment resulted in some fine examples of LEGO building and also demonstrated the potential of an active learning environment for practically exploring concepts like scale and the built environment. We plan to expand this program in the future and include other digital methods for

Figure 11.2. Seminole Tribe of Florida's Ahfachkee School students display some LEGO model concepts during the Tribal Historic Preservation Office/Museum LEGO Summer Program. *Left to right*: Avery Bowers, Dayne Billie, Tony Billie, Joy Murphy (Museum Educator), and Lania Bert. By permission of Juan J. Cancel, Chief Data Analyst, Seminole Tribe of Florida Tribal Historic Preservation Office.

visualizing the environment (such as the popular computer game Minecraft), giving young Tribal members the opportunity to practically engage their capacity for spatial thinking in relation to their own environment on the reservation. Our hope is that such programs will lead to a greater understanding of the environment and increase participation in its preservation.

The LEGO project was a positive experience. Initially the project was designed as a way to get involved with the Tribal youth. However, over the course of six weeks, the project evolved into something with much more meaning. We were able to impact the lives of Tribal children by helping them develop an understanding that their education and ideas about the world around them could be enriched through something as simple as working with LEGO bricks. During the project end evaluation, we realized that this is the type of project that has much room for growth and could be turned into a long-term collaboration involving the THPO, the museum, and Education Departments. Our goal is to increase the number of students and develop the LEGO project into an after-school program. The program will continue to involve tangible items such as LEGO bricks and incorporate digital programs that involve spatial connectivity. The opportunities are there to connect this type of project to the current use of our GIS programs like storytelling mapping, and we are hopeful that they will inspire students to pursue careers in GIS, or heritage and environmental management, molding them to become future leaders of their Tribe.

Case Study 3—GIS Portal

The development of GIS Portal is a recent trend that has been gaining interest both within and outside the GIS community (Dangermond 2015). The justification for the project arose from the plethora of information silos that were being created within our office, largely as a result of the need to review off-reservation National Historic Preservation Act Section 106 actions (see Mueller, this volume). With these projects, our own researchers, external researchers, and Tribal historians were generating a tremendous amount of historically important cultural information that lacked a clear framework for storage, retrieval, and synthesis. We were faced therefore with a pressing need to create a system to share historically and culturally significant information with other staff in our office, Tribal members, and even select outside researchers. To be successful, we realized we needed to create a GIS simple and efficient enough that any individual, regardless of technical background, could easily use it.

The system needed to be versatile enough to capture the stories of a Tribal member's family or twenty years of academic knowledge from a professor studying one Seminole-related site. The solution we have developed is GIS Portal. GIS Portal, or GIS Online, is a simple and efficient manner of displaying shared mapping data across an open network, typically the Internet, to other users. The interface is beneficial as it strips away the great number of tools and buttons present in a desktop version of GIS, thereby removing a large obstacle to adoption—technological intimidation. We maintain the data in an isolated work space and are especially cognizant of the secure and sensitive nature of the Tribal history and culture being stored in the system. Working collaboratively with the Tribe's GIS department has helped us address this concern by publishing GIS Portal as a closed network within the Tribe's digital infrastructure.

The project was born from an intern-driven semester-long pilot and has now been adopted throughout the office. Initial database and environment design required some technical expertise not apparent to users on the front end. We created multiple layers and appropriate symbology to capture the geographic representation of the end users' knowledge. The result is an open yet controlled community environment where the larger discussion of Tribal history and culture can be examined and common questions shared. Key questions as to what constitutes the broad geographic area associated with the ancestral Seminole population can be explored through integrated access to state site file databases. Archaeological sites in danger of being destroyed can be rendered in detail and discussed with cultural advisors and leadership during heritage management strategy sessions.

Once built, GIS Portal allows users to continue to add data. The results six months after implementation are staggering. Crowdsourcing data entry to multiple experts within a controlled data schema has allowed us to visualize new patterns not apparent with more conventional means. An excellent illustration of the power of this system came within the first month of creating the Portal environment. The THPO had the privilege of hosting a meeting between a research associate studying Seminole history in the Florida panhandle and the leadership of the Tribe. The researcher was presenting the results of his study, which in isolation were extremely significant to the history of the region. However, when the results were viewed in the broader context of the Portal environment, the interpretation was amplified substantially. James Billie, Chairman of the Seminole Tribe of Florida, began to connect the physical archaeological and documentary evidence configured on GIS Portal to the legends of the Tribe. Working within this environment, he traced the history of a particular community represented in the archaeological site file to a legend regarding the evolution of the current landscape of Florida. The Portal came to life with information and stories as the Chairman wove a narrative connecting the cultural universe with the physical realities on the ground today. The experience underscored the value of a platform that encourages participation and intuitive exploration. We continue to see the power that such a system provides in allowing users to connect tangibly with their culture and history. This realization is strengthened by the fact that the Tribe's history stretches throughout parts of nine states in the southeastern portion of the North American continent. Today, much of the tangible history of the Tribe is inaccessible on private land. GIS Portal provides one bridge to connect to that otherwise hidden history and an opportunity to reconnect with the past.

Conclusion

The Archaeometry Section of the STOF THPO exists to facilitate communication. The tools we use to undertake this task are technologically based. We have found our major challenge is to engage the Tribal community in a common dialogue about their heritage using these tools. Participatory programs prove to be an extremely useful method to involve different sections, and oftentimes cross sections, of Tribal society in heritage thinking. The THPO, as a branch of Tribal government, is charged with implementing the rules set out in the Tribal Cultural Resources Ordinance (C-01-16, see Appendix). Interpreted in a strictly bureaucratic sense, the implementation of these rules could serve as a further administrative barricade, isolating communities from active participation in programs that reflect Tribal government oversight of their heritage. The types of programs initiated by the Archaeometry Section are designed to break down these barriers and allow participation at the grassroots level. We are only now beginning this process, but the ideal is one shared by the entire office. A recent survey conducted by the Bluestone Strategy Group (2015) indicates that it is the THPO and museum programs working with Tribal communities that have earned these programs the high rating of "most important" departments of Tribal administration. At the end of the day, we want to supply the tools to Tribal members to write and communicate their own heritage values, and we will continue to take steps toward this important goal.

Figure 11.3. Juan J. Cancel.

References Cited

Barker, Craig. 2015. "Lego Pompeii Creates Less Pomp and More Yay in the Museum." *The Conversation*, January 22. http://tinyurl.com/q9ef56b.

Bodenhamer, David J., John Corrigan, and Trevor M. Harris. 2010. *The Spatial Humanities: GIS and the Future of Humanities Scholarship*. Bloomington: Indiana University Press.

Dangermond, Jack. 2013. "GIS—Transforming Our World." Plenary speech presented at the 28th ESRI International User Conference, San Diego, Calif.

———. 2015. "GIS: Creating Our Future." Plenary speech presented at the 30th ESRI International User Conference San Diego, Calif.

Darvill, Timothy. 2009. *The Concise Oxford Dictionary of Archaeology*. 2nd ed. Oxford: Oxford University Press.

ESRI. 2008. Proceedings of the 28th Annual ESRI International User Conference. http://proceedings.esri.com/library/userconf/proc08/.

Garbarino, Merwyn S. 1986. *Big Cypress: A Changing Community*. Long Grove, Ill.: Waveland Press.

Sturtevant, William C. 1954. "The Mikasuki Seminole: Medical Beliefs and Practices." Ph.D. diss., Yale University.

Tribal Historic Preservation Office. 2014. *Tribal Historic Preservation Office 2014 Annual Report: Preparing for the Future*. Clewiston: Seminole Tribe of Florida.

Verplanke, Jeroen. 2009. "Mobile GIS to Manage Indigenous Technical Knowledge in Developing Countries." Paper presented at the 29th ESRI International User Conference. San Diego, Calif.

12

Let's Celebrate!

The Red Barn as Community Heritage

CARRIE DILLEY AND LEWIS GOPHER

The vernacular architecture of the Seminole Tribe of Florida has largely been given short shrift by architectural historians who tend to celebrate bricks and mortar construction able to last hundreds of years. Traditional Seminole chickee construction emphasizes sustainable building techniques. Chickee structures were built for the needs of a population that frequently moved as a result of the relentless pursuit of the U.S. Army and the ongoing search for available resources. Approaching the issue of architectural heritage management is therefore significantly different in an on-reservation setting. While necessary as part of the National Historic Preservation Act Section 106 review process, opportunities for the architectural historian to engage in meaningful projects with the community were extremely limited. Against this background, the Red Barn project represents a sea change in the history of the Tribal Historic Preservation Office (THPO) and as a partner for community heritage activism.

Author Bios

Carrie Dilley, Visitor Services and Development Manager at the Ah-Tah-Thi-Ki Museum, worked as the Architectural Historian of the THPO from February 2008 to November 2013. She spent nearly six years working to understand what "architectural significance" means from a Tribal perspective. Coming fresh to the THPO out of college, where her Master's in Architectural Studies and Historic Preservation Certificate program focused solely on architectural preservation, she wrongfully believed that historic preservation was synonymous with architectural preservation. It was a shock to see that archaeology was the focus of all historic preservation activities of the

THPO. After she got her feet wet in the office, and started to understand the cultural dynamic of the Tribe, it began to make perfect sense. Dilley's first major task at the THPO was to nominate the Red Barn—a simple vernacular structure with ties to the Seminole cattle industry—to the National Register of Historic Places (the nomination was approved and the property listed in December 2008). Her journey through this process, followed by working to preserve the barn by raising awareness and conducting historic preservation projects, became the hallmark of her time spent as Architectural Historian. Though her official job title has changed, Dilley still works with the THPO on architectural projects and helps share the story of how the built environment represents Seminole history.

Lewis Gopher, Seminole Tribal member from the Brighton Reservation, sees the importance of preserving the Red Barn because it represents such a significant part of his own history. He stresses the fact that cattle raising was the first major financial venture for the Seminoles and paved the way for future business successes. Gopher views the Red Barn as the Hard Rock International franchise purchase of its time—a powerful symbol of self-sufficiency. He believes that education is the key to raising awareness about significant cultural properties. If families do not teach their children the importance of places such as the Red Barn, irreplaceable pieces of Tribal history may be lost.

Introduction

People are naturally drawn to the things they can see, touch, and experience. Therefore it makes sense that architecture exists as a visual representation of history. By preserving this tangible component of our past, we allow history to live on. As of 2014, the Seminole Site File had over 400 properties in its database, and only 20 of those (5 percent) were buildings or structures. Compare those statistics from the same year to the entries in the Florida Master Site File, where approximately 146,000 of the 181,000 resources were historic buildings or structures (81 percent). The number of standing historic buildings or structures on-reservation is disproportionately small compared to the state of Florida as a whole. This is most likely because, on-reservation, it is often the archaeology and other remnants of Seminole culture that tug at people's heartstrings—remainders of camps once occupied by matrilineal families, pieces of pottery that tell stories, beads from jewelry or clothing, plant-gathering areas where medicine was collected, broken pieces of a chickee that was once a home. Aging buildings seem nearly obsolete on the modern-day reservations, thus the need to preserve them is not a priority.

The Seminole Tribe has experienced rapid growth and development over the past few decades. As such, it is easy to forget that up until the 1970s, the Seminoles were still living en masse in chickees (open-sided, thatched-roofed homes made from palmetto and cypress). This may certainly be the case if you drive past the flashing movie screen plastered on the side of the Hard Rock Hotel and Casino on the Hollywood Reservation. That is the Seminole Tribe people know today—a tribe with great wealth and independence. Luxury cars and beautiful modern homes dot the reservations. Despite this rapid advancement, Seminoles still maintain their cultural heritage. Even a cursory glance at reservation property reinforces the way in which the Tribe holds on to its most important piece of architectural history through the building and maintaining of chickees. Most homes feature at least one modern chickee structure, but all the "old" buildings are nearly gone.

At one point, the thought of spending the Tribe's resources (financial or manpower) on saving aged buildings seemed ludicrous. "Why spend money on an old building when you can just knock it down and build a new, better one?" we were asked. Just a few short years later, however, we are working on our first architectural preservation project, completely supported by the Tribe.

History of the Red Barn

The Red Barn represents many firsts for Seminole historic preservation—the first property listed in the National Register of Historic Places, the first building nominated to our in-house Tribal Register of Historic Places, the first site at which we placed a commemorative historical marker, the first site we honored with a community celebration, and the first property we are working diligently to restore. At first glance, the Red Barn might appear to be little more than a modest agricultural structure, but the events that happened within those walls helped shape the modern Seminole Tribe of Florida.

The idea of nominating the Red Barn to the National Register did not originate in 2008. Internal discussions began years before the THPO had an Architectural Historian, before the existence of the THPO, and even before the creation of the Ah-Tah-Thi-Ki Museum in 1997. A 1994 memo from the Seminole Tribal Museum Authority shows correspondence between two Tribal employees (non-Tribal members) about nominating the Red Barn to the National Register (memo on file at the THPO, Big Cypress Reservation). In 2002, the THPO was established by the Seminole Tribal Council, and in 2004 the THPO contracted a cultural resource management (CRM) firm to prepare the National Register nomination. Although these plans never came to fruition, they serve as evidence that people were aware of the Red Barn's significance.

A monumental event occurred in 2006. The Tribal Historic Preservation Officer position was created by a Tribal Resolution, and in October of that year, the THPO entered into an agreement with the National Park Service (Backhouse, this volume). This agreement authorized the Seminole Tribe to assume the functions of the State Historic Preservation Officer with regards to administering the National Historic Preservation Act on reservation land. It suddenly became the duty of the THPO to identify and nominate eligible Tribal properties to the National Register of Historic Places, with the authority to bypass the SHPO altogether. Though any person in the THPO would have been capable of preparing the National Register nomination packet for the Red Barn, the Tribal Historic Preservation Officer thought it best left to an architectural historian—a position created and filled in 2008.

The Red Barn was central to the foundation of the modern Seminole cattle industry on the Brighton Reservation. Historically speaking, however, Seminole cattle keeping did not initiate when the reservations were established. Early evidence of Seminole involvement with cattle dates back hundreds of years. Creek Indians and other tribes of the Creek Confederacy moved south into Florida in the mid-1700s, and followers of the Oconee Creek Ahaya, or Cowkeeper, settled around Alachua, near present-day Gainesville (Sturtevant 1971, 103). Creek Indians had prior experience with raising cattle and obtained herds from the Spanish colonists to continue cattle ranching in their new territory (Cattelino 2004, 69). The importance of cattle to the Seminole people waxed and waned throughout the 1800s and early 1900s.

By the 1930s, the viability of raising cattle once again came into question. Roy Nash, Special Commissioner for the Office of Indian Affairs (later named the Bureau of Indian Affairs, or BIA), was sent to report on the condition of the Seminoles living in the Everglades in 1930. He reported, among other things, that almost no Seminoles owned cattle at that time (Nash 1931, 38). He felt strongly, however, that owning cattle could lead to economic success and stability. James L. Glenn, Christian minister and friend of the Seminoles, was appointed as Seminole agent in 1931. He shared Nash's belief that cattle could help lead to economic independence (Kersey 1989, 29).

The Brighton Seminole Indian Reservation opened on June 13, 1935, as a 2,500-acre rural plot of land north of Lake Okeechobee (Kersey 1989, 96). According to Willie Johns, Brighton resident and Seminole historian, the modern Seminole cattle industry began about seven months later when the U.S. government shipped 700 head of Hereford cattle to Brighton from the

Apache Reservation in Oklahoma. A journey that should have taken only a few short days instead took an entire month. By the time the cattle finally made it to the reservation, only 200 out of 700 head were still alive. The cattle that ultimately survived the journey arrived in poor condition (Willie Johns, personal communication with Carrie Dilley, February 23, 2008). The modern Seminole cattle industry got off to a rocky start, but U.S. government representatives such as Nash and Glenn held steadfast to the belief that cattle could bring income and self-sufficiency to the Tribe.

Although government agents played an important role in bringing cattle back to the Seminoles, it was Fred Montsdeoca who fully organized the Brighton cattle program. Montsdeoca, Florida Agricultural Extension Agent, led the program beginning January 1, 1937, and helped the Tribe gain financial stability (Kersey 1989, 99–100). He believed the Seminoles had a special knack for working with cattle, and noticed that livestock, even the most unruly animals, took to them quite easily (West 2003, 48). Montsdeoca worked specifically with Seminoles who had previous experience with cattle—Frank Shore, Charlie Micco, Naha Tiger, and Willie Gopher—but taught many of the Brighton residents how to properly care for the herds (Montsdeoca 1972). By 1938, the Brighton Reservation had grown to over 35,000 acres, with ample grazing pasture (Kersey 1989, 96). The Brighton cattle industry soon became an economic success, and the burgeoning program ushered in additional changes for the Seminoles.

The cattle industry encouraged the development of democratic ideals that served as the foundation for the first Tribal government. In the fall of 1939, Seminoles elected three Representatives (approved by the BIA Superintendent and the Commissioner of Indian Affairs) to conduct the governmental business of the cattle program. At that turning point, the cattle program changed from a federally funded program to a self-sufficient Tribal program. As such, the Seminoles would now need to repay the government for their expenditures (Covington 1980a, 61). The Brighton Agricultural and Livestock Enterprise formed in 1945, and both cattle trustees and Tribal trustees were elected under this new system. The new Tribal trustees, in theory, were chosen to represent the entire Seminole Tribe. Seminoles on the nearby Big Cypress Reservation followed the model set up at Brighton by acquiring their own herds of cattle and electing their own cattle trustees in 1945 to form the Big Cypress Agricultural and Livestock Enterprise. In 1957, the Tribal government assumed its current form when the Seminoles created their own constitution and by-laws and became the federally recognized Seminole Tribe of Florida (Covington 1980b, 33–36). The cattle industry paved the way for future economic and political endeavors for the Seminoles, and the Red Barn stands today as a reminder of this path to Tribal sovereignty.

Civilian Conservation Corps–Indian Division

The Red Barn is one of the oldest structures still standing on any Seminole reservation. It was built around 1941 as a product of the Civilian Conservation Corps–Indian Division (CCC-ID), based upon plans created by the BIA. A special division of the CCC (one of President Franklin D. Roosevelt's New Deal Programs), the CCC-ID helped "to bring material aid to reservations, to encourage self-administration by Indians, and to conserve and even add to the Indians' considerable land resources" (Gower 1972, 4).

Though little was recorded about the program in its nearly ten years of existence (1933–1942), its benefits were immense. In fact, it is considered one of the most popular New Deal programs overall (Gower 1972, 12). The program provided employment for over 85,000 Native Americans (Franco 1994, 243). One of the most important characteristics of the CCC-ID is that it did not encourage assimilation, but instead supported existing ways of Tribal life. In a 1972 article about the program, author Calvin W. Gower describes the organization:

> The CCC-Indian Division was strongly supported by the Indian Service, for the reason that the CCC did not force the Indians to adjust to the white man's way of living but instead—following the recommendations of Indian Service leaders—deliberately altered the organization, administration, and program to harmonize with the ways of reservation life. . . . By providing financial assistance to working Indians to improve their most tangible asset—their land—the CCC had been a valuable program for American Indians. (Gower 1972:13)

CCC-ID projects on the Seminole Reservations in Florida from January 1934 to August 1939 included the construction of 46 miles of range fence, twenty-one wells, 15 miles of truck trails, and 12 miles of road. Under the CCC-ID, Seminoles also developed over 1,200 acres of range and 14 acres of campground, and planted over 2,000 shrubs and trees ("Florida Seminole CCC" 1939, 20–22). Furthermore, the CCC-ID supplied the funds and facilitated the manpower for the construction of the Red Barn in 1941. Geneva Shore, a Tribal member who grew up on the Brighton Reservation, recalls that Byron Yates was the foreman for the project (Geneva Shore, personal communication with Carrie Dilley, February 26, 2008). Yates had been part of the Seminole CCC-ID from the beginning and had supervised most of the CCC-ID projects on the Seminole reservations (Kersey 1989, 102).

The Brighton Red Barn was not unique in its existence. A second "red barn" was built around the same time period on the Big Cypress Reservation but has since been demolished. Other versions based upon the same BIA plans were rumored to have existed on reservations throughout Indian Country. It is unknown if any other "red barns" are still standing.

The Red Barn dates to the early reservation period. At that time only a few other non-chickee structures existed in Brighton—a school, a headquarters/Tribal office, and a small number of wooden-frame buildings. The Red Barn predates the CBS (concrete block and stucco) structures that fill the reservation today. The Red Barn is not only significant for what it represented to the cattle industry and development of Tribal government but also because it is one of the few pieces of architectural history still standing from that era.

Red Barn Preservation Attempts

The Red Barn has been vacant for decades. Once the center of the cattle industry on the Brighton Reservation, this horse barn eventually became a "town hall" meeting place that housed discussions of forming a Tribal government in the 1950s. The barn was also used for other meetings and gatherings after the constitution was signed under the Council Oak at the Hollywood Reservation in 1957. Some remember the Red Barn as the site of family reunions; others remember it as a place of 4-H haunted houses. And some, even fewer, remember it actually being used as a horse barn. Many of the families who grew up in the camps surrounding the Red Barn remember it fondly. For many Tribal members born and raised on the Brighton Reservation, myself (Gopher) included, the Red Barn has always been a place of significance. My family stressed the importance of the barn to me since I was a small child. My grandfather was even one of the original cattle committee members, and my father was a cattle owner as well. Some children were advised to stay away from the Red Barn because it was "haunted"—possibly a tactic used by parents to keep their children from vandalizing the historic building.

When the Red Barn was listed in the National Register of Historic Places, the next logical step was to plan its preservation. It was in a sad state of disrepair—vines covered the exterior surfaces, grass around the site was overgrown, wood on the east and west facades was mostly rotten or completely missing, the barn was plagued with termites, the stall doors hung by a thread, and the only evidence that doors once covered the entrance were some rusty hinges. The Red Barn stood as the epitome of a building suffering from neglect.

The Red Barn was not completely left alone over the years, however. In its nearly seventy years in existence, it had received a few coats of paint. The wooden shingle roof that once covered the structure was replaced with a red metal roof, and pieces of siding were changed out over time. In 2005, the THPO facilitated the installation of a new metal roof, which effectively held the aging Red Barn together. Even though the Secretary of the Interior's Standards for the Treatment of Historic Properties were not applied when performing these tasks, the efforts helped keep the barn relatively intact.

Even after the Red Barn was listed in the National Register, we found that overall interest from the community was lacking. Was it that other people did not care or just that the THPO did not know whom or how to ask? The THPO and certain key individuals within the community understood the significance of the Red Barn to be beyond what we could see. The challenge was how to communicate our own enthusiasm to the community at large.

In 2009, we began searching for a structural engineer. It was unclear how far the project would proceed at that point, but the THPO decided we should at minimum perform a structural stabilization. We hired an engineer, had the construction drawings in hand, and even hired a contractor to conduct the necessary structural work before the project came to a screeching halt. Due to budget constraints, a problem pertaining to arsenic contamination, and an overall lack of enthusiasm, the Red Barn project was put on hold for an indeterminate amount of time. The THPO tried unsuccessfully for the next three years to raise awareness and build momentum for preserving the aging barn.

Red Barn Celebration

In April 2012, two staff members from the Seminole Media Productions Office (one of whom is a Seminole Tribal member) discovered the Red Barn's National Register listing. They questioned why the THPO had never made a big announcement of the listing, and it was determined we should have a belated celebration to honor the historic building. At that point we were merely set on honoring the Red Barn, but we never lost sight of our preservation pipe dreams. The Red Barn Celebration was set for October 6, 2012.

Party planning built momentum in June. The number of committee participants continued to grow throughout the Brighton Reservation, allowing key community leaders and advocates to become involved and develop public understanding and enthusiasm for the event. At the meetings, our discussion soon extended beyond the celebration itself as we brainstormed ideas about the preservation and future uses of the site, including creating a "Red Barn park" to showcase the Tribe's history and provide a place for the community to gather. We reached out to Brighton residents via a community meeting early in the planning process and shared our ideas with them. We gave them a chance to address their questions and concerns; surprisingly, many people came forward to express their happiness that we were trying to save the old barn.

We presented three different options for preservation at this early community meeting. Option One was to leave the barn alone and let it deteriorate on its own. Option Two was to only conduct structural stabilization based upon the engineer's plans. Option Three was to conduct a full restoration, bringing the barn back to its 1941 appearance. The site could then be utilized to teach visitors about the cattle program or perhaps be turned into a park. While there was no poll taken at the community meeting, it was clear for the first time that the consensus was preservation—Option Three. We were shocked and elated.

Tribal members spoke up about their memories of the Red Barn. "The Red Barn was very important to the Seminole Tribe of those days; not only the cowboys but everyone hung around out here," a Brighton senior shared. He continued: "It was sad when it went into disrepair. I think everyone out here will be overjoyed to fix that old barn up." Another senior expressed her interest in the project: "There's nothing I'd like to see more than a photo of the Red Barn the way it looks today in The Seminole Tribune," she said. "Everyone needs to see the Red Barn and get behind this project" (Gallagher 2012). It was encouraging to see so much enthusiasm for the project. But another area of concern still loomed—how could we financially make the preservation project happen? The budget for the THPO was small, and other sources of funding seemed difficult to obtain.

A Seminole Tribune article describing the community meeting was published at an opportune time. The Director of the Tribe's Community Planning and Development Department (CPD) read about our plight in the Tribe's newspaper and expressed interest in helping with the project. She offered funds from her department to support the cause. The CPD Director grew up on the Brighton Reservation, and it touched her that we were trying to save a building important to her family's history. She became our advocate and offered to put the Red Barn preservation project on the Tribe's capital improvement plan, which secured all necessary funding. At last it seemed we had the support we needed to move forward and truly save the barn. With financial backing and community support, we started planning a structural stabilization for the upcoming months. Everything suddenly fell into place. We contacted the same engineer and contractor from three years prior and found they were still interested in completing the project. They conducted additional site assessments and made slight updates to their drawings to reflect the changes that had occurred during the time we were at a standstill.

In July 2012, we held two planning meetings. The first meeting had modest attendance, but the second meeting included our committee members along with the engineer and contractor. At that meeting we all gave updates on the status of the celebration planning process and made a site visit. This connection proved critical; we were able to get both the engineer's and contractor's perspectives and the Tribal community's perspective on the stabilization. Everyone was in agreement about the steps of the project. Stabilization work began in November.

We overcame several hurdles within the next few months. Though support for the celebration remained steady throughout August, the atmosphere began to change in September. Our committee continued to grow, but with this growth came new opinions and concerns. Some people felt the event was expanding far beyond its modest roots. Others thought the attention brought on by this celebration might actually bring harm to the barn, such as vandalism. Wavering enthusiasm and skepticism from the growing planning committee placed doubts in the mind of the community at large. A last-minute date change caused the momentum to decline even further. Fewer and fewer people started showing up for the planning meetings. It suddenly felt as though the two of us were carrying the weight of the event on our shoulders without the support of the community. We were not expected to come out victorious. The project became a fight to save a significant piece of Seminole history and to show that the THPO was relevant to the Brighton community.

Despite dwindling momentum, the committee still met twice in October 2012. At that point in time there was no rescheduled date for the celebration. The committee met twice again in November with pitiful attendance, but we selected January 26, 2013, as the new date. We decided to scale back the event in many ways (including budget). During those months, it often seemed as though only a few of us cared anymore.

The English textile designer William Morris once stated: "These old buildings do not belong to us only, they belong to our forefathers and they will belong to our descendants unless we play them false. They are not in any sense our own property to do with as we like with them. We are only trustees for

Figure 12.1. Red Barn celebration on January 26, 2013. The cattle drive, which originated at the Marsh Pens, reached the Red Barn as the band began playing in the background to kick off the event. Photo by author.

those that come after us" (Morris 1877). Although Morris was not an architect, he was an early preservation advocate and environmentalist. His words reminded us why we truly wanted to make a difference—we wanted to save the Red Barn for future generations of Seminoles. Even though we were set up for failure, we pushed on. Our persistence finally paid off, and two weeks before the event the support began to pour in again. We saw a renewed enthusiasm. We once again had hope. The words of architect and urban planner Daniel Burnham echoed in our minds: "Make no little plans. They have no magic to stir men's blood. . . . Make big plans; aim high in hope and work" (Moore 1921, 147). We kept persevering.

A Day to Celebrate

On January 26, 2013, the Red Barn Celebration went off without a hitch (Figure 12.1). The event featured a cattle drive, hayride, barbeque, live music, and stories that forever changed people's attitude about architectural and cultural history. Three hundred people (approximately 90 percent Tribal members) showed up to provide their support. We raised awareness and made connections. Tribal members were particularly intrigued by the historic photos we placed around the barn, and the event was a time to reminisce about the past. Although Chairman James Billie had fond memories of the Red Barn, he admitted he had been skeptical that anyone actually cared. Other members of the Tribal Council and Board of Representatives weighed in on why they thought the Red Barn was an important part of the Tribe's history. Tribal elder Happy Jones, age eighty-six, spoke in Creek about how she used to play at the Red Barn as a young girl. Her words truly touched audience members. Tribal members of all ages shared their words and memories about the barn.

> We need this. For years to come at least we'll have something to look back on and say, "You know ol' Willie lived here at one time, Wanda lived here at one time and she left. Here's something that reminds us of where she lived." It's history. . . . We need to have this show every year, make it an annual event.—Stanlo Johns, cattleman and event emcee

> I guess I took it kind of lightly. It's just an old barn. You know how it goes through your head. Who the heck wants to go see an old barn? Next thing I know, it took momentum, and even this morning I thought, "Who the heck is gonna be out here?" I drove around the corner and I saw all of these cowboys, all you people. Thank goodness we got something going. It's monumental, something we can look at for a long time. I'm glad you folks came out to give this old barn a little revitalization here.—Chairman James E. Billie

> We need to do this. We need to preserve things like this. That's what my mom tells me. She says you got to know where you came from before you can know where you're going. This is a very important building to us. This is the grandfather of our businesses for the Seminole Tribe. You see the casinos and the commercials, but that's like the granddaughter, the grandson. This is . . . where it all started, right here, for the Seminole Tribe. We kept horses here to take care of our cattle. . . . You can't put a dollar amount on what this means to us.—Lewis Gopher

Even though the event was free for attendees, we managed to raise over $3,000 to support the preservation project. More important, we raised widespread awareness about historic preservation. We also received the blessing of the Tribe to continue our efforts with restoring the Red Barn.

Reflecting on Success

In order for the community to not only attend the celebration but be engaged by what the event represented, we first went through some trials and errors.

We answered many tough questions and encountered criticism along the way. But the most important component of our journey was that we persevered and made the Red Barn project something to which every person could relate. We showed how the events that occurred at the Red Barn laid the groundwork for the future successes of the Tribe, including the purchase of the Hard Rock franchise in 2006.

The celebration took place amid the structural stabilization, which was completed approximately a month later. Since completion of the stabilization, we have seen regular maintenance and upkeep of the site, and we receive constant inquiries about the status of the project. The Red Barn is once again a source of pride for the Seminole Tribe and particularly the Brighton community.

The Red Barn Celebration came at a time when the THPO needed to fully engage with the Tribal community or risk becoming completely irrelevant. Our office had the reputation of being in existence just to annoy Tribal members by digging up their yards and holding up the construction process. While the project ultimately rested on the shoulders of the Architectural Historian, it helped change the image and working practices of the entire THPO. The community wanted to see that we had heart; we proved that the passion we had for the Red Barn was real and modeled a strong THPO/Tribal community relationship. Overall, this enthusiasm paved the way for other historic preservation projects on the Brighton Reservation, including the protection and rebuilding of historic camps.

According to the Washington Trust for Historic Preservation's website: "Architecture is a direct and substantial representation of history and place. By preserving historic structures, we are able to share the very spaces and environments in which the generations before us lived. Historic preservation is the visual and tangible conservation of cultural identity." There is no better embodiment of this statement than Brighton's Red Barn.

Though the celebration fostered a sense of community pride in the Red Barn, the Tribe's financial priorities have once again shifted. We hired an architect in 2014 to complete restoration plans, but funding was reallocated before construction began. The THPO and Brighton Community have not lost hope that the Red Barn will someday be restored to its full glory—an ever-present reminder of the resilience and success of the Seminole Tribe of Florida.

Figure 12.2. Carrie Dilley (*left*) and Lewis Gopher (*right*). By permission of *The Seminole Tribune*.

References Cited

Cattelino, Jessica. 2004. "Casino Roots: The Cultural Production of Twentieth-Century Seminole Economic Development." In *Native Pathways: Economic Development and American Indian Culture in the Twentieth-Century*, edited by Brian C. Hosmer and Colleen O'Neill, 66–90. Boulder: University of Colorado Press.

Covington, James W. 1980a. "Brighton Reservation, Florida: 1935–1938." *Tequesta* 36:54–65.

———. 1980b. "Seminole Leadership: Changing Substance, 1858–1958." *Tequesta* 40:31–38.

"The Florida Seminole CCC Sponsors a Community Celebration." 1939. *Indians at Work* 6(12):20–22.

Franco, Jere. 1994 "Beyond Reservation Boundaries: Native American Laborers in World War II." *Journal of the Southwest* 36(3):242–254.

Gallagher, Peter. 2012. "Red Barn Project Presented at Brighton Community Meeting." *The Seminole Tribune*, June 27.

Gower, Calvin W. 1972. "The CCC Indian Division: Aid for Depressed Americans, 1933–1942." *Minnesota History* 43(1):3–13.

Kersey, Harry. 1989. *Florida Seminoles and the New Deal*. Boca Raton: Florida Atlantic University Press.

Montsdeoca, Fred. 1972. Interview by Tom King. Samuel Proctor Oral History Program Collection. University of Florida, Gainesville, December 4.

Moore, Charles. 1921. *Daniel H. Burnham, Architect*. Vol. 2, *Planner of Cities*. Boston: Houghton Mifflin Harcourt.

Morris, William. 1889. Address at the Twelfth Annual Meeting of the Society for the Protection of Ancient Buildings. London, July 3.

Nash, Roy. 1931. "Survey of the Seminole Indians of Florida. Technical Report." Washington, D.C.: Government Printing Office.

Sturtevant, William C. 1971. "Creek into Seminole." In *North American Indians in Historical Perspective*, edited by Elaeanor Burke Leacock and Nancy Oestreich Lure, 92–128. New York: Random House.

Washington Trust for Historic Preservation. "Benefits of Historic Preservation." N.d. http://preservewa.org/Benefits-Historic-Preservation.aspx.

West, Patsy. 2003. "A Chronology of Seminole Cattle Raising since 1740." In *Florida Cattle Frontier: Over 400 Years of Cattle Raising*, 37–61. Kissimmee: Florida Cattlemen's Association and the Florida Cracker Cattle Breeders Association.

13

Bringing the Ancestors Home

DOMONIQUE DEBEAUBIEN AND KATE MACUEN

The enactment of the Native American Graves Protection and Repatriation Act (NAGPRA) created a powerful tool that in theory affords tribes greater opportunity to bring their ancestors home to rest. Implementation is a different issue. The bulk of the NAGPRA workload undertaken by the Seminole Tribe of Florida is completed by the Tribal Historic Preservation Office (THPO) Bioarchaeologist who works within the Collections Section. The Bioarchaeologist provides an interface between individual institutions and the THPO by protecting the broader Tribal community from having to deal directly with an issue not culturally appropriate for discussion. Because of the subject matter, the Bioarchaeologist must prepare information sufficient for the NAGPRA Review Committee while staying within culturally appropriate parameters to encourage input from the designated spiritual advisors within the Tribal community.

Author Bios

As a Bioarchaeologist, Domonique deBeaubien initially started working for the THPO in 2011 to help identify fragmented human remains in the field or in the laboratory, so that human burials would not be unknowingly disturbed on-reservation. As she became more familiar with the inner workings of a THPO, it became evident that there was a significant need to address the vast backlog of NAGPRA documentation that had accumulated over the decades. As a non-Native, deBeaubien has adopted the challenge of NAGPRA in hope that she may use her position to work closely and sensitively within the Tribal community to give the long deceased a voice in the repatriation process. For many members of the Seminole Tribe, the act of discussing human remains and burials is considered taboo. For cultural reasons, most members of the Seminole Tribe prefer not to discuss death openly or handle human remains, making it exceptionally challenging for a traditional Seminole Tribal member to participate in many aspects of NAGPRA. DeBeaubien's current role for the Seminole Tribe has encouraged open and thoughtful discussions of repatriation, and she hopes to continue to help strengthen the relationships between the Tribe and repatriating institutions in the future.

Since 2009, Kate Macuen has been the Collections Manager for the THPO. While her work with NAGPRA began in 2012 for the Tribe, her previous collection positions with museums out west provided her with many opportunities to experience and observe the implementation of the law for the past ten years. Macuen received her M.A. in museum science from Texas Tech University, and it was here, while taking a museum law class, that she was really exposed to the challenges and struggles tribes are often faced with when navigating through NAGPRA. Working for the Seminole Tribe has allowed her to take on those challenges by fostering positive relationships between the Tribe and museums and promoting the ethical obligations museums have toward consultation and repatriation.

Introduction

The passage of NAGPRA in 1990 was a meaningful step toward rectifying the indiscriminate collection of Native American human remains, grave goods, and items of cultural patrimony. While numerous repatriations have been conducted throughout the country, there are still significant setbacks that can overburden and undermine the repatriation process. The law's reliance on "good faith effort" is oftentimes inadequate, and striking a balance between legal mandate and ethical responsibility is a constant challenge faced by tribal communities and museums alike. Tribes and museums must cooperate to uphold the integrity of the law, while incorporating a tribal perspective into the practice of NAGPRA. The purpose of this chapter is to expose the reader to this tribal perspective and the valuable lessons that the authors have learned through NAGPRA on strengthening tribal and museum relationships, conducting successful consultations, and encouraging ethical responsibilities. These lessons are also being shared to benefit others who are beginning their own journey of bringing their ancestors home.

NAGPRA: An Overview

NAGPRA was groundbreaking and long overdue. Yet over the last two decades it has been both a blessing and a curse for those with the task of understanding and implementing the regulations. At the Seminole Tribe of Florida Tribal Historic Preservation Office (STOF THPO), NAGPRA-related issues are reviewed by a small committee made up of THPO employees and Tribal elders. Both authors sit on the STOF NAGPRA Committee and are responsible for most of the day-to-day workload relating to NAGPRA compliance.

NAGPRA was promulgated to address an important issue: that federally recognized Native American tribes have not been given an equal amount of respect when it comes to their human ancestral remains and culturally sensitive objects. NAGPRA has created an avenue for museums that receive federal funding (excluding the Smithsonian Institution, which has its own repatriation law) and federal agencies to return cultural material within their collections back to lineal descendants, culturally affiliated Indian tribes, and Native Hawaiian Organizations (NHOs). These cultural items include human remains, associated and unassociated grave goods, sacred items, and items of cultural patrimony. NAGPRA applies both to collections held in museums and to inadvertent discoveries on federal and tribal lands made after November 16, 1990. The regulations differ slightly depending on the object type (human remains or funerary object), and if it is a new discovery or part of an existing museum collection. The implementation of NAGPRA is quite demanding in both time and resources and is a task that is not taken lightly.

Museums and federal agencies that hold Native American cultural material are required to submit inventories of human remains and associated funerary objects, and/or summaries of cultural items housed within their collections, to the National Park Service and all potential culturally affiliated tribes. Through consultation with tribes, museums can determine the cultural affiliation of human remains and identify cultural objects. This process is intended to be completed in consultation with tribes under 25 U.S.C. 3003(b)(A); however, this step is often overlooked. Once affiliation has been determined by the federal agency or museum, it must publish a Notice of Inventory Completion describing those objects and listing the affiliated tribes. Affiliated tribes are then able to make a claim for or request those objects; control of the objects is then legally transferred, and the tribes have the final say of disposition.

When human remains or associated funerary objects are newly discovered on tribal land, or any land that is considered part of a reservation or held in a trust by the U.S. government, ownership lies with the lineal descendant(s) of the deceased Native American. If a lineal descendant cannot be determined, the Indian tribe or NHO on whose tribal land the remains or objects were discovered takes ownership. Unassociated funerary objects, items of cultural patrimony, and sacred objects also belong to the Indian tribe or NHO on whose tribal land the objects were discovered.

The inadvertent discovery of human remains and associated funerary objects is slightly different when on federal land. Those objects belong to the lineal descendants of the deceased Native American, but if no lineal descendants can be determined, ownership is given to the closest culturally affiliated Indian tribe or NHO that can establish cultural affiliation. The same applies to unassociated funerary objects, sacred items, and objects of cultural patrimony. If cultural affiliation cannot be ascertained, control can be given to the requesting Indian tribe that is identified as having aboriginal land claims where the objects were discovered. Aboriginal land is considered any federal land that was evaluated by the Indian Claims Commission of the U.S. Court of Claims and was determined to be the native lands of an Indian tribe (*The Seminole Indians of the State of Florida v. The United States*, 13 Ind. Cl. Comm. 326 [1964]). For the STOF, aboriginal lands encompass the entire state of Florida.

In the past, some federal agencies have expressed confusion over how to interpret the rulings of the Indian Claims Commission courts. Though the Indian Claims Commission excludes several counties within Florida (referred to in the court ruling as The Picolata Purchase, The Forbes Purchase, and The Pensacola Purchase), the Tribe is still associated with this land for both consultation and repatriation purposes. This technical exclusion is due to an additional Indian Claims Commission finding that the Tribe had already been compensated financially for this land (*The Seminole Indians of the State of Florida v. The United States* [1964]). This ruling does not suggest that the Tribe lacks ancestral ties to these counties or to any of the neighboring states in which the Seminole Tribe claims an interest, but rather that the Seminoles had already legally sold these tracts of land to the British, and the Seminoles were therefore not entitled to be compensated again by the U.S. government. We should bear in mind that these courts were established to determine financial culpability, not to write an accurate interpretation of Seminole history. These rulings are just one useful form of documentation federal agencies can use to determine which tribes to contact for consultation or which tribe may have a stronger connection if there are competing claims for remains.

Navigating through NAGPRA

While NAGPRA provides a sound foundation for repatriation efforts, both tribes and museums still face many obstacles (Watkins 2004; Hemenway

2010; Colwell-Chanthaphonh 2012). Though the law has been in effect for over two decades, the burden that repatriation places on tribes has not yet been eased. Many of the issues tribes encounter are also faced by museums: limited time and financial resources, unclear regulations, and an overwhelming abundance of process and paperwork. Other obstacles are faced by tribes alone (for example, cultural implications and religious decisions), and there is not always a clear-cut answer within the tribe as to how they can be resolved.

For most tribes, the process of implementing NAGPRA is, in itself, a large undertaking. Since its inception, hundreds of NAGPRA inventories, summaries, and inadvertent discovery notifications have been sent to the STOF for comment and review. Many tribes lack the resources to support the integral role of a permanent NAGPRA coordinator, or the position must be funded through temporary grants. From the late 1990s to his passing in 2004, Billy L. Cypress worked on NAGPRA claims for the Seminole Tribe. This was only one of his many responsibilities while Director of the Ah-Tah-Thi-Ki Museum. To date, the STOF still does not have the capacity to support a full-time NAGPRA position; rather, the STOF relies on a committee to work through cases. A lack of response from tribal leadership may give museums the impression that tribes are uninterested in making NAGPRA claims, but without reliable financial support and associated staff to handle the work, repatriations are slowed or cannot be conducted.

This leads to an interesting point of discussion. While a lack of capacity to implement NAGPRA within tribes is an obvious obstacle, it also reveals a larger issue. The law did not take into account how tribes and museums would actually staff and fund this essential process. Many museums' role in NAGPRA will eventually come to an end, and they may not have to permanently fund NAGPRA-related positions, budget for NAGPRA-related supplies, or host consultations. Overall, many museums' lack of capacity regarding NAGPRA is finite. But for a tribe, it can potentially be an endless involvement (for example, inadvertent discoveries). How would the process have looked today if NAGPRA had addressed the issue of capacity in the beginning? The following in-depth look into the activities of our THPO has been included to give readers an insider's perspective of how a Tribal department with a diverse and experienced staff strives to build the capacity to effectively and efficiently manage NAGPRA.

The National Tribal Preservation Program was established in 1992 by the National Park Service through amendments to the 1990 National Historic Preservation Act. Through this program, federally recognized tribes can establish a THPO (NPS THPO Program 2014), which assumes many of the responsibilities of the State Historic Preservation Office, but on tribal lands. Through a THPO, tribes can better govern their own cultural resources. For the STOF, one of the most essential priorities of the THPO is to serve the Seminole Tribal community as a whole. This means that we must prioritize the incoming workload to offer the greatest amount of benefit to Tribal members and the communities that we serve.

The majority of THPO resources are used toward the review of on-reservation development and construction projects. The completion of a project from start to finish typically involves every staff member within the THPO. The process begins with the Tribal Archaeology Section, which is responsible for completing archaeological fieldwork and necessary reports. The Collections Section preserves the archaeological material and prepares it for curation. The Archaeometry and Compliance Sections provide supporting technical documentation and maps, as well as internal reviews of our own archaeological reports before they are sent to the Bureau of Indian Affairs (BIA). Each project clearance takes approximately sixty days from start to finish. The THPO receives several hundred on-reservation project requests annually (Mullins, this volume).

The THPO also devotes a significant amount of time to off-reservation compliance (Mueller, this volume). Our office is responsible for reviewing federal undertakings within the Seminole Tribe's area of interest, which has been defined as any land that is considered aboriginal or ancestral to the STOF. Currently, this land base encompasses six states in the southeastern United States, as well as the Tribe's own six reservations. In 2013 alone, the THPO received over 3,600 off-reservation project notifications. The STOF THPO must function at the highest level of efficiency to keep up with the large amount of work that comes our way. A creative balancing act is often needed to tackle the NAGPRA workload.

Fortunately, at the STOF THPO we all wear many hats, allowing us to carry out the implementation of NAGPRA without having an official NAGPRA coordinator. The protection and repatriation of human remains are carried out under the STOF Cultural Resource Ordinance (Appendix) and are important matters to the Tribal community and fundamental to the mission of the THPO. In 2012, with the strong support of Tribal leadership, the STOF THPO formed a diverse and dedicated committee to begin the long process of bringing Tribal ancestors home. The committee is made up of seven members: five THPO employees and two Tribal elders, one of whom serves as Chief Justice in the Tribal court system. Each member provides a different area of expertise, from legal to cultural and historical research to logistics. Together, the STOF NAGPRA Committee selects priority cases, makes decisions about consultations, and executes the NAGPRA process. The establishment of this committee has eased the burden of work for any one individual, and we have found it to be a successful way for our office to better manage NAGPRA.

The committee meets once a month to review active cases and introduce new notifications. A progress report is provided to document where the THPO currently stands in the NAGPRA process on current cases. Selection of new cases is based upon the existing workload, and often cases are prioritized based upon their cultural significance. All NAGPRA matters have significant cultural value; however, because staff resources are limited, cases must be prioritized. For example, if human remains in a NAGPRA inventory have individual names, come from a historic Seminole context, or have storage conditions that do not meet cultural standards, they are typically given a high priority status. This process is dynamic, and often changes in priority are made based upon evolving circumstances—for example, new research and the political atmosphere that might make some cases of more immediate concern.

Even though decisions are made as a team and tasks are divided among the committee's members, working through NAGPRA takes diligence and time. Hundreds of inventories and notices to review come to the Tribe from all over the United States. NAGPRA correspondence is not limited to the state of Florida or even the Seminole Tribe's aboriginal lands. Museums from all across the country hold collections from explorers or scientists who made expeditions to the wild lands of Florida in the nineteenth and early twentieth centuries to conduct excavations on Indian mounds. Thousands of human remains made their way back into these collections and have lingered there in untouched boxes over the decades. NAGPRA has required museums to reexamine the contents of these collections, which has resulted in notifications from thirty-seven different states and 195 institutions to date. A great amount of respect is given to those institutions that diligently follow their obligations under NAGPRA, sending notices to sometimes numerous culturally affiliated tribes. However, a museum must only manage what it has in its control, whereas a tribe may quite literally have interest in the holdings of hundreds of museums all across the country and even the world.

A Long Journey Home: University of Massachusetts and Amherst College Repatriation

Our first formal NAGPRA repatriation project began in 2012 with the University of Massachusetts–Amherst and the Beneski Museum of Natural History, Amherst College. The THPO soon came to learn that the remains we were working to repatriate had a long and complicated history. Originally excavated by Amherst College in the 1920s as part of a university geological expedition, the remains were taken from multiple burial mounds along the east coast of Florida. F. B. Loomis, a professor of geology at Amherst College at the time, was keenly interested in mammal evolution and taxonomy, and conducted several expeditions to Florida to investigate Ice Age megafauna. Loomis encountered numerous "burial heaps," or mounds, and took the liberty of excavating and collecting the individuals interred within.

Unfortunately, very little is known about the context from which the remains were removed. Field notes were either lost or never completed, and the supposed original location of excavation has long since been developed. Loomis did publish several accounts of his excavations in Florida, claiming that some of the remains were found in the same context and of the same age as Ice Age megafauna (Cooke 1926; Gidley 1926). Unfortunately, it is impossible to know if there is any truth to this claim or even if the remains described are the same that ended up in the museum collections. The *Boston Globe* summarized the Amherst College excavations and described an encounter with Loomis in 1925: "On one table was the skull of some human, on another a forearm and still another pair of jaw bones. . . . Probably they are not human bones at all, but a camel or a turtle" (*Boston Globe* 1925). As illustrated by this newspaper passage, 1920s archaeology left something to be desired. The evidence we have left to piece back together is largely conjecture, and probably inaccurate. What we do know is that the remains came from burial mounds from the east coast of Florida, and that based on osteological analysis, they were hundreds of years old. In the end, the remains were taken back to Massachusetts and housed by Amherst College until the 1980s, when the collection was divided and most of the remains were transferred to the University of Massachusetts–Amherst.

While both institutions were eager to see the remains repatriated, there had not yet been any input from culturally affiliated tribal communities that may have wanted to claim them. Formal consultation with any potentially affiliated tribe is one of the first and most important steps toward repatriation. Consultation allows tribes to have a voice about their ancestors and provides an official channel for tribes to make recommendations about treatment, storage, and disposition. Amherst College and the University of Massachusetts invited the STOF, as well as other potentially affiliated tribes, to participate in consultation. This can be a delicate process, and there is no standard format of how consultation should be conducted. As long as institutions are receptive to tribal requests and conduct the process with honesty and respect, consultation can be an incredibly effective tool. Fortunately, in this instance consultation was a positive process. All three tribes present agreed to jointly claim the remains, and the STOF was selected to take the lead on planning logistics.

Once consultation is concluded, museums must publish a document in the *Federal Register* called a Notice of Inventory Completion (NIC) that determines which tribe(s) may physically claim the remains (25 U.S.C. §3003 1990). In this instance, the museums worked together to publish separate notices for the remains in their individual collections. The same tribes were listed as culturally affiliated in each museum notice (*Federal Register* 2012a, 2012b). There is no set timeline on how quickly the transfer must occur, but any tribe listed in the NIC is able to take possession. As the lead agency for this repatriation, one of the first priorities for the Tribe was to address the issue of funding. Many museums do not or cannot budget the financial resources to cover the cost of repatriation, and often the responsibility of securing funding rests entirely on the Tribe. The cost of any repatriation is highly variable, depending on the volume of material being returned and the distance being traveled. Using outside funding, such as grants, has become a crucial key in supporting repatriation projects, especially when internal budgets may not always cover these costs.

The National NAGPRA Program offers consultation/documentation and repatriation grants that are available to both museums and tribes, and according to National NAGPRA, over two-thirds of grant monies are awarded to tribes (NPS National NAGPRA Program 2009). Thirteen repatriation grants were awarded with a total of $162,269 in 2013, and the STOF was one of ten tribes that successfully received a grant to fund the return of their ancestors, while only three recipients were museums (NPS National NAGPRA Program 2013). It took several months to write the grant and over a year to secure that funding and coordinate all of the travel logistics for the physical transfer of remains.

Working for a tribal government means there are many checks and balances in place for large-scale projects, and grants are no exception. First, a grant must be approved by multiple Tribal departments, including the Legal and Risk Management Departments, and then presented before the Tribal

Council to receive a Tribal resolution, which is required for the grant application. The Tribal Council is the Tribe's own internal governing body and is made up of a Chairman, Vice-Chairman, and Representatives from three of the Tribe's reservations: Hollywood, Brighton, and Big Cypress. Bringing a resolution before the Council illustrates the importance the Tribe places on NAGPRA matters. Resolution C-151-13 (repatriation grant for the University of Massachusetts and Amherst College repatriation) was unanimously passed on March 8, 2013, marking another major milestone for the Seminole Tribe and our NAGPRA Committee.

During this time, communication between the University of Massachusetts, Amherst College, and our office was essential to keep all parties updated and to make the museums aware of our own internal processes. Once the grant was awarded, logistical planning began and details from hotels to travel routes were coordinated. Even the smallest of details were worked out in advance to help avoid travel delays. Although the overall process of securing funding is time consuming, it placed the financial responsibility on National NAGPRA and helped ease the financial burden for the Tribe.

When all of the financial hurdles had been cleared, the final step in the repatriation was formally transferring legal possession to the STOF and safely transporting the Seminole ancestors to their final resting place. After flying in from Florida, the drive from Massachusetts took four days, and strict courier procedures were put into place so the remains were never left unattended. When the reinterment location was reached, the remains were peacefully laid to rest, prayers were said, and the Seminole ancestors were finally put back into the earth. Overall, it was a positive experience for everyone involved. The tribes were genuinely grateful to the dedicated museum staff that saw the process through to the end, and felt that the repatriation from start to finish had been completed with respect and dignity toward the ancestors.

Experiences with other institutions have not always been as positive, but have been used as learning experiences to give us a better understanding of the shortfalls within the NAGPRA legislation, and how to use those gaps to better the process. A few of the main limitations that need to be addressed include funding obligations, consultation procedures, and how museums classify objects and human remains under NAGPRA.

As already briefly discussed, repatriation should be a joint effort, with all parties willing to work together through the process, especially when it comes to funding the repatriation. From a Tribal perspective, the NAGPRA process could be improved if museums were more proactive in acquiring funding for repatriations. The National NAGPRA Program offers two different types of grants: consultation/documentation and repatriation. Repatriation grants are noncompetitive and easily cover the cost of most repatriation projects. Sharing the financial obligations is one way to increase cooperative partnerships between tribes and museums. Ideally, the issue of funding should be discussed early during consultation. Having a mutual understanding of all parties' responsibilities helps to ease the process and encourage transparency.

For most tribes, the NAGPRA process really begins with consultation. NAGPRA is based on the premise that tribes and institutions will come together and have meaningful conversations about human remains and sacred and cultural objects in their collections. This means putting aside the common Eurocentric view of history and actually listening to what tribes have to say. The idea of meaningful, two-way consultation may seem like an easy concept to understand, but more often than not, consultation involves a tribe being told the story of their past through an outsider's interpretation of Native American material culture. Hundreds and thousands of artifacts and individuals have already been categorized as "nonfunerary" or "culturally unidentifiable" without going through the consultation process or giving appropriate deference to tribal interpretations. As of August 2014, National NAGPRA lists 7,265 sets of human remains as culturally unidentifiable from the state of Florida, as determined by the holding institution (NPS National NAGPRA Program 2014a). The STOF did not contribute to the culturally unidentifiable (CUI) determinations for any of those remains; they were made solely by the museums that house them.

A case brought before the NAGPRA Review Committee in 2012 highlights this discrepancy in object interpretation. Between 1995 and 2006, the Tlingit T'akdeintaan Clan of Hoonah, Alaska (represented by the Huna Totem Corporation and the Hoonah Indian Association), began the formal process for the return of thirty-nine sacred objects and objects of cultural patrimony with the University of Pennsylvania Museum of Archaeology and Anthropology (Penn Museum) (NPS National NAGPRA Review Committee 2012). The Tlingit asserted that these objects hold deep spiritual meaning and were used for a variety of ceremonial and religious purposes. The Penn Museum purchased the objects in 1924 from Archie White, a member of the Snail House, which makes up part of the T'akdeintaan clan of the Tlingit (Putnam 2014). The Tlingit contend that while the objects may have been sold, White did not have the authority to do so, which can only be given by the clan as a whole. In this case, the Penn Museum had to make a determination not only of the objects' cultural significance but also of which party had the legal right of possession.

Under NAGPRA, sacred objects are defined as "ceremonial objects which are needed by traditional Native American religious leaders for the practice of traditional Native American religions by their present day adherents" (25 U.S.C. §3001[2] [C–D] 1990), and an object of cultural patrimony is described as "an object having ongoing historical, traditional, or cultural importance central to the Native American group or culture itself" (25 U.S.C. §3001[2] [C–D] 1990). In 2009, and after years of negotiations, the University of Pennsylvania made the determination that these objects were not sacred to the claiming tribes, nor were they objects of cultural patrimony. The Penn Museum also determined that the objects were purchased fairly, despite having been sold in a manner that clashed with Tlingit traditional conventions. These decisions did not consider the traditional or cultural values of those groups, and an academic institution was allowed to define the cultural practices of the Hoonah people and the objects they consider sacred.

By honoring and giving due diligence to the consultation process, disputes such as these can be easily avoided. Creating an open dialogue between tribes and museums, where both parties come to the table as equal players, is the responsibility of everyone involved. It is important that museums do not independently decide what is sacred to any tribe because many museums are not always equipped with the specialized knowledge to make accurate determinations of what is sacred, what is CUI, or even what types of objects may be funerary. Discussions about traditional beliefs and values are not always easy for either party involved, but through meaningful dialogue, a mutual respect and appreciation of shared goals can be achieved.

A recent addition to NAGPRA legislation addresses one of the more perplexing issues of assigning objects or human remains to certain tribes. There are thousands upon thousands of human remains and objects listed in inventories with the designation CUI. Often this is due to collections with poor provenience, inadequate record keeping, or a lack of effort in making accurate identifications. The nearly endless inventories of CUI remains are a constant source of frustration for many indigenous communities. Investigation of NAGPRA inventories frequently reveals that many of these remains are easily identifiable by the tribes with the appropriate knowledge. Confusingly, many of the CUI inventories actually list affiliated tribes, leaving many to wonder why remains are listed as CUI.

In a rush to comply with NAGPRA legislation, many museums placed human remains on the CUI inventories and then forgot about them. Because of the challenges of repatriation under previous regulations, these remains have sat in limbo for decades. New regulations, amended in May 2013, implement procedures for the disposition of CUI Native American human remains (25 U.S.C. §3001 [8][c][5] 1990). Museums must now initiate consultation with potentially affiliated tribes, and if affiliation cannot be attributed, tribes may still request disposition of the remains without having to go before the NAG-PRA Review Committee, which oversees repatriation activities. Tribes with evidence that the human remains were taken from tribal lands, or aboriginal lands as determined by the Indian Claims Commission, may now claim the remains and have them returned (NPS National NAGPRA Program 2014b).

It is unclear how the new regulations will increase the ability of tribes to claim CUI human remains, but for the STOF, it is significant. The Indian Claims Commission was established in 1946 for tribes to file grievances, primarily land claims, against the U.S. government. The commission determined in 1964 that the STOF had aboriginal land claims to nearly the entire state of Florida (*The Seminole Indians of the State of Florida v. The United States* [1964]). In essence, the STOF has legal standing to claim any human remains excavated from the state of Florida now housed in museum collections across the country. A tribe is never obligated to pursue repatriation under NAG-PRA, but this will greatly aid the Seminole Tribe when making repatriation claims, and should, in theory, help many other tribes claim unaffiliated remains as well. Additionally, the expanded opportunity for an open dialogue during consultation should help more tribes and museums identify cultural affiliation for the unidentified remains in their collections, which both sides readily agree is an important benefit of the legislation.

Ethics

Although NAGPRA is widely considered human rights legislation and the act of repatriation is strongly grounded in the ideals of ethics, there are no specific ethical guidelines established in the NAGPRA regulations. It is up to each institution to decide how it will interact with tribes and treat the human remains and objects that are housed in its collections. Many regulations in NAGPRA are based upon the principle of a "good faith effort." Museums and tribes do not always agree on the interpretations of what is required under the designation of good faith or within the spirit of the law. It is expected, although not regulated, that museums will exercise ethical decision making (American Alliance of Museums 2000). But what happens, for example, when a tribe makes a request regarding the treatment of sensitive cultural material and a museum chooses not to respond? What are a museum's ethical obligations (not under the law) according to the consensus of museum professionals?

What recourse does a tribe have when museums deny cultural requests, and intentionally slow down the repatriation process?

Many would find any of those scenarios shocking—for example, a tribe making specific requests regarding the treatment of their ancestors only to have this request denied by the holding institution. However, it does happen. During a current repatriation project regarding the cultural treatment of Seminole ancestors, the STOF THPO experienced firsthand the challenges faced when a tribe and museum do not agree on what is ethically or morally acceptable. The remains in question are in the collection of a large university museum. Many are women and children who died during the enforced Indian Removal period in the 1830s. There are also Seminole warriors whose crania were removed by battlefield surgeons during the Second Seminole War. Several of these are known individuals and are likely connected to living members of the Seminole Tribe.

This case first came to the THPO's attention when a letter was sent to the STOF's Ah-Tah-Thi-Ki Museum from an outside researcher asking for help connecting the 1830s Seminole crania to living members of the Tribe. It was the first time the THPO had ever heard of these remains, and the Tribe wanted to know more about their history and how they came to rest in a museum collection. The Tribe made a formal request for all of the museum's documentation relating to these remains; however, months passed and no documentation was received. Request after request was made to the museum, and each time the Tribe was asked to be patient. In the meantime, the remains stayed accessible within the museum's collection, university researchers continued their analysis and examinations, and papers were publicly presented on the Seminole remains without the Tribe's consent.

Within the STOF Tribal community, research on human remains is typically considered inappropriate. Those who have passed on were meant to stay where they were originally placed or buried, and their removal and study is akin to a cultural nightmare. In this particular case, the STOF THPO respectfully requested that the museum cease research on the Seminole ancestors and hold the remains privately within their collections. Tribes are sensitive to the formal NAGPRA processes that museums must navigate through and are aware that repatriations are not able to happen instantaneously. However, while consultation occurs and the paperwork and notices are completed, a museum can act on their good faith effort by storing remains and controlling access in a manner that is respectful to tribal beliefs in anticipation of the physical transfer. The THPO's cultural requests were ignored, and the Tribe was left virtually powerless when it came to protecting their deceased ancestors. Short of pressing legal action, the Tribe simply had to wait until the museum was ready to move forward. Exactly one year after the initial request, the STOF THPO received the museum's complete inventory and almost immediately began to pursue formal consultation.

This particular case study demonstrates that there are still challenges for museums and tribes to find a common ground through NAGPRA. It helps to pose the question of how NAGPRA compliance could be handled better in the future. In this instance, National NAGPRA had not properly enforced its own rules: the museum had denied the Tribe's request to serve as a culturally appropriate repository for Seminole remains, and the museum had still not fulfilled its legal obligation to provide documentation and formal consultation in a timely manner.

Formal consultation was held at the museum in the fall of 2013. It quickly became a classic example of two very different worlds coming together: the realm of academia, on the one hand, and, on the other, a sovereign nation deeply rooted in religion and tradition. The consultation began with several of the museum's Repatriation Committee members explaining their anthropological research interests in detail. In past experiences, most consultations have begun with a traditional prayer and the direction of the conversation was agreed upon by all parties involved. To tribes, these types of consultations can be a deeply private and spiritual meeting, and it is always important for everyone to feel like respected and equal players at the table. One of the Seminole Tribe's most respected Medicine Men, Bobby Henry, later described his discomfort inside that room. He felt the museum had created such a controlled environment that his words had become trapped, that they were not free to speak for his ancestors as they needed to.

Additionally, during consultation, the museum's Repatriation Committee appealed to Tribal elders and stated that the museum could provide a better home for the remains than the Tribe and asked them to respect the museum's desire to continue analysis on remains it has had in its possession for over 150 years. In the end, the needs of the Seminole Tribe went unheard, and the STOF's repatriation committee walked away from the consultation feeling disheartened. Although this case highlights many issues, the first and most crucial is the lack of respect for indigenous peoples and their ancestors. There are still some museums that tend to see human remains as their possessions; they collected them, they house them, they own them.

Strained relationships between tribes and museums will not improve until attitudes shift away from ownership and focus more on what is ethically appropriate. A representative from the American Indians Against Desecration simplified the purpose of repatriations by saying, "This has nothing to do with ownership. It's about respect for ancestors—everybody's ancestors. I respect your ancestors, my ancestors, and the way to respect them is by taking care of them, trying to make sure that they can continue their journey to the spirit world" (King 2002, 103–111). Decisions on how human remains are treated should be made in conjunction with the relevant tribes, not by museum professionals alone, even when the human remains are in museum control. While it is nearly impossible to regulate a moral obligation, realistic time lines for providing a tribe with documentation and conducting consultation are clearly within the intent of the law. Clear and easily enforceable penalties for museums that do not comply would also help eliminate the intentional stall tactics used by some institutions. Further conditions within the law that would offer tribes the opportunity to help decide how human remains are treated while in museum control would benefit all parties.

Second, the museum's behavior is not representative of a good faith effort, nor did its actions fall within the spirit of the law. And while NAGPRA may not lay out an ethical roadmap to be followed by museums, this cannot be used as an excuse for the lack of a good faith effort. Many museums, especially accredited institutions, follow a strict code of ethics, setting moral and professional standards of what it means to go above and beyond the letter of the law. We have seen firsthand museums that, through tribal consultation, have made institutional and policy changes that take into consideration a tribe's spiritual and cultural traditions, such as creating restricted access to NAGPRA objects still within the collection or adjusting handling procedures (Harms 2012). Even the act of turning an object toward a specific cardinal direction at the request of a tribe is a simple example of a good faith effort.

As one of the most trusted types of institutions in our society, museums have a significant role and responsibility in educating the public, setting high standards and guidelines for professional practice, and preserving both the tangible and intangible cultural heritage of tribes. Yet sometimes museums still hold on to antiquated methodologies and push for scientific advancements and research at the cost of human rights. The recent challenges our own NAGPRA Committee has faced have been a reminder that museums must be activists for the preservation of Tribal cultural heritage. Museums that are implementing NAGPRA should use their role as trusted educational and cultural institutions to set an example of strong ethics and morals while creating open dialogue as they work toward successful repatriations with tribes.

Summary

NAGPRA has laid the groundwork for repatriation across Indian Country. It has created a platform for museums and tribes to work collectively toward the return of tribal ancestors and sacred objects. However, the past two decades have shown us that there is still work to be done in order to make the law more tribally mindful and effective. Additional provisions should be made to further protect these significant objects while in a museum's custody and to provide clearer definitions and regulations on ethical considerations, which can often be interpreted differently by tribes and museums. We have learned many lessons through the work of other tribes who have helped pave the repatriation path, along with our own current work with NAGPRA. And while there are many museums carefully and respectfully seeing the NAGPRA process through, others are still learning about the process, and still others are navigating their way through the sometimes unfamiliar territory of cultural sensitivity. We are optimistic that many of these pressing issues will be resolved. Until then, tribes will continue to press forward by advocating change and collaborating with museums to create open and meaningful dialogues. With each successful repatriation, museums and tribes steadily create a middle ground where tribal voices are of equal status and bringing ancestors home is the shared goal of all.

Figure 13.1. Domonique deBeaubien. By permission of Kate Macuen, Collections Manager, Seminole Tribe of Florida Tribal Historic Preservation Office.

Figure 13.2. Kate Macuen. By permission of Katie Gregory.

References Cited

American Alliance of Museums. 2000. "Code of Ethics for Museums." http://www.aam-us.org/resources/ethics-standards-and-best-practices/code-of-ethics.

Boston Globe. 1925. "Amherst Party Finds Skeletons of Animals of 800,000 Years Old." November 1.

Colwell-Chanthaphonh, Chip. 2012. "The Work of Repatriation in Indian Country." *Human Organization* 71(3):278–291.

Cooke, Wythe. 1926. "Fossil Man and Pleistocene Vertebrates in Florida." *American Journal of Science* 12(71):441–452.

Federal Register. 2012a. "Notice of Inventory Completion: Beneski Museum of Natural History, Amherst College, Amherst, MA." *Federal Register* 77(243). December 18. 74872–74873.

———. 2012b. "Notice of Inventory Completion: University of Massachusetts Amherst, Department of Anthropology, Amherst, MA." *Federal Register* 77 (243). December 18. 74868–74869.

Gidley, James W. 1926. "Fossil Man in Florida." *American Journal of Science* 12(69):254–264.

Harms, Cecily. 2012. "NAGPRA in Colorado: A Success Story." *University of Colorado Law Review* 83(2):593–632.

Hemenway, Eric. 2010. "Trials and Tribulations in a Tribal NAGPRA Program." *Museum Anthropology* 33(2):172–179.

King, Thomas. 2002. *Thinking About Cultural Resources Management: Essays From the Edge*. Walnut Creek, Calif.: Altamira Press.

NPS National NAGPRA Program. 2009. "Journeys to Repatriation: 15 Years of NAGPRA Grants (1994–2008)." Washington, D.C.: National Park Service, U.S. Department of the Interior.

———. 2013. "FY2013 Final Report: National NAGPRA Program." Washington, D.C.: U.S. Department of the Interior.

———. 2014a. "National NAGPRA Online Databases, Culturally Unidentifiable (CUI) Native American Inventories Database." http://grants.cr.nps.gov/CUI/index.cfm.

———. 2014b. "Indian Land Areas Judicially Established 1978." http://www.nps.gov/nagpra/DOCUMENTS/ClaimsMAP.htm.

NPS National NAGPRA Review Committee. 2012. "Native American Graves Protection and Repatriation Review Committee Findings Related to the Identity and Return of Cultural Items in the Possession of the University of Pennsylvania Museum of Archaeology and Anthropology, Philadelphia, PA." *Federal Register* 77(243). December 18. 74875.

NPS THPO Program. 2014. "Tribal Preservation Program." http://www.nps.gov/tribes/tribal_historic_preservation_officers_program.htm.

Putnam, L. Jennifer. 2014. "NAGPRA and the Penn Museum: Reconciling Science and the Sacred. Concept 37." http://concept.journals.villanova.edu/article/view/1718.

Watkins, Joe. 2004. "Becoming American or Becoming Indian? NAGPRA, Kennewick and Cultural Affiliation." *Journal of Social Archaeology* 4(1):60–80.

14

Consultation and Compliance

Then and Now

BRADLEY M. MUELLER

Consultation: The act of exchanging information and opinions about something in order to reach a better understanding of it or to make a decision (*Cambridge Dictionaries* Online 2015).

Today most people view the land base (and therefore Area of Interest [AOI]) of the Seminole Tribe of Florida (STOF) as the relatively small five reservations dotting the landscape of South Florida. This misleading demographic situation masks the sovereignty of a people who historically lived throughout a large portion of southeastern North America. The responsibility for consultation with relevant agencies within the aboriginal, ancestral, and ceded lands of the STOF is therefore no small task, as this land base comprises a large portion of nine individual modern states. With a staff of just two people who work back-to-back out of a single office, the compliance team must sift through the 99 percent of projects that do not impact sites of significance to the Tribe in order to find the 1 percent that do. Cross-referencing state archaeological site files, historical documentation, and tribal oral histories makes this task even more daunting. The 1 percent is, however, incredibly important. The example of Egmont Key, a small island just off of the coast from the modern city of Tampa, is a great case in point. During the Third Seminole War (1855–1858), Tribal members were forcibly taken to this island to await steamships and removal to the West. Years of fighting and lack of provisioning meant that, for many, it was the last land they would see. Today the dark history of the island lies hidden as sea levels rise and erosion threatens to submerge it forever. Consultation on beach stabilization confronted all stakeholders with a difficult history but one that eventually presented an opportunity for collaboration and cultural understanding.

Author Bio

Bradley M. Mueller is presently the Compliance Review Supervisor for the Seminole Tribe of Florida Tribal Historic Preservation Office (STOF THPO). Prior to his current posting, he was an archaeologist with the THPO Tribal Archaeology Section (TAS). Mueller earned his B.A. in general science from Webster University in St. Louis in 1986. In 1987, he began graduate studies in physical anthropology–primatology at Tulane University of Louisiana before relocating back to St. Louis to pursue a developing interest in archaeology. In 1991, he was awarded an M.A. in anthropology from Washington University in St. Louis.

Mueller's understanding of archaeology and cultural resources is heavily influenced by his twenty-plus years of experience in contract archaeology/cultural resources management. His first field project, undertaken while he was still attending Washington University, consisted of Phase II testing of a small prehistoric site in eastern Missouri. During the intervening twenty-four years, Mueller has participated in Phase I, II, and III investigations in various capacities, from field technician to project manager. He has worked extensively in the Southeast and Midwest and along the Gulf Coast, and less extensively in the Southwest, Great Basin, Plains, and Northeast. This work was performed for universities, for private companies (large and small), and for Native American tribes (briefly for the Navajo Nation and now for the STOF). As field director and project manager, Mueller has contributed to over 160 technical reports as author, coauthor, illustrator, or editor.

In his current capacity as Compliance Review Supervisor, Mueller draws on his knowledge of the types of culturally important resources that can be encountered in the field, his understanding of the appropriateness of employing specific methodologies to avoid or investigate these resources, and his sensitivity to the advice, counsel, and direction provided by Tribal members. His understanding of federal preservation law and the rights and responsibilities of Native American tribes under those laws continues to evolve.

Background

The National Historic Preservation Act (NHPA) (Pub. L. No. 89–665; 16 U.S.C. §470 et seq.) was signed into law on October 15, 1966. The 1966 act created the Advisory Council on Historic Preservation (ACHP), the National Register of Historic Places (NRHP), and the State Historic Preservation Offices (SHPOs). The law requires that federal agencies evaluate the impact of all federally funded or permitted projects on "historic properties," and it provides a process, the Section 106 process, by which these requirements can be met. Historic properties refer to districts, sites, buildings, structures, and objects determined to be "significant" in American history, architecture, archaeology, engineering, or culture. These properties may date to either prehistoric or historic time periods, with historic period properties usually having to be at least fifty years old (there are exceptions). Generally regarded as the most effective preservation legislation in the United States, the act does not directly guarantee the preservation of any particular property, but it does establish a process that requires, among other things, a dialogue (consultation) between interested parties over the treatment of important cultural resources (that is, historic properties). Among others, interested parties include Native American tribes and Native Alaskan villages.

Although NHPA 1966 established SHPOs and the position of State Historic Preservation Officer, it was not until the act was amended in 1992 that Indian tribes were allowed to establish THPOs and Tribal Historic Preservation Officers and to assume the role of SHPOs on tribal lands. It is important to note that some tribes had effectively, if not "officially," already established historic preservation offices and assumed many of the roles of a historic preservation officer prior to the 1992 amendments. The role of tribal consultant for Section 106 purposes may or may not be the responsibility of a THPO. Tribes that do not currently have federally recognized THPOs are still legally entitled to participate in the 106 process and may designate a person or persons of their choosing (tribal or nontribal) for consultation. The designated contact could be a tribal Chairperson, Chief, Elder, Medicine Person, and so forth.

On October 3, 2006, the Tribal Historic Preservation Officer of the STOF assumed the duties previously performed by the SHPO (see Backhouse, this volume). From its inception, the STOF THPO has divided consultation responsibilities between two entities. Currently, on-reservation consultation is performed by the Deputy Tribal Historic Preservation Officer, while off-reservation consultation is performed by the THPO Compliance Review Section (CRS). Although the STOF allows the THPO to conduct consultation on its behalf, guidance from Tribal government and Tribal cultural advisors is routinely solicited, especially on more complicated or problematic issues. The Tribal Chairman can, and does, consult directly with federal agencies at his discretion. While consultation over routine matters generally occurs at a fairly rapid pace, especially sensitive or complex consultations can be lengthy in order to ensure that the Tribe has time to develop its position and to make its position known to the THPO. Federal agencies and other nontribal entities often have difficulty dealing with the length of time it may take a tribe to "develop its position" and to respond to a request for comments. It is important for these nontribal groups to keep in mind that many of the issues that tribes have to deal with, especially issues involving the relocation or reburial of human remains, have no historical precedents within the tribe; it was never expected that ancestors would be excavated and reinterred. Tribal consideration of these issues and consensus building can be long, difficult, and painful.

The CRS is one of four sections within the THPO. The other three sections include Archaeometry, Collections, and Tribal Archaeology. The THPO can also draw on the expertise of an Architectural Historian who is on the staff of the Ah-Tah-Thi-Ki Museum. All of these sections report to the Deputy Tribal Historic Preservation Officer, who in turn reports to the THPO. Staffing levels within the CRS have varied over time as the section responds to changing demands and improved efficiencies. Currently, the CRS is comprised of two individuals, a Compliance Review Supervisor and a Compliance Review Specialist. In addition to its primary responsibility of conducting Section 106 off-reservation consultation, the section also performs other duties, including:

- conducting research, both document-based and ethnographic, on cultural sites of importance to the STOF;
- conducting research on the off-reservation Area of Responsibility (AOR);
- maintaining an off-reservation Geodatabase;
- participating in the STOF THPO Native American Graves Protection and Repatriation Act (NAGPRA)/Florida Statute 872.05 Committee;
- participating on the STOF Tribal Register of Historic Places (TRHP) Committee;
- non-Section 106 consulting with the state of Florida SHPO concerning statute 872.05 issues (unmarked human burial law);
- reviewing and editing on-reservation TAS reports for Section 106 sufficiency;
- reviewing and editing on-reservation reports for STOF Cultural Resource Ordinance (C-01-16) sufficiency; and
- other tasks as assigned.

Introduction

Since its Tribal inception in 2002 and its National Park Service recognition in 2006, the STOF THPO has committed itself to strengthening departmental capacity, defending Tribal interests and Tribal sovereignty through the consultation process, and improving the timeliness and the quality of these consultations. The remainder of this chapter is devoted to examining three topics directly related to the ability of the CRS to assist the THPO in conducting its business and fulfilling its Tribal mission. These topics are: dealing with the increasing volume of consultation requests; delineating a Tribal AOI; and providing a Tribal perspective on the consultation process.

Requests for consultation received by the CRS have steadily increased over the years. These requests originate with multiple (mostly federal) agencies and encompass a wide geographic area. Information concerning the quantity of documents received and processed by the CRS and the variety of agencies generating these documents is presented below in the section entitled "Consultation Demands."

Despite advances that the CRS has made in processing consultation requests and managing its workflow and its documents database, several challenges still exist that affect its ability to consult successfully. One of the challenges to providing quality and timely consultation originates with the STOF's geographically large AOI. Large AOIs tend to result in large numbers of consultation requests, which challenges the review capacity of the CRS staff. Issues related to how the STOF determines its AOI will be examined in the section entitled "Area of Interest versus Area of Responsibility."

The way in which formal consultation is initiated by federal agencies, as well as differing attitudes on the nature and extent of how the consultation process should be conducted, creates additional challenges for the CRS. These issues are commonly discussed by THPO staff and other Tribal representatives attending annual meetings and conferences. Under Section 106, consultation is the responsibility of the lead federal agency. However, not only is there a lack of uniformity between agencies, in many cases there also appears, from an etic perspective, to be a lack of consistency within agencies. Finally, differing views between what the THPO expects out of consultation versus what lead agencies expect, and are willing to do during consultation, create discrepancies between the goals and needs of the consulting parties. The section entitled "Consultation—A Tribal Perspective" examines this issue.

Consultation Demands: 2006–2015

Records management within the Compliance Review office has evolved through several stages, originating with "little to none" (piles of paper on a desktop or in the corner of an office) to paper documents stored in filing cabinets and in cardboard boxes (also sometimes in the corner of an office), to electronic documents stored in searchable databases. Each project notification, consultation request, or other important document received by the CRS is assigned a unique THPO number. In 2006–2007, Paul Backhouse, then Chief Data Analyst for the Archaeometry Section, developed and implemented a Microsoft Access–based system referred to as the "Incoming Correspondence and Tracking Database" (ICTD). The first document was entered into the ICTD on March 26, 2007, and was assigned THPO #000007. The last ICTD entry, THPO #011025, was made more than five years later on November 15, 2012.

Recognizing the ICTD's limitations, the THPO had conducted a search for a more functional document management system, and on November 19, 2012, the CRS transitioned to a proprietary system developed by Perceptive Software called ImageNow. ImageNow creates documents that are 100 percent searchable (not limited to "key words"), stored in a single database, and can be inserted into a user-defined "work-flow." This work-flow can be used to alert designated individuals to the presence of documents that require their attention or action. Over the five-plus-year period that the ICTD was in use, 11,018 THPO numbers were assigned. Although the correlation is not exact, this number roughly corresponds to 11,018 project notifications or consultation requests; this represents an average of almost 2,000 notifications/requests per year. The number of THPO numbers assigned does not correspond to the number of pages of documents entered into the ICTD. Each THPO number can, and usually does, have several related documents subsumed under it, and each of these documents can, and usually does, consist of multiple pages of text and/or graphics.

A similar analysis can be done for ImageNow documents. Between November 19, 2012, and June 30, 2015, over 6,152 documents had been entered into the ImageNow database. This averages to slightly over 2,400 documents per year and, as with the ICTD database, represents tens of thousands of pages of material.

In 2013, former THPO Compliance Analyst Alison Swing conducted a more detailed analysis of the ICTD database in preparation for a Southeastern Archaeological Conference presentation. Her analysis focused on "new project" requests received per year, which differs somewhat from either the amount of correspondence (documents) received or the number of THPO numbers assigned. Swing found that from March 2007 to December 2007, approximately 1,315 project requests were received. If ICTD had been in place for all of 2007, the count was projected to be 1,753. For subsequent years, 1,118 requests were logged for 2008; 2,279 requests for 2009; 2,716 requests for 2010; 1,872 requests for 2011; and 1,957 requests for 2012. ICTD was discontinued in mid-November 2012. A projected number of project requests for all of 2012 would be 2,237.

The important point here is that the CRS staff, which has varied between two and three individuals, must maintain a database of tens of thousands of pages of documents while sorting through 2,000 to 3,000 consultation requests annually in order to identify Tribally important projects and to meaningfully consult on those important projects within prescribed review deadlines.

The challenge then is to be able to successfully "triage" the incoming documents and to determine which of the projects or undertakings are of greatest importance to the Tribe. Undertakings may range in scale from a single Housing and Urban Development (HUD) funded house renovation to a several-thousand-acre U.S. Army Corps of Engineers (USACE) Everglades water project. In these examples, the decision over which project to devote the most time to is obvious—the project with the greatest potential to impact cultural resources important to the STOF, that is, the USACE project. But between the two extremes is an enormous range of undertakings that transition gradually from one end of the spectrum to the other—a new Federal Communications Commission (FCC) permitted cell tower, a 10-acre HUD funded housing development, a 100-acre Natural Resource Conservation Service (NRCS) funded Environmental Quality Incentives Program (EQIP) project. With limited review resources and time—and it is likely that every Compliance Review Section of every SHPO/THPO has limited resources—the CRS has to make decisions daily on what to review and what not to review.

Unlike state SHPOs, who, because of their legal obligations under Section 106, have less flexibility in deciding in which consultations they choose to participate, the STOF CRS deals primarily with off-reservation undertakings and has considerably more flexibility. The CRS gets to decide on what it focuses, but since the CRS serves the Tribe, these decisions are designed to reflect the Tribal consensus. Understanding the Tribal consensus requires THPO's own "internal" consultation process with Tribal representatives. The danger in choosing not to provide comments on an undertaking or respond to a request for consultation is the possibility of overlooking something important to the Tribe. To minimize this risk, the CRS is actively engaged in researching off-reservation sites, areas, and locations that are important to the Tribe, either historically or presently. While the purpose of "triaging" consultation requests is to allow for a shift in emphasis from quantity to quality, by reducing the demand for staff resources, there are sometimes unintended consequences—recent efforts by the CRS to reduce the time spent on HUD projects were not entirely successful.

A decision was made to restrict HUD consultation to only projects that involved new ground-disturbing activities in areas previously undisturbed. This turned out to be problematic in two ways: HUD delegates its 106 consultation responsibilities to "responsible entities" (frequently municipalities or not-for-profit groups) that often lack the background, training, and skills necessary to conduct 106 consultation, or to reliably interpret the meaning of "new ground-disturbing activities"; and the "responsible entities" continued to request letters from the CRS stating our intent not to comment on their project if they had not received a response from us within thirty days of their initial consultation/comment request. When the CRS decides to consult or provide comments on a particular consultation request, a chain of activities is set in motion, including capturing all relevant documents in ImageNow, assigning a THPO number, composing and sending a CRS response letter, and so forth. Each of these actions is time-consuming. Past experience has demonstrated that to fully process a single consultation request, even the simplest one, requires on average thirty minutes. Individually this may not seem like a great deal of time, but multiplied by roughly ten HUD requests per week, it begins adding up to significant amounts of time—time that could be devoted to more important projects. If the intent of our HUD experiment was to eliminate time spent sending "no comment" letters, it was not successful.

Area of Interest versus Area of Responsibility

A key underlying component of Tribal consultation is the concept of an AOI. Simply defined, an AOI is the geographic area over which a tribe feels it has a legitimate cultural interest. Areas incorporated into an AOI may include aboriginal, ancestral, and modern territories, and these may include lands currently belonging to the Tribe or areas ceded by the Tribe. Unlike state SHPOs whose consultation is usually restricted by political boundaries, tribal AOIs often cross state boundaries. An AOI may extend for hundreds or possibly even thousands of miles, especially in the case of displaced tribes, and encompass thousands of square miles. It is often easy for consulting agencies to overlook the fact that the tribes they need to be consulting with may reside hundreds of miles away from an undertaking.

While not being constrained by political boundaries can be a blessing, in that it allows tribes to be actively engaged in the consultation process for all those areas they decided are important to them, it is also something of a curse. Accepting the responsibility for consulting on a 323,000-square-mile area, for example, presents significant challenges. This is especially true for the STOF THPO and the Compliance Review staff because we take our role as advocates for the Tribe and as active participants in the 106 consultation process very seriously. We won't conduct substandard project reviews or half-heartedly engage in consultations even if we know that a SHPO, federal agency, or even another THPO may be there to catch our mistakes. Large AOIs tend to produce large volumes of consultation requests (with their correspondingly large volumes of accompanying documents). This can tax staff capacity and prevent staff from being able to identify and devote time to priority projects.

A variety of resources are used by the THPO in order to help delineate the STOF AOI. These sources can include: state site files, reports of archaeological investigations, historic period maps, journals, letters, and military records. Especially valuable guidance is provided by Tribal members themselves based on firsthand knowledge or histories and traditions passed down to them.

The original AOI map developed by the THPO dates to around 2007 (Figure 14.1) and was based in large part on the Lamar Culture Area, centered on the Lamar Mounds and Village site located in central Georgia along the banks of the Ocmulgee River. The site was occupied from about a.d. 1350 to 1600, and the inhabitants of the area are thought to be ancestral to the later Creek Indians and would, therefore, be ancestral to the Seminoles. Added to this Lamar area was the rest of Florida, which represents the historic and modern areas of the Seminole peoples. To capture the largest area of potential interest, a fairly large buffer area, including Mississippi and portions of Louisiana, Alabama, Tennessee, North Carolina, and South Carolina, were also incorporated into the first iteration of the AOI. This first version encompassed an area of more than 300,000 square miles—representing roughly twice the size of the state of California (or approximately the size of the country of Namibia).

Unlike state SHPOs, the STOF AOI boundaries are not permanently fixed and unchanging. As additional research is conducted and as Tribal interests change, the map boundaries can also change. Over the past two years there has been a development in how the CRS views the STOF AOI. This development results from an attempt to reconcile the Tribe's interest with

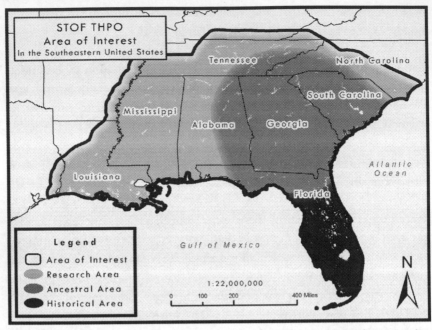

Figure 14.1. Seminole Tribe of Florida Tribal Historic Preservation Office original Area of Interest map. Created by Juan Cancel, Chief Data Analyst, Seminole Tribe of Florida Tribal Historic Preservation Office.

recognition of the practical real-world limits placed on staffing levels and available resources with the CRS. To fill the role of effective off-reservation Tribal advocate by balancing Tribal interests with limited resources, the CRS is now making a distinction between an AOI and an AOR (Figure 14.2). The AOI will continue to reflect all those areas in which the STOF has some level of interest. Smaller in size, the AOR will represent those areas the Tribe is especially concerned with and for which the CRS assumes the responsibility of active, comprehensive consultation. Currently, the CRS, in conjunction with the THPO Archaeometry and Collections Sections, the Tribal Ah-Tah-Thi-Ki Museum, and the Tribal community, is engaged in the development of an off-reservation Geographical Information Systems (GIS) database. The purpose of the database is to identify and to document specific off-reservation sites and locations of importance to the Tribe. A similar database already exists for on-reservation use. As research into Tribal history continues and as Tribal government and Tribal advisors/community members continue to guide the THPO, it is likely that changes will periodically be made to both the AOI and the AOR. It is easy to imagine that portions of the AOI may become of sufficient concern or interest to the Tribe that they become incorporated

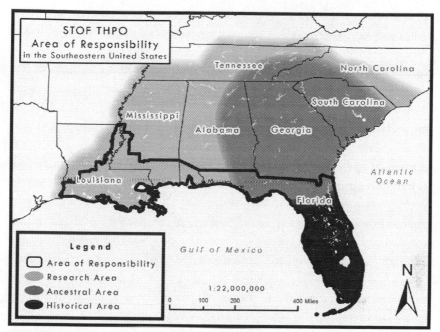

Figure 14.2. Seminole Tribe of Florida Tribal Historic Preservation Office, current Area of Responsibility map. Created of Juan Cancel, Chief Data Analyst, Seminole Tribe of Florida Tribal Historic Preservation Office.

into the AOR. Federal agencies may view the reality of changing STOF AOR boundaries with some confusion and perhaps consternation, so it will remain incumbent on the CRS to provide timely updates to the agencies as changes occur.

Consultation—A Tribal Perspective (Why, Who, What, When, Where, How)

Despite the fact that federal agencies have been engaged in the Section 106 consultation process with tribes for more than forty years, there is an amazing variety in the quality of these consultations. They can range from very good to poor (little to no real consultation). There is inconsistency not just between federal agencies but often within an agency—either between departments or between regional offices. Let me be clear that I am not classifying the quality of a consultation based solely on its outcome. The CRS recognizes the parties engaged in consultations do not serve the same constituency and that there will be differences of opinion and interpretation and recommendations. The CRS recognizes that its role in off-reservation consultation is essentially advisory in capacity. Lead agencies are charged with making final determinations, and their determinations may not be desirable outcomes from the Tribal perspective. The Tribe does, however, expect to be treated fairly, respectfully, and in a manner consistent with the law. So let's spend the remainder of this chapter examining what the STOF THPO believes consultation is and what we would like to see by way of meaningful consultation. I will do this by posing and then answering the questions why, who, what, when, where, and how.

Why consult at all? The simplest answer is because the law requires it. On the federal level, Section 106 of the NHPA and NAGPRA both require consultation with tribes, Alaskan villages, and Native Hawaiian Organizations under certain conditions. Moving beyond the issue of legally mandated compliance, however, there is, or should be, a moral component based on a respect for the cultural and religious beliefs of Native peoples. This moral dimension is clearly reflected in an early definition of the "federal trust responsibility": "The United States Trust responsibility toward the American Indians is the unique legal and moral duty of the United States to assist Indians in the protection of their property and rights" (TallBear 2014).

Who consults? This appears to be pretty straightforward. Governmental agencies and tribes consult. While by volume most of our consultation occurs at the federal level, we do consult with states, primarily with the state of Florida, on a routine basis. Our consultations with Florida most often relate to Florida statute 872.05, which concerns unmarked human burials. This falls outside of Section 106 and isn't a consultation in the NHPA sense, but the state does keep us informed of 872.05 issues and does solicit the Tribe's opinion. We also rub elbows with the state when providing comments on federal undertakings and have developed a respectful enough working relationship that the CRS is not afraid to pick up the phone and exchange ideas or solicit advice from the SHPO.

Since tribes are sovereign nations, consultations under Section 106 should occur on a government-to-government basis. Who the appropriate consulting parties are can be problematic in at least two ways. First, federal agencies may want to delegate some of their consultation responsibilities to state agencies, local governments, or even nongovernmental organizations pursuant to Section 800.2 (c) (4). Some agencies seem to forget delegation requires the concurrence of the Tribe and that the delegating agency still remains legally responsible for all findings and determinations resulting from the consultation. A second factor complicating the "who" of consultation occurs when a nondesignated party (environmental or cultural resource consultants, architectural and engineering firms, real estate developers and land owners, and so forth) contact the THPO directly in order to enter into discussions regarding particular projects. Sometimes this is done with an expectation of future federal involvement eventually initiating the 106 process, and sometimes it is done even after a federal agency has initiated the 106 process. We often find the nondesignated party does not inform the lead federal agency of its Tribal contact.

While the Tribe always reserves the right to talk with whom it chooses, generally the 106 process works best when the consultation remains between the federal agency and the THPO or SHPO. There are, however, at least two exceptions to this rule. The CRS supports the THPO not just by serving as the off-reservation contact for compliance issues but also by assisting the THPO in providing information to the Tribal government and community on a wide range of topics having the potential to affect their lives. We live in an age of almost instantaneous communication, when information is readily accessible to the STOF community. If this information concerns projects that might impact the STOF, it is increasingly expected that the THPO will be aware of these projects and assess possible impacts to the Tribe, whether or not Section 106 has been or will ever be initiated.

Case in point: the proposed River of Grass Greenway (AECOM 2014), which would connect the east coast and west coast of South Florida via a biking/hiking trail, had been well publicized (Miami–Dade County 2013) before the CRS was ever officially asked to consult on the project (or a portion of the project) by the Florida Department of Transportation (Federal Highways Administration 2013). It is no longer acceptable for us to say we do not know anything about, for instance, oil and gas exploration in South Florida but that if it ever becomes a 106 issue we will learn about it. The THPO is expected to anticipate some of these pre-106 or non-106 concerns, and, with its off-reservation focus, the CRS will support that effort. One way that effort can be supported is by monitoring local, state, and federal news outlets; another is by attending public meetings (non-Tribal, federal, state, or county agency presentations, and so forth) in order to collect general information about specific projects.

A second expectation of the government-to-government consultation preference occurs when parties wish to discuss proposed off-reservation projects with the Tribe for the purpose of providing the Tribe with a background briefing and/or seeking the Tribe's assistance in locating or avoiding Tribally sensitive areas. The CRS has engaged in these types of presentations and will consider requests for these types of briefings. Whenever these briefings occur, it is always with the clear understanding that the meetings are informal in nature and do not constitute a formal consultation. At the appropriate time, the CRS will consult with the appropriate federal lead agency and will provide that agency formal comments as necessary. Despite these warnings, it is not uncommon for nonagency meeting participants to believe they are participating in a consultation and tell a federal agency they have already conducted a Tribal consultation.

What is consultation? A synthesis derived from statements issued and adopted by various federal government agencies results in the following definition of the key term "consultation": consultation generally consists of meaningful and timely communication between agency officials and elected or duly appointed tribal government officials or their authorized representatives in developing agency actions that affect tribes. Consultation means open sharing of information, the full expression of tribal and agency views, a commitment to consider tribal views in decision making, and respect for tribal self-government and sovereignty.

The *American Heritage Dictionary* (2014) defines "consultation" as "a conference at which advice is given or views are exchanged." For the Tribe, the notion of views being exchanged is critically important. Consultation should be an opportunity for a dialogue between parties and not a soliloquy directed at the Tribe. The *Merriam-Webster's Dictionary* (2014) offers the following definition of "consultation": "a discussion about something that is being decided." It doesn't say "that *has* been decided." If the "exchange of views" is to be meaningful and constructive, they have to be listened to with open minds. The THPO is not happy when agencies coming into a consultation, especially the early stages of a consultation, have already reached a conclusion or made a determination, and present the appearance that it doesn't matter what the Tribe says since they won't be changing their minds. At worst this represents a violation of the agency responsibility under the law, and at the very least it won't win the agency any friends in the THPO.

An example of how not to respectfully exchange views occurred in a fairly recent consultation meeting between the STOF THPO and a large federal agency concerning an especially troublesome and problematic issue for the Tribe (burial resources). A federal agency senior archaeologist told the STOF Chairman that the Chairman didn't have to worry about possible impacts to precontact period mounds present within the area of potential effect (mounds known to contain burial resources) because these resources were not affiliated with the Seminoles. This official clearly failed to recognize the importance of possible ancestral affiliations to the Tribe even if, from the non-Tribal perspective, the ancestors didn't call themselves "Seminoles." While Western science might label mounds and sites "prehistoric" and not see their connection to modern tribes, the label is arbitrary and disrespects a tribe that views those "prehistoric" peoples as ancestors. It is certainly inappropriate for an agency official to tell a Tribal leader or any Tribal member what he or she should or shouldn't be concerned with.

Moving on to the "when" question: when should consultation begin? Tribes might not agree on everything, but if there is one opinion that seems to be universally held it is that consultation should begin "as soon as possible." We recognize that government agencies operate under various constraints. For example, a private developer engaged in a construction project of some kind will eventually require a wetlands permit from the U.S. Army Corps of Engineers. A great deal of planning, design work, even cultural resources investigations may occur before a permit application is even submitted to the Corps. The Corps cannot begin 106 consultation with the Tribe until the application is submitted. Another example might be an electric utility considering several alternate transmission line corridors. Until the federal nexus is triggered (that is, it becomes a Section 106 issue), the tribe is out of the picture. These are cases where, as previously stated, the CRS may seek project information outside of the 106 consultation (informal briefings, public meetings, and so forth). So again—begin the consultation as soon as possible, and if there is some way to notify us about an undertaking coming along later, by all means let us know.

The next consultation question to be asked is where should consultation occur? There are several options, and no one option is going to be the right choice all of the time. Our experience has been that it is easier to establish productive working relationships through face-to-face meetings. Even though budget limitations often preclude this, for consultations that are likely to be protracted or problematic, every attempt should made to arrange at least an initial face-to-face meeting. If an in-person consultation is being scheduled, then the CRS highly recommends the agency make arrangements for that meeting to take place at the THPO. We believe this demonstrates a level of respect for the sovereignty of the Tribe on the part of the agency. It also allows the THPO an opportunity to familiarize the agency representatives with the THPO facilities and staff. We also recommend that agencies that have routine dealings with the Tribe try to make at least annual or semiannual visits, even if the visit is not linked to a particular project but is more informal. Let me add one other reason for in-person meetings—to paraphrase something I once heard said—it's harder to say you're crazy to someone sitting in the same room with you. A certain level of forced civility is not necessarily a bad thing; perhaps it makes us look for more reasoned, constructive ways of presenting our views. If subsequent consultations need to take place via teleconferencing, then the groundwork has already been laid by in-person meetings and relationships have already been established.

One last suggestion on the consultation process concerns the "how." How should consultation be initiated? Consultation should begin with a formal letter addressed to the Tribal Historic Preservation Officer, Paul Backhouse, and courtesy-copied to the Chairman of the Tribe. Since the THPO is authorized to engage in Section 106 consultation on behalf of the STOF, the THPO will remain the point of contact for the majority of consultation issues. Consultation issues can be elevated by the THPO to the Chairman and leadership as needed. Routine Section 106 consultations and 872.05 matters are then directed by the THPO to the Compliance Review Section.

Once an initial letter is received, a decision can be made concerning the nature of the consultation and what the appropriate method of future contact or interaction should be. Fortunately, the majority of the consultations we do can be handled through e-mails and telephone calls. Many federal agencies engaged in consultation with multiple tribes—the Federal Emergency Management Agency (FEMA), for example—rely heavily on webinars and teleconferences. Agencies using such media must be sensitive to the fact that for reasons deriving from sovereignty or privacy issues, many tribes are not comfortable with discussing tribal concerns in group settings and will only consult one-on-one. It is the responsibility of the federal agency to accommodate these concerns. Here I must emphasize that "notification" is not equivalent to "consultation." Simply notifying a tribe of a proposed undertaking or decision regarding a project without affording the tribe an opportunity to participate in the decision-making process violates the letter and the spirit of the law. While the CRS often participates in phone conversations with federal or state agencies, most of the time these conversations are intended to be informal discussions and are not meant to be construed as formal comments on any particular project. THPO CRS formal comments come in the form of a written document, usually on Tribal letterhead and attached to e-mails.

To summarize the STOF THPO–CRS view of consultation, and borrowing from an Environmental Protection Agency (EPA) document (Environmental Protection Agency 2009), consultation means:

+ openly sharing information;
+ fully expressing Tribal and agency views;

+ considering Tribal interests in decision making;
+ respect for Tribal self-government and sovereignty; and
+ consultation is different from input and interaction or collaboration and outreach; consultation is government to government.

Conclusion

Any number of topics related to the challenges that the CRS faces and to their perspective on Tribal consultation could have been presented here. I chose to briefly examine issues relating to the increasing demands on staff time created by increasing numbers of consultation requests and how some of these demands can be managed by narrowing our AOR. This was followed by a discussion of the why, who, what, when, where, and how of the consultation process. One final word of caution: each tribe's perspective is unique, and the experiences and the expectations of the STOF THPO–CRS are just that, unique, and not transferable to any other group. The challenge for any agency engaged in tribal consultation is to recognize that uniqueness and to adapt to it.

Figure 14.3. Bradley Mueller. Image by Kate Macuen, Collections Manager, Seminole Tribe of Florida Tribal Historic Preservation Office.

References Cited

AECOM. 2014. "River of Grass Greenway Feasibility Study and Master Plan." Prepared for the National Park Service, RTCA Program.

Environmental Protection Agency. 2009. "The Office of Air Quality and Standards, Consulting with Indian Tribal Governments, April 10, 2009." Environmental Protection Agency. http://www.epa.gov/oar/tribal/pdfs/OAQPSConsultation-Policy%20april%202009.pdf.

Federal Highways Administration. 2013. "River of Grass Greenway PD&E." U.S. Department of Transportation, Federal Highways Administration. May 13.

Miami–Dade County. 2013. River of Grass Greenway Community Workshops and Interactive Project Website Launch. Miami–Dade County, Parks, Recreation and Open Spaces, January 25.

TallBear, Kimberly M. 2014. "Understanding the Federal/Tribal Relationship and Barriers to Including Tribes in Environmental Decision Making." http://www.iiirm.org/publications/Articles%20Reports%20Papers/Environmental%20Protection/unders~1.pdf.

15

Preservation of Culture in Connection with the Largest Environmental Restoration Project Ever

Lessons Learned

JAMES CHARLES AND PAUL N. BACKHOUSE

The vast scale projects currently being undertaken within the Everglades, collectively referred to as Everglades restoration, represent an enormous challenge in terms of Tribal consultation. In broad terms, few people relate the Everglades to a cultural environment, and most research undertaken to date has been biologically driven. Despite the intensity of research, basic questions regarding the building blocks of the Everglades ecosystem, tree islands, remain largely unanswered. Archaeological research demonstrates that as long as the Everglades has existed, people have lived within this environment. Discussion regarding restoration therefore must include a cultural voice. The enormity of the task is made clear by referencing the wall-size Comprehensive Everglades Restoration Plan map that adorns the wall of the Tribal Historic Preservation Office (THPO). Each component of the overall project is given an individual designation and assigned a project management team. The challenge, as with many interrelated projects occurring at any given time, is how can a Tribal voice be heard?

Author Bios

James Charles works closely with Tribal governments, assisting and representing them with government-to-government consultations; developing and implementing strategies to protect Tribal interests on and off Tribal lands (cultural, environmental, and natural resources); developing and negotiating agreements with local, state, and federal agencies; enhancing Tribal self-governance/self-determination; and developing Tribal infrastructure and capacity. His passion for working with Tribal governments began with his assisting the Seminole Tribe of Florida in protecting its cultural and environmental interests in connection with Everglades restoration. This passion carries forward as his greatest satisfaction is working collaboratively with Tribal governments to develop Tribal capacity for self-governance and preserve Tribal culture and heritage for future generations.

For Paul N. Backhouse, see chapter 3.

Introduction

In this chapter, we seek to convey a story of our experiences working for the Seminole Tribe of Florida (hereafter "Seminole Tribe") in connection with Everglades restoration. Specifically, our experiences revolve around efforts to protect and preserve the cultural/religious values associated with the Everglades that are significant to the Seminole Tribe, a task the Seminole Tribe's leadership charged us to perform. It was our responsibility to effectively navigate the maze of federal and state processes so that the Seminole Tribe's cultural interests were meaningfully heard, understood, and included. Considering the unprecedented scope and complexities of Everglades restoration, we did not have the benefit of being able to learn from prior case studies or projects. Therefore, we had to develop innovative solutions to navigating the non-Native processes while preserving both the Seminole Tribe's cultural identity and cultural resources.

While this chapter discusses relevant laws and approaches protecting cultural interests, it is not intended to be a conservation guidebook or a "How-To" manual. Instead, it is intended to convey a story from a Tribal perspective to be shared with other tribal governments in the hope that they can learn from our experiences and share their stories with us as well. It is through this sharing of stories that we can all learn from each other and preserve the cultural values for future generations. Because the Seminole Tribe traditionally views Americans as European colonists and not indigenous to Florida, the term "European" is frequently utilized to include the people of the United States along with the English and Spanish. Our experiences are from the perspective of working for the Seminole Tribe; however, it is important to note that the Miccosukee Tribe of Indians of Florida has long participated in Everglades restoration and in the protection of cultural resources significant to the Miccosukee people.

Background

Who Are the Seminoles?

As discussed in more detail in the first chapter, the Seminole Tribe is a unique confluence of culture and circumstances. The Seminole people are descendants of Native American people living in the Southeast at least 12,000 years before European colonization. In efforts to distance themselves from the expanding European colonization, the Seminole people resettled in Florida, which had been historically utilized by the Seminole people. As European colonization expanded in Florida, conflicts between the Seminole people and Europeans were inevitable. After a series of protracted warfare waged against them by the U.S. government in the early to mid-nineteenth century, the remaining survivors were primarily protected by the cover of the Everglades. In addition to surviving warfare, the Seminole people also survived, as a culturally distinct people, federal policy eras of: (1) relocation, where Indian tribes were forcibly removed from their homelands; (2) assimilation, where the federal government attempted to divest Indian tribes of their cultural identity; and (3) termination, where the federal government refused to acknowledge Indian tribes' legal status. The story of the Seminole people is a story of survival and adaptation whereby the Everglades plays an important role in that story. This determination and ability to adapt have allowed them to thrive in the modern world while still embracing their cultural/religious heritage.

The Historic Everglades—"Grassy Water"

It is helpful to first describe what the Everglades was and is before sharing our experiences with Everglades restoration. The Everglades is one of only three wetland ecosystems designated by the United Nations Educational, Scientific, and Cultural Organization (UNESCO) as having global importance. Prior to European colonization and drainage, the Everglades was a web of interconnected marshes, tree islands, and prairies. The connection between these ecosystems was subtle and frequently in flux (size, location, and existence). Although it has been radically altered by humans since the early nineteenth century, the Everglades still remains a dominant feature of the Florida landscape. The Everglades watershed historically began with the Kissimmee River near Orlando flowing south discharging into Lake Okeechobee. When water levels exceed the capacity of the Kissimmee River floodplain and Lake Okeechobee, the excess water slowly sheet flowed across the landscape for approximately 100 miles into Florida Bay (Figure 15.1). This constant, slow-flowing water

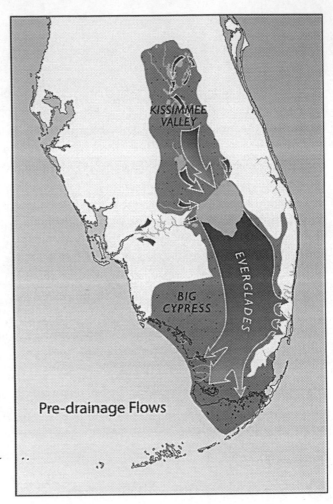

KISSIMMEE VALLEY

EVERGLADES

BIG CYPRESS

Pre-drainage Flows

Figure 15.1. His-
toric Everglades
watershed. By
permission of the
South Florida Wa-
ter Management
District.

was so vast that the first European military surveyors initially perceived the
sheet flow as the beginnings of a sea. The Seminole Tribe historically called
it "Pa-hay-okee," meaning "Grassy Water." The dominant feature driving the
Everglades was, and still is, water.

How to Break the Everglades and Everglades Restoration

In 1840, an anonymous military surveyor described the Everglades, "no county
that I have ever heard of bears any resemblance to it; it seems like a vast sea
filled with grass and green trees, and expressly intended as a retreat for the
rascally Indian, from which the white man would never seek to drive them"
(Tebeau 1968, 66–67). The Everglades and its "unforsaken and impenetrable"
character would begin to change after Florida became a state on March 3, 1845.

The Everglades was extensively drained and altered between 1845 and 1947 in order to make the swamps suitable for agricultural and inhabitation by the Americans. The drainage of the Everglades resulted in numerous problems, including soil subsidence, saltwater intrusion, flooding, and muck fires. Two devastating hurricanes in the late 1920s resulted in the construction of a long dike, known as the Herbert Hoover Dike, around the southern edge of Lake Okeechobee and a long canal through the Caloosahatchee River. These flood control efforts significantly altered the Everglades ecosystem by starving it of water, its driving force.

In 1947, the Everglades National Park was officially designated (16 U.S.C.A. §410 established the Everglades National Park in 1934 provided that the necessary land was acquired, which occurred in 1947, officially establishing the Park). In the same year as the Park was officially established, the citizens and elected officials of Florida successfully petitioned the U.S. Congress to further assist with flood control after another hurricane caused significant property losses. Consequently, the Central and Southern Florida Project for Flood Control and Other Purposes (C&SF) was approved in 1948. In implementing the C&SF, the State of Florida and the U.S. Army Corps of Engineers (USACE) determined the best approach to fix the problems caused by the extensive drainage was to (1) divide the previously interconnected Everglades into separate basins and (2) to construct over 1,400 miles of canals, levees, and other structures. The flood control measures significantly diminished the water flows within the remaining natural areas. As a result of the extensive man-made water management, agriculture, and development, the European population grew exponentially in South Florida, further taxing the water demands for the Everglades.

While the C&SF was effective in flood control, it had significant adverse impacts on the Everglades. Waterfowl, wading birds, and fish populations began to significantly decline. In addition, water pollution from agricultural operations and metropolitan uses was significantly impacting the Everglades. One USACE Commander later characterized the C&SF as "innocent ignorance" (Godfrey and Canton 2011, ix). What resulted were numerous court battles, including one where the federal government sued the State of Florida for operating a federal project, specifically, the C&SF (Godfrey and Canton 2011, chapters 12–14). Ultimately the U.S. Congress enacted the Comprehensive Everglades Restoration Plan (CERP) to restore portions of the Everglades. The CERP is being implemented through a 50–50 partnership between the State of Florida and the federal government. The CERP seeks to undo fifty years of damage caused by the C&SF by proposing more than sixty water control projects over thirty years. It is a massive undertaking that encompasses sixteen counties and over 18,000 square miles. Several other Everglades restoration programs accompany the CERP, including the Everglades Construction Project, the Everglades Forever Act, and Florida's Expedited Projects. Overall, Everglades restoration is the largest environmental restoration project ever attempted by man.

Perspectives of the Everglades and Everglades Restoration

Implementation of Everglades restoration involves numerous stakeholders. It is not uncommon for a specific project to have over a dozen state and federal agencies involved in the process, along with Tribal governments and the public. Each stakeholder brings different views and interests to the table. One of the first lessons we learned while representing the Seminole Tribe's interests was that the stakeholders in Everglades restoration all had different views of the Everglades. We came to this conclusion by working with the various stakeholders during the consultation process, taking the time and energy necessary to understand how they viewed the Everglades. Understanding the different perspectives and acknowledging them became instrumental in the Seminole Tribe gaining a meaningful voice in Everglades restoration and protecting the associated cultural values. While it can be dangerous to generalize something as complex as Everglades restoration, we have considerably simplified three basic perspectives for the readers: (1) the Seminole Tribe's perspective; (2) the implementing agency's perspective, and (3) the layman's perspective.

The Seminole Tribe's Perspective

While the Seminole people trace their ancestral presence in Florida to a time long before European colonization, it was during the 1800s that the Seminole people utilized the Everglades as a refuge against European encroachment, forced removal, and termination. Europeans deemed the Everglades "unforsaken" and "impenetrable," but this unique ecological region characterized by a ridge and slough landscape and punctuated by tree islands became a sanctuary for the Seminole people and instrumental to their survival as a distinct cultural people. Seminole families and wider clan groups occupied the higher tree islands within the Everglades. They were not, however, sedentary and frequently moved from tree island to tree island by means of poled canoes. These tree island homes were central places within a broader pattern of movement that took families west to the pine flatwoods during the rainy season to hunt and east to the Atlantic Coastal Ridge to harvest the root of the coontie plant

Figure 15.2. Seminole man pulling dugout canoe through the Everglades during a rain event, capturing a scene of traditional everyday life for the Seminoles. Image #48131. By permission of the American Museum of Natural History Library.

(*Zamia integrifolia*). During these expeditions, the Everglades and adjoining Big Cypress swamp formed a backdrop that could be relied upon for protection and security.

As such, the Everglades landscape holds more than just historic value to the Seminole people; it embodies the Seminole cultural identity. The variety of resource types found within the Everglades (for example, land features and vegetation) has been imbued with value by the Seminole people as an expression of the Tribe's beliefs, traditions, and cultural practices. Miccosukee-speaking Seminoles have a unique word for the tree islands that extend upward from this watery environment. They call these features *kantakle* (islands). This word differs from *yakne oke*, *kaa-chokoôle*, *yanh-kaa-chokó*, which is used to signify islands encountered in an oceanic context. The usage of *kantakle* in the Miccosukee lexicon demonstrates the unique traditional ecological knowledge bound up in the Seminole worldview. Indeed, during an interview on Big Cypress, former Seminole Medicine Man Josie Billie individually identified and described the traditional use for more than 300 unique floral species (Sturtevant 1954). These values make the Everglades essential to the Seminole people, whereby preservation of this landscape is also preservation of the Seminole people's identity. The Seminole people traditionally viewed the Everglades as embodying heritage, culture, and survival (Figure 15.2).

Burials are also important components of the Everglades landscape, holding significant cultural value to the Seminole people. As the Seminole Chief Coacoochee stated, "My father Philip always told me I was made of the sands of Florida, and that when I died, my brothers and my people would sing and dance over me" (quoted in Sprague 2000, 327). Consequently, avoiding man-induced disturbances to burials is an important belief of the Seminole people. In particular, the unnatural inundation of burials is especially abhorrent to the Seminole people. Everglades restoration encompasses engineered projects that will substantially alter hydrological regimes within Central and South Florida. As a result, Everglades restoration poses the threat of unnaturally inundating burials, adversely impacting the Seminole people if their beliefs are not adequately considered.

The Implementing Agency's Perspective

As noted earlier, the Everglades has been significantly altered with numerous water control projects constructed and operated by state and federal agencies. Essentially what was once a natural sheet flow has become a complex plumbing network of canals, levees, pumps, and dikes (McVoy et al. 2011). These water control projects are the result of sophisticated modeling and engineering designed to restore environmental functions while balancing competing flood control and water supply needs of the urbanized and agricultural areas. One can imagine that the South Florida water control networks, with their channelized, linear canals, resemble a schematic of a computer chip more than a natural system. For example, the A-1 Reservoir, located south of Lake Okeechobee in an area known as the Everglades Agricultural Area, features straight-line canal structures similar to conducting lines on a computer chip (Figure 15.3). The A-1 features are representative of the water control systems that populate the modern-day Everglades. For the agencies that design, construct, and operate such water control projects, Figure 15.3 is representative of what the Everglades has become: (1) flood control; (2) undoing past mistakes; and (3) sustaining natural areas like the Everglades National Park while sustaining growth in agricultural and urban areas.

The Layman's Perspective

It is also important to understand the public's general perception of the Everglades because the public is a major stakeholder in Everglades restoration. In order to get a feel for the general public's perception, we informally distributed several images to a small group of colleagues and friends not intimately familiar with wetland ecosystems, asking them to select the picture that best

Figure 15.3. Aerial photograph showing the A-1 Reservoir project located south of Lake Okeechobee in an area known as the Everglades Agricultural Area. By permission of the South Florida Water Management District.

depicts the Everglades. The majority of those surveyed picked an image showing cattails as being the one that depicts the "ideal" Everglades (Figure 15.4). While the most popular image has a natural appearance, especially compared to the engineered configuration of water control systems (Figure 15.3), it depicts cattails rather than sawgrass. Cattails are commonly referred to as the "grave makers" for the Everglades as they indicate eutrophication of the area due to unnaturally high nutrient levels (Godfrey and Canton 2011, 192, 197). It was interesting and instructive for us that the layman's perception of the natural Everglades was one that is also disturbed by man.

In summary, it became apparent to us that the non-Tribal stakeholders had a different view of the Everglades and thus had different motivations. This was an important lesson because acknowledging the different perspectives allows us to not only understand other stakeholders but also put us in a better position to be understood. It was through this mutual understanding that we overcame differences when negotiating agreements. We also learned that making mutual understanding a priority resulted in fewer impasses and conflicts. Essentially, by acknowledging different views and motivations, we did not attempt to change those views or motivations. Instead, we attempted to redirect those views and motivations to be invested in the common goal of protecting culturally significant burial resources.

Figure 15.4. Image of the Everglades, selected by a majority of a small study group as being representative of the "ideal" view. By permission of the South Florida Water Management District.

Must Fully Understand Your Goals and Objectives

Prior to 2008, the Seminole Tribe's participation in Everglades restoration from a cultural perspective was ad hoc (that is, project by project). An overarching comprehensive view of all the Everglades restoration projects in the context of cultural values was lacking. Consequently, there was no consistency in the consultations or the Seminole Tribe's participation and no consideration of the cumulative impacts to cultural resources caused by the incremental impacts of all the restoration projects taken together. The cultural values associated with the Everglades were being chipped away project by project almost unnoticed. That changed when one project resulted in the excavation and relocation of two aboriginal cemeteries without the Seminole Tribe's knowledge (hereafter "Project X," unnamed for cultural reasons). Project X motivated the Seminole Tribe to (1) become more actively involved from a cultural perspective and (2) voice concerns of the cumulative impacts to cultural resources that could collectively result from Everglades restoration projects rather than reviewing individual projects in isolation.

What became apparent to the Seminole Tribe was that the ad hoc approach did not facilitate the development of clear goals or objectives for cultural values. It therefore became important to clearly define what the short-term and long-term goals and objectives were for cultural values associated with Everglades restoration. The established goals and objectives operated as the Seminole Tribe's strategic plan for cultural preservation, allowing the Tribe to be more successful in planning for and protecting cultural values. That plan directed the Tribe's actions, allowing purposeful allocation of resources. It also encouraged Tribal leadership, Tribal members, and Tribal staff to be invested in a common purpose. Tribal expenditures of time and resources were directed to implementation of the plan, which facilitated economy of effort. This discipline would prove critical as the Everglades restoration projects can be complex and enormous. For example, the Central Everglades Planning Project has an Area of Potential Effect of approximately 1.5 million acres (larger than Rhode Island), with 23,499 recorded cultural resource sites and potentially many more unknown sites (USACE 2014). The Everglades Restoration Transition Plan project is nearly the size of Rhode Island, with numerous known sites as well (USACE 2011). Although there have been several geographically large-scale archaeological surveys completed within the Everglades (Carr 2002; Griffin 2002; Schwadron 2005), there have been no comprehensive archaeological surveys conducted to date. Despite the lack of comprehensive archaeological surveys, many of the project areas are known to contain numerous cultural sites (USACE 2011, 2014). Economy of effort and focused direction would become essential for the Seminole Tribe to logistically navigate Everglades restoration successfully.

It became important for us to enumerate the goals and objectives rather than simply stating them. By enumerating them, they became a permanent fixture in the Seminole Tribe's approach to Everglades restoration and provided Tribal staff with clear direction. We also learned that the goals and objectives had to be flexible to adjust to changing circumstances. Generally, the short-term and long-term goals stayed the same; it was the objectives that had to be modified as projects and agency personnel changed. Most important, enumerating goals and objectives facilitated purposeful actions rather than being reactive. Such was the case with Project X. The initial reaction was understandably one of anger and pain. Acting on such emotions may have been satisfying but could have precluded the results desired, which was reinternment of the ancestors to their original resting place.

The Seminole Tribe basically had two choices: (1) seek revenge by suing the acting agencies and berating them personally in the press, or (2) seek to resolve the matter by building stronger relationships. The former had a high probability of success and would have been emotionally satisfying; however, the project was just one in a whole suite of projects. It was determined that successfully "beating up" the agencies in court and in the press could have negative long-term consequences for other projects and end up causing more harm to cultural values than it could protect. The Seminole Tribe team concluded that this upsetting incident provided a platform by which the Seminole Tribe could have a stronger voice in the process. Consequently, the Seminole Tribe sought to achieve the short-term goal of reinternment while opening the door for the long-term goal of greater protection for burials. This was accomplished by developing an agreement for the reinternment of the ancestors. This agreement would serve as the foundation for a stronger relationship with the agencies and for subsequent agreements protecting burials. Through this objective of improving the working relationship, the Seminole Tribe has been able to enhance the protection of cultural values, particularly burials, while allowing for agency objectives to be achieved (that is, a win-win outcome).

In summary, one of the most important lessons learned from the Everglades experience so far is that you must have a clear understanding of your goals and objectives before you can expect the agencies to understand your interests. Without a clear set of goals and objectives, you are acting without purpose or direction. Further, a project-by-project approach is time-consuming, unpredictable, and ineffective. Establishing goals and objectives helps develop a more comprehensive approach to cultural resource preservation that is more cost effective. The approach also encourages investment from Tribal leadership, Tribal members, and Tribal staff.

Know the Conventional Toolbox and Its Limitations

In order for the Seminole Tribe to be more effective in protecting cultural values, it became apparent that a better understanding of the "rules of the game" (that is, the relevant laws) was needed, along with a firm grasp of their limitations. By knowing the scope and limitations of the laws that are routinely administered by the acting agencies, the Seminole Tribe became more aware of the agencies' limitations and more successful in participating in the process. While there are several relevant laws, this chapter briefly summarizes three federal laws that are relevant to Everglades restoration.

First, the National Historic Preservation Act (NHPA) of 1966 (Pub. L. No. 89-665; 16 U.S.C. §470 et seq.) provides for the maintenance and expansion of a National Register of districts, sites, building, structures, and objects of significance in U.S. history, architecture, archaeology, and culture. The Act requires federal agencies to consider the effects of their actions on properties eligible or listed in the National Register (that is, historic properties). In addition to consideration of effects, the Act is intended to require acting agencies to identify and assess historic properties and seek ways to avoid, minimize, or mitigate adverse effects. The Act also directs the acting agencies to consult with interested Native American tribes and afford the Advisory Council on Historic Preservation reasonable opportunity to comment on the agency actions.

Second, the Native American Graves Protection and Repatriation Act (NAGPRA) (Pub. L. No. 101-601, 25 U.S.C. §3001 *et seq.*) provides protection to Native American burial sites and human remains. The Act basically provides for two processes. The first requires federal agencies and all museums receiving federal funds to inventory their collection of Native American human remains and associated funerary objects so that culturally affiliated tribes can seek repatriation of those burial resources. The second process addresses intentional and inadvertent discovery of Native American burial resources on federal lands, whereby the federal agency must consult with culturally affiliated Native American tribes on the proper treatment of said resources.

Third, the Archaeological Resources Act (ARPA) of 1979 (Pub. L. No. 96-95; 16 U.S.C. §§470aa–470mm) protects archaeological resources on federal lands by prohibiting the removal, damaging, or alteration of artifacts of archaeological interest without a permit. The Act provides for civil and criminal penalties against violators. Generally, when an inadvertent or intentional discovery under NAGPRA occurs, an ARPA permit is required for final disposition of the burial resources.

While all three federal Acts include terms like "protection" and "preservation," the reality is that these three Acts are primarily procedural and do not prevent agencies from implementing Everglades restoration projects that adversely impact cultural sites. The lack of substantive protection/preservation is a limitation that should be understood by Tribal practitioners. So long as the procedures are followed, compliance is almost assured even if the resources are not protected or preserved. With regard to NAGPRA and ARPA, the acting federal agency is usually the land manager, which means the acting agency is same agency that would issue the ARPA and NAGPRA approvals. Charging the acting agency as the permitting agency for its own actions is essentially a perfunctory task. In our case, the federal agencies argued that NAGPRA and ARPA generally did not apply because most of the land was under state ownership and the existence of federal Everglades projects was not sufficient federal control to trigger these Acts. It is important to note that the Seminole Tribe did not subscribe to the federal agencies' arguments.

It has been our experience that the most significant limitation of these three Acts, especially NHPA, is the fact they are not written from a Tribal perspective. As such, the cultural values the Seminole people attribute to cultural sites are much more significant than the consideration required under these three Acts. Generally speaking, the unnatural inundation of burials is culturally abhorrent to the Seminole people. Under the NHPA, it is unclear whether the federal agencies consider unnatural inundation to be an adverse impact. Further, not all burials would be considered eligible for the National Register.

The Federal Trust Responsibility—A Tool to Overcome Conventional Limitations

Rather than argue about the application of NAGPRA/ARPA and the interpretation of adverse impacts under NHPA, we learned that it was much more effective to find an alternative approach to addressing the cultural concerns, which were mainly focused on protecting burials. The alternative approach chosen was the Federal Trust Responsibility. The Trust Responsibility is much broader in scope than the federal and state laws protecting cultural resources and focuses on Tribal interests. Fortunately, the agencies implementing Everglades restoration had previously developed a trust policy, so the concept was not entirely new. However, its implementation had been problematic, as evidenced by Project X, which was the first project to be subject to said trust policy.

What Is the Federal Trust Responsibility?

The Federal Trust Responsibility defines the relationship federally recognized Native American tribes have with the federal government. Despite its incredible importance, it is a vague, often misunderstood, and confusing concept (American Indian Policy Review Commission 1977, 125). Over 180 years ago, the Supreme Court described the relationship between the federal government and Native Americans as "perhaps unlike that of any other two people in existence" (*Cherokee Nation v. Georgia*, 30 U.S. 1, 16 (1831)). This unique relationship was first derived from treaties entered into by the federal government and Native American tribes. It is the legal obligation under which the federal government "has charged itself with the moral obligation of the highest responsibility and trust" toward Indian tribes (*Seminole Nation v. United States*, 316 U.S. 286, 297 (1941)); American Indian Policy Review Commission 1977, 133). It is the cornerstone of the federal government's relationship with

Native American tribes, including the Seminole Tribe. It is a special, fiduciary obligation that carries the duty to act "with good faith and utter loyalty to the [Indian tribe's] best interests" (American Indian Policy Review Commission 1977, 133).

While the Trust Responsibility was first discussed by the Supreme Court in *Cherokee Nation v. Georgia* (1831) as being borne from treaties (American Indian Policy Review Commission 1977, 4, 574), Native Americans generally viewed it as a binding promise. It is the promise that the federal government will protect the rights of tribes and their way of life from intrusions in exchange for the cessions of land from the Tribes to the United States (Suagee 1999, 494; American Indian Policy Review Commission 1977, 574). What it specifically means to the Seminole Tribe, in connection with Everglades restoration, is that the federal government has a fiduciary obligation to protect cultural and natural resources for the benefit of the Seminole Tribe. The Seminole Tribe views the Trust Responsibility as a substantive obligation. So, whereas the NHPA, NAGPRA, and ARPA are primarily procedural, not dictating a specific result, the Federal Trust Responsibility does—namely, that federal agencies act in the Seminole Tribe's best interests with regard to protecting cultural values/sites.

Limitations of the Federal Trust Responsibility

It is important to note the limitations of the Federal Trust Responsibility in order to effectively utilize it as a tool for cultural preservation. As noted above, the major limitation of the Federal Trust Responsibility is that it is not clearly defined. It is a vague and amorphous concept that is based on common law principles of fiduciary law created from doctrines of international law (Cohen 2012, 412–413). As such, federal agencies often misunderstand the Federal Trust Responsibility. This problem is augmented by the fact that each federal agency interprets and implements the Trust Responsibility differently. This leads to inconsistent application and results from agency to agency. Further, the courts have eroded the power of the Trust Responsibility over time, limiting its application and enforceability.

Ultimately, proper implementation of the Trust Responsibility is dependent on agency staff and the working relationship Tribal governments have with agency staff. Consequently, the human factor can potentially be the principal obstacle to full utilization of the Trust Responsibility. Acknowledging the importance the human factor plays in the implementation of the Trust Responsibility is a prerequisite to being able to use the Trust Responsibility as an effective tool. For example, Project X was the first Everglades restoration project subject to a specific Trust Responsibility policy. As noted earlier, Project X resulted in the relocation of two aboriginal cemeteries without the Seminole Tribe's knowledge—a result that the Seminole Tribe felt was contrary to the Trust Responsibility. While we were able to secure an agreement mandating the burials be placed back to their original resting places and perpetually protected from any further human disturbance, the initial implementation of the Trust Responsibility was questionable.

The lesson learned from Project X was that the problem was not with the Trust Responsibility but with its implementation. Therefore, we still viewed the Trust Responsibility as a potential useful tool that is Tribally focused and addresses Tribal interests that enacted laws do not. As an analogy, simply because a person hits his thumb with a hammer does not mean the hammer is not the right tool to drive a nail into wood. Instead, it means the person using the hammer needs to learn how to effectively use the hammer. Similarly, we needed to put the Seminole Tribe and the federal agencies in the best position to effectively utilize the Trust Responsibility. Such a task required the Seminole Tribe to critically revisit its internal operations to improve the relationship with the federal agencies and facilitate meaningful application of the Trust Responsibility by agency staff. Implementation of the Trust Responsibility requires meaningful effort by both the federal agencies and the Tribal governments.

After resolution of Project X, the Seminole Tribe sought to utilize the broad scope and flexibility of the Trust Responsibility to address cultural interests that conventional statutory acts and reviews often overlook. Our efforts resulted in the Seminole Tribe and the USACE entering into multiple trust agreements that ultimately led to the development of one statewide Trust Responsibility agreement that set forth burial protection and consultation protocols for USACE's regulatory and civil works programs. While the agreements are sound, the human factor remains the key element affecting successful implementation. Therefore, it has been imperative for us to continue to facilitate mutual understandings and a working relationship with the USACE and other stakeholders. This is an ongoing investment in the protection of ancestral burials and our government-to-government relationship with federal and state entities. It also has been imperative for us to critically analyze mistakes in the implementation of these agreements and to develop strategies to ensure those mistakes do not reoccur. This requires us to continue to educate ourselves and the relevant federal and state entities, with the ultimate goal of improving implementation and our relationships.

In summary, the Federal Trust Responsibility had the potential to enhance protection of burials in connection with Everglades restoration, despite its limitations. It was under this broad umbrella that the Seminole Tribe negotiated agreements for the protection of burial resources from anthropogenic disturbances, including unnatural inundation, in connection with specific projects that followed. We were also able to negotiate a Trust Responsibility agreement with the USACE that establishes a trust process to protect all Native American burials within the State of Florida that may be impacted by the USACE's regulatory and civil works programs. Unlike agreements under the NHPA, these trust agreements were based upon the Seminole Tribe's cultural beliefs and addressed Tribal concerns. In the end, we learned that it was critical to fully understand the conventional protection mechanisms (NHPA, NAGPRA, ARPA, and so forth) and their limitations. Based on this understanding, the Seminole Tribe was able to recognize unresolved issues and find alternative mechanisms to address those issues within the authority of the agencies.

Consultation Process

While consultation on cultural resources is discussed in detail in chapter 12, it is worth discussing again in this chapter as several lessons were learned from consultation on Everglades-related projects.

What Is It?

Whereas the Federal Trust Responsibility is the cornerstone of the United States' relationship with Native American tribes, its hallmark component is the duty to consult with tribes on issues that may affect their interests and resources, including cultural resources. This duty has been formally confirmed by Presidential Executive Order 13175 (Clinton 2000) and is the basic building block of the trust obligations. Although such statutes as the NHPA include a specific requirement for federal agencies to consult with Native American tribes, the duty to conduct consultation is primarily a trust obligation. Often federal agencies view consultation in the context of the NHPA alone, and the fiduciary responsibilities that are required by the Trust Responsibility are overlooked.

Consultation under the Trust Responsibility requires federal agencies to consult with Native American tribes on a government-to-government basis. This is an important concept because meaningful consultation inherently implies acknowledging the tribes as culturally distinct people that have the right of self-determination. It is this government-to-government process that is the primary mechanism by which federal agencies communicate with Native American tribes.

What Were/Are the Barriers?

As the Seminole Tribe became more actively involved in preserving cultural values associated with Everglades restoration, we quickly ran into barriers. The first barrier was the volume of consultation generated by Everglades restoration projects. As noted earlier, these projects can be massive, encompassing hundreds of thousands of acres with numerous known cultural sites. These projects also involved complex modeling, engineering, and reports. It also seemed like there was an endless supply of Everglades-related projects that commanded the Seminole Tribe's attention. The sheer volume of projects magnified by the volume of associated documents was precluding the Seminole Tribe from effectively being able to consult with the agencies. The Seminole Tribe also encountered resistance from agency staff that were accustomed to the ad hoc approach to consultation whereby the agencies dictated the nature of consultation (the when, how, and where). The Seminole Tribe perceived consultation as being one-sided.

The Seminole Tribe learned that it was important to identify the barriers and find ways to overcome them in cooperation with the agencies. Our first step was to take more control of the consultation process rather than having it control the Tribe. We accomplished this by developing a policy on how the Tribe will conduct formal consultation. This policy was distributed to the agencies and established when and how formal consultation would occur. Essentially, this approach turned a one-way process into a two-way conversation. Subsequently, the Seminole Tribe has collaboratively developed consultation protocols based on the Trust Responsibility with the USACE.

We also learned that persistence was the only way to overcome resistance to change. In order for the Seminole Tribe to gain a more meaningful voice, a behavioral change had to occur internally (Seminole Tribe staff) and externally (state and federal agency staff). The Seminole Tribe repeated the same story over and over again: "meaningful consultation is early and often." Slowly the message became the narrative for consultation on both sides. Now the consultation process is much more manageable, and the acting agencies are reaching out to the Seminole Tribe during the early stages of project planning.

Finally, we learned from past mistakes that being unprepared during consultations effectively silenced the Seminole Tribe's voice. Therefore, we made it a point to be prepared as much as possible. If the agencies did not provide sufficient time or information for us to be prepared, then we made it clear that any meeting or discussion was not formal consultation until the Tribe had time to be sufficiently informed. The lesson learned was that consultation protocols, persistence, and preparation ultimately reduced conflicts and misunderstandings.

In summary, the most important lesson learned about the consultation process was that it could be a burdensome and ineffective process if not managed. Taking control of the process by defining in writing what consultation is, when it should occur, and how it should occur was the key to having the process be meaningful. It was incumbent on us to take the initiative to define the consultation process rather than wait on the agencies. Equally important was the need to account for the agencies' needs in the consultation process so that all parties can be invested in the process. The end result has been improved consultations (that is, timely, effective, and a meaningful discussion between equals).

Understanding the Obstacles and Making Them Your Friend

The Seminole Tribe's efforts to have a more meaningful role in Everglades restoration and preserve cultural values have been a process rather than an event. It was important for us to acknowledge this as we faced obstacles. The process required behavioral changes internally and externally. Understanding that such changes take time and are not an event helps keep the ultimate goals and objectives in focus, especially during difficult times. The following highlights the top three obstacles the Seminole Tribe has faced in its efforts to enhance the process and preserve cultural values.

Lost in Translation

When the Seminole Tribe first sat down with state and federal agencies to resolve Project X, all parties seemed to leave the meetings frustrated. The parties were frustrated because we each were stating our points, and the other parties did not seem to be understanding. Each party felt their points were obvious and could not understand why they were not accepted by the others. It became apparent that important messages were being lost in translation. Even though consultation took place in a common language (English), the cultural differences made it difficult to understand each other. We thus made it a point to go into every meeting with a simple motto, "I must first understand before I can expect to be understood." This motto is consistent with how the Seminole Tribe handles disputes internally, focusing on listening rather than speaking. It requires that we must first acknowledge the other parties' views. It also requires acknowledging that they have different motivations and interests, but that does not mean issues cannot be resolved. Essentially, it required us to first listen to what the agencies were saying and understand their point of view before we would attempt expressing our views—a simple concept that takes a lot of self-discipline to implement. However, it did allow us to have a better understanding of the circumstances surrounding an issue. Consequently, we were better prepared to express our views in a manner that could be understood as well.

We also learned that each person hears differently and to stop assuming every person at the agencies were the same. It was therefore incumbent on us to learn how each person sitting at the table heard. A classic example of this was a conversation we had with a USACE Colonel. The Colonel is an intelligent and honorable man. However, he asked us why he must go through all the formalities of consultation. He wanted to know why he could not just call us up out of the blue and talk things over instead of being so formal. We explained to him that the law requires that he communicate with the Seminole Tribe by formal consultation. His response was that he understood the law but wondered why could we not be less formal. We then explained to him that by conducting formal consultations, he was respecting the Seminole Tribe as a sovereign government. Further, formal consultation shows that he respects the Seminole people as a distinct people and the promises made to them. His response was that he respected the Seminole Tribe and their sovereignty but just did not understand why the process had to be so formal. Finally, we explained to him that Executive Order 13175 requires formal consultation when an agency action could affect Tribal interests. We further explained to him that this Executive Order was more than an executive directive but was a standing order from a superior officer, the Commander and Chief of the Armed Forces, and that failure to strictly follow that standing order was insubordination punishable under Article Fifteen of the Military Code of Conduct. Essentially, we spoke "military" to him, and the understanding was immediate as he declared that formal consultation was a part of his mission and a standing order for every project. At that point we knew we had a mutual understanding. It could be easy to blame the Colonel for taking three attempts to understand the message; however, it was our fault for not speaking to be heard. Once we understood how he could hear the message we were trying to convey, it was easy finding common ground with him. Understanding how a person hears required us to first take the time to understand him or her and his or her unique traits. It can be time-consuming but is worth the results.

Another lesson we learned from a Tribal elder was that it was our responsibility to educate the agencies about the Seminole point of view. An elder asked us why do Europeans want to dig up graves, a concept that is abhorrent to the Seminole Tribe. The question caught us off guard and left us searching for an answer. The first answer that came to our minds was that nobody had taught them differently. The elder's response was simple and brilliant: "then it is your job to teach them" and not assume they know such things. From that time forward, we have made it a point to educate the agencies about the Seminoles and their interests within culturally permissible parameters. Through this effort of educating the agencies about us, we have also learned more about how the agencies work. This mutual immersion has helped us build a stronger relationship and understanding when addressing cultural issues.

Change the Way of Thinking

During the negotiations with the agencies, we began to notice that the law was driving the process and not what the parties thought the outcomes should be. Preservation of cultural values became the slave to the minimum requirements of the law instead of the law being a tool to accomplish preservation. Once this was recognized, the anchor of the conversation for the Seminole Tribe became "what should we do and how can the law help us do it." Such an approach opened the door for all the parties to think beyond the minimum requirements of the law and see the full potential of the laws. The consultations went from arguing about what was minimally required to what protection measures were legally possible (focusing on the ceiling versus the floor). In asserting our interests, it was important that we accounted for the agency needs. Such thinking helped us find ways for both the project and preservation goals to coexist rather than to be mutually exclusive. Overall, viewing the law as a tool to accomplish collective goals rather than the driving force of the process benefited all parties.

In the past, we simply advocated our interests, as did the other stakeholders. Essentially, all parties were thinking two dimensionally, only focusing on plotting their interests. This way of thinking made finding agreement difficult because every party had different motivations. We learned we had to change our approach to a three-dimensional way of thinking. Instead of focusing on just our interests, we also focused on the other stakeholders' motivations. This three-dimensional approach allowed us to fashion solutions that addressed our issues and addressed the motivations of other stakeholders. Essentially, we focused on outcomes and finding a way to tailor those outcomes to satisfy the motivations/interests of all the stakeholders (plotting mutually acceptable outcomes rather than individual motivations). Simply stated, we created solutions that other parties could agree to even if they were agreeing for different reasons.

Understanding Tribal Capacity

The capacity of the Seminole Tribe to manage the volume of consultations and pursue preservation of cultural values was a limiting factor that had to be addressed. Dealing with the world's largest environmental restoration effort, in addition to the thousands of other consultation requests received each year, taxed our capacity to the breaking point. We learned that it was essential to understand our baseline capacity to handle cultural issues on- and off-reservation. It was also essential to understand the Seminole Tribe's goals and objectives for cultural preservation. Understanding what the current capacity can achieve helped us understand how to better allocate resources.

As noted earlier, it was also important for us to understand that cultural preservation was a process and not an event. This kept us moving forward toward a goal, even if things did not always turn out the way we wanted for a given matter. It was easy to be overwhelmed by the sheer nature of Everglades restoration and the thought of trying to preserve hundreds of sites within a given project. The analogy we used to ground us was that we would not start by selling a simple farming village a space shuttle; instead, we would sell them a cart because it is something they can understand and use. After a while, we would come back to the village and ask them how the cart was working out for them and what else can we put wheels on? After a while, the village would go from a cart to a wagon, to a car, to an airplane, to a space shuttle. This same gradual process of building upon each success took us from simply securing the reinternment of two aboriginal cemeteries (our cart) to finalizing burial resource protection agreements on individual projects to finalizing a burial resource trust agreement to govern the USACE throughout the State of Florida (our space shuttle).

We also learned the value of having the Tribe and Tribal staff invested. This was accomplished by being involved in the community and providing opportunities for outside consultants/attorneys to be invested in the Tribal community. The proposition for us was that we cannot expect the state and federal agencies to be invested in preserving our cultural values if we are not internally invested in such an outcome.

Finally, we learned that it was important to recognize opportunities and when to be patient. An elder from a tribe in Arizona taught us that not only do we need to speak to be heard but that we also need to know when the other person is ready to hear us. Prematurely acting or telling a story can delay achieving preservation goals or destroy them completely. Waiting until the state and federal agencies are ready to hear the Seminole Tribe's story was important in our success. We recognized that Project X put the state and federal agencies in a position to hear the Seminole Tribe's cultural interests. As we progressed from the reinternment to subsequent agreements, we were patient to wait until the next chapter of the Seminole story was ready to be told and heard. It has truly been a process for the Seminole Tribe, not an event—probably the most important lesson that has guided us for the past eight years.

In summary, by understanding the obstacles that are in the way of reaching your goals, you put yourself in a better position to overcome them. This takes discipline and the willingness to critically evaluate yourself and not just critically judge others. If this can be accomplished, then obstacles can become tools for achieving your goals.

Conclusion

The Seminole Tribe has been on a long journey to protect those cultural values associated with the Everglades. During that journey, we have learned several lessons (good and bad). We are thankful for the opportunity to share some of them with other tribal governments. Everything we have discussed in this chapter can be summed up as the price of freedom is persistence and that what seems impossible is possible with the right planning and determination.

Figure 15.5. Paul Backhouse (*left*) and James Charles (*right*). By permission of Anne Mullins.

References Cited

American Indian Policy Review Commission. 1977. Final Report Submitted to Congress, May 17. Washington, D.C.: Government Printing Office.

Carr, R. 2002. "The Archaeology of Everglades Tree Island." In *Tree Islands of the Everglades*, edited by Fred H. Sklar and Arnold Van Der Valk. Dordrecht: Kluwer Academic Publishers.

Clinton, William J. 2000. "Executive Order 13175 Consultation and Coordination with Indian Tribal Governments." *Federal Register* 65:218. November 9.

Godfrey, Mathew C., and Theodore Catton. 2011. *River of Interest: Water Management in South Florida and the Everglades, 1948–2010*. Washington, D.C.: U.S. Army Corps of Engineers.

Griffin, John. 2002. *Archaeology of the Everglades*. Edited by Jerald T. Milanich and James J. Miller. Gainesville: University Press of Florida.

McVoy, Christopher W., Winifred Park Said, Jayantha Obeysekera, and Joel Van Arman. 2011. *Landscapes and Hydrology of the Pre-drainage Everglades*. Gainesville: University Press of Florida.

Newton, Nell Jessup, ed. 2012. *Cohen's Handbook of Federal Indian Law*. Lexis-Nexis Law Publishers.

Schwadron, Margo. 2005. "Big Cypress National Preserve." In *Archeological Overview and Assessment*, Vol. 1. Southeast Archeological Center Accession 1396. Tallahassee, Fla.

Sprague, John T. 2000 (1848). *The Origin, Progress, And Conclusion of the Florida War*. Tampa, Fla.: University of Tampa Press.

Sturtevant, William C. 1954. "The Mikasuki Seminole: Medical Beliefs and Practices." Ph.D. diss., Yale University.

Suagee, Dean B. 1999. "The Cultural Heritage of American Indian Tribes and the Preservation of Biological Diversity." *Arizona State Law Journal* (Summer).

Tebeau, Charlton. 1968. *Man in the Everglades: 2000 Years of Human History in the Everglades National Park*. Miami: University of Miami Press.

U.S. Army Corps of Engineers (USACE). 2011. "Everglades Restoration Transition Plan Final Environmental Impact Statement December 2011 Volume I."

———. 2014. "Central Everglades Planning Project Final Integrated Project Implementation Report and Environmental Impact Study July 2014."

16

The Significance of People and Preservation

Tribal Archaeology, Traditional Cultural Properties, and Section 106 of the National Historic Preservation Act

TIMOTHY A. PARSONS

Although they serve different communities with differing cultural belief systems, both the Tribal Historic Preservation Office (THPO) and the State Historic Preservation Office (SHPO) share very similar preservation-centric goals. Florida is a very large state, and the relationship between the SHPO (in Tallahassee) and the THPO (in Big Cypress) presents a challenge to employees of both offices with little opportunity for interaction. Nevertheless, the similarity in mission and cooperative personnel has resulted in a fruitful relationship between the two institutions. This is not to say that culturally mandated project-based disagreements don't exist. They do. However, staff at both offices demonstrate the cultural and professional respect necessary to work well with one another. Opportunities to collaborate on projects of mutual interest have strengthened this relationship, and we have found much common ground. A view from outside the THPO is always welcome as we learn from each another.

Author Bio

Timothy Parsons is the Division Director and the State Historic Preservation Officer at the Florida Division of Historical Resources. He has more than fifteen years of archaeological research and applied cultural resource management (CRM) experience in the United States and Europe. Parsons received a B.A. from Millsaps College in 2003 and his Ph.D. from Florida State University in 2011. He lives in Tallahassee with his wife and daughter.

Introduction

Tribal archaeology has a context; it does not exist in a disciplinary vacuum. It is, after all, archaeology, and its practitioners are archaeologists. Its methods and theoretical frameworks are rooted in the ethnohistorical approach of mid-twentieth-century processualists and late twentieth-century postprocessual interpretive approaches, as well as a dose of ethnography that serves as a living link between the archaeological record and the interpretation of past human behavior. While their purpose may differ from many contemporaneous archaeologists, tribal archaeologists draw upon mainstream theoretical approaches that have shaped the discipline since its beginnings as a scientific, methodological endeavor.

What distinguishes tribal archaeology from conventional approaches to the discipline are not the methods, theoretical frameworks, or middle-range bridges used to link material culture to human activity. The goals of tribal archaeologists are distinct from their contemporaries, and they address current issues facing modern Indian tribes in addition to questions of identity and culture history. The tribal approach assumes that archaeology viewed through an indigenous lens can speak to more than just the culture and social organization of their ancestors. It gives Indian tribes in North America the opportunity to actively shape the description and interpretation of their pasts—to control their own historical narratives and to exert sovereignty over their histories. Until recently, these histories have been written almost exclusively by Europeans and European Americans.

As Native American tribes in Florida and elsewhere develop archaeology programs built around reflexive interpretive approaches (Backhouse, this volume), their growing influence in the legal environment of CRM and research contributions will have implications for archaeological interpretation of the past, and for how archaeology is practiced in the United States. An interpretive framework that directly incorporates the perceptions and interpretations of living cultural entities will require us to rethink the concept of *significance* and force us to ask a deceptively simple question: "significant to whom, and why?"

This chapter approaches the issue of archaeological and historical significance through the lenses of CRM and preservation law, the development of archaeological theory in America since about 1950, and the concept of the Traditional Cultural Property (TCP)—a historic property type that inherently lends itself to use in the tribal archaeological approach. Since it is impossible to address all of the challenges inherent to American CRM in a single chapter,

I hope that any omissions or shortcomings in the following pages are seen as opportunities to expand the discussion rather than to pejoratively criticize the legal, theoretical, and methodological environment in which we work, or the broader concept of historic significance. Embedded in the challenges that arise in the course of resource management is the opportunity for flexibility, creativity, and positive outcomes. Tribal archaeology can make unique and important contributions to this field, as part of a broad and inclusive approach to managing and preserving America's irreplaceable and important cultural resources.

Obligations, Considerations, and Significance: CRM in America

> The spirit and direction of the Nation are founded upon and reflected in its historic heritage. (National Historic Preservation Act)

Compliance with the National Historic Preservation Act of 1966 (NHPA)—and specifically Section 106 of that act—created the institutions and practice of CRM as we understand it today (Pub. L. No. 89-665; 16 U.S.C. §470 *et seq.*). Section 106 requires federal agencies to "take into account" the effects of their activities and funding on any historic property listed or eligible for inclusion in the National Register of Historic Places (NRHP), and its implementing regulations (36 CFR Part 800) dictate the responsibilities of the State Historic Preservation Officers (SHPOs) and Tribal Historic Preservation Officers (THPOs) and lay out a step-by-step process for federal agencies to follow as they go about the business of conducting, funding, and approving all manner of projects. In the 1970s and 1980s, the CRM industry experienced rapid growth led by enterprising archaeologists who capitalized on the requirements of the law. They established consultation firms to conduct historic property identification inventories and assessments of National Register eligibility for federal agencies and their funded delegates, who lacked the resources to comply on their own. The "gray literature" produced as the result of compliance with Section 106, which is housed in state site files throughout the country and increasingly in online repositories like The Digital Archaeological Record (www.tdar.org), contains data on the identification, assessment, excavation, and interpretation of thousands of archaeological sites in North America.

Section 106 was a boon to American archaeologists, but the phased identification process dictated by the federal regulations (identify, evaluate, excavate) relies entirely on the eligibility standards for the NRHP. If a site fails to meet the criteria as judged by the consultant, the SHPO, and the federal agency, it receives no further consideration in the Section 106 process. Such a narrow definition (especially for sites eligible under Criterion D, which emphasizes a site's potential to yield information important in history or prehistory) sets an arbitrary boundary that doesn't account for multicultural perceptions of what makes a site significant. Although input from THPOs and the public is required as part of Section 106, concurrence on determinations usually is not. This means that the identification and evaluation process relies almost exclusively on the judgment and interpretation of nontribal archaeologists and compliance officers to make determinations of eligibility. The entire scope of "significance," from an anthropological or multicultural perspective, is not always captured.

In 2002, a group of Florida cultural resource professionals addressed the issue of archaeological significance and the value judgments made by field archaeologists, staff at SHPOs, and federal agencies (Austin et al. 2002). Although the volume approached the concept of significance from a variety of perspectives, an emphasis on context was a thematic link between chapters. Broadly speaking, significance derives not from the material cultural present at an archaeological site or a site's physical integrity, but from how that site can be placed into the framework of what we know about the culture that formed the site, and whether research at the site could further that understanding in a meaningful way (Hardin 2002; Tesar 2001, 186–187). A scientific, research-based contextual approach to significance works well for archaeologists and is compatible with state and federal compliance laws. However, it fails to capture a broader perspective on significance employed by some Native American tribes. Dayhoff and Terry (2002) discussed how, to the Miccosukee Tribe of Indians of Florida, the significance of an archaeological site does not derive from scientific potential, but from its association with the tribe's ancestors as a broader part of tribal identity. The authors argued that all archaeological sites are significant and should be preserved because of their sacred association with ancestors. As a result, the Miccosukee believe that "no more archaeological digs are necessary" and that "what is in the ground should stay in the ground" (Dayhoff and Terry 2002, 112).

Although there is undoubtedly room for middle ground, the Section 106 process often fails to consider elements of site significance that transcend the four criteria for National Register eligibility. This occurs despite well-meaning attempts to identify and evaluate archaeological sites. Fortunately, publications like the *Thinking about Significance* volume are available to CRM professionals who see the value in looking beyond National Register criteria when considering what makes a place important to living cultures.

Laws other than the NHPA are in place that require federal agencies to account for Native American perspectives on places of religious or cultural significance. Most notably, Executive Order 13007, issued by President Clinton in 1996, directs federal land-managing agencies to accommodate Native Americans' use of sacred sites for religious purposes and to avoid adversely affecting the physical integrity of sacred sites (Clinton 1996). Similarly, the American Indian Religious Freedom Act (AIRFA) requires agencies to evaluate policies and procedures in consultation with Native American religious leaders and to make necessary policy changes to protect and preserve Native religious rights and practices (American Indian Religious Freedom Act 1978). Integrating Executive Order 13007 with the older AIRFA is straightforward: federal agencies should consult with tribes if their actions might affect traditional religious sites and should preserve Native rights of access and traditional religious use. There is also overlap with Section 106. The Advisory Council on Historic Preservation notes that some sacred sites covered by Executive Order 13007 and/or AIRFA may be considered TCPs (whether or not they are archaeological sites) and may meet the criteria for listing on the National Register. Despite the clear relationship between places of religious or cultural significance and the National Register, the CRM emphasis on identification and evaluation of archaeological sites as part of the Section 106 process leaves less rigorously defined historic or religious landscapes underrepresented and infrequently evaluated compared to archaeological sites and buildings.

In the midst of the alphabet soup of various federal laws and regulations is the more ephemeral "Federal Trust Responsibility." The trust responsibility is a legal obligation under which the United States "has charged itself with moral obligations of the highest responsibility and trust" toward Indian tribes (*Seminole Nation v. United States* [1942]). Foundationally, it is a fiduciary obligation to protect tribal treaty rights, lands, assets, and resources. It also requires the U.S. government to carry out the mandates of federal law with respect to Native American tribes. The trust responsibility includes and extends beyond the protection of archaeological sites, but it nonetheless meshes uncomfortably with Section 106 since most other consulting parties to the process—notably SHPOs—do not share this federal obligation and may interpret federal acquiescence to some tribal requests as inconsistent with the Section 106 regulations. This is especially true when an undertaking is not taking place on federal or tribal land, and therefore does not require concurrence on determinations of effect from the tribe/THPO (for example, mitigation banks or environmental restoration projects on state-owned land, or federally permitted activities on private or state-owned property).

Federally recognized tribes can advocate for consideration and protection of cultural resources under the federal trust responsibility, and they can exercise their legal right to participate in the Section 106 process. While the avenues for tribal participation in the federal decision-making process are well established, the concept of *significance* as defined by the NHPA still does not encompass the culturally specific Native American perspectives on what makes archaeological, religious, and spiritual sites important. The emergence of tribal archaeology during the last several decades has affected how federally recognized tribes participate in the evaluation of historic properties and define significance within the Section 106 consultation environment, but what makes places important to tribes still receives less consideration than significance based on the National Register criteria. As a bridging mechanism between scientific study and a group's interpretation of its own past, tribal archaeology plays an important role in bringing Native American concerns to the forefront of Section 106 consultation.

Archaeological Thought and Perspectives on the Past

Tribal archaeology did not develop in isolation from the broader discipline, nor is it defined simply as Indian tribes participating or sponsoring archaeological fieldwork. By the mid-1980s, archaeologists in the United States and Canada began to write explicitly about the development of "native archaeologies" and the need for a productive dialogue between "traditional" scientific approaches to the discipline and Native perspectives on interpreting the past (Denton 1985). This is notable, as the first clearly organized and defined recognition of tribal archaeology occurred roughly contemporaneously with the development of CRM standards for the inventory and treatment of archaeological sites, and with an explosion in the number of archaeological sites investigated and excavated as part of the Section 106 process. Furthermore, this discussion developed alongside a broadening discourse of archaeological theory that began in the 1970s and continued throughout the next decade. The postprocessualist (postmodern) critique of positivist, data-driven archaeology, and the shift in emphasis away from the empirical aspects of cultural history and toward a more emic, reflexive archaeology, made the emergence of tribal archaeology at this time a logical step in the development of archaeological thought (Nicholas 2008).

The position that there exists multiple valid interpretations of past human behavior based on the physical archaeological record, as part of the postprocessualist critique, set the stage for tribal archaeology as a component of modern archaeological method and theory. Indeed, it could be more than "archaeology with, for, and by indigenous peoples" (Nicholas and Andrews 1997); it could contribute to the breadth of archaeological knowledge in a meaningful and constructive way. That said, it is impossible to separate indigenous perspectives on archaeology as an avenue for understanding the past from the broader context of colonialism and marginalization. The list of Native American objections to archaeological excavations is long, and entire laws—such as the Native American Graves Protection and Repatriation Act (NAGPRA)—were created to address more than a century of perceived bad behavior on the part of archaeologists. The use of archaeological methods by Indian tribes to investigate their pasts and exert control over how their histories are written is a powerful component of sovereignty, and of control over their cultural patrimony.

Though tribal archaeology has a distinct purpose that goes beyond explaining past human behavior, theoretical differences should not exclude Native American perspectives from the archaeological discussion. In 1989, the renowned archaeological historian Bruce Trigger noted that the ultimate goal of archaeological fieldwork has long been under debate (1989, 370). From the material culture component of cognitive archaeology (Clarke 1968) to explanatory positivist approaches (Binford 1962; Dunnell 1971, 1979), to symbolic approaches disconnected from the scientific method and hypothesis testing (Hodder 1991), no unified goal for the whole of archaeological research was established during the twentieth century. As we approach the third decade of the present century, most undergraduate and graduate students are trained as theoretical jacks-of-all-trades and select broadly from the theoretical smorgasbord (or at least have the opportunity to do so).

For most of these students and professional archaeologists, the purpose of archaeology is usually clear, at least in a broad sense: to understand human behavior and social organization in the past. The theoretical frameworks for achieving this purpose are tool kits for interpreting what we remove from the ground and the data that we collect. Tribal archaeology, which interacts with living indigenous values, knowledge, practices, ethics, and sensibilities (Nicholas 2008), has a broader purpose serving an extant cultural group. Though the goals of the tribal framework focus on contributions to living cultures instead of (or as well as) understanding past ones, such divergent priorities should not dissuade cultural resource professionals from considering and utilizing knowledge presented by tribal archaeologists in their decision making. Archaeologists have for many decades developed and refined theoretical and practical approaches to the discipline. An implicit applied approach to archaeology, or even advocating a particular interpretation of the past, does not discredit the practice of tribal archaeology. Furthermore, the multidisciplinary integrated approach to understanding culture and behavior taken by indigenous archaeological approaches recalls the "middle-range" anthropological perspective advocated by Binford (1962) and adherents to the processualist model. As such, tribal archaeology's holistic approach fills a gap between a positivistic approach to archaeology and the reflexive process of CRM.

Negotiating Difference and Redefining Significance in the Section 106 Process

During the Section 106 consultation process, archaeological sites are usually assumed to be the primary concern of Native American tribes and THPOs. In the real world this is an accurate situation at least as often as not, though archaeological sites do not represent the compendium of locations important or sacred to tribes. They do, however, receive a disproportionate amount of attention. As a result, archaeological sites became synonymous with cultural resources, and the consultation environment often prioritizes archaeological sites over historic landscapes, TCPs (including places of great religious and cultural significance that may not have an archaeological signature), and historic structures. While the focus on archaeological sites is appropriate in many CRM situations, archaeology is only one part of a broad spectrum of CRM.

Though cooperation is the goal, the Section 106 consultation environment is fraught with the potential for disagreement. Many federal agencies consider compliance with the NHPA as much a burden as a legal requirement, and Section 106 often takes a backseat to environmental compliance requirements. Compliance with the NHPA can be resource and time intensive due to the consultative nature of the law and the various interests of the consulting parties. SHPOs are charged with assisting federal agencies in completing their Section 106 obligations, but they also have the opportunity to advocate for the preservation of historic properties in consideration of other federal, state, and local laws. And the opinion of the SHPO might ultimately reflect the best interests of the taxpayers of the state in which they work, the political whims of the state's governor (the SHPO is an appointed position, with varying degrees of autonomy from state to state), or a mix of both. The THPOs may have more in common with SHPOs than with federal agencies as concerns responsibilities under the law, but they face the additional challenge of representing the religious, spiritual, and cultural beliefs of tribal members.

The THPO's responsibility to tribal members is complex. The NHPA sets forth criteria and guidance for assessing significance and making determinations of National Register eligibility, but the legal definitions of terms like "eligibility" and "significance" do not necessarily align with tribal perspectives on what is culturally important. Fortunately, the NHPA and the Section 106 regulations provide for identifying and evaluating many kinds of historic properties—even if such properties must occasionally be made to fit uncomfortably into existing categories. The reflexive, anthropological, and multidisciplinary approach of tribal archaeology can therefore make the THPO's input all the more valuable. The fact that the interpretive frameworks of tribal archaeology are rooted in ethnography and living, traditional belief systems can benefit the consultation process, since a multicultural perspective is invaluable to consulting parties and federal agencies seeking to accomplish their goals and fulfill their legal responsibilities in good faith. As part of this effort, tribal archaeology is an effective means of bolstering arguments for the National Register eligibility of historic properties that have special significance for Indian tribes. One possible avenue for accomplishing this task is the consideration of an often maligned and misunderstood element of the NRHP: the TCP.

TCPs and Section 106: Finding Places That Matter

Parker and King (1990) coined the term "traditional cultural property" in *National Register Bulletin* 38. What distinguishes TCPs from other historic properties is that their significance lies in their importance to living communities rather than in their physical characteristics, potential for contributing important information about the past, or association with specific people or historical events. According to Parker and King, a TCP "can be defined as one that is eligible for the National Register because of its association with cultural practices or beliefs of a living community that (a) are rooted in the community's history, and (b) are important in maintaining the continuing cultural identity of the community" (1990, 1). In the case of Native American communities, a TCP could be a location associated with a tribe's traditional beliefs about its origins, its cultural history, or the nature of the world. This does not limit TCPs to Indian tribes. A TCP can be a rural community or an urban neighborhood that is reflective of the cultural traditional of its long-term residents; a specific location where a community has carried out economic, social, or artistic cultural practices that are important for the maintenance of its fundamental identity; or a building or place that holds special religious meaning for a community and is important for maintaining the cultural identity of that community (King 2003). For example, the significance of the Tarpon Springs Greektown Historic District—listed in the NRHP as a TCP in 2014—is rooted in the standard National Register criteria. However, the district also contains the Tarpon Springs Sponge Docks, which are integral to the cultural identity and sponge-fishing economy of the Greek population in Tarpon Springs, Florida. As a result, the district is considered a TCP for the purposes of the NRHP. Even though the docks along the Anclote River, near Tampa, have been rebuilt and are not significant due to age or architecture, their historical and continued use by the residents of Tarpon Springs are fundamental to the maintenance of the community's identity.

In the course of a Section 106 consultation, the TCP concept can be useful for identifying and evaluating a property's significance to Indian tribes that might not be immediately obvious as eligible for the National Register (as an archaeological site rich in features or an architecturally significant structure might be). Although a TCP must still meet one or more criteria to be considered eligible for the National Register, its *significance* is determined not by archaeologists, ethnographers, or historians, but by the community that values it. This can be confusing, especially in a field with a strong sense of how sites should be identified and evaluated. The fact that TCPs are neither fish nor fowl, in that they do not have to correspond to a "type" of historic property in order to be considered eligible, means that many federal agencies, SHPOs, THPOs, and CRM consultants are unfamiliar with how to recognize a TCP when they see one.

To set the confusion aside, what makes a location a TCP is relatively straightforward. It must be a tangible place; be important to a living community and play the same role in the community's present as it did in the past; have been important for at least fifty years, though that importance does not have to be continuous; have integrity of location, design, setting, materials, workmanship, feeling, and association in order to be eligible for the National Register; and have definable boundaries (which for some spiritual sites or geographic landmarks can be a challenge) (Parker and King 1990). A cultural practice itself is not a TCP, and neither is a belief. But the location associated with the practice or belief, if it has played the same role for fifty years and demonstrates a pattern of use or continued value, could be a TCP.

Good Faith Consultation and TCPs: Working Together
to Understand Significance

A discussion of TCPs offers an opportunity to examine how we define "signifi-cance" and emphasize the importance of good faith tribal consultation. Proper-ties considered culturally significant by a Native American tribe might not be obvious to non-Native archaeologists, historians, or ethnographers employed or contracted by a federal agency. Indigenous communities are often unwilling or unable to discuss certain cultural practices, beliefs, or important places with outsiders. Or a property might not demonstrate obvious significance from an outsider's perspective. Properties eligible for the National Register as TCPs can be easily missed during the identification phase of the Section 106 process. Tribal archaeologists familiar with Native religious and cultural beliefs are in a better position to recognize and identify these properties and ensure that they are considered in the federal decision-making process.

While the legal responsibility for the identification and evaluation of TCPs and other historic properties rests with the lead federal agency consulting un-der Section 106, many agencies—though well intentioned—fail to adequately consult with federally recognized Indian tribes as part of their "good faith ef-fort" to identify and consider culturally important sites. While SHPOs can, and sometimes do, try to fill in the knowledge gaps, they usually do not possess the specialized knowledge on Native American cultural values to adequately advise agencies on how to address sensitive cultural or religious sites. Unfortu-nately, an emphasis on expediency often leads to an inadequate determination: no historic properties are documented within the area of potential effect, the SHPO concurred with a *no adverse effect* determination, and so the project can move forward.

Case law demonstrates that this is faulty thinking on the part of federal agencies (King 2013, 134). In the 1995 case *Pueblo of Sandia v. United States*, the Tenth Circuit Court of Appeals ruled that the U.S. Forest Service had failed in its good faith consultation efforts with the tribal government of the Sandia Pueblo. After receiving SHPO concurrence on a *no adverse effect on historic properties* determination, they chose to move forward, implementing a man-agement plan in the Las Huertas Canyon of New Mexico's Cibola National Forest that included road construction and the development of recreational facilities. The Forest Service wrote to local tribes asking for comment on their plans, but the tribes declined to provide sensitive cultural information to the agency, noting only that the canyon contained important spiritual sites. The Sandia Pueblo maintained that the entire canyon was essentially a TCP, and the Forest Service failed to sufficiently account for the sensitive cultural areas within it.

The court said that the Forest Service could not ignore the possibility of historic properties within the canyon just because the tribes would not provide the specific information that the agency requested. Furthermore, the decision noted that "the information communicated to the Forest Service as well as the reasons articulated for the lack of more specific information clearly suggest that there is a sufficient likelihood that the canyon contains traditional cultural properties to warrant further investigation" (*Pueblo of Sandia v. United States* [1995]). The court felt that the Forest Service should have known that tribes are reluctant to divulge specific information about religious and cultural sites as discussed in *Bulletin* 38. It was further persuaded by the fact that the Forest Service had omitted documentation of consultation with an anthropologist and tribal members regarding the cultural importance of secrecy in the material it provided to the SHPO, and on which the SHPO's concurrence was based.

Several things can be learned from the *Pueblo of Sandia* case. First, SHPO concurrence does not constitute a good faith consultation effort, in and of itself. This is especially true when an agency selectively omits important information from consultation documents. Second, federal agencies should not expect SHPOs or tribes to do their work for them. The court's ruling was clear in stating that even minimal information provided by the tribes should have been sufficient for the Forest Service to undertake additional identification and evaluation efforts in making the determination of effect. Finally, despite the ruling, SHPOs, THPOs, and other consulting parties should not rely solely on the efforts of federal agencies to identify and evaluate historic properties. Communication and cooperation between the consulting parties remains the most critical component of Section 106 consultation.

Putting the Pieces Together: Tribal Archaeology, TCPs, and Section 106

To bring this chapter full circle, I need to return to the earlier discussion of the development and place of tribal archaeology within the wider archaeological discipline. Although anthropological archaeology is not a new idea ("American archaeology is anthropology or it is nothing" [Willey and Phillips 1958, 2]), the scope of the discipline was broadened by the acknowledgment that a multicultural perspective—meaning multiple points of view—could contribute to our understanding of past human behavior. If ethnohistorical information remains useful for archaeology as an analog to past human activity (Binford

1962), then tribal archaeologists have an opportunity to engage with members of a living culture about their past and their present, giving them a chance to contribute to and design their own historical narrative. Simultaneously, tribal archaeologists can contribute to the archaeological discipline by presenting and publishing the results of their archaeological and ethnographic studies.

More pertinent to the topic of Section 106 consultation, tribal archaeologists are the best equipped party to provide information on culturally and spiritually significant places to federal agencies—even if the extent of the importance to the tribe cannot be completely divulged to the SHPO or to the federal government. The intangibles of what makes a place culturally important can, however, be described through an anthropological archaeological approach viewed through an indigenous interpretive lens. This can describe significance in a way that contributes to and maintains tribal sovereignty, and is also appropriate for the Section 106 process as it exists today. Utilizing the TCP concept as a tool for identification, evaluation, consultation, and preservation could provide Indian tribes with a louder voice in the CRM process.

The National Park Service's guidance on TCPs provided in *Bulletin* 38 has been embraced more in the western United States than in the Southeast. In Florida, only two TCPs have been listed on the National Register as of 2014. The first, the Council Oak on the Hollywood Seminole Indian Reservation, played an important role in the tribe's history and continues to function as a symbol of its identity and culture. The second listed TCP, the above-mentioned sponge docks in the Tarpon Springs Greektown Historic District, is not of particular significance to any Indian tribe but is important to the Greek community in and around Tarpon Springs. Neither TCP was identified or nominated and listed on the National Register as the result of a Section 106 consultation.

As of 2015, few surveys associated with cultural resources compliance have been conducted specifically with TCPs in mind. The one notable example was undertaken as part of the U.S. Army Corps of Engineers Comprehensive Everglades Restoration Plan (CERP) project. "You Just Can't Live Without It: The Ethnographic Study and Evaluation of Traditional Cultural Properties of the Modern Gladesmen Culture" (Smith et al. 2011) was completed following a series of public meetings where speakers stated that the CERP project could adversely affect TCPs associated with the Gladesmen/Swamp Folk culture in South Florida. As part of its Section 106 responsibilities, the Corps of Engineers sponsored a survey and report aimed at identifying and evaluating TCPs associated with the Gladesmen culture in the project area. Throughout the production and publication of the report, Corps cultural resources staff and consultants met with self-identified Gladesmen to discuss the survey and its results. Ultimately, leaders in the Gladesmen community agreed with the report's conclusions—that of the thirteen properties identified and evaluated, two were determined eligible for listing in the National Register as TCPs. Those properties (Mack's Fish Camps and the Airboat Association of Florida) now receive consideration for avoidance from adverse effects by federally sponsored projects. And, if any future adverse effects are unavoidable, they would need to be appropriately mitigated through consultation with the property owner, the Gladesmen community, and the Florida SHPO.

An obvious question given the consideration of Gladesmen TCPs during the CERP Section 106 process is, what about tribal TCPs? Were the Seminole and Miccosukee Tribes contacted as part of the Corps' consultation process? According to the Corps of Engineers, Florida's federally recognized tribes were part of the planning process and were contacted about the potential identification of TCPs in the CERP project area, but the response was tepid. This is entirely plausible. At the time that CERP Section 106 consultation began, the Seminole THPO was a recently established organization still getting on its feet. The Miccosukee, like many tribes, are reluctant to discuss the location and nature of culturally sensitive tribal locations. Another challenge, from the tribal perspective, is the impracticality of locating distinct TCPs within such a vast area. Important areas may be transitory, making them difficult to encompass with a defined boundary, or they may not be in continual use (Paul Backhouse, personal communication, 2014). According to the Corps' Gladesmen report, defined boundaries and continuous use over a period of at least fifty years are critical elements of TCPs (Smith et al. 2011), though it must be mentioned one of the authors of *Bulletin* 38 disagrees with the Corps' identification and evaluation approach as practiced during the CERP project (King 2014), and with how the Corps and the authors of the Gladesmen report interpreted the *Bulletin*'s guidance. That said, the National Park Service has stated that the TCP is not a separate category of historic property, but is an "overlay of traditional cultural significance that may be associated with a property otherwise listed in or eligible for listing in the National Register" (Abernathy 2013). This means that a property must otherwise be eligible or listed under Criteria A, B, C, or D in order to be considered a TCP. The National Park Service is currently in the process of updating *Bulletin* 38, and I hope that the refinements will refine our understanding of what a TCP is and is not. But I will be disappointed if landscapes sacred to tribes are excluded from this designation simply because they cannot be easily circumscribed with arbitrary boundaries.

Conclusion: Moving Forward with Anthropological Tribal Archaeology and Section 106

Tribal archaeology, as a sophisticated and theory-driven extension of the broader discipline, has an important role to play in the world of compliance with the NHPA. Indeed, "traditional" archaeological approaches and tribal archaeology do not stand at odds—archaeology has a century-long history of developing interpretive lenses through which to view the past. Archaeologists love to shatter aged perceptions and develop synthetic theoretical frameworks for describing and understanding human behavior. In this context, tribal archaeology fits right in.

The significance of a site, structure, or place is shaped by one's cultural experience and can be understood differently by tribes, cultural resource professionals, and federal agencies. Archaeology can be a tool for bridging gaps and understanding difference. By utilizing a reflexive and reciprocal anthropological approach to understanding a tribe's past and defining its present, tribal archaeologists are in a unique position that allows them to advocate for historically, culturally, and spiritually significant historic properties that matter to living people. These kinds of properties might be overlooked by federal agencies, SHPOs, and CRM consulting firms, despite honest efforts to identify them. The question nontribal cultural resource professionals must ask is not whether tribally sensitive sites are significant, but *how* and *why* are they significant to living people? Taken a step further, how do federal agencies and SHPOs evaluate the National Register eligibility of historic properties that may not conform to traditional archetypes of eligible sites, and how can they comfortably consider them as part of the federal planning process?

I hope that this chapter demonstrates that significance is in the eye of the beholder, and that preservation is about people—living people and people in the past. Furthermore, I encourage CRM professionals to view TCPs as appropriate avenues within the Section 106 process for considering properties that have special cultural and spiritual importance to Indian tribes. Unless we divorce the concept of National Register eligibility from the Section 106 process—which has been proposed as a good idea by Tom King (personal communication, September 1, 2014)—significance and eligibility will remain entwined within the Section 106 regulations, guidance from the National Park Service, state standards set by SHPOs, and tribal decisions made by THPOs and tribal leadership. While tribal archaeologists should not ignore other property types, TCPs allow THPOs and tribes to define significance on their own terms, and are less reliant on outside measures of importance. They are therefore well suited to description via tribal archaeology's ethnohistorical theoretical framework. And they shift the focus from preservation of the past to living, breathing human beings—without whom no preservation would be worthwhile.

Figure 16.1. Timothy A. Parsons. Photo by author.

References Cited

Abernanthy, Alexis. 2013. "Traditional Cultural Properties." Presented during National Park Service Webinar, *Progress on Updating National Register Bulletin 38*. May 23.

American Indian Religious Freedom Act. 1978. 42 U.S.C. §1996.

Austin, Robert J., Kathleen S. Hoffman, and George R. Ballo, eds. 2002. *Thinking about Significance: Papers and Proceedings, Florida Archaeological Council, Inc., Professional Development Workshop, St. Augustine, Florida*. Riverview, Fla.: Florida Archaeological Council.

Binford, Lewis R. 1962. "Archaeology as Anthropology." *American Antiquity* 28(2):217–225.

Clark, D. L. 1968. *Analytical Archaeology*. London: Methuen.

Clinton, William J. 1996. "Executive Order 13007 Indian Sacred Sites." *Code of Federal Regulations* 61:711. May 24.

Dayhoff, Fred E., and W. Stephen Terry. 2002. "Micosukee Tribal Beliefs Concerning Archaeological Significance." In *Thinking about Significance: Papers and Proceedings, Florida Archaeological Council, Inc., Professional Development Workshop, St. Augustine, Florida*, edited by Robert J. Austin, Kathleen S. Hoffman, and George R. Ballo, 15–36. Riverview, Fla.: Florida Archaeological Council.

Denton, D. 1985. "Some Comments on Archaeology and Northern Communities." Heritage North 1985 Conference. Yellowknife, Northwest Territories.

Dunnell, R. C. 1971. *Systematics in Prehistory*. New York: Free Press.

———. 1979. "Trends in Current Americanist Archaeology." *American Journal of Archaeology* 83:437–439.

Hardin, Kenneth W. 2002. "Archaeological Significance: A Deconstruction of the Florida Approach." In *Thinking about Significance: Papers and Proceedings, Florida Archaeological Council, Inc., Professional Development Workshop, St. Augustine, Florida*, edited by Robert J. Austin, Kathleen S. Hoffman, and George R. Ballo, 15–36. Riverview, Fla.: Florida Archaeological Council.

Hodder, Ian. 1991. "Interpretive Archaeology and Its Role." *American Antiquity* 56(1):7–18.

King, Thomas F. 2003. *Places That Count: Traditional Cultural Properties in Cultural Resource Management*. Walnut Creek, Calif.: Altamira Press.

———. 2013 [1998]. *Cultural Resource Laws and Practice*. 4th ed. New York: Altimera.

———. 2014. "How to Write Off Traditional Cultural Properties: The Gladesmen Report." http://crmplus.blogspot.com/2014/07/how-to-write-off-traditional-cultural.html.

National Historic Preservation Act of 1966. 16 U.S.C. §§470(b)(1) (2006).

Nicholas, George. 2008. "Native Peoples and Archaeology (Indigenous Archaeology)." In *The Encyclopedia of Archaeology* 3:1660–1669. Oxford: Elsevier.

Nicholas, George, and Thomas Andrews. 1997. "Indigenous Archaeology in a Post-Modern World." In *At a Crossroads: Archaeology and First Peoples in Canada*, 1–18. Burnaby, Fla.: SFU Archaeology Press.

Parker, Patricia L., and Thomas F. King. 1990. "Guidelines for Evaluating and Documenting Traditional Cultural Properties." In *National Register Bulletin* 38. National Register of Historic Places. Washington, D.C.: National Park Service.

Pueblo of Sandia v. United States, 50 F.3d 856 (1995).

Seminole Nation v. United States, 316 U.S. 286 (1942).

Smith, Greg C., Susan Perlman, and Mary Beth Reed. 2011. "You Just Can't Live Without It: The Ethnographic Study and Evaluation of Traditional Cultural Properties of the Modern Gladesmen Culture." *Comprehensive Everglades Restoration Plan (CERP), Southern Florida*. Prepared for U.S. Army Corps of Engineers, Jacksonville District.

Tesar, Lewis D. 2001. "Archaeology: A Personal Perspective." Unpublished ms. on file at the Florida Bureau of Archaeological Research.

Trigger, Bruce. 1989. *A History of Archaeological Thought*. Cambridge: Cambridge University Press.

Willey, G. R., and P. Phillips. 1958. *Method and Theory in American Archaeology*. Chicago: University of Chicago Press.

17

"What May Look Like Nothing to You, Is Everything to Someone Else"

Growing up Seminole and the Future of Tribal Historic Preservation

QUENTON CYPRESS AND STEPHEN BRIDENSTINE

What are the future heritage concerns of the Seminole Tribe of Florida? How will the Tribal Historic Preservation Office (THPO) be relevant to that discussion in the next five, ten, twenty, and more years? Working with Tribal youth is one of the most important aspects of the office and one in which we are most proud of our achievements to date. Two tribal government programs allow the opportunity for Tribal youth to work within the department through the Summer Work Experience Program for high school students and the Tribal Work Experience Program for adults. These programs are immersive, allowing students to learn more about the processes of working in a THPO. There is no doubt the students have themselves fundamentally shaped the broader staff and the program itself. In this way, the THPO can operate as a cultural learning vehicle allowing Tribal youth to be more than passive learners of their culture. They are tasked to seek out, learn, and protect cultural knowledge through the various projects undertaken by the THPO. The resultant learning experience is meaningful, reflexive, and vibrant—for example, a photograph identification project offering opportunities for youth to engage the seniors during lunch—offering opportunities for transmission of cultural knowledge that might have otherwise been lost.

Author Bio

Quenton Cypress is a citizen of the Seminole Tribe of Florida and a member of the Wind Clan. He has lived his entire life on the Big Cypress Reservation,

Figure 17.1. Quenton Cypress (*facing camera*). By permission of Juan Cancel, Chief Data Analyst, Tribal Historic Preservation Office.

where he attended the Ahfachkee Tribal School from first grade through high school. The school offers a formal curriculum like science, reading, and math as well as Seminole cultural classes like woodworking and Eláponke, the Miccosukee Seminole language.

In the summer of 2013, Cypress worked part-time at the THPO and Ah-Tah-Thi-Ki Museum through the Seminole Education Department's Tribal Professional Development Program. He then worked a formal internship with the THPO Archaeometry Section during his senior year of high school the following winter. After graduating, he returned to the Tribal Work Experience Program in July 2014.

On July 15, 2014, Cypress sat down with Ah-Tah-Thi-Ki Museum Oral Historian Stephen Bridenstine to discuss his recent work experiences with the museum and the THPO. In this insightful interview, Cypress shares some of his experiences growing up as a modern Tribal youth on the Big Cypress Reservation, his involvement with the THPO and Ah-Tah-Thi-Ki Museum, and his hopes for the future of the Seminole Tribe and himself.

STEPHEN BRIDENSTINE: I understand you grew up here on the Big Cypress Indian Reservation. Is that right?

QUENTON CYPRESS: Yes, I grew up here all my life. I lived with my parents, Celesta and Cicero Osceola, although I am adopted.[1]

SB: Could you tell us a little bit about growing up here? You didn't grow up in a chickee did you?

QC: No, I just grew up in a normal home. It was the house my father and mother got built for us the year my sister was born. I think the first year of me being born though, we lived behind the church.

SB: Growing up, what different roles did different family members have? Your parents, aunts, uncles, grandparents, etc.?

QC: I have aunts and uncles everywhere. I have a few aunts in Hollywood, I have a few aunts in Oklahoma because we have family up there, and then I have an aunt that lives up in Tampa. We don't really see them often living down here. I have relatives down here, but they don't really stop by all the time as much as I guess some people's do.

SB: And in your household growing up, what language did you all speak?

QC: Well, considering the fact that my father is fluent but my mother is a Cherokee from Oklahoma, they always spoke English to communicate.

SB: And your father spoke Miccosukee?

QC: Yeah, he spoke Miccosukee. My father is from down here. He's Seminole.

SB: Where did you go to school growing up?

QC: Growing up I came to school here at the Ahfachkee Tribal School on the Big Cypress Reservation. I've been there all my life. I've never gone to any other school. It's really good though because they teach you your language and back home my father always spoke English, but every now and then he would speak in our language.

SB: Can you tell us how a culture class at Ahfachkee differs from a normal school class?

QC: At other schools they have Spanish or French, our school has our language, Eláponke, also known as Miccosukee. We have Eláponke I and Eláponke II. I've never been to another school so I don't know how much it differs from other language classes. One big difference is that our language, as written out, is relatively new. It has only been about eight years since our language was first written. Even our teachers, they're learning as they go because they grew up knowing the language by their parents talking to them. They never learned it written down so they're trying to learn it now and then teach it to us. So I guess it is basically just how other language classes are, they break up the words, tell you what means what, and how to put them together.

We also have arts and crafts so they teach us both aspects of our culture. They teach us our language and then what the women and men do. They teach the women how to bead and sew and make baskets, and they teach the men how to do woodcarving. We carve little canoes or a big canoe or a tomahawk or something. That's mainly something we picked up to make a profit for us as a Tribe because originally Seminoles didn't make tomahawks. We didn't make any of that kind of stuff. All we made were canoes and bows and arrows, but as far as I know, there are not many elders left today that know how to make a bow and arrow, the proper way anyway.

SB: Do Tribal elders contribute to the culture classes at the school? Do they teach some of the crafts?

QC: Yes. We're trying to get a wood-carving class going for our school again, but this past year they haven't been able to do that. We do offer wood-carving over at the Frank Billie Field Office here on Big Cypress. Victor Billie does the wood-carving over there. And then also, at the back of the museum, Jeremiah Hall does the wood-carving back there.

SB: To go a different direction now, I understand you're a skateboarder. How did you get into that?

QC: When I was younger, I didn't really know what I liked doing. I saw my father playing golf all the time, and I kind of liked golf so I was into that. Then my older brother Billy—his name is Billy Cypress, he passed away recently—I used to see him skate all the time. He always used to come to the school and skate around. I always thought it was cool. Then my older brother Ryan. He didn't really do tricks or anything but he just skated back and forth, and so that's just one more thing that got me into it. I remember getting one of my first boards. It was actually from Walmart. (laughter) It was a little cheap board, and you tried pushing on it and it barely took you anywhere. I forget how old I was when I got my first real board, but I believe it was from a company named Blind. And it's pretty cool because on the board it had South Park characters and the Blind company logo. So mainly it was my two brothers that got me into skateboarding.

SB: Do you have friends that skateboard here?

QC: Yes. I do have a few friends that skateboard down here. Mainly my cousins: Tyrus and Jalen. They both skate. It's kind of weird though how I got into it because everyone on the Rez plays basketball, and that's one main thing everyone expects you to get into. So sometimes at school, if a teacher doesn't really know me and they see that everyone else plays basketball, they ask me, "Do you like basketball?" or "What team do you go for?" And I'm like, "Uhh, I watch the X Games."

(laughter)

Figure 17.2. Poster created by Quenton Cypress for his Tribal Government class at the Ahfachkee School. Foam core board, 10″ × 36″ (25.4 cm × 91.4 cm). (ATTK catalog no. 2013.24.1)

SB: But there's a skate park, right?

QC: Yeah, we do have a skate park on the reservation, but I don't know how that got started. When I was younger, I'd say about six or seven, there were a lot of people about ten years older than me that skated. That's how my older brother got into it. But as they grew up, they started playing basketball more and they just dropped skateboarding. So my cousins and I ended up being some of the few ones that never went to basketball and kept skateboarding instead. We're trying to make skateboarding a bigger sport for the reservations. Skateboarding is a fun sport, and not everyone has to play basketball.

SB: What do you think are some of the common misconceptions or misunderstandings that people outside the Tribe have about the Seminole Tribe?

QC: There are tons of misconceptions. I'll just start off by naming a few of them. So Seminoles, we receive per cap or a dividend, and the main thing a lot of people outside the Rez—non-Tribal members, non-Indians, I've even heard this from other Indians—they think since we get money, all we do is sit around. A lot of them think we're a bunch of drunks. That's the common Native American misconception. So a lot of them think we don't work. They think we don't appreciate things like working and having an actual independent lifestyle. And for me, whenever I hear someone say, "Oh, you don't appreciate anything. You just receive that money and don't do nothing," I just laugh at them

What may look like nothing to you, is everything to someone else.

TRUE BEAUTY

*This billboard was made by Quenton
from The Ahfachkee Day School*

because that is the total opposite of me. I love working. I'm starting a job here at the museum in two weeks actually and will be doing something I like to do. I don't want to be sitting around, some house bum who does nothing but drinks Coke and eats pizza all day. (laughs) So that's one of the misconceptions.

SB: So speaking of work and the museum, I know that you worked a summer experience here back in 2013. Can you tell us how that got started and what that entailed?

QC: At my school, we have a class called Tribal Government. We get to learn more about our Tribe and how our Tribal government works. My teacher, Jarrid Smith, thought it would be cool to do a project with us that was kind of like a billboard. There's a picture on the left-hand side of the billboard, and you type in whatever comes to mind about it on the right. Under that you type a word like "true beauty" or "culture" or "family." Mine has an old black-and-white aerial photo of the Big Cypress Reservation and says, "What may look like nothing to you, is everything to someone else." And then under that I wrote "TRUE BEAUTY." When I finished it, we took it to the museum with the others to put them on display. My teacher thought it would be cool to present them in the museum so that when visitors walk by they can see what the Native American students are doing nowadays and what they do in their school.

As that went on display, Paul Backhouse saw it, and I guess it got his attention or he thought it was really cool. So he asked Jarrid Smith to ask me to contact him about working here. So that's how that came about. I decided the museum sounded pretty cool, so I took the offer and I came here and I liked working here. Everything I got to do here is pretty cool, and I got to see that there is more to the museum than just mannequins.

(laughter)

SB: Yes. We have a lot of mannequins. But growing up here in Big Cypress, did you visit the museum before you worked here that summer?

QC: Yes, there were a few times when our school would actually take us on field trips here for the AIAC [American Indian Arts Celebration] and other different events.[2] That was usually when I was younger, we'd come through here. The first thing you do when you walk into the museum is they greet you. Then you watch the video that talks about our Tribe called "We Seminoles." You then walk through the museum and look at the mannequins. Being younger, you don't really read what it says, you just listen to the tour guide. They say, "Oh, look at the cousin—err, look at that mannequin." And I accidentally said cousin because they're actual molds of people's faces from down here.[3] My cousin is in there so I always laugh when I see it. So I went through there and I thought it was pretty cool, but it never occurred to me that this would be something that I would like to come to and work with one day. So when Paul asked me to work here, I got to see all the behind-the-scenes things that go on in the museum and all these other cool things with the animal bones and setting up events and education. I saw all that and saw how cool it was, so I said, "Hey, I like it. I'm going to stick with it."

SB: And I understand you also worked with the THPO. Can you tell us about some of the different sections you joined and the different projects you worked on?

QC: When I got to work here, it was with museum and THPO. I got to work with almost all the sections. The ones that I really enjoyed and I think fit me were the GIS section [Archaeometry Section], outreach, education, and exhibits. Those are the four that mainly interested me and I thought that I would be good at. Education I thought would be good because when a school from outside the reservation comes down here on a field trip, education helps by having almost like a cultural exchange. They talk to them about our culture, and I thought that was pretty cool.

And also, if I work with education, that gives me a chance to come back and talk to our students on the reservation and our Tribal members about jobs other than just working at the gym or something like that. It just helps me because I want to help my family and the younger generations and all of our Tribal members. So working with education helps me open doors to everybody else and also helps the museum get more involved with our Tribal members.

And then working with GIS, that was pretty cool because I got to work with Juan Cancel and Moriah Joy and Joshua Ooyman. They are really good people. They helped me learn more about GIS, which is basically mapping out the Rez. I got to see parts of the Rez that I don't really get to see every day because I don't say, "Hey, I'm going to go to this side of the Rez today." But the GIS crew had to go to that side of the Rez for work, and since I got to go with them, I got to see more of the reservation and learn that there's more stuff out there than just trees. There are campsites and there are actually the remains of an old railroad that used to come through here.

And then working with outreach is pretty cool because you get to go out to different places and talk to non-Tribal members about our Tribe. Schools teach kids about the American government and American history, but few of them teach you what happened, how they got here, and what they did when they got here. People talk about, "Oh they came here and Indians attacked them." No, and if we did attack them it was because they were on our land. They were trying to wipe out our homes and in order for them to live somewhere, they said, "Oh, well all these people that live here, we're going to go ahead and move them somewhere else." Nobody wants to be moved from their own homes so we fought back and they call that attacking them. So that's another misconception. People think we're just a bunch of savages or ignorant people. There's more to it than just attacking the Americans. So in outreach, we get to go out and tell people about what actually happened and why we fought them and why there were three Seminole Wars.[4] That's why I like outreach. I also liked working with exhibits because you get to set things up, and one main thing that I'm happy to work with is the "Ramp It Up" exhibit which deals with skateboarding.[5]

SB: Yeah, tell us about that.

QC: Okay. Well, it's still in the works right now, but it explores how skateboarding and graffiti art intertwine with Native Americans and how it's becoming a big thing in Native American culture nowadays. I don't really know too much about it, but I know one of the things that I'm going to do is help them set up the exhibit. We're also hopefully going to have some skate competitions, if we can get some kind of ramp in here.

SB: Did this first work experience change your understanding of Seminole history or your understanding of preservation and what the employees do here at the museum and the THPO?

QC: Well, when I got a chance to work here with each of the sections, it helped me understand more of what the museum and THPO do and how much work they put into helping our Tribe. Also, it helped me understand myself because it taught me more about my Tribe, about our culture and our history. So it really helped me because I got to understand more about why our reservations are here, why it's even called a reservation, and why we have the land that we do now. It helped me learn some of the things we had to go through to even get here, to be the Tribe that we are now.

But one main thing I really liked about it was the workers. You guys. Because there are people here around the reservation, like my father, who heard one of the Tribal employees who wasn't a Tribal member say something that wasn't right. He said this isn't his Tribe so why should he bother helping. Hearing that from a Tribal employee makes me think, "Wow, I wonder what all the other Tribal employees are thinking?" But working here, I really got to see a bunch of workers who are non-Tribal really enjoy working there and really enjoy helping us, helping our Tribe.

Like right now, we have the FPL power plant. They're talking about putting a power plant just outside the reservation, and even though it's not physically on the reservation, it's still part of our land and it drinks up 22,000 gallons of water a day so you can wonder what that's going to do to our ecosystem down here. And we have workers here that really don't like that idea either. Seeing some of the workers down here who talk to me about that and say how much they don't like that. It shows me that they do care for our Tribe and they will do whatever it takes to help us as a Tribe. You have to like working here if you're driving over an hour every day to get here.

SB: And then you came back for an internship in 2014. Why did you want to come back again? Did you get to choose your work?

QC: For my senior year of high school, I only needed four credits, which allowed me to have some incentive classes. At first they wanted me to choose a class, but then I asked them if I could work with the museum and THPO and they thought that would be a great idea. I thought that would be cool because I could work at the museum and THPO and I could bring what I learned there back here to the school and again help out my peers and open their eyes up to more opportunities around the reservation. I wish it was longer, but they had to do all this paperwork first, which took time. I wanted to come back because I liked it, and the museum and THPO is something I want to stick with for the rest of my life. It's something that I'm always going to go back to.

SB: So what did you do exactly for your internship?

QC: I worked with one section through the internship: GIS, Geographic Information Systems [Archaeometry Section]. I got to work on a project called "THPO Archaeological Predictive Modeling: Understanding the Relationship between Archaeological Sites and Elevation Values." Basically all I had to do was find an area of the reservation to do my project on, and then I was supposed to find whether higher elevation would give us a higher possibility of finding a historical site. That was my hypothesis. Throughout the whole thing, we found out that not just higher elevation but higher elevation plus location of the area, meaning if there's a body of water around or tree hammocks around, would help us find a site. We even found sites in lower areas sometimes because the site was good and didn't really flood as much as other places.

SB: You passed your class right? Did you get a grade for this?

QC: Yes. They graded me weekly on remembering what I did the day before. They graded me on paying attention, basic stuff. One thing I did have trouble with was communication because there were some days when the principal at my school would ask me to emcee at our different school events so that would interfere with my internship. Other than that, I had great grades through the whole thing.

SB: Did you present your internship to anyone?

QC: Yes, that was one thing I forgot to mention. After I finished my project, I had to present it to some of the students, eleventh grade and twelfth grade. I got to speak to them about my project and about what I did, why we came up with doing that, and just about the project itself. I got to explain GIS to them, what it is, why we need it down here, and why the THPO uses it. After I finished telling them that, I also got to tell them more about the museum. I got to tell them there's more job positions open there than just working in the main building. There's both the museum and the THPO. And it was all pretty cool, having that experience with the THPO and then combining it with my school.

SB: So I hear you just graduated from Ahfachkee. Congratulations!

QC: Thank you.

SB: Do you have any future plans for your education?

QC: Eventually I want to go to school at Lynn University. I actually applied and already paid the fee. I just have to turn in a 500-word essay. I was thinking of sports management but then I also like working with the museum so I would have to study museum studies. I believe they have something like that, but if they don't and I do decide to do museum studies, I want to go to Florida Atlantic University [FAU] so I can learn more about museum studies. FAU is in Boca Raton right next to Lynn University.

SB: Cool, good luck with that. So I want to ask you a few questions about the THPO office and archaeology. Could you maybe tell us in your own words, what does the THPO do? What service does it provide to the Seminole Tribe?

QC: Well you see there's the museum, which is out there in front for the people. They come by and see the museum, which teaches them about Seminoles' daily life, what they did a long time ago, before it became what it is today. But then there's the THPO side, and THPO is behind the scenes. The THPO has a few different sections. It has a GIS section [Archaeometry Section]. There's a compliance section. And then archaeology. That's one main one actually. In terms of a service, I'm not exactly too sure everything they do.

SB: Well, one of the big things that THPO does is they help preserve Seminole heritage. Could you maybe say why that is important for the Tribe? Why is that important for you?

QC: Okay, I couldn't think of a way to say it. Yeah, the THPO preserves Seminole culture and Seminole history and that's very important because if one day all of our gaming and other things that bring in profit for our Tribe for some reason get shut down or taken away, then we won't have money to pay our employees. We won't have any job positions down here. And the employees are important, THPO is important, because let's say a Tribal member wants to build a house on a home site. Before that Tribal member gets the okay to have the house built there, the THPO has to go out and do a field analysis. They have to do some shovel tests. And let's say they find some animal bones, historic animal bones. If it's just bones there and they don't see any historical significance in why it's there, then it would be okay to build there. But if they find a whole bunch of bones, and maybe some arrowheads or some pottery, they'll see that there's possibly a campsite there. Then the Tribal member won't be able to build their house because we have history there. You also don't want to build where there could be an old Seminole grave. It's important to know this kind of stuff because we want to know where our families lived before and we want to know more about our history. If they can find any remains of our sites, that's important to our Tribe because we get to have that history. That physical history.

SB: In any of your work with the THPO or the museum, did that change your identity at all, how you see yourself as a Seminole person?

QC: I don't know if it changed my view about myself, but I know before I worked here, I didn't really know what I was going to do. I wasn't sure what my interests were. I was still trying to figure out what I wanted to do, what direction I wanted to take my career in. But as I said, working here I really got to see more into our culture and more into our Tribe and into our workplaces. It really helped me set up myself for my future, what I want to be doing with myself in the future. I know I want to become Councilman one day, but I can't just be a Councilman out of nowhere.[6] I want to be somebody who is well known, at least be respected by a fair amount of Tribal members. And working here, I get to work with a lot of people. I get to work with employees, different Tribal members, and even our elders.

I think that's one thing that's great because I get to work with my elders. They can tell me some of the history and they can share their perspective about the Tribe with me and I can share mine with them. Like recently, we did a three generations panel [for the Army Corps of Engineers Cultural Immersion Workshop]. We had three Tribal members: an elder, someone in their thirties, and then me, which is our younger generation. It was good because we got to talk to the Army Corps of Engineers employees, who are non-Tribal members, and tell them about our culture. But also listening to our elder talk and tell his stories was good because I got to hear some of what our Tribe had to go through. I got to hear from our elder's perspective [Willie Johns], then I got to hear from a midgeneration perspective [Everett

Osceola], and then they got to hear what I thought about our Tribe and where we're going.

SB: Do older and younger generations in the Seminole Tribe have different feelings about the THPO and archaeology and digging in the ground?

QC: Well, I know I've heard that some of our elders don't like that. They say, "Why are you digging that up? That's supposed to stay there." I hear that from them and then I hear the workers' perspective, which is that they don't have to dig the thing out but they have to know what's there and why it's there so that they can preserve something for us as well. So hearing that from an elder, I understand them. I understand why they wouldn't want that touched or even being bothered with. Then hearing it from the employee, it helps me because I know in the future if they ask me if it's okay if we look at this or if I see them digging something up, I know not to just jump out and tell them, "Hey that's not right. You're not supposed to do that." I will see it as something that's okay because I know they're not trying to mess with it or sell it on eBay or anything. They're just preserving it for us.

But a lot of the younger people my age, they don't really know that kind of stuff because they've never worked here. They don't know what goes on behind the scenes. So if they hear something, they're going to hear it from their elder, from their grandpa or grandma, and they're going to hear it as something bad. So they may think, well the museum is doing all these dumb things, and they won't want to work here. So getting to work with THPO and seeing it from my point of view, I can go ahead and tell them that it's not wrong. It's okay. They're just preserving it for us.

SB: In your time working here with the museum and THPO, have there been any big surprises?

QC: Working here I found out that mammoths got to roam around here years and years ago. They found a mammoth tooth when they were draining out a ditch. It was stuck in the mud. They picked it out and I thought that was pretty cool. It also surprised me too to see how many of the workers here actually enjoy working here and working with Tribal members. That was one thing I enjoyed seeing.

SB: This book is aimed at several groups, including THPO programs at other tribes, state and federal agencies and officials, CRM [cultural resource management] contractors, museum professionals, and academics. Speaking to that audience, what do you want them to know about the Seminole Tribe and the THPO so that they can do their jobs better?

QC: That's something that I was actually recently thinking about. I think it's cool that I get to be a part of this book because if other THPOs and agencies see a younger Tribal member working with this THPO, it'll help them see that they might want to involve their tribal community more. And I guess in a way, it'll help them do their job better, seeing what we're doing here. After seeing how you all work closely with our Tribal members, maybe they might work more closely with their tribal members. It's mainly something that'll open their eyes and see that working with tribal members helps them learn more about their culture. It helps them with the museum too. It helps the museum understand more about the tribe and help educate the people that come through the museum.

SB: Last question. Where do you see the Seminole Tribe heading into the future? You know, twenty, fifty, one hundred years down the line. Where do you want it to head?

QC: Well, I actually have a few things to say about that. Some negative things, some positive things. I'd really love for our Tribe to keep carrying on, and I want our bloodline to keep carrying on. That's one thing the Tribe is kind of struggling with. I think that's the same thing with any other tribe. Keeping our bloodline within our bloodline because you have a lot of people that are meeting non-Tribal people. And it's natural to love or like whoever you want, but it's something people don't really think about. They aren't sitting there thinking about, well if I have kids with this non-Tribal member, that thins out our blood. And let's say a person who is half has kids with a non-Tribal member, their children will now be a quarter, and if those quarter kids find another non-Tribal member when they're older, that child is now a descendant. Therefore, the bloodline stopped. There's no more Tribal member. And I know one thing, we have a lot more quarters than full bloods nowadays. I really hope our Tribe doesn't thin out and die out just because of that reason.[7]

But on the positive side, I see our Tribe doing a lot of good things, a lot of big things. We're trying to branch out into different companies, like I know right now we just started selling energy drinks, which is pretty cool. I love energy drinks. I know we sell cigarettes, cigars, and we sell water. Obviously, everyone knows we have the Hard Rock

Casinos. I definitely see our Tribe opening up to more things as well, like starting a T-shirt company, something with music, or even skateboards. I know another tribe has their own skateboard company, and it would be great for our Tribe to have a skateboard company because we have Tribal members that skateboard.

And our school is only getting better as it goes. I only hope for our Tribe's education to further and get better and teach our younger generations more about our culture and more about our language. I believe that's one thing that's going to get better. I've seen little kids walk around knowing words that I don't know, so I see our Tribe doing all the good things in the future and hopefully getting better with the qualities that we happen to lack right now. And if I become Councilman, I'll do the best I can for us and further our Tribe's education, further our Tribe's finances, all that kind of stuff. But I see our Tribe doing a lot of good things.

Notes

1. Intratribal adoption is a fairly common practice within the Seminole Tribe of Florida.

2. American Indian Arts Celebration is an annual two-day event hosted by the Ah-Tah-Thi-Ki Museum that highlights Tribal food, dance, arts, music, and culture.

3. The Ah-Tah-Thi-Ki Museum features fifty lifelike mannequins in its galleries, each with a face based on a Tribal member.

4. The Seminole Wars were a series of armed conflicts between the U.S. federal government and the Seminoles. Historians have split them into three main conflicts: First Seminole War (1817–1819), Second Seminole War (1835–1842), and Third Seminole War (1855–1858). In reality, the period from the Creek War (1813–1814) until 1858 marked a period of intense conflict and hardship. Citizens of the Seminole Tribe of Florida are descended from those who remained in Florida at the end of the Third Seminole War (Sturtevant and Cattelino 2004).

5. "Ramp It Up" is a Smithsonian Institution traveling exhibit originally on view at the National Museum of the American Indian. It was on view at the Ah-Tah-Thi-Ki Museum from September 15 to November 23, 2014.

6. The Seminole Tribal Council consists of a Chairman, Vice-Chairman, and three Councilmen who represent the Hollywood, Brighton, and Big Cypress Reservations.

7. Membership in the Seminole Tribe of Florida currently requires a one-quarter blood quantum, meaning that one grandparent must be full Seminole.

Reference Cited

Sturtevant, William C., and Jessica R. Cattelino. 2004. "Florida Seminole and Miccosukee." In *Handbook of North American Indians Southeast*, Vol. 14, edited by Raymond D. Fogelson, volume editor, and William C. Sturtevant, general editor, 429–449. Washington, D.C.: Smithsonian Institution.

18

The Promise and Potential of Seminole Tribal Historic Preservation and Archaeology

BRENT R. WEISMAN

More than twenty years have elapsed since the federal nexus for the creation of Tribal Historic Preservation Offices (THPOs) occurred, yet the work of the THPO remains unevaluated holistically. What are the contributions that have been made socially, culturally, politically, academically, and economically? With little organizational or mission-centric uniformity between individual programs, should we expect greater homogenization of institutional forms in the future? Or does the diversity in programs underscore the very different cultural groups that comprise the modern political configurations of the indigenous people of North America? The Seminole Tribe of Florida THPO is a case study of one well-resourced office that is attempting to build capacity and pull up a seat to sit squarely at the table. The relative successes, or otherwise, of this strategy will ultimately be judged by the community it serves.

Author Bio

Brent R. Weisman's involvement in Seminole archaeology dates to 1983, when, with a newly discovered diary of Second Seminole War army officer Lt. Henry Prince in hand, he went trekking through the swamps of the Withlacoochee River in search of Seminole Indian villages described in the diary. During this period of immersion, Weisman came to realize that an archaeology of the Seminole past could not be disconnected from who the Seminoles are today. The results of the Withlacoochee project, the first of its kind to explore the archaeology of Seminole villages during the war years, was published in 1989 as *Like Beads on a String: A Culture History of the Seminole Indians in North Peninsular Florida* (University of Alabama Press). Since then, Weisman has published numerous essays, articles, and book chapters on Seminole Indian history and archaeology, including his 1999 book, *Unconquered People: Florida's Seminole and Miccosukee Indians* (University Press of Florida).

Weisman has been active in Florida archaeology for more than thirty years, first as an archaeologist for the Florida Division of Historical Resources and, from 1995 to 2015, as a faculty member at the University of South Florida, where he -taught courses on public archaeology, historical archaeology, North American Indians, museum methods, and, of course, Florida archaeology. His interests range across many Florida topics, but his longest involvement is with the archaeology of the Seminole people.

Weisman received his Ph.D. from the University of Florida. He served as President of the Seminole Wars Historic Foundation for ten years (and shared many memorable hours of conversation with Billy Cypress and John Mahon) and continues his research on Seminole topics as Professor Emeritus.

Sovereignty and Its Consequences

The primary function of the THPO is to serve the interests of the Seminole Tribe by implementing and complying with federal historic preservation mandates (Tribal Historic Preservation Office 2014). Several chapters herein detail this process from the perspective of those tasked with implementing these mandates from within the Tribe. The THPO serves as a conduit for the flow of the federal reach into reservation life and also as a gatekeeper or check valve for the regulation of that flow. The THPO translates the intent of federal action and mediates the effect of that action on the citizens of the Tribe. To Tribal citizens, the THPO can be seen as an agent of the federal government intruding where it doesn't belong, even trespassing into personal and cultural domains. Indeed, until its recent success in crafting a Tribal Cultural Resource Ordinance approved by the Tribe and permissible under federal law, the THPO's contribution to expanding the role of the Tribe in managing its own cultural resources was not a guaranteed outcome.

"Nation to nation" is the phrase often used to characterize the sovereign relationship between federally recognized Indian tribes and the federal government. The history of treaties between Indian nations and the federal government attests to the long political recognition of this sovereign status. Nations make treaties with each other. The federal government, as the political embodiment of the will of the people of the United States, engages in treaty-making with other nations whose status as autonomous, self-governing legitimate polities is not questioned. Engaging with the Indian nations similarly throughout the course of U.S. history has conferred upon them the same status (Wilkinson 2004; Rockwell 2010). Or so it would seem, as one way to look at the history of U.S.-Indian relations. And in that version the THPO, like the Bureau of Indian Affairs (BIA), the Indian Gaming Regulatory Act, indeed, the very act of federal recognition, abridges the inalienable and fully independent condition of sovereignty, like sovereign nations possess. And although that view of sovereignty might be idealistically pure in wishing away the very presence of European-derived people on this continent, harkening back to a time before European contact, it does not square with the reality of U.S. history in which the practicalities of politics and law have acknowledged Indian national sovereignty, but sovereignty with conditions (Lytle 1980).

This conditional sovereignty recognizes that the very existence of the United States as a sovereign body impinges on the ability of the Indian nations to exercise full and unfettered sovereignty. They exist as geographically bound units within a much larger and more powerful sovereign domain that owes its very existence to having gained for its own what was once tribal land and what were once tribal natural resources. This taking greatly reduced the capacity of the Indian nations to act as full sovereigns. This sovereign capacity was further reduced by the political reality that the Indian nations, subsumed as they are within the larger nation of the United States, are not recognized to have the right to engage as sovereigns with nations other than the United States. One way around this, of course, is for the Indian nations to exercise a corporate sovereignty, as the Seminoles have so remarkably done with their many enterprises (Fletcher 2014), most visibly with their 2006 purchase of Hard Rock International (Merced 2006). We need to understand the realities of a limited sovereignty to appreciate the significant and legitimate contributions of the THPO to capacity-building and to make sense of why the THPO exists.

The concept of indigenous sovereignty dates to the earliest era of contact when Europeans recognized that the coveted lands they hoped to conquer and colonize were already inhabited by people who possessed their own structured forms of social and political organization, were generally orderly in their legal and personal affairs, and lacked only a belief in the Christian God (Bragaw 2006) to separate them from Europeans. This view, most cogently expressed by the Spanish monk Francisco de Vittoria in a critique of his own government's colonial policies, was later embraced by the founders of the United States, most thoughtfully by Thomas Jefferson. Jefferson's Indian policy reflects the contradictory bind that came to characterize much of U.S. Indian policy throughout the nineteenth century (Abel 1906; Sheehan 1973; Keller 2000). Although the Indian nations met all the standards to qualify as sovereign nations, that very fact made them a thorn in the heel of American expansionism. How could the United States fulfill its destiny if other sovereign nations were allowed to exist within it? One solution would be to persuade these sovereigns, in their own best interest, to voluntarily relocate in a territory all their own where they could exist unthreatened and apart from the bulging expansion of the new American nation. Jefferson's Louisiana Purchase in 1803 made this solution feasible (Abel 1906). The political will to make this happen was slow in coming and suffered from the usual factional interests, finally and unfortunately culminating in the Indian Removal Act of 1830. Meanwhile, another solution to the Jeffersonian dilemma presented itself in the so-called Marshall Trilogy Supreme Court rulings in 1823, 1831, and 1832 (Wilkinson 2004).

The Marshall rulings explicitly defined Indian nations as "domestic dependent nations," a sovereign condition unique to them due to the unique contingencies of American history. Domestic dependent nations have the right of self-government but are not foreign nations and have sovereignty status only in relationship to the U.S. government. Like the many paradoxes that characterize American Indian law, the Marshall rulings affirmed the sovereignty of the Indian nations and exempted them from state authority but also, as dependents, placed them under the protection of the United States. Here we see the origins of the nation-to-nation relationship so often referred to today and also the beginnings of the trust system, still in existence, through which the U.S. government exercises paternal control over the Indian nations by providing social services, holding reservation lands and natural resources in trust, regulating tribal membership, and overseeing the conduct of tribal government.

Domestic dependency and the trust relationship work hand in hand, each made logically necessary by the existence of the other. They bind together the Indian nations and the federal government in what seems to be a kind of mutualism. The government owes the nations "consultation," a defined process through which the tribes gain a seat at the table in discussing federal actions that will impact them (Wilkinson 2004). The Native American Graves Protection and Repatriation Act (NAGPRA) falls into this category; after all, repatriation is a federal action that, however sympathetically intended, has both positive and unintended consequences for the tribes. The tribes owe the feds compliance—with Section 106, for example—again a stark reminder of conditional sovereignty and trust paternalism. It is in this context of constraint and dependency that the THPO engages in capacity-building. In my view, this means the capacity to build a Seminole-defined past and a historic preservation agenda independent of federal definitions. So the THPO complies and consults but also, and most important, creates.

Creating a Seminole Past

And again, the paradox. The Past as it exists in the Present is created by the living to serve the interests of the living. These interests can be as varied and diverse as the people themselves. Each variation is a version of the story, a medium through which Past and Present come together. The Past can be preserved because it tells the story of a grand national narrative, a political script intended to unite people of different histories and different origins into a shared vision of what they stand for and who they are. As a narrative, this Past is usually shaped from afar, in an office or conference room, scripted through a prescribed process that elicits the voices of stakeholders only to then submerge them under the headings and subheadings of themes and contexts. This Past stands as the representation of that interaction and is given back to the people as history, the way your story contributes to the bigger picture.

The Past can exist as it is passed down orally, in family histories, or in stories of how the world and the things in it came to be. These, too, are shaped and reshaped in the interaction between teller and audience. A story told today of how the Creator made the Earth or how the first people came into being is different than that same story told 200 or 500 years ago. Today, everybody knows that this story is not the only version of Creation and that it coexists with, competes with, and is in fact preserved and valued because it is not the dominant narrative. In the United States, multiculturalism has become one of the core values espoused at the national level (Floyd 2001) to give both cause and explanation of what America stands for, what freedom in America means. Indigenous views of history and indigenous religious beliefs, once suppressed in the name of assimilation, are now celebrated because they serve as bastions of cultural diversity (Pease 2011). The teller knows this. The audience knows this. What was once intended to be private, in a time when there was only private, has now become public in a time when true privacy has fallen out of respect. This is the world in which the THPO exists, and in this world the THPO has become both protector and an agent of change.

The THPO creates a version of the Seminole Past suitable for the outside world. In so doing, it changes the ways in which the Seminoles see themselves as participants in what this world sees as history. To the extent the THPO helps the people write their own story for their own purpose and benefit, the THPO is a catalyst in heritage-making. An unremarkable pole-and-frame stable built by federal work-relief labor in the 1940s becomes the Red Barn, a National Register site celebrated for its role in launching the Seminole cattle enterprise on the Brighton Reservation. This is heritage in the making. The story of the Red Barn, recounted here in chapter 12, is an excellent primer on how to build heritage by engaging people with the commonplace aspects of their history, perhaps even things taken for granted.

The Red Barn is real; it is a visible part of the everyday environment of people living on the Brighton Reservation—a place that stirs memories in the minds of the older residents (once stirred); a place, once identified by the THPO as being culturally significant in the formal sense, that provided a natural bridge for the THPO to enter the community life of the reservation. The chickee inventory project is another example of that logical connection (Dilley 2015). Not so with archaeology. The strangeness of archaeology to the Seminole people has made the archaeological mission and function of the THPO less accessible to them, even on occasion triggering anger and suspicion. To the extent that archaeology becomes tolerated or accepted by the Seminole people, the THPO again is acting as an agent of acculturation. The Seminoles do have a concept of history, a concept of people and events in a distant time before the present. This is the basis of their oral traditions. They also understand that history can be embedded in things. Each object wrapped up in a medicine bundle (Sturtevant 1954) tells a story of power and wisdom passed down from a time before memory. These objects are alive in the present because they have meaning by bringing health and well-being to the group of people who share in opening the bundle. This is a very personal connection to the past. Archaeology does no such thing. It is not immediately apparent to many Seminoles what is to be gained by disturbing objects that have been left in the ground. Seminole history is what has been passed down by the elders.

If this archaeology is contributing to a larger view of Seminole history, framed by concerns with chronology and culture process, then this is a Seminole history for outsiders. If this archaeology unearths the broken pottery and food bones from more ancient people, what does this have to do with us? Justifying archaeology only as part of the Section 106 process doesn't help. Rather, it shows yet another federal intrusion into daily life. This challenge is requiring the THPO to figure out what is truly important to the Seminoles and then how these needs can be served archaeologically, which, after all, is the THPO's mandate. Archaeology must be seen as useful, but getting there requires a cultural sensitivity that is one of the hallmarks of successful tribal archaeology. It requires listening to people who don't speak archaeology. It requires hearing what they say. And it requires responding in a way that honors the integrity of their voice. These are skills not typically cultivated in the standard archaeological training but are skills the successful THPO absolutely must possess. Learn how the needs of the people intersect with the requirement to do archaeology, then do archaeology that makes sense to them.

The efforts of the THPO strengthen the capacity of the people to participate in what has been defined for them as a sovereign process. But still this is very delicate terrain. The THPO is an outsider that must be let in. This depends on a relationship built on trust. Not the large and abstract paternal trust pledged by the U.S. government, but a person-to-person trust that emerges from honest and direct conversation. The THPO must act with integrity—again, not a quality that can be taught. The THPO has listened and has heard and has learned several things that have become critically important to its success. First, the Seminoles do not want to build their houses on top of places once occupied by ancient people. Such places are known to the THPO and to all archaeologists as archaeological sites. The archaeological surveys required to make sure this doesn't happen show the THPO in action to serve the interests of the Seminole people and help justify archaeology by its usefulness. This kind of archaeology truly is beneficial to the community in the most basic sense. Also, at this level, it is not public archaeology; the people don't need to be educated about the value of archaeology. There is no need for the archaeologists to tell a story about the wonders of archaeology. Nor do the people want to be told that archaeology brings knowledge about the lifeways of nameless ancient cultures. Archaeology has done its job.

A Seminole Archaeology?

Can there be an archaeology of the Seminole past that makes sense to the Seminole people? THPO archaeologists hope the answer is in the family-level reconstructions of camp life on the reservations. This is the archaeology of the very recent past, connected to people who are still alive. I am reminded of Charles Fairbanks's 1978 gem "The Ethno-Archeology of the Florida Seminole," published in a volume of essays titled *Tachachale* and edited by Jerald T. Milanich and Samuel Proctor. Placing this recent period of Seminole history in the "Modern Crystallization Phase," Fairbanks goes on to state (1978, 189): "Studies directed at a better understanding of the development of modern

Seminole culture as it is revealed in material objects would be intensely valuable for knowledge of culture change and to help solve the many problems of the people today. Archaeology would, of course, cause considerable opposition among many segments of the present society. It is nearly certain that no systematic archaeology could be done unless the direct and immediate benefits to the group could be demonstrated well in advance." I don't think the THPO archaeologists know this chapter (they don't cite it), but here, in 1978, long before the existence of the Seminole THPO and at a time when Fairbanks himself couldn't anticipate such a role residing within the Tribe, we see the blueprint for what was to come.

Demonstrate the usefulness of archaeology, then let it be used by the people to tell their own story on their own terms. This seems to be the very commitment to which the Tribal archaeologists have pledged themselves. And in so doing, they have found that not all Tribal members are opposed to the practice of archaeology. Some are very able and interested in digging shovel tests and shaking screens. Some see how broken pieces of pottery and discarded food bones can tell the only story of how people lived on this land in that time before memory. Further, these few (so far) believe in scientific archaeology and see their role as a human bridge between science and cultural tradition. Does this demonstrate the effectiveness of the THPO as an agent of culture change? Perhaps. But we should also remember that historically, some Seminoles have been eager to embrace things and ideas coming from the outside world (MacCauley 1887; Weisman 2012). The existence of the THPO now provides a present opportunity for this to happen. If there is an unrequited challenge still remaining in the Fairbanks assessment of 1978 it is this: archaeology used to "help solve the many problems of the people today" (Fairbanks 1978, 189). What does this mean for the Seminole people of the twenty-first century? The THPO must provide the answer for its mission to stay relevant in the future.

THPO Archaeology in Florida

The Seminole Tribe isn't the only party with a stake in the THPO. THPO archaeology is scrutinized by the community of Florida archaeologists and judged by its contribution to Florida archaeology. Indeed, because the geography of the two largest reservations contains landforms and ecosystems unique to the United States, archaeologists everywhere who research the relationships between cultural development and environmental history pay attention to the archaeology of South Florida. The influential American anthropologist

Alfred Kroeber was one of the first to recognize South Florida as a distinct natural area comprised of ecological subareas (Kroeber 1939, 69). In his view, incorrectly as later archaeology would show, Native cultures here were meager and diminished due to their distance from the major cultural centers in the lower Mississippi valley and mainland South America.

Florida archaeologist John Goggin, like Kroeber a proponent of the culture area approach, gave Florida its own cultural hearths (Goggin 1949) and worked on the ground, site by site, to lay the groundwork (Goggin 1948, 1950) for the more sophisticated evolutionary perspectives that prevail today (Widmer 1988; Marquardt 2014). One key to understanding the emergence of cultural complexity as evidenced by the massive shell mounds of the adjacent Gulf Coast is in recognizing the coordinated fishing-gathering-hunting that took place in both coastal wetlands and interior freshwater environments. If the mound-dwelling coastal populations dispersed seasonally in small bands to hunt and fish the interior ponds, marshes, and sloughs, then the archaeology of these locations is critical to an understanding of the overall cultural strategy we now know persisted for some 3,500 years (Griffin 2002).

This is why the archaeology of the Tribe's 52,610-acre Big Cypress Reservation is of interest to a much wider audience. Sitting on a shallow limestone shelf perched slightly above the Everglades (the change in elevation between the two areas is easily seen on "Alligator Alley," Interstate 75 at exit 49), the reservation includes essentially the northern shoulder of the Big Cypress Swamp, most of which is contained within the Big Cypress National Preserve (Roybal 2006). Natural habitats include "strands" (freshwater hardwood swamps growing in shallow linear depressions in the limestone), seasonal marshes, cypress-fringed wet and dry prairies, sloughs (shallow treeless troughs with slightly flowing water), and hammock uplands vegetated by cabbage palm, palmetto, pine, and various hardwoods (Ewel 1990). Some of the larger features have been named—Kissimmee Billy Strand, Cow Bone Island, Cow Bell Slough—reflecting modern Seminole use of the area. The seasonal pulse is driven by the wet (April–October) and dry (November–March) periods (Chen and Gerber 1990) and the regenerative power of wildfires. We don't know which season was preferred by the prehistoric residents of the Big Cypress: the dry season was particularly favorable because the fish, reptiles, mammals, and birds they counted on as a food source would be concentrated at the permanent water sources, but in the wet season deer would be concentrated on the few areas of high ground.

Most known archaeological sites, many of them identified in the National Park Service surveys of the Big Cypress Preserve (Ehrenhard et al. 1980), are located adjacent to water sources and are comprised of small mounds of dark, organically rich soil loaded with the well-preserved bones of animals and small bits of pottery. Called "black dirt" or "black earth" middens, most are not large spatially or in volume; some are little more than sheet layers right on top of the bedrock. This is a case where quantity matters as much if not more than quality. The more of these sites there are, the more human activity is indicated, either by small groups of people moving from place to place within a given season or by a larger number of people divided into small groups and occupying small territories simultaneously. Each site is but one sample filling in one more dot on the map of a prehistoric cultural geography, a bird's-eye view of a landscape made useful by people living in a very different world than our own.

The early reservation Seminoles stepped into the modern world, a world in which living off the land yielded only a marginal existence. Their concern was with surviving, even prospering, as a community in a rural isolated setting. Land was drained, prairies and hammocks cleared and opened up so cattle could graze. Eventually, tracts with well-drained sandy soil were planted in citrus, roads and houses were built, the community grew. Each of these activities altered the natural ecosystems in the way humans do, not entirely obliterating the natural relationships between water, soil, and habitat, but reducing them, obscuring them, replacing the wild with the tame (McVoy et al. 2011).

Looking for archaeological sites on the Big Cypress Reservation is different than looking for them in the Big Cypress Preserve. On the reservation, archaeologists must learn how to predict the locations of sites in disturbed conditions. Add to these the invasion of exotic plants that thrive in disturbed locations, Brazilian pepper for one, and you get field conditions that are less than optimal for archaeological reconnaissance and shovel testing. Using their predictive models, THPO archaeologists need to see the land as it once was and find sites that, to our present eye, are where they shouldn't be. Thus we see THPO archaeologists in cow pastures, along the edges of graded roads, or in thickets of invasive exotics. Reality for them is what was, not what is. There are lessons here for the uses of predictive modeling in the larger world of cultural resource management (CRM).

Archaeology on the 36,541-acre Brighton Reservation meets with similar opportunities and challenges. Brighton is located just above the northwestern shore of Lake Okeechobee on a landform slightly higher in elevation than Big Cypress but still low enough for a landscape of hammock-dotted prairies. And like Big Cypress, the annual seasons are driven by rainfall, divided into wet and dry periods (Snyder et al. 1990). Small creeks, ponds, and wetlands that occur throughout the area did not provide the bountiful food resources of the Gulf Coast estuary. Prehistoric people here had to hunt, fish, and gather broadly across much greater distances, taking what they could of all consumable plant and animal life (Hale 1984). Early Spanish accounts indicate that Native peoples of the Lake Okeechobee area had gained some prominence for their ability to produce a flourlike substance from the roots of a plant (perhaps Zamia, or coontie) (Fontaneda 1945, 27). Still, the several large earthen mound complexes in the region are not easy to explain (Willey 1949).

One of these, named Fort Center after a Seminole War fort located there (Covington 1981, 31; Thompson 2014), is just outside the southern boundary of Brighton; another, the Ortona Mounds (Goggin n.d. 2:326–331; Carr et al. 1995), is located about 11 miles away. These sites typically cover 10 acres or more and consist of constructed sand mounds, linear sand earthworks of various configurations, black-earth-type midden deposits, burial mounds (or, in the case of Fort Center, a burial mound and a mortuary pond [Sears 1982]), and, in some cases, canals ultimately linking them to the Caloosahatchee River. Archaeology indicates that these sites were used for about 2,500 years, from about 1000 b.c. to the sixteenth century a.d. (Sears 1982, 192–201). The native peoples of the Okeechobee region created a level of social organization and achieved a certain cultural stability in this environment that, although survivable by a foraging people, does not have the resource overabundance usually associated with cultural complexity. How, then, did it happen? The role of corn, if any, is debatable and likely minimal at best prehistorically. What circumstances gave rise to mound building in the scrub and hammocks of the Okeechobee prairies?

Again, as in Big Cypress, archaeologists must seek answers away from the big sites themselves and look to the broader landscapes on which prehistoric peoples imprinted their daily life in small ways, in small sites containing the discarded food remains of animal bone, small sherds of everyday pottery, charcoal from cooking hearths, and tools of bone and shell thrown away when they were no longer of use. These are the kinds of prehistoric archaeological sites found on Brighton. THPO archaeologists can contribute significantly to an understanding of the Okeechobee mound builders through their systematic and persistent work to discover archaeological sites. Further, figuring out time periods of use for sites or discrete portions of sites and then estimating numbers of people living in the Brighton area at different times would greatly advance our understanding of the population history in the Okeechobee drainage. This is basic archaeological research, with no immediate direct application to the needs of the Seminole Tribe. But its value might be crucial nonetheless.

To the extent that the success of the THPO depends on demonstrating its credibility and contribution to the larger realm of archaeological professionals, then basic research does benefit the Tribe by strengthening the position of the THPO (Backhouse et al. 2014).

CRM archaeology also can learn from survey methods used by the THPO. Seminole people made Brighton into a usable landscape. The cattle tradition runs deep (as evidenced by the Red Barn); pastures, not preservation, were their first priority. Roads, bridges, canals, housing, and public buildings altered the natural terrain of Brighton as the reservation community grew. Now, THPO archaeologists are tasked with finding archaeological sites that have been obscured from easy view by recent human activities. The CRM profession (and other THPOs for that matter) should watch very closely how they integrate sophisticated computer technology (Cancel and Backhouse 2012), radar and other noninvasive subsurface techniques, basic shovel archaeology, and community-based approaches to create what could be a model for all archaeology of the twenty-first century.

The THPO is a new endeavor for the Seminole Tribe and a new presence in the archaeology of Florida and the Southeast. It has set an ambitious agenda reaching far beyond the modern reservation boundaries. The THPO is both creating and preserving a Seminole past. As in all acts of creation, many influences—from the individual to the cultural—contribute to the form and shape of the representation. The THPO has gained credibility within the Tribe by respecting the integrity of the Tribal decision-making process. This has allowed the THPO to make great strides in accomplishing a most difficult task of bridging the interests of the Seminole Tribe with federal historic preservation law. The THPO sees its role in this relationship as enlarging the sovereign capacity of the Seminole people to act on their own behalf in preserving what is important to them. Through the enactment of the Cultural Resource Ordinance the Tribe is now poised to act on its own behalf, without BIA oversight, in concurring with the National Historic Preservation Act's Section 106 review process. When this becomes reality, the Seminole Tribe will have removed at least one of the dependent conditions inherent in Justice Marshall's concept of dependent sovereignty invoked those many years ago.

To get to this point the THPO has exerted remarkable skills of diplomacy and shown a deep and true commitment to eliciting Seminole visions of the past and future. It has looked without flinching on its role as an agent of culture change and is involved in the ongoing and never-ending negotiation of what that means. Above all else, it is that process of reflection that stands as a model to be emulated by the rest of the archaeological world.

Figure 18.1. Seated behind Brent Weisman (*left to right*): Seminole Tribe of Florida Chairman James E. Billie, Bobby Henry, and Danny Tommie. By permission of Peter Gallagher, *The Seminole Tribune*.

References Cited

Abel, Annie H. 1906. "History of Indian Consolidation West of the Mississippi." *Annual Report of the American Historical Association for the Year 1906*, 233–454.

Backhouse, Paul N., James K. Feathers, Maureen Mahoney, and Kate Macuen. 2014. "An Initial Assessment of the Applicability of Luminescence Dating to Developing an Absolute Chronology for the Production and Use of Sand Tempered Plain Ceramics in South Florida." *Journal of Archaeological Science* 45:150–158.

Bragaw, Stephen G. 2006. "Thomas Jefferson and the American Indian Nations: Native American Sovereignty and the Marshall Court." *Journal of Supreme Court History* 31(2):155–180.

Cancel, Juan J., and Paul N. Backhouse. 2012. "Seminole Geography: Using GIS as a Tool for Tribal Historic Preservation Offices." In *Tribal GIS: Supporting Native American Decision Making*, edited by Anne Taylor, David Gadsden, Joseph J. Kerski, and Heather Warren, 26–32. Redlands, Calif.: ESRI Press.

Carr, Robert S., David Dickel, and Marilyn Masson. 1995. "Archaeological Investigations at the Ortona Earthworks and Mound." *Florida Anthropologist* 48(4):227–264.

Chen, Ellen, and John F. Gerber. 1990. "Climate." In *Ecosystems of Florida*, edited by Ronald L. Myers and John J. Ewell, 11–34. Gainesville: University Press of Florida.

Covington, James W. 1981. *The Billy Bowlegs War*. Chuluota, Fla.: Mickler House.

Dilley, Carrie. 2015. *Thatched Roofs and Open Sides: The Architecture of Chickees and Their Changing Role in Seminole Society*. Gainesville: University Press of Florida.

Ehrenhard, John E., Robert Taylor, and Gregory Komara. 1980. "Big Cypress National Preserve, Cultural Resource Inventory, Season 4." Southeast Archaeological Center, National Park Service, Tallahassee, Fla.

Ewel, Katherine C. 1990. "Swamps." In *Ecosystems of Florida*, edited by Ronald L. Myers and John J. Ewell, 281–322. Gainesville: University Press of Florida.

Fairbanks, Charles H. 1978. "The Ethno-Archaeology of the Florida Seminole." In *Tacachale*, edited by Jerald T. Milanich and Samuel Proctor, 163–193. Gainesville: University Press of Florida.

Fletcher, Matthew L. M. 2014. "The Seminole Tribe and the Origins of Indian Gaming." *FIU Law Review* 9(2):255–275.

Floyd, Myron F. 2001. "Managing National Parks in a Multicultural Society: Searching for Common Ground." *Managing Recreational Use* 18(3):41–51.

Fontaneda, Do. D'Escalante. 1945. *Memoir of Do. d'Escalante Fontaneda Respecting Florida, Written in Spain About the Year 1575*. Edited by David O. True. Translated by Buckingham Smith. Coral Gables, Fla.: Glade House.

Goggin, John M. 1948. "Florida Archaeology and Recent Ecological Changes." *Journal of the Washington Academy of Sciences* 38(7):225–233.

———. 1949. "Cultural Traditions in Florida Prehistory." In *The Florida Indian and His Neighbors*, edited by John W. Griffin, 13–44. Winter Park, Fla.: Rollins College.

———. 1950. "Stratigraphic Tests in Everglades National Park." *American Antiquity* 15:228–246.

———. n.d. "Archaeology of the Glades Area, Southern Florida." 2 vols. Ms. in the Goggin Collection, University of Florida Libraries, Special Collections.

Griffin, John W. 2002. *Archaeology of the Everglades*. Gainesville: University Press of Florida.

Hale, H. Stephen. 1984. "Prehistoric Environmental Exploitation Around Lake Okeechobee." *Southeastern Archaeology* 3:173–187.

Keller, Christian B. 2000. "Philanthropy Betrayed: Thomas Jefferson, the Louisiana Purchase, and the Origins of Federal Indian Removal Policy." *Proceedings of the American Philosophical Society* 144(1):39–66.

Kroeber, Alfred. 1939. *Cultural and Natural Areas of Native North America*. Berkeley: University of California Press.

Lytle, Clifford M. 1980. "The Supreme Court, Tribal Sovereignty, and Continuing Problems of State Encroachment into Indian Country." *American Indian Law Review* 8(1):65–77.

MacCauley, Clay. 1887. "The Seminole Indians of Florida." In *Fifth Annual Report of the*

Bureau of Ethnology to the Secretary of the Smithsonian Institution, 1883–84, 469–531. Washington, D.C.: Government Printing Office.

Marquardt, William H. 2014. "Tracking the Calusa: A Retrospective." *Southeastern Archaeology* 33(1):1–24.

McVoy, Christopher W., Winifred Park Said, Jayantha Obeysekera, Joel A. VanArman, and Thomas W. Dreschel. 2011. *Landscapes and Hydrology of the Predrainage Everglades*. Gainesville: University of Florida Press.

Merced, Michael de la. 2006. "Florida's Seminole Tribe Buys Hard Rock Cafes and Casinos." *New York Times*, December 28.

Pease, James L. 2011. "Parks and Under-served Audiences: An Annotated Literature Review." www.nps.gov/hfc/services/interp/InterpPlanning/literatureReview.pdf.

Rockwell, Stephen J. 2010. *Indian Affairs and the Administrative State in the Nineteenth Century*. New York: Cambridge University Press.

Roybal, Art. 2006. "Big Cypress Basin Conceptual Ecological Model." Comprehensive Everglades Restoration Plan, U.S. Army Corps of Engineers and South Florida Water Management District. http: www.evergladesplan.org/.

Sears, William H. 1982. *Fort Center: An Archaeological Site in the Lake Okeechobee Basin*. Gainesville: University Press of Florida.

Sheehan, Bernard W. 1973. *Seeds of Extinction: Jeffersonian Philanthropy and the American Indian*. Chapel Hill: University of North Carolina Press.

Snyder, James R., Alan Herndon, and William B. Robertson Jr. 1990. "South Florida Rockland." In *Ecosystems of Florida*, edited by Ronald L. Myers and John J. Ewell, 230–274. Gainesville: University Press of Florida.

Sturtevant, William C. 1954. "The Medicine Bundles and Busks of the Florida Seminole." *Florida Anthropologist* 7:31–70.

Thompson, Amanda D. Roberts. 2014. "The Archaeology and History of Fort Center during the Second and Third Seminole Wars." *Florida Anthropologist* 67(1):5–22.

Tribal Historic Preservation Office. 2014. 5 Year Strategic Plan 2015–2020. Ms. on file, Seminole Tribal Historic Preservation Office, Big Cypress Reservation, Fla.

Weisman, Brent R. 2012. "Chipco's House and the Role of the Individual in Shaping Seminole Indian Cultural Responses to the Modern World." *Historical Archaeology* 46(1):161–171.

Widmer, Randolph J. 1988. *The Evolution of the Calusa: A Non-Agricultural Chiefdom on the Southwest Florida Coast*. Tuscaloosa: University of Alabama Press.

Wilkinson, Charles. 2004. *Indian Tribes as Sovereign Governments*. American Indian Lawyer Training Program: Oakland, Calif.

Willey, Gordon R. 1949. "Excavations in Southeast Florida." *Yale University Publications in Anthropology* 42. New Haven, Conn.: Yale University Press.

Cultural Resource Ordinance

The Seminole Tribe of Florida Cultural Resource Ordinance (C-01-16) was presented and unanimously approved by the Tribal Council of the Seminole Tribe of Florida at a packed meeting held on the Big Cypress Seminole Indian Reservation on October 11, 2013. The ordinance represents the culmination of years of work to allow the Seminole Tribe of Florida greater control over its own resources on-reservation. The ordinance sets out clear guidelines for the issuance of permits for those whose work on the reservation may affect sites of cultural significance to the Seminole people. The ordinance also sets up a Seminole Site File and Tribal Register program, which allows for the preservation of places not meeting National Register of Historic Places (NRHP) criteria. This site file structure also allows the Tribe to keep cultural information confidential while protecting critical resources. It is our hope that the version contained here may be of use to other tribes seeking to take control of their own resources.

RE: CULTURAL RESOURCE ORDINANCE

SEMINOLE TRIBE OF FLORIDA

HOLLYWOOD, FLORIDA

ORDINANCE NO. C-

WHEREAS,   the Seminole Tribe of Florida is an organized Indian Tribe as defined in Section 16 of the Indian Reorganization Act of June 18, 1934, as amended; and

WHEREAS,   the Tribal Council of the Seminole Tribe of Florida is the governing body of the Seminole Tribe of Florida; and

WHEREAS,   pursuant to Article IV of the Bylaws of the Amended Constitution and Bylaws of the Seminole Tribe of Florida, all final decisions of the Tribal Council on matters of general and permanent interest to Members of the Seminole Tribe of Florida and to Tribal administration are to be embodied in Ordinances; and

WHEREAS, on October 11, 2013, the Tribal Council of the Seminole Tribe of Florida enacted Ordinance C-01-16, the Cultural Resource Ordinance; and

WHEREAS, in order for undertakings on Seminole Tribe of Florida lands to be reviewed by the Tribal Historic Preservation Office under the regulations of the Cultural Resource Ordinance, rather than the regulations promulgated by the Advisory Council on Historic Preservation, Ordinance C-01-16 must be amended; and

WHEREAS, the Tribal Council of the Seminole Tribe of Florida is otherwise fully advised,

NOW THEREFORE BE IT ENACTED that this Ordinance cancels and replaces Ordinance C-01-16 and shall govern the protection and treatment of cultural resources; and

Part I. General Provisions and Definitions

1.1. Name and Short Title

(a) This Ordinance may be cited as the "Seminole Tribe of Florida Cultural Resource Ordinance" and is referred to herein as the "CRO."

1.2. Applicability

(a) Unless otherwise provided, the provisions of this CRO are applicable to: (1) areas within the reservation lands and (2) to the extent they do not conflict with any applicable laws or regulations, areas where the Seminole Tribe of Florida ("Seminole Tribe") has defined customary usage rights and Seminole Tribe land holdings that are not reservation lands.

(b) Any person(s) who enters onto Seminole Tribe reservation lands shall be subject to this CRO and shall be deemed to have consented to the jurisdiction of the Seminole Tribe and to be bound by the lawful ordinances of the Seminole Tribe.

(c) The Tribal Council of the Seminole Tribe of Florida ("Tribal Council"), by request or on its own initiative, may grant, at its discretion, a variance, with or without conditions, to any provision of this CRO, including incorporated documents, for good cause as determined by the Tribal Council.

1.3. Purpose and Finding

(a) The purpose of this CRO is to preserve the cultural heritage of the Seminole Tribe throughout its reservation lands, tribal land holdings, and ancestral lands.

(b) The Tribal Council finds and declares that:

(i) The cultural heritage of the Seminole Tribe should be preserved as a living part of the Seminole Tribe's community life and cultivated for future generations of tribal members;

(ii) The Seminole Tribe's cultural heritage contributes to the cultural legacy of the Seminole Tribe providing guidance and direction for the Seminole Tribe;

(iii) Cultural resources and property, in part, make up the Seminole Tribe's cultural heritage;

(iv) Cultural resources and property, on and off of reservation lands, including historic resources, archaeological, ceremonial, and sacred (including burials) sites, hold cultural and religious significance to the Seminole Tribe;

(v) These cultural properties and resources have been adversely impacted or are endangered/potentially in danger of being adversely impacted;

(vi) The Seminole Tribe's language, music, stories, dances, and traditions also form the cultural heritage of the Seminole Tribe;

(vii) The preservation of the Seminole Tribe's irreplaceable cultural heritage is of the utmost importance to the Seminole Tribe;

(viii) It is in the Seminole Tribe's interest to preserve its cultural heritage and legacy as a distinct group of people;

(ix) Increased knowledge of the Seminole Tribe's cultural resources/heritage and establishment of more accurate means of identifying them fosters preservation of the Seminole Tribe's cultural heritage and improves the planning of development;

(x) Although the preservation of cultural resources on and off of reservation lands has primarily been the result of federal laws and policies, the Seminole Tribe finds it essential that the Seminole Tribe expand its cultural resource protection programs and activities to achieve the preservation goals set by the Seminole Tribe; and

(xi) The health and welfare of the Seminole Tribe will be enhanced by the Seminole Tribe's regulation and preservation of cultural heritage, which are essential to the continued well-being of the Seminole Tribe and self-governance.

1.4. Policy

(a) It shall be the policy of the Seminole Tribe to:

(i) Use appropriate measures to preserve cultural resources so that cultural heritage can coexist in productive harmony with the Seminole Tribe's present and future;

(ii) Provide leadership in the preservation of the Seminole Tribe's cultural heritage;

(iii) Administer cultural resource protection in a spirit of stewardship for the present and future generations

(iv) Cooperate with local, state, and federal governments for the preservation of cultural resources;

(v) Cooperate with and encourage private entities for the preservation of cultural resources;

(vi) Treat cultural resources as the communal property of the Seminole Tribe requiring treatment with respect in accordance with traditional customs; and

(vii) Take primary responsibility for the proper management of cultural resources and cultural heritage.

1.5. Authority

(a) This CRO is adopted and will be implemented as an exercise of the Seminole Tribe's inherent sovereignty and pursuant to Article V of the Constitution and Bylaws of the Seminole Tribe of Florida.

(b) This CRO and any associated regulations, procedures, standards, guidelines, or operational plans/manuals necessary to implement the requirements or to achieve the purpose of this CRO shall not be construed as a waiver, limited or otherwise, of the Seminole Tribe's sovereignty including sovereign immunity.

1.6. Severability

(a) The provisions of this CRO are severable; therefore, if any portion of this CRO or the application therefore is held to be invalid by the Seminole Tribe or federal court, then the invalidity shall not affect other provisions of this CRO that can be given effect without the invalid provisions or application.

1.7. Repealer

(a) The provisions of all prior ordinances which are in conflict with this CRO are hereby repealed except the provisions of Tribal Resolution No. C-0185-02 shall take precedence in case of a conflict with this CRO.

1.8. Effective date

(a) This CRO shall become effective immediately upon being approved by the Tribal Council.

1.9. Interpretation

(a) In the interpretation and application of the provisions of this CRO, the CRO and any associated regulations, procedures, standards, guidelines, or operational plans/manuals shall be liberally construed in favor of the Seminole Tribe and shall not be deemed a limitation on the Seminole Tribe's authority or sovereignty.

(b) Confidentiality of the traditional, cultural, and religious values is imperative and thus cannot be enumerated in this CRO. Therefore, this CRO and any associated regulations, procedures, standards, guidelines, operational plans/manuals are not intended to be comprehensive regulations or policies concerning cultural resources.

(c) This CRO and any associated regulations, procedures, standards, guidelines, or operational plans/manuals shall not be construed to limit or define traditional practices and beliefs. Further, the Tribal Council may, at its discretion, elect to waive any or all the requirements of this CRO when it deems such waiver is in the best interest of the Seminole Tribe or a situation would be best served in accordance with traditional laws and customs not provided for under this CRO.

(d) The provisions of this CRO are not intended to diminish the responsibilities of other tribal divisions, departments, programs, agencies, authorities, enterprises or any other instrumentality of the Seminole Tribe. To the extent this CRO creates overlapping responsibilities, the Tribal Council directs the affected instrumentalities to develop protocols to jointly administer shared responsibilities.

1.10. Definitions

(a) Several defined terms herein are terms defined pursuant to the National Historic Preservation Act, Native American Graves Protection and Repatriation Act, and the Archaeological Resources Protection Act. It is the intent of this CRO to expand upon the federal definitions of these shared terms, when appropriate, in order to reflect the Seminole Tribe's cultural beliefs and expand the scope of cultural resource protection. These shared terms shall not be interpreted or applied under this CRO so as to diminish their definition under the above referenced federal Acts. Where terms are not defined under this CRO, but are defined in the above referenced federal Acts, the federal definition will be applied by the Tribal Historic Preservation Officer ("THPO"), accounting for the Seminole Tribe's cultural beliefs. Where terms are not defined in the CRO or above referenced federal Acts, the terms will take their ordinary meaning, taking into account the Seminole Tribe's cultural beliefs.

(b) "adverse effect" is found when an undertaking may alter, directly or indirectly, any characteristic of a cultural resource or historic property that makes the resource (1) significant to the Seminole Tribe and/or (2) eligible for either the Seminole Tribe of Florida Register of Historic Places or National Register of Historic Places, and in a manner that would diminish the significance to the Seminole Tribe and/or diminish the integrity of the property's location, design, setting, materials, workmanship, feeling, or association.

(c) "ancestral lands/homelands" means any and all lands that were historically or traditionally utilized by people of the Seminole Tribe and their ancestors.

(d) "Archaeological Resources Protection Act" means the federal Act codified at 16 U.S.C. §§470aa-470mm, and its implementing regulations governing the excavation of archaeological sites on federal and Indian lands and the removal and disposition of archaeological collections from those sites. Short cited as "ARPA."

(e) "area of potential effect" means the geographic area or areas within which an undertaking may directly or indirectly cause alterations in the character or use of cultural resources, including historic properties, if any such resources exist. The area of potential effect is influenced by the scale and nature of an undertaking and may be different for different kinds of effects caused by the undertaking.

(f) "building" is a structure created to shelter any form of human activity, such as a house, barn, church, hotel, or similar structure. Building may refer to a historically or culturally related complex such as a house and barn.

(g) "burial resources" means the subset of cultural resources that includes human remains, funerary object and objects of cultural patrimony.

(h) "burial/burial site" means that immediate geographic area that can be reasonably defined as containing burial resources.

(i) "control" means having a legal interest in a cultural resource.

(j) "cultural resources" means (1) any product of human activity culturally or historically significant to the Seminole Tribe; (2) any object or place culturally or historically significant to the Seminole Tribe; and (3) any flora, fauna, scenery, landscape, or other product of nature culturally or historically significant to the Seminole Tribe. This term includes the location containing cultural resources ("site"). This term may include archaeological resources, historical resources, Seminole Cultural Sites, burial resources, or historic properties.

(k) "cultural resources overlay district" means a planning tool that establishes cultural resource protection requirements within a specific area that requires special attention and may be superimposed upon/over other land use maps or zoning districts, or other land use planning maps.

(l) "custody" means ownership or control of a cultural resource.

(m) "customary usage rights" means, and is intended to capture, those activities by the Seminole Tribe and/or its members that are usual, habitual and defined by continued practice. It includes those activities that would have been "customary" but for displacement of tribal members and/or the Seminole Tribe. In interpreting and applying the term, it is acknowledged that the Seminole Tribe's customary usage is evolving over time and is not restricted to usage associated with a particular point in time.

(n) "district" means a geographically definable area possessing a significant concentration, linkage, or continuity of cultural resources. A district may also comprise individual elements separated geographically but linked by association, history, or culture.

(o) "effects" means alteration to the characteristics of a cultural resource, including historic properties, making it culturally or historically significant to the Seminole Tribe or qualifying it for inclusion in or eligibility for the National Register of Historic Places or the Seminole Tribe of Florida Register of Historic Places.

(p) "funerary objects" means items that, as part of the death rite or ceremony of a culture, are reasonably believed to have been placed intentionally at the time of death or later with or near individual human remains.

(q) "Historic Property" means any prehistoric or historic district, site, building, structure, or object included in, or eligible for inclusion in, the National Register of Historic Places maintained by the Secretary of the United States Department of the Interior or the Seminole Tribe of Florida Register of Historic Places maintained by the THPO. This term includes artifacts, records, and remains that are related to and located within such properties. The term includes properties of traditional religious and cultural importance to an Indian Tribe.

(r) "historic resources" means the subset of cultural resources that includes items of historic significance to the Seminole Tribe and historic properties.

(s) "human remains" means all physical remains of a human body, even if in fragmentary form, unless it is determined that the human remains had been freely given or naturally shed by the individual from whose body they were obtained, such as hair made into ropes or nets or individual teeth. Human remains incorporated into a funerary object, sacred object, or object of cultural patrimony must be considered as part of that item and as a cultural resource item.

(t) "inadvertent discovery" means the unanticipated encounter or detection of cultural resources under or on the surface land.

(u) "instrumentalities" means any official administrative and/or governmental body of the Seminole Tribe, including but not limited to, tribal agencies, departments, offices, and programs. The term also means any commercial entity or enterprise owned in whole or in part by the Seminole Tribe.

(v) "land use" means any action that involves the use of land requiring land/ground disturbance.

(w) "land/ground disturbances" means any activity or action which moves the surface of the land, including, but not limited to, construction, digging, site preparation, excavation, silviculture, agriculture on uncultivated soils, dredging, drilling, filling, mining, demolition, and landscaping.

(x) "National Environmental Policy Act" means the federal Act codified at 43 U.S.C. §4321 et seq, and its implementing regulations establishing a national environmental policy and goals for the protection, maintenance, and enhancement of the environment and providing a process for implementing these goals within the federal agencies. Short cited as "NEPA."

(y) "National Historic Preservation Act" means the federal Act codified at 16 U.S.C. §470 et seq, and its implementing regulations creating the National Register of Historic Places, State Historic Preservation Offices, and Tribal Historic Preservation Offices. The Act is intended to preserve historical and archaeological sites in the United States of America. Short cited as "NHPA."

(z) "Native American Graves Protection and Repatriation Act" means the federal Act codified at 25 U.S.C. §3001 et seq, and its implementing regulations governing the Native American burial resources, including museum collections, inadvertent discoveries, planned excavation, and repatriation. Short cited as "NAGPRA."

(aa) "no adverse effect" is found when the undertakings' effects do not meet the criteria for adverse effect or the undertaking is modified or conditions are imposed to avoid adverse effects.

(bb) "object" means a material thing of functional, aesthetic, cultural, historical, or scientific value that may be, by nature or design, movable yet related to a specific setting, environment or site.

(cc) "object of cultural patrimony" means an item having ongoing historical, traditional, or cultural importance central to the Seminole Tribe itself, rather than property owned by an individual tribal or organization member. Such objects must have been considered inalienable by the culturally affiliated Seminole Tribe at the time the object was separated from the group.

(dd) "other Indian Tribes" means an Indian tribe, band, nation, or other organized group or community, including a native village, regional corporation, or village corporation, which is recognized by either the United States Bureau of Indian Affairs or by the Seminole Tribe.

(ee) "ownership" means having the legal right to possess a cultural resource.

(ff) "person" means any individual, corporation, partnership, association, business trust, legal representative, administrative or governmental body, or any organized group of persons.

(gg) "place" means an identifiable location, not necessarily identifiable by meets and bounds, at which an event occurred or is given cultural or historic significance by the Seminole Tribe.

(hh) "possession" means having physical custody of a cultural resource.

(ii) "public" unless otherwise provided, means enrolled members of the Seminole Tribe.

(jj) "reservation lands" means those lands held in trust for the benefit of the Seminole Tribe.

(kk) "resolution of adverse affects" means to sufficiently avoid, minimize, and mitigate adverse impacts to cultural resources and historic properties under this CRO.

(ll) "restoration" means, for purposes of administrative remedies in Parts VIII and IX of this CRO, remedial action that is intended to return a disturbed, altered, damaged, excavated, removed, desecrated, or taken cultural resource to its original condition.

(mm) "sacred object" includes specific ceremonial objects which are needed by traditional Native American religious leaders for the practice of traditional Native American religions by their present day adherents.

(nn) "Section 106" means Section 106 of the National Historic Preservation Act (16 U.S.C. §470f), and its implementing regulations, which requires federal agencies to take into account the effects of their undertakings on historic properties.

(oo) "Seminole Cultural Site" means the subset of cultural resources that includes sites that are associated with cultural practices or beliefs of the Seminole Tribe that (1) are rooted in that community's history (2) are important in maintaining the continuing cultural identity of the community and/or (3) are locations that have been determined by the Seminole Tribe to hold significant cultural value that defines and embodies their cultural identity.

(pp) "Seminole Tribe land holdings/tribal land holdings" means any land not in trust that the Seminole Tribe, or one of its instrumentalities, owns a fee simple or less than fee simple interest.

(qq) "site" means the location and/or feature of a cultural or historic event, occupation, activity, building or structure, whether standing, ruined, or vanished, where the location and/or feature itself possesses cultural, or archaeological significance to the Seminole Tribe regardless of the significance of any existing structure.

(rr) "sponsor/responsible person" means the person(s) who has decision making authority over a particular undertaking.

(ss) "structure" is used to distinguish from buildings those functional constructions made usually for purposes other than creating human shelter.

(tt) "substantially effected person" means any person that will suffer an adverse effect to any interest protected or furthered under this CRO.

(uu) "traditional activities/use" means, and is intended to capture, those activities by the Seminole Tribe and/or its members that are usual, habitual, customary, or defined by continued practice. It includes those activities that would have been "traditional" but for displacement of tribal members and/or the Seminole Tribe. Interpretation and application of the term will acknowledge that the Seminole Tribe's traditional activities are evolving over time and will not be restricted to usage associated with a particular point in time.

(vv) "undertaking" means a project, activity, or program that can result in changes in the character or use of cultural resources, including historic properties, if any such cultural resources are located within the area of potential effects. The project, activity, or program must be under the direct or indirect control/jurisdiction of a Sponsor. Undertakings include new and continuing projects, activities, or programs not previously considered under the authority of this CRO.

1.11. THPO Operational Plan and Operational Manuals

(a) The THPO Operational Plan and Operational Manuals, as may be amended, are incorporated and made a part of this CRO.

(b) In addition to any other Operational Manuals the THPO deems necessary, the THPO will develop and update, as needed, Operational Manuals for:
　(i) Archaeometry;
　(ii) Architectural History;
　(iii) Collections;
　(iv) Compliance Review; and
　(v) Tribal Archaeology

(c) The THPO shall update the Operational Plan and all Operational Manuals as needed, subject to Tribal Council approval for any updates that are deemed by the THPO to be major substantive or procedural changes warranting Tribal Council approval.

Part II. Cultural Resources Preservation Program

2.1. The Tribal Historic Preservation Office

(a) On or about July 15, 2002, the Tribal Council established the Tribal Historic Preservation Office, which serves in the capacity of a tribal department. The Tribal Historic Preservation Office shall continue to exist under this CRO and be directed by a Tribal Historic Preservation Officer appointed by the Tribal Council to administer this CRO and any other responsibilities assigned by the Tribal Council.

2.2. The Tribal Historic Preservation Officer

(a) Creation: The Seminole Tribe of Florida Tribal Historic Preservation Officer position was created by Tribal Resolution No. C-0185-02. On or about October 8, 2006, the Agreement Between The National Park Service, U.S. Department of The Interior And The Seminole Tribe Of Florida For The Assumption By The Tribe of Certain Responsibilities Pursuant to the National Historic Preservation Act (16 U.S.C. 470) (hereafter "THPO-NPS Agreement") was executed which authorized the Seminole Tribe to assume the functions of the State Historic Preservation Officer in administering the National Historic Preservation Act on reservation lands. The THPO-NPS Agreement, as may be amended, is incorporated into this CRO by reference. In connection with the appointment of the THPO, the Seminole Tribe created the Tribal Historic Preservation Office.

(b) Purpose: The THPO acts as the director of the Tribal Historic Preservation Office and shall be the lead agency for identification, protection, preservation, and management of cultural resources and cultural heritage programs on and off of Seminole Tribe reservation lands as provided by this CRO.

(c) Authority:

(i) The THPO has such authority and obligations as enumerated in the THPO-NPS Agreement, which includes, but is not limited to:

a. Direct and conduct comprehensive surveys of all reservations and maintain an inventory of historic and culturally significant properties;

b. Identify and nominate eligible properties to the National Register of Historic Places ("National Register") and otherwise administer applications for the historic properties on the National Register;

c. Develop and implement comprehensive historic preservation plan(s) for all reservations covering historic, archaeological, and traditional cultural properties;

d. Advise and assist, as appropriate, federal and state agencies and local governments in carrying out their historic preservation responsibilities;

e. Cooperate with the Secretary of the Department of the Interior, the Advisory Council on Historic Preservation, and other federal agencies, state agencies, local governments, organizations, and individuals to ensure that historic properties are taken into consideration at all levels of planning and development;

f. Provide information, education, training, and technical assistance to the public regarding historic preservation;

g. Consult with the appropriate federal agencies in accordance with Section 106 of the NHPA; and

h. Carry out the Seminole Tribe's responsibilities to review undertakings under Section 106 of the NHPA.

(ii) In addition to the authority enumerated in the THPO-NPS Agreement, the THPO has the authority to carry out the requirements of this CRO; including, but not limited to:

a. Develop, publish, and implement such procedures, standards, guidelines, management/protection plans, or operational plans/manuals necessary to implement the requirements of or to achieve the purpose of this CRO, the THPO-NPS Agreement, and any other responsibilities assigned by the Tribal Council;

b. The preservation and management of cultural resources and heritage;

c. Management planning for cultural resources and heritage;

d. Review undertakings proposed to be carried out by divisions, departments, programs, agencies, authorities, enterprises, and any other instrumentality of the Seminole Tribe, if such undertakings are subject to the clearance requirement set forth in Part IV of this CRO;

e. Represent the Seminole Tribe in consultations with local, state, and federal agencies regarding cultural resources;

f. Negotiate agreements with local, state, and federal agencies concerning cultural resources with the understanding that all agreements must be ultimately reviewed by the Seminole Tribe's Office of the General Counsel ("General Counsel") and approved by the Tribal Council;

g. Compile, update, and maintain cultural resource databases for reservation lands, traditional use lands, and ancestral lands;

h. Develop and implement appropriate education programs regarding the Seminole Tribe's cultural heritage;

i. Review and update the Tribal Historic Preservation Office Operational Plan, as needed, subject to Tribal Council approval for any updates that are deemed by the THPO to be major substantive or procedural changes warranting Tribal Council approval;

j. Prepare, on a yearly basis, a brief report summarizing the THPO's achievements during the preceding year and issues that merit consideration by the Tribal Council;

k. Review and update, as needed, all THPO Operational Manuals in consultation with the Tribe's Historic Preservation Review Board subject to Tribal Council approval for any updates that are deemed by the THPO to be major substantive or procedural changes warranting Tribal Council approval;

l. Employ and supervise sufficient multi-discipline staff necessary to carry out the responsibilities of the THPO;

m. Appoint designees necessary to carry out the functions and responsibilities of the THPO;

n. Enter into cooperation and/or operational agreements with other tribal instrumentalities related to or affecting cultural resources. Such agreements may provide for consolidation of facilities, equipment, or personnel, cross-deputization of enforcement personnel, and/or provide such other relationships as may be deemed beneficial to the interest of the Seminole Tribe; and

o. Develop and conduct such other activities or programs necessary to achieve the purposes of this CRO or that are in accordance with the Operational Plan/Manuals.

(d) Operation: The THPO was initially established to operate under the Museum Department, which is a program of the Tribal Council. Upon enactment of this CRO, the THPO shall operate as a standalone department, independent of any other tribal department. The THPO shall report directly to the Tribal Council or whomever the Tribal Council designates. The THPO shall carry out its responsibilities in coordination with the Seminole Tribe's Historic Preservation Review Board. The THPO shall also carry out its responsibilities in cooperation with the Museum Department and other tribal instrumentalities including, but not limited to, divisions, departments, programs, agencies, authorities, and enterprises.

2.3. Seminole Tribe of Florida Museum

(a) At the discretion of the THPO, the THPO may enter into agreements with the Seminole Tribe of Florida Ah-Tah-Thi-Ki Museum on the Big Cypress Seminole Indian Reservation to act as the repository for all cultural resource items collected in a manner consistent with the relevant Operational Manual. Nothing herein shall preclude the THPO from entering into agreements with other repositories.

2.4. Historic Preservation Review Board

(a) Pursuant to the THPO-NPS Agreement, the THPO is required to consult, as needed, with traditional cultural authorities through membership on the Historic Preservation Review Board, also known as "Cultural Advisors," when evaluating the significance of and impact on historic properties under the National Historic Preservation Act and cultural resources under this CRO.

(b) In carrying out its responsibilities under this CRO, the THPO and staff of the Tribal Historic Preservation Office shall be guided by the wisdom and expertise of the Historic Preservation Review Board.

(c) Consultations with the Historic Preservation Review Board, including those regarding eligibility of sites on the Seminole Tribe of Florida Register of Historic Places ("Tribal Register") and National Register shall be closed to the public unless directed by the Tribal Council or by request of the Historic Preservation Review Board.

(d) When necessary, the THPO shall make a good faith effort to consult with the Historic Preservation Review Board. In cases where the THPO must timely act but the Historic Preservation Review Board is not available for consultation, the THPO will not be precluded from acting after making a good faith effort to consult with the Tribal Council or its designee.

(e) Upon enactment of this CRO, the THPO, in consultation with the members of the Interim Historic Preservation Review Board, the Tribal Council, and the General Counsel, shall develop for inclusion into the appropriate operational manual:

   (i) A policy statement on the roles and responsibilities of the Historic Preservation Review Board, which may include provisions for the payment of compensation to the members of the Review Board for their services to the Seminole Tribe in this capacity;

   (ii) Procedures for Appointment to the Historic Preservation Review Board; and

   (iii) Procedures for substitution, vacancy, and interim appointments for the Historic Preservation Review Board, including procedures for when the Tribal Council may act as the Historic Preservation Review Board.

(f) Until such time as a Historic Preservation Review Board is appointed pursuant to the Policy Statement and Procedures for Appointment referenced in subsection (e) above, the THPO shall continue to consult and coordinate efforts with select Cultural Advisors who have been acting as the Interim Historic Preservation Review Board.

Part III. Historic and Cultural Resource Protection

3.1. Seminole Tribe of Florida Site File

(a) The THPO shall develop and maintain a database of all known cultural resource sites (i.e., archaeological, structures, heritage, ceremonial, sacred, Seminole Cultural Sites) that are or may be significant to the Seminole Tribe's heritage and culture, regardless of eligibility for inclusion in the Tribal Register or National Register. This database shall be known as the "Seminole Site File."

(b) The Seminole Site File may, at the THPO's discretion, include sites on and off of reservation lands.

(c) Information from the Seminole Site File will not be distributed, published, or shared in any manner with persons not enrolled as Seminole Tribal members, unless specifically authorized by THPO in consultation with the Historic Preservation Review Board and Tribal Council, or as otherwise provided for in this CRO.

(d) Information from the Seminole Site File may be shared with tribal divisions, departments, programs, agencies, authorities, enterprises, or any other instrumentality of the Seminole Tribe at the discretion of the THPO in consultation with the Historic Preservation Review Board.

(e) Unless directed by the Tribal Council, nothing herein shall be interpreted to preclude the THPO from sharing information from the Seminole Site File with the Historic Preservation Review Board or enrolled Seminole Tribal members. If the THPO believes sharing information from the Seminole Site File could jeopardize the cultural resources, or interfere with traditional practices associated with such cultural resources, the THPO may refrain from sharing such information pending direction from the Tribal Council.

3.2. Seminole Tribe of Florida Register of Historic Places

(a) The THPO shall create, expand, and maintain a Tribal Register. The THPO, in consultation with the Historic Preservation Review Board, shall develop an Operational Manual establishing criteria for eligibility and determination procedures for the Tribal Register. The THPO shall also include in the Operational Manual criteria and procedures for the identification, nomination, inventorying, evaluation, and registration of Tribal Historic Places.

(b) Eligibility for the Tribal Register includes places within reservation lands, within Seminole Tribe land holdings not in trust, within areas where the Seminole Tribe have customary usage rights, and within ancestral lands.

(c) Eligibility criteria for the Tribal Register will be in accordance with the Operational Manual referenced in subsection (a) herein.

(d) Determination of eligibility for the Tribal Register will be made jointly by the THPO and the Historic Preservation Review Board consistent with the applicable Operational Manuals and the procedures set forth in Part II of this CRO. For purposes of administering the Tribal Register, the THPO will act as the Keeper of the Tribal Register of Historic Places.

(e) The THPO shall consult with the Historic Preservation Review Board in a manner consistent with the procedures set forth in Part II of this CRO. In the event the THPO and the Historic Preservation Review Board should disagree on the eligibility of site for the Tribal Register, the decision on eligibility will be made by the Tribal Council.

(f) Nothing in this Part precludes the Tribal Council from adding a property to the Tribal Register on its own initiative.

(g) Determinations under this Part are not subject to appeal or subsequent review, except by the Tribal Council.

3.3. National Register of Historic Places

(a) Consistent with the THPO-NPS Agreement and relevant Operational Manuals, the THPO shall develop and maintain a program to identify and nominate eligible properties to the National Register and otherwise administer applications for listing historic properties on the National Register

(b) In determining whether to nominate a property to the National Register, the THPO shall consult with the Historic Preservation Review Board. The THPO shall also consider (1) places that are eligible for both the Tribal and National Registers, and (2) places that are eligible for the National Register but are not eligible for the Tribal Register.

(c) The THPO will consult with the Historic Preservation Review Board in identifying and nominating eligible properties to the National Register.

(d) Any Seminole Tribal Member may appeal, pursuant to 36 C.F.R. 60.12, to the Keeper of the National Register of Historic Places the failure or refusal of the THPO to nominate a property located on reservation lands that the Tribal Member considers to meet the National Register criteria for evaluation. No other determinations or actions under this Part are subject to appeal or subsequent review.

(e) The THPO, in consultation with the Historic Preservation Review Board, is authorized to suggest properties off of reservation lands that may be eligible for inclusion in the National Register to the appropriate state or federal agency.

3.4. Effects of Listing

(a) For purposes of this CRO and its administration, the Seminole Site File, the Tribal Register and the National Register are designed to primarily identify and preserve the Seminole Tribe's cultural heritage. To this effect, the Registers and Seminole Site File will be administered as a planning tool for the Seminole Tribe, tribal members, and tribal instrumentalities to ensure appropriate avoidance, minimization, and mitigation of impacts to cultural resources, including listed sites or sites potentially eligible for either the Tribal or National Registers, resulting from undertakings including development and land disturbance.

(b) All divisions, departments, programs, agencies, authorities, enterprises, and any other instrumentality of the Seminole Tribe that proposes an undertaking will consult with and seek the necessary authorizations from the THPO as early as possible in the planning process and before any land disturbance.

(c) All persons who are deemed to have consented to the jurisdiction of the Seminole Tribe under this CRO that propose an undertaking, will consult with and seek the necessary authorizations from the THPO as early as possible in the planning process and before any land disturbance.

(d) The THPO may, in consultation with the Historic Preservation Review Board, nominate sites included in the Seminole Site File, Tribal Register, or the National Register that are located within the Seminole Tribe's jurisdiction and/ or ownership to the Seminole Tribe of Florida Land Use Committee to be set aside for cultural conservation purposes consistent with the rules and procedures of the Land Use Committee. Cultural conservation areas may only be taken out of conservation by the Tribal Council.

(e) While the Seminole Site File, Tribal Register, or the National Register should serve as planning tools for local, state, and federal governments in connection with undertakings off of reservation lands, the Registers are not intended to serve as a comprehensive list or as a substitute for meaningful government to government consultation. It is also understood that the location of some sites may be so culturally sensitive that the Seminole Tribe may choose not to list them or share information regarding them.

3.5. Determination of Archaeological and Cultural Significance

(a) The Tribal Council may, for cultural, traditional, religious, or other reasons in the best interest of the Seminole Tribe, determine archaeological and cultural resources: (1) are not or are no longer of interest to the Seminole Tribe and therefore not considered resources under this CRO or (2) are culturally or historically significant to the Seminole Tribe.

Part IV. Prohibited Activities, Permitting and Resolution of Impacts

4.1. Assumption of Federal Programs

(a) The THPO is hereby authorized to coordinate with the appropriate federal agencies the development of an agreement(s) that will authorize the Seminole Tribe to substitute its own review procedures for those established by the Advisory Council on Historic Preservation (36 C.F.R. Part 800). The THPO is also authorized to coordinate with the appropriate federal agencies the development of an agreement(s) regarding the Archaeological Resource Protection Act program including the permitting and enforcement components. Any such agreement(s) shall require approval by the Tribal Council before taking effect. During the interim, the THPO will administer the following review and permitting procedures for all cultural resources regardless of ultimate eligibility under the National Historic Preservation Act. In the event of any conflict with the following procedures in connection with a property eligible for the National Register, the THPO will follow the Advisory Council on Historic Preservation review procedures.

4.2. Prohibited Activities

Unless otherwise provided, this Part shall not apply to activities conducted by the THPO and THPO employees or agents in furtherance of its/their responsibilities.

(a) No person shall carry out an undertaking, including land disturbance, without first consulting with and obtaining all necessary permits from the THPO.

(b) No person shall: (1) disturb, take, excavate, remove, damage, destroy, desecrate, or alter any cultural resource or historic properties or (2) conduct any investigation relating to any cultural resource or historic properties, or (3) conduct an exploratory excavation to determine the presence of any cultural resource or historic properties without first obtaining a permit from the THPO.

(c) No person shall sell, purchase, exchange, transport, receive, or offer to sell, purchase, exchange, or transport, any cultural resource or historic property in violation of:

(i) the prohibitions in paragraph (b) of this Section;

(ii) the conditions of any permit issued pursuant to tribal or federal law; or

(iii) any rule, ordinance, or other provision of tribal or federal law in effect at the time of the conduct.

(d) No person shall conduct ethnological or archaeological studies related to the Seminole Tribe's heritage without first obtaining a permit.

(e) Consistent with Section 1.2, no person, except enrolled Seminole Tribal Members, shall conduct historical, cultural, or other research, oral or written, scientific or non-scientific, or make recordings of any kind, regardless of the technology used, related to the Seminole Tribe's heritage without first obtaining a permit.

4.3. Clearance Requirements for Undertakings

(a) In order to ensure the protection of cultural resources and historic properties, the sponsor of any undertaking (including any land disturbance activity not otherwise subject to exception) that may affect cultural resources and/or historic properties must obtain sufficient approval from the THPO to proceed prior to commencement, implementation, or authorization of any undertaking by the sponsor. To adequately protect cultural resources, the presence of cultural resources is presumed to exist and be affected by an undertaking until such time as the THPO has completed its review of the undertaking. The sponsor shall give the THPO a reasonable opportunity to review the undertaking, investigate the area of potential effect, consult with the Historic Preservation Review Board, when appropriate, and determine the effects the undertaking is likely to have on cultural resources and/or historic properties. The THPO shall formulate its determination of potential effects in writing informing the sponsor of the need for a permit under this CRO.

(b) Identification and Evaluation of Cultural Resources

(i) In reviewing any proposed undertaking, the THPO shall determine and document the area of potential effect.

(ii) In reviewing any proposed undertaking, the THPO will, in a manner consistent with the protocols set forth in the appropriate operational manual(s), determine: (1) the scope of identification of cultural resources and historic properties and (2) identify cultural resources and historic properties. The THPO shall make a reasonable and good faith effort to carry out the appropriate identification efforts.

(iii) The THPO shall evaluate the cultural and historic significance of all cultural resources and historic properties identified and evaluate eligibility for the Tribal Register and National Register in a manner consistent with the protocols of the applicable operational manual(s). The THPO will consult with the Historic Preservation Review Board when appropriate.

(iv) The THPO shall also determine if the proposed undertaking will have an effect on any cultural resources and historic properties. For cultural resources under this CRO, the evaluation of effect shall result in either a determination of "no cultural resources affected" or "cultural resources affected." With regard to historic properties under the National Historic Preservation Act, the THPO shall make a finding of either "no historic properties affected" or "historic properties affected" in order to be consistent with various agreements between the Seminole Tribe of Florida and federal agencies concerning NHPA review. It is important to note that, under this CRO, historic properties may also be a subset of cultural resources when the properties have cultural or historic significance to the Seminole Tribe.

(v) If the THPO finds that a proposed undertaking will have an effect on cultural resources or historic properties, then the THPO shall assess the adverse effects.

(c) Assessment of Adverse Effects

(i) The THPO shall evaluate each undertaking to determine any adverse effects on cultural resources and historic properties considering the views of the Historic Preservation Review Board and, when appropriate, tribal community based decision-making. An adverse effect is found when an undertaking may alter, directly or indirectly, any characteristic of a cultural resource or historic property that makes the resource (a) significant to the Seminole Tribe and/or (b) eligible for either the Tribal Register or National Register, and in a manner that would diminish the significance to the Seminole Tribe and/or diminish the integrity of the property's location, design, setting, materials, workmanship, feeling, or association.

(ii) Finding of no adverse effect. The THPO may make a finding of no adverse effect when the undertaking's effects do not meet the criteria for adverse effect or the undertaking is modified or conditions are imposed to avoid adverse effects. No clearance under this CRO will be required in connection with a finding of no adverse effect where the effect does not satisfy the criteria for finding an adverse effect. A clearance under this CRO will be required for undertakings that are found to have no adverse effect due to modifications or the imposition of conditions. In such cases, the modifications and/or conditions will be incorporated as special conditions in the permit clearance under this CRO along with any necessary monitoring requirements. Any changes to the proposed undertaking or the discovery of unanticipated cultural resources and/or historic properties will require further review under this CRO.

(iii) Finding of adverse effect. The THPO may make a finding of adverse effect when the undertaking's effects meet the criteria of adverse effect. These decisions require a clearance under this CRO so as to condition the undertaking to avoid, minimize, and mitigate adverse effects.

(d) Resolution of Adverse Effects

   (i) All undertakings determined to have an "adverse effect" finding shall require resolution of the adverse effects. No clearance under this CRO shall be issued if the THPO finds that the adverse effects have not been adequately resolved by modification of the undertaking or imposition of conditions such as to avoid, minimize, or mitigate adverse effects.

   (ii) The priority for resolution of effects shall first consider all reasonable efforts to avoid adverse effects. After consideration of all reasonable avoidance efforts, then reasonable measures to minimize the adverse effects shall be considered. Consideration of mitigation measures shall only be contemplated after full consideration of avoidance and minimization measures are exhausted or unsuccessful.

(e) There shall be three types of permits to proceed for undertakings that have the potential to impact or disturb cultural resources and/or historic properties. Unless otherwise determined by the THPO, all areas will be presumed to contain protected cultural resources. Consistent with relevant agreements with federal agencies, only the THPO, in consultation with the Historic Preservation Review Board, may determine that no cultural resources or historic properties will be affected by an undertaking.

   (i) Land Use Action Permits: Any person seeking to carry out an undertaking, including land disturbance activities that may impact or disturb cultural resources and/or historic properties, must obtain a permit from the THPO prior to commencement of proposed action:

      a. Class A permits shall be issued for undertakings by the Seminole Tribe or any other instrumentality of the Seminole Tribe.

      b. Class B permits shall be issued, to the extent not contrary to applicable federal law, for undertakings by local, state, and federal agencies on reservation lands, including undertakings conducted in partnership with the Seminole Tribe.

      c. Class C permits shall be issued for undertakings by Seminole Tribe tribal members that are not otherwise excluded.

      d. Class D permits shall be issued for undertakings that utilize, affect, or may affect historic structures or historic buildings.

   (ii) Archaeological-Cultural-Traditional Practices Permits: Any person seeking to carry out archaeological, ethnographic, or historical activities and/or studies and any associated activities (including but not limited to identification, inventorying, and excavation or removal of resources), or any person not an enrolled Seminole Tribal Member seeking to carry out traditional practices must obtain a permit from the THPO prior to commencement of proposed action:

    a. Class E permits shall be issued to persons conducting historical, ethnological or archaeological studies/investigations that do not involve excavation and/or removal of resources.

    b. Class F permits shall be issued to persons conducting historical, ethnological or archaeological studies/investigations that do involve excavation and/or removal of resources.

    c. Class G permits shall be issued to traditional practitioners who are members of other Indian Tribes in the event that such persons choose to apply for a permit rather than seeking a waiver.

(iii) General and Programmatic Permitting: The THPO is authorized to develop general permits for any category of activities that involve cultural resources and/or historic properties if it is determined the activities in the category are similar in nature and will cause no or acceptable impacts to cultural resources and/or historic properties when performed separately or cumulatively. General and Programmatic Permits will be utilized to streamline and/or expedite the clearance process when appropriate while ensuring the protection of cultural resources in a culturally sensitive manner and ensuring the protection of historic properties. General and Programmatic Permits cannot be used to authorize impacts to burials or burial resources.

(f) Procedures for Undertakings by Federal agencies: in addition to any permits required by this CRO, the following procedures are required:

(i) Any person seeking to carry out an undertaking requiring a permit under this CRO must inform the THPO if the project, activity, or program:

    a. is funded in whole or in part under the direct or indirect jurisdiction of a federal agency (including those carried out by or on behalf of a federal agency;

    b. is carried out with federal financial assistance; and/or

    c. requires a federal permit, license or approval.

(ii) When one or more federal agencies are involved in the undertaking, the THPO will be designated the lead agency for purposes of fulfilling the collective responsibilities under Section 106 of the NHPA including but not limited to:

    a. Initiation of the Section 106 process;

    b. Identification of historic properties;

    c. Assessment of adverse effects to historic properties;

    d. Developing requirements for resolution of adverse effects;

    e. Section 106 determinations; and

    f. Enforcement.

(iii) Where the THPO is the lead agency, Section 106 compliance will be evidenced by the clearance issued under the CRO.

(iv) The THPO may, at its sole discretion, elect not to be the lead agency for purposes of Section 106. In such cases:

    a. The THPO and the federal agencies will develop protocols for Section 106 review and compliance (such as sharing of information, confidentiality of information, identification and assessment methodologies, and assignment of responsibilities);

    b. All Section 106 determinations will be made in full consultation with the THPO;

    c. Federal agencies will document compliance with Section 106 by Memorandum for the Record executed by both the THPO and the federal agencies evidencing Section 106 obligations have been satisfied.

(g) TI IPO may issue "after the fact" authorization for activities that require a permit to proceed under this CRO but were commenced or conducted without the necessary authorization.

(h) Procedures for obtaining a permit to proceed and issuance criteria

(i) The THPO, in consultation with the Historic Preservation Review Board and the General Counsel, shall include in the appropriate Operational Manual(s) procedures for:

    a. obtaining each class of permit;

    b. evaluating permit applications;

    c. criteria for issuance (including avoidance, minimization and mitigation of impacts);

    d. submission of application for permit to proceed;

    e. archaeological review;

    f. fee schedules;

    g. costs of monitoring and enforcement of permit;

    h. duration; and

    i. renewal, modification, suspension and revocation of permits.

(ii) Until such time as the requirements of sub-subsection (i) above are completed, the THPO will continue to utilize the procedures set forth in its current operational manual(s), including the issuance of one type of clearance letter for all activities.

(i) Permit Conditions

(i) All permits to proceed under this CRO must contain a condition:

    a. concerning the inadvertent discovery of cultural resources or historic properties including any appropriate requirements to cease work;

    b. concerning the confidentially of information;

    c. requiring all activities to be done in a manner respectful of the Seminole Tribe's culture, traditions, and religion;

    d. concerning the treatment of any inadvertently discovered burial resources;

    e. concerning monitoring and status reports;

    f. concerning the collection of data;

g. providing that all cultural resources discovered, excavated, or removed from reservation lands and Seminole Tribe land holdings remain the property of the Seminole Tribe of Florida and that possession, control, and custody of the cultural resources shall be with the Seminole Tribe of Florida; and

h. concerning modification, suspension and revocation of the permit.

(ii) The THPO may require such permit conditions it deems necessary to ensure the appropriate protection of the cultural resources and/or historic properties, including, but not limited to, conditions related to avoidance, minimization, and mitigation of impacts. Failure to fully comply with the terms of a permit, including permit conditions, issued pursuant to this CRO will be considered a violation under this CRO.

(iii) For undertakings on reservation lands conducted in part or in whole by local, state, or federal agencies, the THPO:

a. will develop avoidance, minimization, and mitigation measures in coordination with the non-tribal agencies; and

b. is authorized to develop agreements, subject to Tribal Council approval, with non-tribal agencies for the resolution of impacts to cultural resources and/or historic properties. These agreements, in conjunction with any permit issued under this CRO, will govern undertakings and will be evidence of compliance with applicable legal obligations including the National Historic Preservation Act, Trust Responsibility, and this CRO. When practical, these agreements will be incorporated by special condition into any necessary permit issued under this CRO.

(j) Emergencies

(i) In rare circumstances, all or part of a person's responsibility under this CRO may be temporarily exempt from compliance in order to conduct emergency actions necessary to prevent imminent harm to human life or avoid irreparable damage to property. The responsible person must notify the THPO within three (3) business days of the emergency undertaking. The THPO has three (3) business days in which to concur with the emergency determination or require cessation of all work until proper authorization is perfected. The notice provided by the responsible person shall include:

a. the nature of the event requiring emergency action;

b. the date and nature of the emergency action;

c. a description of the measures taken to avoid and minimize impacts to cultural resources; and

d. a proposed plan to mitigate any impacts to cultural resources that ultimately must be approved by the THPO.

(ii) The THPO may require an "after the fact" permit consistent with the provisions of this Part, including permit conditions for the resolution of impacts to cultural resources.

(iii) The THPO may require the responsible persons to remediate all impacts to cultural resources, including restoration, or THPO may seek recovery of costs incurred by THPO's actions to remediate impacts.

(k) Relationship to Other Permitting Requirements

    (i) The requirement for and issuance of permits under this CRO are independent of any other authorizations required by other tribal programs (such as environmental permits), tribal laws, or applicable local, state, and federal laws.

    (ii) The THPO is authorized to develop, in coordination with other tribal instrumentalities, including, but not limited to, tribal departments, agencies, offices, and programs, streamlined permitting procedures and permits subject to Tribal Council approval.

    (iii) Obtaining permits from other tribal instrumentalities does not relieve any person from the need to obtain any required permit under this CRO nor do permits issued pursuant to this CRO relieve the need for other required authorizations.

    (iv) If a permit from another tribal instrumentality is required for the proposed undertaking in addition to a permit under this CRO, then the permit under this CRO shall be incorporated by special condition in the other permit, when feasible, specifying full compliance with the permit under this CRO is required.

    (v) Permits issued under this CRO to enrolled tribal members or to tribal instrumentalities will operate as an exemption to any permit that may be necessary under the Archaeological Resources Protection Act.

4.4. Activities Determined to Have No Potential to Affect and Exceptions from Clearance Requirements

(a) The following activities have been determined to have no potential to affect cultural resources or historic properties and thus do not require a permit under Part IV of this CRO, unless the THPO determines that a permit to proceed is necessary to prevent adverse impacts to cultural resources or historic properties:

    (i) Renewal or transfer of a lease where no new construction is expected;

    (ii) Changing the name of a lessee;

    (iii) Mortgage Payouts;

    (iv) Renovations of buildings less than fifty (50) years of age;

    (v) Demolition of buildings of less than fifty (50) years of age and where reconstruction will occur within the existing footprint of the previous building or previously disturbed areas; and

    (vi) Landscaping that does not involve the use of heavy equipment.

(b) The following land uses and activities shall be exempt from the clearance requirements outlined in Part IV of this CRO, unless the THPO determines that a permit to proceed is necessary to prevent adverse impacts to cultural resources or historic properties:

(i) Renewal, or transfer of a lease that includes construction of improvements when the existing lease was approved by either the Seminole Tribe or the United States Bureau of Indian Affairs;

(ii) A new lease for an area which has been surveyed and found not to contain cultural resources and/or historic properties, provided that the supporting documentation for the THPO's finding includes a copy of, or reference to, the survey, when the survey is deemed sufficient by the THPO;

(iii) A new lease for an area which has been surveyed by the THPO and, although it contains one or more cultural resources and/or historic properties, conditions have been included in the lease to avoid any adverse effects on any cultural resources and/or historic properties;

(iv) Activities by enrolled Seminole Tribal Members directly related to traditional practices and visitation of cultural resources;

(v) THPO and tribal employees engaged in properly authorized official business relating to cultural resource or historic property management under this CRO;

(vi) Activities within areas listed in the Seminole Site File but not included in the Tribal or National Registers f when the THPO, in consultation with the Tribal Historic Preservation Review Board, determines the site or sites are not significant such as to require a permit or preservation under this CRO; and

(vii) Other exceptions designated by the Tribal Council.

(c) Persons who are not employees of the Seminole Tribe, including employees of federal and state agencies and persons serving as agents of the Seminole Tribe, are not exempt from the permit requirements of this CRO. The THPO may, in the appropriate operational manual(s), establish expedited permit procedures for such persons. The THPO may negotiate agreements with federal agencies to provide that employees of such agencies may perform their authorized duties without obtaining permits that would otherwise be required.

(d) The THPO, in consultation with the Historic Preservation Review Board and Tribal Council or its designee, may waive, on a case-by-case basis, the applicable permit requirements to allow access to cultural resources by traditional practitioners from other Indian Tribes.

(e) Notwithstanding the exceptions listed above, all persons conducting activities otherwise excluded shall monitor their activities for the discovery of cultural resources and historic properties, immediately contact the THPO upon discovery of such resources, and avoid disturbing the resources. This subsection does not apply to traditional activities conducted by enrolled tribal members that require discovery and disturbance of cultural resources.

4.5. Modification, Suspension or Revocation of Permits

(a) The THPO may reevaluate the circumstances and conditions of any permit issued pursuant to this CRO at any time and initiate action to modify, suspend, or revoke a permit as may be: (1) in the best interest in the preservation of cultural resources and/or historic properties or (2) in the best interest of the Seminole Tribe of Florida.

(b) The THPO may develop procedures for modification, suspension, or revocation of permits in consultation with the Historic Preservation Review Board and General Counsel. Until such time as these procedures are developed, the THPO will be guided by the following protocols:

(i) Modification—Upon request by the permittee or as a result of reevaluation of the permit circumstances and conditions of a permit, the THPO may require a modification of the permit conditions or terms when the THPO determines that it is in the best interest of the cultural resources, the historic properties, and/or the Seminole Tribe. The THPO will notify the permittee in writing, including electronic mail, of the need for modification and order cessation of all work until the permit is appropriately modified. If permittee and the THPO cannot agree on the modifications, then the Tribal Council will determine the need for and scope of any modification. If the Tribal Council elects not to make such a determination, then the modifications proposed by the THPO will be required. Until such time as the modification is finalized, all work must cease unless specifically authorized in writing from the THPO.

(ii) Suspension—The THPO may suspend any permit after preparing a written determination and finding that immediate suspension would be in the best interest of the cultural resources, the historic properties, and/or the Seminole Tribe. The THPO will immediately notify the permittee in writing, including electronic mail, that the permit has been suspended with the reasons justifying the suspension, and order the permittee to cease all work.

(iii) Revocation—Following completion of the suspension procedures, the THPO may revoke the permit. The permittee will be notified in writing, including electronic mail, of the revocation.

4.6. Relationship to Section 106 of the National Historic Preservation Act and National Environmental Policy Act

(a) The mere issuance of a permit to proceed in accordance with this CRO does not constitute an independent undertaking requiring compliance with Section 106 of the National Historic Preservation Act (16 U.S.C. 470f), nor does it constitute a major federal action requiring National Environmental Policy Act review. However, the authorized project and/or activities may otherwise be subject to the National Historic Preservation or the National Environmental Policy Act requirements.

Part V. Additional Provisions for Protection of Burial Resources

5.1. Sanctity of Burials and Burial Resources

(a) Burials, burial sites, and burial resources are, by definition, cultural resources that hold the utmost cultural and religious significance to the Seminole Tribe. In addition to the requirements outlined in this CRO applicable to all cultural resources, the provisions in this Part shall apply to burials and burial resources.

(b) The THPO is also authorized to coordinate with the appropriate federal agencies the development of an agreement(s) relating to the Native American Graves Repatriation and Protection Act and the Archaeological Resources Protection Act through which the Seminole Tribe may assume certain responsibilities for the implementation of such Acts. Any such agreement(s) are subject to Tribal Council Approval. Until any such agreement is executed, the THPO shall be the designated tribal official to receive notices under both Acts.

(c) The THPO shall develop, in consultation with the Historic Preservation Review Board, a general tribal burial policy that will be suitable for disclosure to local, state, and federal governments. The burial policy will be subject to Tribal Council approval. The THPO shall also develop for inclusion in the appropriate operational manual(s) procedures and protocols for identification, assessment, and treatment of burials, burial sites, and burial resources.

(d) In connection with burials, burial sites, and burial resources, only those activities minimally necessary to comply with the notice requirements of the Native American Graves Protection and Repatriation Act and its implementing regulations shall be authorized under this CRO.

(e) The THPO is authorized to identify burials and burial resources of importance to the Seminole Tribe that have been excavated or removed from their original resting place. The THPO is further authorized to take appropriate action, under the guidance of the Historic Preservation Review Board and Tribal Council, to retrieve and repatriate said burials and burial resources.

Part VI. Research and Education

6.1. Research and Education Initiatives

(a) For purposes of preservation, the THPO shall, in cooperation with tribal members and other tribal instrumentalities, study and/or research Seminole Tribe of Florida heritage

(b) The THPO shall coordinate with appropriate tribal instrumentalities (such as schools and Cultural Heritage Departments) to provide educational opportunities regarding Seminole Tribe of Florida heritage.

6.2. Ancestral Lands Initiative

(a) The THPO shall identify culturally important areas in the Seminole Tribe's ancestral homelands that have not been significantly impacted by development and could potentially be suitable for purchase. The THPO will coordinate this responsibility with the Historic Preservation Review Board, General Counsel, and Seminole Tribe Real Estate Department.

(b) The THPO shall brief the Tribal Council on this initiative as needed or upon request.

Part VII. Cultural Resource Overlay

7.1. Authority, Purpose and Intent

(a) The THPO is authorized to establish cultural resources overlay districts for reservation lands.

(b) Development of cultural resources overlay districts is intended to ensure protection of cultural resources within reservation lands while streamlining the process for development review under other tribal programs.

(c) Cultural resources overlay districts will be implemented as a planning tool to direct development away from areas of high probability and provide for special development requirements for all areas of probability.

7.2. Applicability

(a) Once established, all development within a cultural resources overlay district will be subject to the cultural resource protection and development requirements for the given district.

7.3. Development within Cultural Resource Overlay Districts

(a) The THPO will develop specific cultural resource protection and development requirements for all cultural resource overlay districts.

(b) The cultural resource protection and development requirements will be commensurate with the level of probability for various zones within the overlay district (i.e., unknown, low, medium and high probability zones).

7.4. Coordination

(a) The THPO will consult with the Historic Preservation Review Board in the development of all cultural resources overlay districts.

(b) The THPO will also coordinate with other Seminole Tribe instrumentalities, including, but not limited to, the Seminole Tribal Community Development Department, in development of the cultural resources overlay districts. The Community Development Department and the THPO are directed to fully coordinate on the development of cultural resources overlay districts in conjunction with the development of any land use plan or zoning codes. The THPO shall provide the Tribal Council yearly reports of the development of the overlay districts including a summary of the coordination efforts.

Part VIII. Administrative Remedies and Enforcement

8.1. Authority

(a) When appropriate, and at its discretion, the Tribal Council or its designee, the THPO or the Seminole Police Department may resolve any violation of or address any action pursuant to this CRO through the administrative process set forth in this Part and Part IX.

8.2. Investigations

(a) The THPO and the Seminole Police Department, in cooperation with the THPO, are authorized to investigate compliance with permits issued pursuant to this CRO and potential unpermitted activities being conducted in violation of this CRO. All persons with knowledge of any possible violation of this CRO, or who are persons of interest in an investigation, shall fully cooperate with the investigating authority. Cooperation includes, but is not limited to, responding to written and oral inquiries. All information gathered during an investigation may be used in any enforcement proceeding. Failure to fully cooperate or providing false information is in itself a violation of this CRO.

(b) Both the THPO and Seminole Police Department have a duty to investigate possible violations of this CRO. Upon receiving a credible report, complaint, or information, the THPO shall, in conjunction with the Seminole Police Department or other cooperating agencies, perform a thorough investigation of any alleged violations. The THPO and Seminole Police Department are authorized to enter any area connected with an alleged violation.

(c) All persons subject to the Seminole Tribe's jurisdiction have a duty under this CRO to timely notify the Seminole Police Department and the THPO of any possible violation of this CRO and to cooperate fully with any resulting investigation or enforcement action.

8.3. Notices of Violation

(a) When the THPO and/or the Seminole Police Department in conjunction with the THPO has determined that a violation exists, the THPO and/or the Seminole Police Department shall take appropriate action to timely notify, via Notice of Violation, the responsible persons and those persons with a property interest in the land where the violation occurred or is occurring.

(b) All Notices of Violation shall be in writing and include at a minimum:

(i) a concise statement of the facts believed to constitute a violation;

(ii) specific reference(s) to the provision(s) of this CRO and implementing procedures, standards, guidelines, or operational plans/manuals allegedly violated;

(iii) the proposed administrative remedy or a statement that such remedies will be determined after completion of any investigation;

(iv) a statement describing additional remedies that may be imposed if the alleged violation continues to occur or is repeated after service of the Notice of Violation;

(v) an explanation of any administrative rights under this CRO; and

(vi) a statement of any other legal action that may be pursued by the Seminole Tribe of Florida, including civil lawsuits and criminal prosecution under applicable laws.

(c) Service of all Notices of Violation may be performed by the THPO, Seminole Police Department, or by a private service processor when service will occur off of reservation lands.

(d) A Notice of Violation can include a request to the recipient of the Notice of Violation to appear: (1) before the THPO and/or Seminole Police Department and/or the Tribal Council for investigation purposes or (2) before an administrative hearing at a specified time and date. Failure to appear will be considered a violation of this CRO, which shall be noted in a statement within the Notice of Violation requesting the appearance.

(e) A Cease and Desist Order may serve as a Notice of Violation.

8.4. Administrative Remedies

(a) Cease and Desist Orders

(i) The Tribal Council or its designee, the THPO, and the Seminole Police Department have the authority to issue Cease and Desist Orders for any violation or threatened violation under this CRO. All Cease and Desist Orders must be in writing and include all the minimum statements required for the Notice of Violation along with a statement demanding the responsible person to cease and desist in the conduct that constitutes a violation and that failure to comply with the order is in itself a violation of this CRO.

(b) Retroactive Compliance

(i) The Tribal Council or the THPO, at its discretion, may require all responsible parties to apply for and obtain an "after the fact" permit under this CRO.

(c) Restoration

(i) The Tribal Council or the THPO may require that any violation be abated by restoring or reconstructing affected cultural resources to their original condition prior to the violation. The violator must obtain a permit under this CRO prior to restoration. The Seminole Tribe, through the THPO, may perform the restoration and recover the costs from the violator. Restoration costs shall be the sum of the costs already incurred for restoration or repair work, plus those costs projected to be necessary to complete restoration and repair.

(d) Administrative Citations

(i) The Tribal Council or its designee, the THPO, or the Seminole Police Department may, at its discretion, issue a written administrative citation to any person alleged to have violated this CRO. The citation will explain:

a. the conduct that has violated the CRO;

b. the date(s) the violation occurred;

c. the provision(s) of this CRO that has been violated, including its contents;

d. the steps that must be taken to remedy the violation, including how to avoid repeating violations;

e. the date by which the responsible person must comply with the CRO;

f. the potential administrative penalties or other legal remedies that may be imposed or pursued if the offender continues to violate the CRO;

g. the contact information for THPO; and

h. any administrative rights under this CRO.

(ii) A record of the citation will be maintained. Reoccurring violations may include increased penalties.

(iii) The THPO shall coordinate with the General Counsel to develop an administrative citation fee schedule for all violations, including reoccurring violations, under this CRO within ninety (90) days of the effective date such that no fee shall exceed $10,000.00 per violation.

(e) Other Administrative Remedies

(i) The Tribal Council may elect to impose one or more of the additional administrative remedies:

a. for any person who does business on Seminole Tribe reservation lands or land holdings determined to have violated any provision of this CRO, such person may have the privilege of doing business on said lands revoked;

b. for any person who is authorized to enter into Seminole Tribe reservation lands or land holdings determined to have violated any provision of this CRO, such person may have the privilege of entry revoked;

c. for any person deemed to have violated the provisions of this CRO, the Seminole Tribe's investigative costs, administrative costs, court or hearing costs, and reasonable attorney fees may be imposed.

(f) Any person who is not an enrolled Seminole Tribal Member who visits or inspects cultural resources without the appropriate tribal authorization(s) shall be committing trespass. Any person deemed to have committed trespass under this CRO shall be deemed to have consented to the jurisdiction of the Seminole Tribe consistent with the Part I of this CRO.

(g) The administrative remedies set forth in this Part are supplemental to any other legal actions or enforcement available under applicable law including civil lawsuits and criminal prosecution. Further, the administrative remedies set forth in this Part are alternative and not mutually exclusive such that one or more of the remedies may be imposed for any given violation of the CRO.

Part IX. Administrative Review

9.1. Administrative Hearings

(a) Unless otherwise provided by this CRO, any person whose interests are substantially affected by any decision, determination, action, or enforcement action (including the imposition of administrative remedies) under this CRO may request an administrative hearing within thirty (30) days after receipt of notice of said decision, determination, action, or enforcement action or receipt of a Notice of Violation, Cease and Desist Order, or Citation under this CRO. All persons waive the right to a hearing for failure to timely request a hearing. Except for the review processes provided in subsections (g) and (h) of this section, the administrative hearings process provided by this section is the sole review process. However, if a court of competent jurisdiction should rule that other civil or administrative review is available, the administrative remedies under the CRO must first be exhausted. Failure to initiate the administrative review procedures under this Part will act as a waiver of all rights.

(b) All requests for administrative hearing must be timely filed by certified mail with the THPO and the General Counsel. Once a sufficient request has been received, the TI IPO will appoint a hearing officer to preside over the proceeding, which may include appointment of an attorney from the General Counsel.

(c) The THPO, the Seminole Police Department, or the Tribal Council or its designee may initiate, at its discretion, an administrative hearing to resolve any violations or action under this CRO. Nothing herein shall preclude the Seminole Tribe from bypassing the administrative hearing process and filing an action in a civil court of competent jurisdiction to resolve any violation under this CRO or other applicable laws.

(d) The THPO and the General Counsel will develop procedures for administrative hearings under this CRO within ninety (90) days of the enactment of this CRO including, but not limited to, procedures governing administrative hearings, identification of who may request an administrative hearing, detailed notification requirements, enumerate documentation requirements, and include any other elements necessary to carry out the purpose of this Part. These procedures will, at a minimum, provide the substantially affected person notice of any hearing and the opportunity to be heard related to the matter in question, including providing testimony and introducing evidence.

(e) Administrative review by the hearing officer shall be limited to review of the administrative record created during the administrative/enforcement action taken by the THPO and/or Seminole Police Department. The administrative hearing officer shall uphold the decision of the THPO and/or Seminole Police Department unless it finds that the decision was arbitrary and capricious or ultra vires. The petitioning party bears the burden of proving from the record that the THPO and/or Seminole Police Department decision was arbitrary and capricious or ultra vires.

(f) As a part of its ruling, the hearing officer may require an unsuccessful petitioner to pay investigation costs, administrative costs, hearing costs, and reasonable attorney fees.

(g) Decisions by the hearing officer may be appealed to the Tribal Council. All requests for appeal to the Tribal Council must be in writing and filed by certified mail with the General Counsel and THPO within fifteen (15) days of the administrative hearing officer's order being filed with the General Counsel. As a part of its ruling, the Tribal Council may require an unsuccessful appellant to pay administrative costs, hearing costs, and reasonable attorney fees. There is no right to appeal the administrative hearing and the Tribal Council may, at its discretion, elect to deny any request for appeal under this CRO.

(h) Any enrolled Seminole Tribal Member whose interests are substantially affected may, in lieu of an administrative hearing under this Part, request that a matter be decided by a traditional community-based decision-making process consistent with the Seminole Tribe's traditions. Such requests will be honored at the discretion of the Tribal Council. Decisions from a traditional community-based decision-making process are final and cannot be appealed. Any person requesting a traditional community-based decision-making process waives all rights to file an action in or appeal to any court of competent jurisdiction and agrees to be bound by the decision resulting from the traditional community-based decision-making process.

(i) At any time, the Tribal Council may, at its discretion, require any request for administrative hearing or any ongoing administrative hearing initiated by an enrolled Seminole Tribal Member be heard through a traditional community-based decision making process, which will foreclose any administrative hearing under this CRO. The Tribal Council may also require any ruling from an administrative hearing initiated by an enrolled Seminole Tribal member be appealed to a traditional community-based decision-making process for final resolution/adjudication. Decisions from a traditional community-based decision-making process are final and all rights to file an action in or appeal to any court of competent jurisdiction will have been deemed to be waived. Further, all parties will be deemed to have agreed to be bound by the decision resulting from the traditional community-based decision-making.

(j) For purposes of this Part IX, when computing any period of time allowed, the day of the triggering act shall not be included. Further, the last day of the prescribed period shall be included unless it is a Saturday or Sunday, or a designated Tribal holiday, in which event the period shall be extended to the next business day. Tribal holidays are those designated by the Seminole Tribe for closure of the Seminole Tribe's government offices and as published on the THPO website, www.stofthpo.com.

Part X. Custody of Cultural Resources

10.1. Ownership, Possession, Control, and Custody of Cultural Resources

(a) Unless directed by the Tribal Council, all cultural resources discovered, excavated, or removed from reservation lands and Seminole Tribe land holdings remain the property of the Seminole Tribe.

(b) Unless directed by the Tribal Council, any person that discovers, excavates, or removes any cultural resources on reservation lands and Seminole Tribe land holdings shall immediately transfer possession, control, and custody of the cultural resources to the Seminole Tribe via the THPO.

(c) All information held, stored, or maintained by the Seminole Tribe concerning cultural resources located within Seminole Tribe reservation lands, Seminole Tribe land holdings, or off of reservation lands is the sole property of the Seminole Tribe and cannot be utilized or disseminated without the express written permission from the Seminole Tribe.

10.2. Cultural Resources off of Reservation Lands or Seminole Tribe Land Holdings

(a) The THPO is authorized, with approval from the Historic Preservation Review Board and the Tribal Council, to identify and secure cultural resources that are not located on reservation lands or Seminole Tribe land holdings. This authority includes the power to negotiate agreements and/or purchasing cultural resources under the direction of the Tribal Council.

10.3. Failure to Comply

(a) Failure to comply with any provision of this Part will be deemed a violation of the CRO except for activities of THPO and tribal employees engaged in properly authorized official business relating to cultural resource management under this CRO.

Part XI. Confidentiality

11.1. Confidentiality of Information Concerning Cultural Resources and Heritage

(a) The THPO will not make available to persons not enrolled Seminole Tribal Members information regarding the nature, location, or significance of cultural resources, unless specifically authorized by this CRO, the Historic Preservation Review Board, or the Tribal Council.

(b) The THPO will only make available to other Seminole Tribe instrumentalities information regarding the nature, location, and significance of cultural resources that is minimally necessary to carry out the THPO official duties and will consult with the Historic Preservation Review Board as needed before sharing said information.

(c) The THPO is authorized to share information, in connection with government to government consultation, with local, state, and federal agencies regarding the nature, location, and significance of cultural resources located off of reservation lands. When practical, the THPO will make a good faith effort to consult with the Historic Preservation Review Board and/or the Tribal Council before sharing said information.

(d) Upon request or on its own initiative, the Tribal Council or Historic Preservation Review Board can direct the THPO to withhold any and all information regarding cultural resources from any person including enrolled Seminole Tribal Members.

BE IT FURTHER ENACTED: that this Ordinance is hereby adopted after motion duly made by _____, seconded by _____ and roll call vote as follows:

Chairman James E. Billie
Vice-Chairman Tony Sanchez, Jr
Council Representative Manuel M. Tiger
Council Representative Andrew J. Bowers, Jr.
Council Representative Christopher Osceola

DONE THIS THE _____ DAY OF _____, 20___ at the meeting of the Tribal Council, duly convened at the _____ Seminole Indian Reservation, with a quorum being present, by a vote of _____ For, _____ Against, with _____ Abstentions.

_____
Chairman
TRIBAL COUNCIL

ATTEST: _____
Secretary
TRIBAL COUNCIL

INDEX

Page number in *italics* refer to illustrations.

Printed in the United States
By Bookmasters